"I have been teaching the biblical book of Job for many years and *Redefining Job and the Conundrum of Suffering* is the most comprehensive treatment of the book I have seen. Adams takes up the problem of suffering and evil with preliterate cultures and moves methodically through the history of religious and philosophical approaches to the problem. She situates Job within its historical and cultural context, and also brings forward the book's handling of questions that are no less relevant today than they were centuries ago. *Redefining Job and the Conundrum of Suffering* is an essential reference for professors, students, and ministers dealing with the book of Job. It is also a valuable resource for all of us who struggle to make sense of unearned suffering in the world. In *Redefining Job and the Conundrum of Suffering*, Adams has baited her hook for Leviathan."

—VIC SIZEMORE

Author of *Goodbye My Tribe: An Evangelical Exodus*

"Steeped in traditional interpretations, philosophically attuned, psychologically sensitive, scientifically informed, Adams—in her modern Christian perspective on Job—seeks a theological understanding of suffering that is considerate of and perhaps even comforting to people who suffer. A special feature is Adams' attention to outlooks and sources behind and beyond the Abrahamic religions."

—EDWARD L. GREENSTEIN

Author of *Job: A New Translation*

"Victoria Adams has taken on the issue of suffering in the world by centering her topic around the classic tale of Job and the scholarship surrounding this beloved, ancient story. She demonstrates a mastery of the published material, provides many topics for class study and discussion; however, her most accomplished task in this book is centering the story of Job and the topic of suffering within the person who suffers. In doing so, Victoria accomplishes two things: she challenges all who suffer to give voice to their experience and, through honest communication with the creative forces religion calls God, to seek restoration and new life from the experience of loss and injustice."

—CHRISTINE KESTERSON

Prison chaplain and founder of Immaculata Home, Inc.

"Remember as a kid how delighted you were to occasionally receive that special sixty-four-crayon box of Crayola crayons, the one with the built-in sharpener? That's what Victoria Adams' book on Job is to anyone fascinated with theology, history, literature, or drama. She offers more nuances and shades of color to understand this timeless tale than you can imagine. This palette of interpretation will serve scholars and lay readers alike."

—MARK WINGFIELD
Executive Director and Publisher of Baptist News Global

"This scholarly yet readable work illuminates the rich social context and profound interpretive legacy of this paradigmatic tale of suffering, faith, resilience, perseverance, and ultimately, joy in the human condition. Adams invites us to rethink what it means to lay our trust in God in the midst of our brokenness. She calls us to develop tenets to live by, through which our own and Job's suffering opens up spaces of compassion, love, and caring as we call ourselves to account for harm, blame, and complacency in crafting a meaningful life."

—ZAYN KASSAM
John Knox McLean Professor of Religious Studies, Pomona College

"This is a masterfully careful and deeply thoughtful look at one of the most important texts on suffering in all of human literature, and one of the most challenging stories in the Bible. I can't imagine a more complete or illuminating treatment of how we can best understand the famous and powerful book of Job. A wonderful book and highly recommended!"

—TOM MORRIS
Author of *Our Idea of God*

Redefining Job and the Conundrum of Suffering

Redefining Job and the Conundrum of Suffering

VICTORIA ADAMS

Foreword by
DAVID VON SCHLICHTEN

WIPF & STOCK · Eugene, Oregon

REDEFINING JOB AND THE CONUNDRUM OF SUFFERING

Copyright © 2020 Victoria Adams. All rights reserved. Except for brief quotations in critical publications or reviews, no part of this book may be reproduced in any manner without prior written permission from the publisher. Write: Permissions, Wipf and Stock Publishers, 199 W. 8th Ave., Suite 3, Eugene, OR 97401.

Wipf & Stock
An Imprint of Wipf and Stock Publishers
199 W. 8th Ave., Suite 3
Eugene, OR 97401

www.wipfandstock.com

PAPERBACK ISBN: 978-1-7252-6244-7
HARDCOVER ISBN: 978-1-7252-6245-4
EBOOK ISBN: 978-1-7252-6246-1

Manufactured in the U.S.A.   JUNE 9, 2020

Cover photograph of Silver Lake, Washington, by Arun Rohila Photography: nonexclusive license.

Maps designed by Julie Witmer, Custom Map Design.

Quotes from and references to Old Testament are reproduced from the *Tanakh: The Holy Scriptures* by permission of the University of Nebraska Press. Copyright 1985 by the Jewish Publication Society, Philadelphia.

Quotations designated (NET) are from the NET Bible® copyright © 1996–2016 by biblical Studies Press, L.L.C. http://netbible.com. All rights reserved.

The Good Person. Reproduced from *Yoruba Proverbs* by Oyekan Owomoyela by permission of the University of Nebraska Press, Copyright 2005 by the Board of Regents of the University of Nebraska.

Excerpt from Philip Pullman's acceptance speech for the Carnegie Medal in 1995 for *"Northern Lights,"* published by Scholastic. Used by permission of United Agents, UK on behalf of Phillip Pullman, all rights reserved, with no intended collaboration on this work.

The Bible and the Comic Vision, J. William Whedbee, Cambridge UP, 1998. Reproduced with permission of The Licensor through PLSclear.

"An Engagement with Marilyn McCord Adams's Horrendous Evils and the Goodness of God," *Scottish Journal of Theology,* 55/4, Cambridge UP, Nov 2002. Reproduced with permission of the Licensor through PLSclear.

Quotations from *Till We Have Faces* by C. S. Lewis copyright © C.S. Lewis Pte, Ltd. 1956 & *The Problem of Pain* by C. S. Lewis copyright © C.S. Lewis Pte, Ltd. 1940. Extracts reprinted by permission.

To my beloved shining star. This work would have never seen the light of day without your earnest support, encouragement, and all those long conversations about wonder, the search for knowledge, and the hope for wisdom.

If history were taught in the form of stories, it would never be forgotten.

—Rudyard Kipling
Riki-Tikki-Tavi.

All stories teach, whether the storyteller intends them to or not. They teach the world we create. They teach the morality we live by. They teach it much more effectively than moral precepts and instructions . . . We don't need lists of rights and wrongs, tables of dos and don'ts: we need books, time, and silence. "Thou shalt not" is soon forgotten, but "Once upon a time" lasts forever.

—Philip Pullman
from his acceptance speech for the Carnegie Medal in 1995.
The award was for *Northern Lights*, published by Scholastic.[1]

---

1. Used by permission of United Agents, UK on behalf of Phillip Pullman, all rights reserved, with no intended collaboration on this work.

Contents

List of Maps and Charts | ix
Foreword by David von Schlichten | xi
Preface | xiii
Acknowledgments | xix

Part I—Nuts and Bolts

CHAPTER 1
Who, What, Where? | 3

CHAPTER 2
A Bit of Exegesis | 15

CHAPTER 3
The Language, the Author, the Date | 26

CHAPTER 4
What Happened | 36

CHAPTER 5
Building a Toolbox | 45

Part II—Theodicy and Philosophy

CHAPTER 6
The Study of Why | 55

CHAPTER 7
The Pillars of Early Christian Thought | 63

CHAPTER 8
Philosophy or Homily? | 77

CHAPTER 9
The Conservative Jewish Philosophers | 93

CHAPTER 10
The Aristotelians | 103

Part III—A Different Point of View

CHAPTER 11
The Dawn of Religion, Preliterate, and Ancient Faiths | 121

CHAPTER 12
Suffering in the Far East | 130

CHAPTER 13
Suffering in the Ancient Near East | 140

CHAPTER 14
Ayyub—The Prophet of Patience | 146

Part IV—Recasting Job

CHAPTER 15
Is Job Really about Theodicy? | 159

CHAPTER 16
God on Trial | 168

CHAPTER 17
When It Gets Real | 175

CHAPTER 18
Can Job Be Understood through Comic Vision? | 184

CHAPTER 19
Suffering in Literature | 192

Part V—Redefining the Conversation

CHAPTER 20
The Gordian Knot | 203

CHAPTER 21
The View from the Author's Window | 217

CHAPTER 22
Consider the Measure of the Earth | 228

CHAPTER 23
Consider Nature | 240

CHAPTER 24
Consider Leviathan and Behemoth | 248

CHAPTER 25
Before I Heard, But Now I See | 260

Bibliography | 271

List of Maps and Charts

Chart 1: Relevant Genealogy | 4

Chart 2: Scripture Key to Relevant Genealogy | 5

Map 1: Middle East and Northeast Africa | 6

Map 2: The Levant | 7

Chart 3: Commentary Timeline | 62

Map 3: The Church Fathers | 90

Chart 4: Key to Church Fathers | 92

Map 4: The Jewish Philosophers | 116

Chart 5: Key to Jewish Philosophers | 118

Foreword

My mother, a devout Christian, hated the book of Job. "I can't imagine that God would play with somebody's life like that," she used to say.

Indeed, the book of Job is almost as challenging as its central issue, namely, why bad things happen to good people. If God is all-powerful and all-loving, then why does God allow horrible things to happen to morally upright people—or indeed, to anyone? We humans have tended to want the universe to operate fairly and not according to evil, or perhaps worse, randomness. Our existence has to mean *something*, and, for many of us, essential to that meaning is a God who ensures that good will ultimately prevail. The book of Job grapples with these issues of morality, fairness, and meaning, but it's a complex book, one that could leave the reader feeling slighted, cheated, or even, as with my mother, outraged.

In *Redefining Job*, Victoria Adams offers a treatment of Job that provides the reader with great guidance through this poetic, profound, often vexing masterpiece of biblical literature. With a breathtaking, encyclopedic scope, Adams contextualizes and scrutinizes the book of Job, turning it over and over to capture every element. With impressive scholarly rigor, Adams examines the socio-historical background of the book, different interpretations throughout the centuries, and how this famous work of Wisdom literature pertains to issues of God and suffering as they have been addressed across the ages, both within and outside of Christianity.

In the process, Adams makes at least three helpful contributions to the study of Job and the issue of suffering. First, she is careful to avoid glib, facile answers to these ponderous questions about the text itself or suffering. Hers is an ambitious project arising from many years of careful study, fitting for a work as sophisticated as the book of Job. Second is the poignantly personal nature of Adams's book. It is evident that this is an intense labor of love for Adams, born out of her own painful experiences and her desire to make sense of a world that frequently strikes one as absurd.

Third, and most important, is the idea of Job being like a knight who is challenging God for answers and whose story challenges the reader to learn more about God and faith and to then engage in meaningful, loving action. Indeed, ultimately, Adams's work is one that compels us forward to overcome misery, not with dismissively easy

Foreword

answers, but with intense intellectual wrestling coupled with dedication to helping those in need.

During my seventeen years as a parish pastor, I had at least one parishioner who would regularly assert that she had questions about the fairness of life but then would hastily add, "But we are not to question God." I was quick to note that the Bible, including the book of Job, does allow us to question God. Indeed, as Adams intelligently argues, the book encourages us to question God. We are only not to give up on God, and we need to be ready for the possibility that we may receive no definite answer except for being urged anew to trust God. We can both challenge and trust in God in a kind of dialectical tension, and Adams's book helps us to do so.

My mother would have benefited from *Redefining Job*, and I pray you will, too.

The Rev. Dr. David von Schlichten, DMin, PhD, MFA.
Greensburg, PA

Preface

"Once upon a time lasts forever."[1] Deep into the process of reviewing one of the final edits of this book, I was challenged to think about voice. How did I want this work to come across and what audience did I want to reach? I developed the material in this book using the accumulated research of many decades. There are also hints of personal experience and something of the pastoral for those in need of comfort. Was it possible to effectively reach multiple audiences and use the same content?

On one hand, we have the scholar or layperson in search of the theological or philosophical discussion. Marilyn McCord Adams, who was a philosopher and a priest in the Episcopal Church, taught that there were three problems with analytical theology when it comes to dealing with evil.[2] One is that the practice of the philosopher or theologian is to develop a vision of a creator God and assume that because creation is agreed to be good, all things that happen within it must also be good.

The second is divine justification. Theologians and pastors often work earnestly to prove that whatever happens to others and us is in God's purview and is justified because we perceive him to be good. In other words, in theology, it is assumed that God is within his rights to do whatever he sees fit regardless of the human cost precisely because he knows best. After all, to think otherwise is to believe in a capricious and often cruel God.

The third is the tendency to look at the bigger questions with no eye for the detail. Consequently, as theologians and philosophers, we become so focused on proving God created the best of all worlds that we lose sight of the day-to-day struggles of the people who live in that world. We ignore life-changing catastrophes and personal tragedies because we are too busy building an indestructible vision of a sovereign, beneficent creator. As McCord Adams explains, theologians and philosophers get so involved in working out the logic of the situation, of defining God and his actions within human reason, that they forget the broken life. They lose sight of the lost child,

---

1. Philip Pullman, from his acceptance speech for the Carnegie Medal in 1995. The award was for *Northern Lights*, published by Scholastic. Used by permission of United Agents, U.K. on behalf of Phillip Pullman, all rights reserved, with no intended collaboration on this work..

2. Loyola Productions Munich, "Marilyn McCord Adams."

the aging parent, or the starving village. Their words fall on barren ground and can cause more pain than succor.

On the other hand, a traditional Christian church upbringing instills key elements used in the interpretation of Job. Job is the exemplification of patience. Even as Job suffers from the unleashed power of Satan, he refuses to bend. The church commonly teaches that someday we will know why people suffer; nevertheless, until that day comes, we must trust that God is right. Somewhere in that mix, some churches teach that the book of Job is most likely quite ancient and that Moses may have been its author. Also, faithful believers sometimes have difficulty getting beyond the misapplied message of Job's visitors. They believe that suffering occurs exclusively as a response to the believer's failings or need for growth. Even today, general catastrophes and tragic life events are blamed on some collective or personal breach of divine code. These teachings, these perspectives, have guided the reactions of believers to personal suffering and shared suffering for centuries.

I was caught somewhere in the middle, doing my best to understand and find comfort while feeling I was missing a crucial piece of the puzzle. When I realized that I was not going to find my answer by listening to the same story told in the same way, I chose to find a new narrative. That meant shuffling through several centuries of embedded theology, as well as approaching modern scholarship with a more open mind. My quest for clarity led me to see the story of Job as a human tale and one that has meaning, regardless of religious background or faith affiliation.

For these reasons, I believe that my story, my "once upon a time," needs to be told from both perspectives. We learn by stories. Whether historical, metaphorical, allegorical, or fantastic, each tale has something to share. Sometimes that sharing is nothing more than an escape, a tale of far away that gives us a moment of peace from the realities we face each day. Sometimes that sharing gives us tools to guide us, arm us, and inspire us each time we face the choices we must make.

The problem with the story of Job is that centuries of retelling embeds a narrow vision of the message in our collective thought. We have allowed the ancient storytellers to do all the work of interpretation for us. In general, the authors of mountains of literature (fiction and nonfiction) have all arrived at conclusions that resolve little. Part of the purpose of this book is to investigate each of the common interpretations, then test those conclusions for validity in the real world of human suffering. For the most part, many of these answers are vague allusions to God's justice, future lives promised to believers, and the need to wait patiently for that day when all will be revealed. Such answers are unacceptable to those who need one most. In addition, such responses fly in the face of the evidence available to us in a perpetually creating universe set upon its course with simple and determinable rules.

If the sources previously known to me did not satisfy me as an answer, then how was I to find a solution acceptable to me? How could I go about retelling a story that is so ancient that the characters and circumstances have become cliché?

Preface

The first step was to investigate the roots of the story. When was it written, and what information was available to the author? Do we know who wrote the book? Is the tale historical or legendary? Changing the setting of the story can influence the development of the characters, the storyline, the conflicts between each character, and the conclusions. To know the story, one must start with where it began.

For instance, to me, Job is not a patient saint bearing his troubles in humility as he is slowly crushed to the ground. He is a knight standing toe to toe with his Maker and demanding answers. Job challenges his Lord even as his friends warn him of impending blasphemy. Scripture is clear that Job is without fault, and yet he suffers. In some parts of the book, he begs for the opportunity to at least have a conversation with his Maker to see if there is some reason or hope of a reason for why he has lost so much.

Several of the commentators examined in this book fall into the previously stated general answers. I differ from all three conclusions. I believe that Job's testimony, "Before I heard, but now I see" (Job 42:5), is a clear declaration that the author of the book did indeed see an answer, or at the very least, part of an answer. The mission of this book is to explore a path to that conclusion and to determine if that message translates well into our lives in the twenty-first century.

The familiarity of the story of Job is at least part of the reason I chose this biblical book as a framework for a deeper study on the subject of suffering. *Redefining Job and the Conundrum of Suffering* explores two fundamental parts of the question, "Why me?"

1. Is theodicy, the vindication of divine goodness and providence given the existence of evil, an answer to suffering? In other words, is there a way to accept the existence of suffering or evil and still believe in the goodness of God?

2. What part, if any, does Providence play in the solution? Must such protection operate on an individual basis to be valid? (Providence is understood to represent the protective care of God or nature as a spiritual power. Providence within this book is used both as a proper title referring to an aspect of God and as the act or function of providence as a noun. Capitalization is an indication of which usage applies.)

Some scholars would argue that Job has nothing to do with these questions. However, whatever labels we choose for the questions, reconciling ourselves to the afflictions in the world is a deep, spiritual need. Therefore, as I was writing this book, it was important to explore how other faiths addressed human responses to suffering. My search for answers included the thoughts and ideas found in classical literature, theological and philosophical commentary, and biblical studies. This book will take you on a journey to the early mists of historical time, and it will lead you through the tenets of some of the most influential faiths of humanity.

Preface

I will show you answers that work in the trenches of everyday life and answers that help you respond to the suffering of so many in the world today. These are conclusions supported by the message of Scripture in general and the book of Job in particular. I also believe that when these tenets become part of our everyday lives, we are better prepared to find comfort, whatever our faith tradition may be. In broad terms, these conclusions are:

1. Sometimes the things we do cause harm to others and ourselves. We need to learn accountability for those events and make sincere efforts to correct the problem and reduce our burden on ourselves and others.

2. We need to break the blame-chain. We must learn to stop blaming ourselves for actions and consequences over which we have no control. We also must learn not to blame others for their suffering when they have little control over the cause or the cure.

3. Whatever our beliefs about the permanency of this earth may be, we must be proactive in the search for ways to make life less crushing. Nothing in Scripture provides us with an excuse to sit back and let the world deteriorate before our eyes. From Genesis to Revelation, the underlying message is to love one another as we love ourselves; we are commanded to care. That means that we are called to use our creative potential to improve the circumstances we find in the world.

Like Job, I wanted assurance that life is not meaningless and that humanity is not victim to random forces. I also found it unacceptable that humanity should be subject to a perpetual, supernatural surveillance system established to catch every infraction, great or small, known or unknown. Like Job, I had to wonder what horrible evil I had committed to make the circumstances of my life necessary. Like Job, I wanted and needed answers. The medieval Jewish philosopher Maimonides taught that the twin fountains of truth were reason and revelation. I ask you to reason together and, perhaps, we will find a revelation.

I cherish Scripture as a sacred heritage, a conversation between Creator and created. I believe that this heritage provides a basis for an ongoing search for meaning. In my experience, the human spirit seems most resilient and creative when in search of a solution to a problem, while exercising a sense of wonder, or in the drive to find answers, sometimes to vaguely formed questions. Such a gift should not be wasted.

In millennia past, we looked to the skies and watched the majestic passage of time played out by points of light. As a species, we came to believe those lights influenced our day-to-day lives and our destinies. Eventually, the study of astrology became the study of astronomy, and we learned that those lights were stars and planets. We also learned that the stars do indeed influence us—they are the *stuff* of which we are made. We learned how and why the planets move, what makes up the stars, and something of how they are born and how they die. From ancient times to modern, researchers and thinkers have sought out order and reason.

Anthropology, in part, studies the past to understand humanity's search for reason. Through these studies, we begin to understand what practices bound us together against threats, both real and imagined. We have learned that ritual, social interaction, and a need to provide a cause for events that occurred aided in the development of our religion, our philosophy, and our astrology. Eventually, our beliefs became organized, and those who assumed leadership roles began to develop the doctrines which formed organized religion.

The ancient writings of humanity—our history, our art, our dreams, and our failures—are a record of those who refused to accept the known and insisted on looking further. We continue to push back the old barriers and stare into the cosmos asking whatever it is that we believe in, "Why?"

God tells Job, "Gird your loins like a man; I will ask, and you will inform Me" (Job 38:3).[3] The voice is *not* dismissing Job as an insignificant bit of humanity who dares to demand an answer from the Creator of the universe. God does *humble* Job by agreeing to statements Job himself has made about God's power and presence. However, God does not *humiliate* Job. The author of Job sees God as delivering a counterchallenge to observe, to learn, and to grow in knowledge and wisdom. In the end, Job declares that before he heard, but now he sees (Job 42:5). Throughout this book, I will show that the author of Job was retelling the story from his place and time. He was using knowledge available to him to revisit the challenging question of undeserved suffering. Now is the time to take up that challenge again.

Becoming part of Job's story requires something of us: the need for "truthfulness."[4] The command given by the voice from the whirlwind was to answer as a mortal, however inadequate that position may seem. I sincerely hope that at the end of this journey, you are not simply better informed about the history of commentary on the book of Job, or what has influenced humanity throughout history in our need to deal with suffering. Rather, I hope you learn to look suffering in the eye and actively prepare to do something constructive for yourself and those who face physical, mental, and socioeconomic challenges. I must warn you that the challenge is not to create your solution based on your perception of a need but to find the best response to meet the needs of the receiver.

Enjoy the journey.

---

3. *Tanakh—The Holy Scriptures.*
4. Greenstein, "Truth or Theodicy?" 238–58.

Acknowledgements

It is difficult to know where to begin when so much of this book is the result of ideas and challenges accumulated over a lifetime. Therefore, I will begin with the dozens of folks that read, challenged, shared sources and ideas, and provided feedback as bits and pieces of this work came together.

Next in line is my initial editor, Cindy Koepp, who patiently picked through the early stages of the manuscript and who helped to grind down the rough edges. She challenged me to seek deeper, to defend with more eloquence, and to build the logic that led to my conclusions. We did not always agree, yet she made sure I was clear, that I understood what the reaction to one idea or another might be, and that I cited every source I drew from. She kept me honest.

I must thank Dr. Zayn Kassam, professor of religious studies, Pomona College, for her kind input regarding my interpretations of the Islamic approach to suffering. My hope is that I incorporated her advice well while staying true to my own goals. She also is responsible for introducing me to the works of J. William Whedbee and his work on the comic vision found within Scripture.

My research regarding the language and the dating of the book of Job as we find it in our current canon would have suffered without the input of Dr. Edward Greenstein of the Salman Shamir Bible Department, Bar-Ilan University. He graciously granted permission for me to quote from our private communication and was quite encouraging based on the excerpts he reviewed to do so. His published works contributed much to my understanding of Job and his story.

Dr. David van Schlichten of Seton Hill University continues to provide his enthusiastic support and is part of my impetus to keep working to the end. He also agreed to review the manuscript for gross errors in presentation and content. He challenged me to be clear and sometimes a bit more compassionate. Still, in the end, what remains is my view, which may not always represent his own conclusions.

Lisa Collins, a friend and colleague, provided the first copyedit. She also provided valuable input from the perspective of psychology and new approaches to dealing with social, physical, and mental challenges in a changing world. She gave so many seemingly small bits of advice that changed the tone of the text and, in my opinion, further matured the final product.

Acknowledgements

Kat Bryant, a friend and professional in the field of edits and writing, has committed to help me through the final review copies. I appreciate her support and her help with stress management. She is also full of ideas on how to get the word out about my hero, Job.

I would also like to thank the team at Wipf and Stock for their active participation in polishing this manuscript and in helping to collect all the pieces that will give *Redefining Job* a chance in today's market. Their faith in me and my work has been the inspiration I needed to walk this book across the finish line.

Of course, any errors remaining are mine; however, these people, each with their own perspective and religious conviction, contributed much to making this work what my late husband always thought it should be. My thanks are a meager expression of my deep gratitude for these and so many other unnamed supporters.

Part I—Nuts and Bolts

Chapter 1

Who, What, Where?

DOES IT MATTER WHO the characters portrayed in the book of Job were, where they lived, or when they lived, or if they lived at all? Part of the reason that the book has such lasting power is that the themes within it are universal and timeless. Our species tends to experience curiosity, anger, or concern regarding the presence of evil and undeserved suffering. Some individuals ponder the question of whether there is Someone out there who cares and can do something to help those who suffer. Nailing down every detail of the text to provide understanding of what the text is saying is not entirely necessary. However, placing the story and the characters in a historical context can help reveal the poet's ultimate message and give depth and lasting meaning to the words.

Knowing something about the times in which the characters lived, where they lived, and what type of culture they lived in, that is, their historical context, can bring clarity to the imagery used by the author. Knowing the sources or background of the book can determine if the text is a parable or if it is a piece of history recounted for edification. The development of the characters within a story and how each one changes helps define what the author is most interested in saying.

Part I—Nuts and Bolts

Chart 1: : Relevant Genealogy

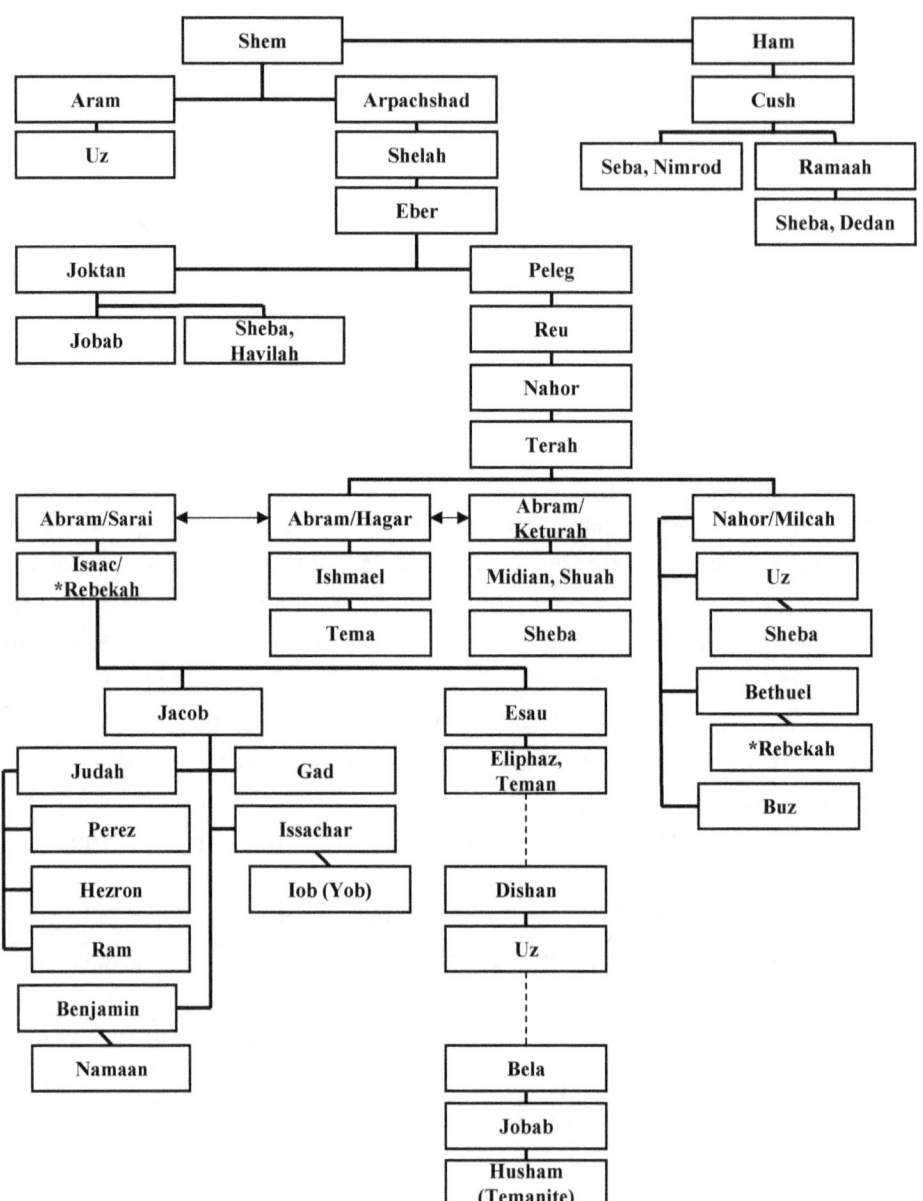

Chart 2: Scripture Key to Relevant Genealogy

Verse Reference	Generation
Gen 5:32	Shem, Ham
Gen 10:6; 10:22	Aram, Arpachshad, Cush
Gen 10:7–8, 23–24	Uz, Shelah, Seba, Nimrod, Ramaah
Gen 10:7; 11:14	Eber, Sheba, Dedan
Gen 10:25	Joktan, Peleg
Gen 10:26, 29; 11:18	Jobab, Sheba, Havilah, Reu
Gen 11:22	Nahor
Gen 11:24	Terah
Gen 11:26, 29; 16:1; 25:1	Abram, Sarai, Hagar, Keturah, Nahor, Milcah
Gen 16:11; 20–22; 25:4	Isaac, Rebekah, Ismael, Midian, Shuah, Uz, Buz, Bethuel
Gen 22:23; 25:13–16, 24–26; 1 Chr 1:32	Jacob, Esau, Tema, Sheba (two different ancestors), Rebekah (Isaac's wife)
Gen 35:22–26; 36:10–11	Benjamin, Gad, Judah, Issachar, Eliphaz, Teman
Gen 46:12, 21	Naaman, Perez, Iob (Yob)
Gen 36:26; 46:12	Hezron, Dishon
1 Chr 1:42; Matt 1:3	Ram, Uz
Gen 36:32–33 (see also 46:21)	Bela
Gen 36:33	Jobab
Gen 36:34	Husham

The charts are not comprehensive. The information provided is a summary of individuals key to the story of Job as well as more familiar names from biblical history to provide a sense of contemporaries. There is no attempt to set these individuals within a specific time frame. Much of biblical literature uses symbols and representations that would have been familiar to the audience. Knowing something about these images and symbols can contribute to understanding the story and the message. Whether the core story is history or legend, the men described within the book of Job represented tribal families. Their heritage should be evident somewhere in the literature of the people who recorded and preserved the tale. One of the few things commentators throughout the ages agree on is that the choice of characters within the book is part of the message the book teaches.

Part I—Nuts and Bolts

Map 1

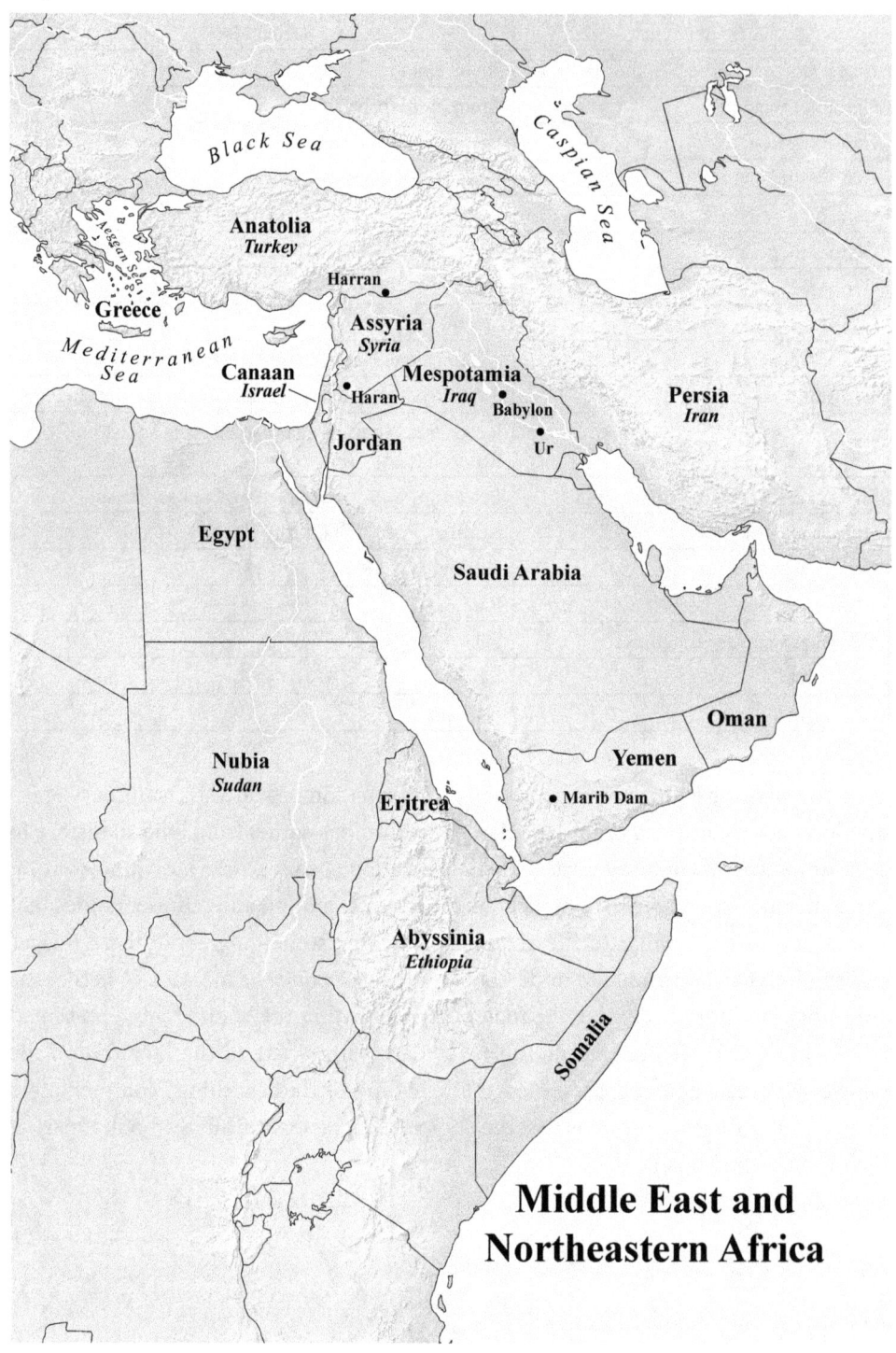

Middle East and Northeastern Africa

Map 2

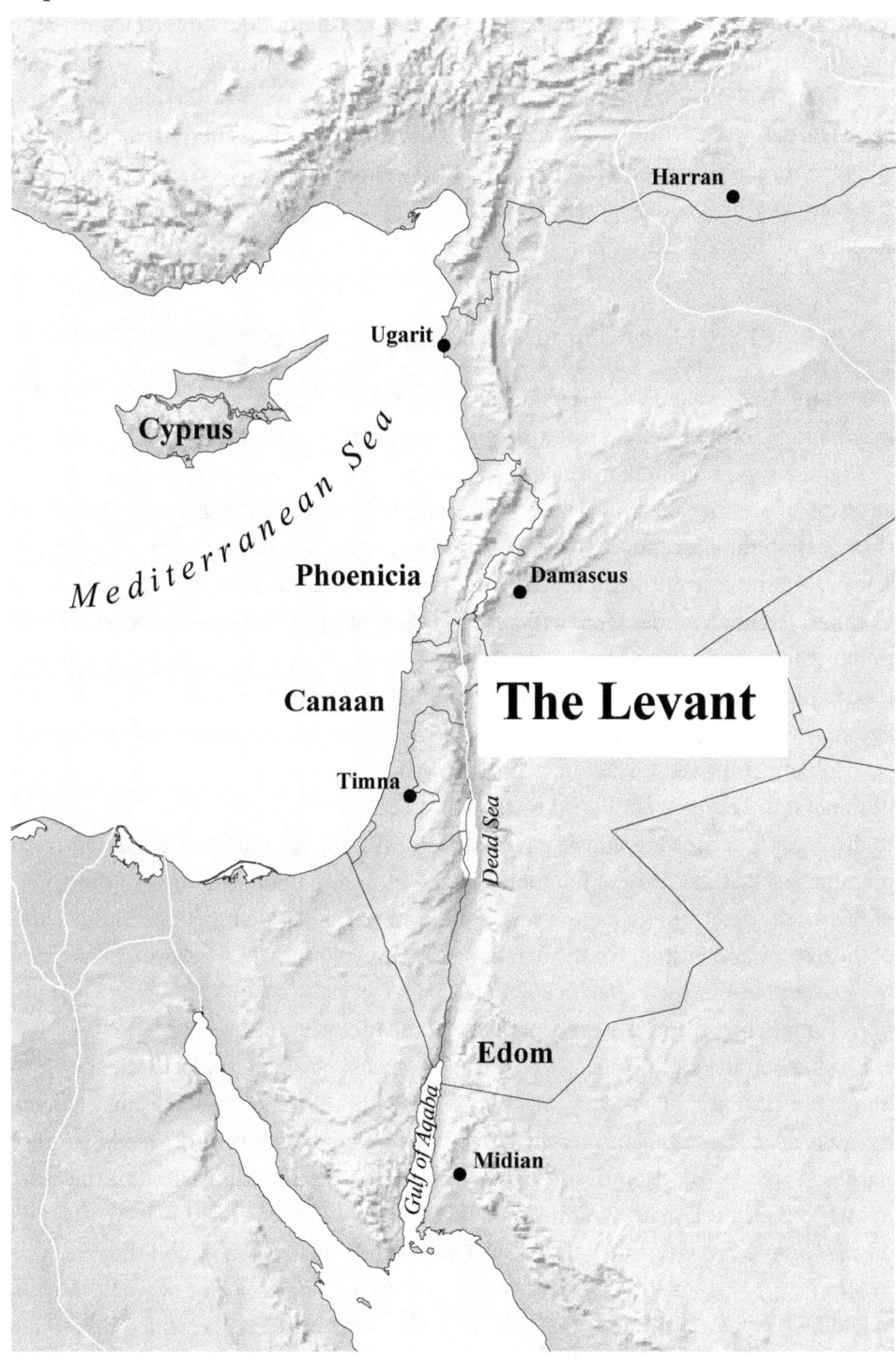

Part I—Nuts and Bolts

As scholars reconstruct the history of the Middle East, the geographic boundaries of the tribes and nations depicted in Scripture are better understood. Such research has also led to unconfirmed, and sometimes contentious, speculation.

There is a plethora of historical responses defining each of the characters and locations described within the book. Each theory has its ardent supporters. Historical and scriptural research pursued in the past few centuries has helped to provide clarity and context. The purpose here is to set the stage of the tale to provide better understanding of the tools the author used to convey the message.

There was a man in the land of Uz called Job.

The name "Uz" frequently appears in Scripture. Chart 1 shows several candidates who may have been the forefather of a tribal group called Uz. First, there is the firstborn of Aram, a son of Shem. Uz is also the brother of Buz, a nephew of Abraham and an ancestor of another of Job's visitors, Elihu. Uz is a name in the genealogy of Edom (Esau). Both the descendant of Shem and Esau are mentioned again in 1 Chronicles 1:17, 42. In the case of the Edomites, a man named Uz appears in the lineage of kings or chiefs. Jeremiah names Uz as a target of God's wrath (Jer 25:20) and as a daughter of Edom whose sins will be exposed (Lam 4:21). From these references, commentators tend to place the land of Uz in or near Edom in an area that lies south of the Dead Sea and north of the Gulf of Aqaba.

Johann Gottfried Eichhorn, a German scholar, living from 1752–1827, was one of the first to compare scriptural texts with other Semitic writings. His purpose was to distinguish between documentary and cultural sources of the Old Testament.[1] His opinion was that the story of Job took place in Idumea, another name for Edom. One of Eichhorn's determining factors was that the author of Job demonstrated knowledge of the history and customs of the neighboring country of Egypt. However, in addition to passages in Job which reference Egypt, the imagery of the book also includes traditions from Babylon and the eastern shores of the Mediterranean.

After centuries of debate, there is no consensus regarding the placement of Job's home. For instance, one theory puts him in the land settled by Aram, a son of Shem, a region near Damascus in present-day Syria. One proponent of this theory, Albert Barnes (1798–1870), proposes in his *Notes on the Bible* that the setting of the story points to a location near Syria in the land of Aramea.[2] He bases this interpretation on the Genesis record, which places Shem's descendants in the East and the reference in Job that he was wealthier than anyone in the East—knowing east of what, though, would be helpful. Barnes uses the speaker as the point of reference, which (assuming a Hebraic source) is what led him to a location east of Canaan rather than south in Edom.

1. Eichhorn, *Introduction to the Old Testament*.
2. Barnes, *Notes on the Bible*.

Another suggested placement for Uz derives from a reference to a Jobab who is a descendant of Joktan (descended from Shem). The *Tanakh* interprets the location provided in Genesis 25:18 as, "They dwelt from Havilah, by Shur, which is close to Egypt, all the way to Asshur, they camped alongside all their kinsmen." This verse describes a large piece of real estate starting in the southern Levant and reaching east and north towards the Upper Mesopotamian Valley. As can be seen, the exercise of assigning a geographic location to many ancient tribes is difficult to do with any precision. However, contextual references to culture, the practice of a monotheistic creed, and the lifestyle depicted indicate that if there was a historical land known as Uz, it existed in or near the tribal lands of Edom.

As a note on the interpretation of places and times, in later biblical translations the word used in Genesis 25:18 is "Assyria." "Asshur" is perhaps more accurate for the age of Job, if not his author. Depending on when the author penned the book of Job, Assyria may not have been a kingdom of any note. Then again, some scholars believe it had already come and gone.

Job is the protagonist in the tale and whether he lived, and if so, when, is also a matter of debate. A man named Job appears in a few passages elsewhere in the Bible. In Ezekiel 14:14, 20, the text indicates that Job's righteousness could only save himself and not his compatriots. James 5:11 remarks on his patience. These brief references attest to the durability of the story and indicate that a person named Job was real enough, or deep enough in Hebrew tradition, that his name invoked specific traits and experiences.

The Arabic form of Job is *Ayyob*. Some sources indicate that the name means, "I repent," or "persecuted." Another meaning for the name in Arabic is "supplanter" (something akin to the meaning of Jacob), and the derivative Jobab can mean "to cry" or "call shrilly." In literature, the meaning behind a name can be significant and not dependent on historical existence. Later chapters in this book investigate this possibility; for now, the goal is to find a historical anchor for the backstory of the book.

For a Job or Jobab, the chart indicates some possibilities that are in the line of Joktan and Edom. Scripture references an idolatrous king in Canaan in Joshua's time (Josh 11:1) and two descendants in the line of Benjamin who precede King Saul (1 Chr 8:9, 18). Neither the Canaanite king nor the later Benjamites seem to fill the role of a wealthy man of the East who is an adherent of a monotheistic faith. An intriguing candidate is a man called Iob listed as a son of Issachar, who was one of those that accompanied Jacob and his clan to Egypt during the drought (Gen 46:13). However, this person would not align well with the heritage of Job's companions, whose tribal affiliations place them much later in biblical history.

Notably, the same sources that place Job near Damascus also suggest that he is the Edomite king referenced in Scripture, a successor of Esau. This theory found past success due to Arabic traditions and references in the Septuagint[3] that Job was a son

---

3. *Septuagint* is derived from the Latin word for "seventy" and refers to a Greek translation of the

of Zare, who was a son of Esau. The problem, of course, is that the distance between Damascus and Timna (an ancient city in southern Edom) is approximately 215 miles (346 kilometers). If Job is a personage of some note in Edom, Damascus is too far away to be a viable home.

And Job's three friends each journeyed from their home.

A substantial portion of the literature on Job analyzes the book based on contextual interpretations of who Job's friends were and what ideology they each represent. This approach requires sorting out where Job's companions may have come from and what ideology they held sacred. The structure of the discourses indicates that the theology or dogma of each of Job's friends contributes something specific to the debate. The prelude to the debates indicates that they held leadership roles within their communities. These were men whose words carried weight.

The problem is that there are varied opinions regarding how old the book of Job is and how old the story of Job might be. The issues created by determining the source and age of the material are interrelated. The best place to begin is with the internal evidence of the book. The book of Job presents itself as a tale of great age about an individual who is not an Israelite. Job is a believer in the God of Abraham and worships El Shaddai. These elements allow a hypothesis that the characters come from within the family of Abraham and his close relations. Here, then, are some suggestions regarding their pedigree. Even if the book of Job proves to be the result of a retelling, the characters and who they may represent may help in the interpretation of the poem.

Eliphaz, the Temanite, opens the dialogue. Eliphaz and Teman, or Tema, are prevalent names in the families of Esau and Ishmael. Some candidates for this tribal heritage include Tema, a son of Ishmael and a grandson of Esau. Eliphaz is also a popular biblical name. The name shows up as a son of Esau, and as the third king of Edom (Husham). A geographical location for Tema also supports both choices for linage. The *Jewish Encyclopedia* places Tema in the southern portion of Edom.[4] As a representative of the wisdom of the Edomites, Eliphaz is a leader within the warrior tribes (Job 6:19) and desert dwellers (Isa 21; Jer 25:23).

The next character in the cast is Bildad, the Shuhite. "Shuhite" is a derivative of Shuah, a name found on the chart as a son of Abraham and Keturah (Abraham's second wife, Gen 25:2). The name Shuah also appears as a wife of Judah (son of Jacob) and as a descendant of Judah, living during the time of Israel's judges. Neither of these latter persons are likely candidates since they appear too late in biblical history. The Shuhites are desert dwellers. One of Shuah's brothers is Midian, an ancestor of the

---

Hebrew Bible completed in Alexandria, Egypt, in the third century BCE. The work is presumed to have been translated and compiled by seventy Jewish scholars. Original texts of the New Testament show evidence that the Septuagint was a frequently quoted source.

4. König and Hirsch, "Eliphaz."

tribe of Jethro who was Moses' father-in-law. The Midianite tribal lands were located far south of Edom along the coast of the Gulf of Aqaba in modern Saudi Arabia. Adhering to a premise that these men are descendants of Abraham and his extended family, Bildad could take his place as a representative of the tribes descended from Abraham through his second wife, Keturah.

Job's third companion is Zophar, the Naamathite. The oldest references to the name Naaman in Scripture are to persons in the family of Benjamin, the son of Jacob (Gen 46:21). These are a grandson and a great-great-grandson through Benjamin's son Bela. Admittedly, this reference rarely appears in study guides, possibly due to the late date such a correlation would produce. Any other references to Naamath are far too late and do not appear to be the heads of any desert tribes. Using the earliest possible reference, if the qualification is to remain within the Abrahamic tradition, Zophar's heritage appears to be from Abraham through Isaac and Jacob.

This analysis gives us a descendant of Abraham through his grandson Esau, his grandson Jacob, and his son Shuah (with Keturah). How the faith of Abraham developed through each of these branches may help interpret the book and the goals of the author.

Suddenly, an angry young man appears.

After a long-winded debate among Job and his three companions, a fifth individual invades the conversation. This new voice, Elihu the Buzite, describes himself as a very angry young man. Elihu is a mystery. Although his speech indicates he has been present for the entire debate, he is silent until all others have spoken. After his outburst, he disappears again and retreats into the background. Before the nineteenth century, Jewish and Christian biblical scholars debated the authenticity of Elihu's contribution. Larry J. Waters contributed an article that provided some history on the matter.[5] He concludes that the Elihu speeches are authentic and are an integral part of the text. Excluding the speeches could be rather unsettling since many of the medieval Jewish philosophers believed that Elihu's speech is pivotal to interpreting the book. If his speech is part of the original text, then his heritage could contribute to the interpretation of the message.

Elihu means "he is my God." In Job 32:2, he is called a son of Barachel, the Buzite, within the family of Ram. Buz is a son of Nahor and a nephew of Abraham (Gen 22:21). Nahor is part of the family line of Rebekah, Rachael, and Leah, the wives of Abraham's son and grandson. There is also a Buz in the genealogy of Gad, one of the tribes of Israel (a son of Jacob) who lived sometime during the period of the judges (1 Chr 5:14). The only alternate reference to someone named Ram is in Matthew in the recitation of the lineage of Jesus. In Matthew, Ram is a descendant of Judah and an

---

5. Waters, "Authenticity of Elihu Speeches," 28–41.

ancestor of David and Jesus (Matt 1:3–4). According to these references, Elihu's heritage sprang from the sons and grandsons of the patriarchs mentioned above, although he may be more closely related to the matriarchs of the family. His heritage also underlines his claim to youth. Buz means "contempt," echoing Elihu's angry and arrogant attitude. His heritage is somewhat convoluted and contributes to the uncertainty of his place in the story. Perhaps this confusion is one of the reasons that some scholars looked at Elihu as an interloper or a construct of a later scribe who was attempting to keep the message more traditional.

The Raiders and Robbers

The book of Job uses contextual references that correlate with extrabiblical recorded history. For instance, the identity of the raiders that struck Job's livestock and carried off his four-footed wealth. The first of these historical peoples mentioned is the Sabeans, the raiders of Job's donkeys and oxen. Some references suggest they are the decedents of the family of Joktan (Shem) or Cush (Ham). The former occupied an area in the southern portion of the Arabian Peninsula (modern-day Yemen) and the latter in east Africa near Egypt. Recent archaeological discoveries strongly support the supposition that the original land of Sheba was in Yemen at or near Marib Dam.[6] Archeological excavations indicate that the kingdom of the Sabeans expanded at some point into Africa, establishing trading posts in countries now known as Eritrea and Somalia.

There are strong traditions in Ethiopia (south and west of these two countries) that the country was the home of the Queen of Sheba and that the country's royal house descended from the queen and Solomon. The historian Josephus speaks of a walled royal city in Ethiopia called Saba, the Arabic form of Sheba. Josephus writes that the conquest of Saba by a young Egyptian prince exposed the prince's identity as the Hebrew slave known to Scripture as Moses. This conquest, of course, would have occurred several centuries before Solomon met the fabled queen.

The *Jewish Encyclopedia* notes that Abraham and Keturah bore a son named Shuah, and he bore a son called Sheba.[7] Bildad, one of Job's companions, came from this same lineage. Based on this information, there are three possible claims to the name "Sabeans": peoples located in Africa in or near the city of Saba (also referenced by Strabo, the Greek geographer), in Arabia, or in Canaan.

Archeologists have been able to identify the Sabeans of southern Arabia as the founders of a kingdom spanning the Red Sea. They were traders marketing such highly prized commodities as frankincense and myrrh. Both spices are the source of resins used in embalming, offerings to the gods, medicines, and perfumes. They also

---

6. Stewart, "A Dam at Marib."
7. Jastrow and Nowack, "Bildad."

traded in the riches of the Far East, bringing silks and a variety of other spices to the ancient Middle East.

The Sabeans were ingenious engineers, having constructed the Marib Dam as early as the seventh century BCE. The dam spanned an 1,800-foot gap and rose fifteen feet above the watercourse. The dam provided the source of water guided by an extensive irrigation system that supported the ancient agricultural economy of the area. In Job 6:19, Sheba and Tema travel in caravans and seek out watercourses in the desert, which indicates a knowledge of the desert and established trade routes. Although the backstory of Job may be more ancient than the engineering feat at Marib, the nature of the Sabean economy supports them in the role of the thieves of Job's agricultural livestock.

The second group of people described in the book are the Chaldeans, the raiders who carried off Job's vast herd of camels. The history of the Chaldeans is rather muddled. According to the Chaldean Community Foundation, Chaldeans are synonymous with, or at least the later descendants of, Babylonians.[8] However, the *Jewish Encyclopedia* develops a different picture.[9] The encyclopedia indicates that the Chaldeans were a Semitic people, possibly originating in Arabia. They migrated at some point to the head of the Persian Gulf, arriving at about the same time that the Arameans appeared in Babylon. Semitic in origin, the Chaldeans expanded into the whole region of southern Mesopotamia and their name became synonymous with Babylon. Assimilated at some point, the Chaldeans remained apart from their neighbors to the degree that many centuries later, Sennacherib (Assyrian king 705–681 BCE) set them apart from their Aramean neighbors in his inscriptions. Sorting out who is a Chaldean and who is a Babylonian can be a bit of a project.

Ur of the Chaldees was the home of Terah before he left to move to Haran (located near the southern border of Turkey). He took Abram, Nahor, and the family of their deceased brother with him. This biblical reference indicates that the Chaldeans established and possibly ruled this southern Mesopotamian country long before the time of Abraham.

In the modern world, these peoples make up part of the indigenous populations of Iraq. Archaeologists set the founding of the city of Babylon around 1867 BCE. The Assyrians conquered the Babylonians around 934 BCE during the expansion of their empire and near at least one date for the reign of Solomon. During the reign of Nebuchadnezzar (a Chaldean), the Babylonians revolted against Assyria and regained prominence in Mesopotamia in approximately 625 BCE. The Assyrians were completely defeated by 609 BCE. Although suggested dates of the Judean exile to Babylon vary, the *Jewish Encyclopedia* cites 597 BCE.[10]

---

8. See the Chaldean Community Foundation, http://www.chaldeanfoundation.org.
9. Hirsch et al., "Chaldea."
10. Gottheil, et al, "Captivity, or Exile, Babylonian."

Is this enough information to set the story within a historical reference? Looking at the chart, most of the reference points for the ancestors of the characters are around the time of the patriarchs (Abraham, Isaac, and Jacob). One would need to move forward in time a few generations to allow sizeable, extended-family households to develop.

One key factor in determining how many generations later is the reference to a son of Jacob in the general area of Canaan. Scripture states that Jacob and his sons moved to Egypt to avoid a drought. According to Genesis, Jacob's entire family migrated to Egypt, and his descendants did not return until some uncertain number of generations later. There is no mention in Scripture that anyone in Jacob's family remained in Canaan. However, biblical scholarship and archaeology over the past few centuries has revealed there may be more to the story. A thesis by Coyt David Hargus describes the conflicting theories.[11] If the heritage of the characters does not resolve the timing of the events, what other clues does the text provide that will help clarify the setting and the meaning of the book?

---

11. Hargus, "Theories of the Israelite Occupation."

Chapter 2

A Bit of Exegesis

Keeping in mind that a goal of this book is to retell the story of Job by starting with the roots of the story, a short lesson in biblical commentary will help. The authorship and circumstances of the book have an impact on the interpretation of the message. Scholars do not have access to the original manuscripts. What they do have is a collection of writings that have survived millennia of retelling and copying, of translating and recompiling, and of synods and conferences. As archeologists unearth the distant past, they continue to find information that elucidates the current understanding of the message and the people who originally put Scripture into words. Ignoring this evidence is not wise if the goal is to understand the heritage passed down to modern times.

There are scholars in the field of biblical criticism who approach Scripture as separate from a personally held faith and some who focus on destroying its usefulness as a spiritual guide. Some scholars are devoted to the support of scriptural heritage as the foundation of faith. Both groups provide a wealth of information that helps the interested student better understand the circumstances, the lifestyle, and the symbology used by the original authors.

Many centuries of analysis contributed to the development of a family tree of scriptural texts. Scholars can determine if a writer or speaker in the New Testament had access to the Greek Septuagint or an Aramaic form of the text by comparing New Testament passages to known surviving texts. These clues can be crucial to the study of biblical manuscripts by providing support regarding whom the author may have been, what they were saying, and to whom.

Did inspired men and women write the Bible? Most certainly yes. However, their inspiration was also a part of the world in which they lived, the challenges they faced, the heartbreaks and joys they knew. An author writes using the imagery shared with the intended audience. For these reasons, knowing the when, where, and how of a message is a fundamental piece of understanding the what. Given this approach, what does the text say about the people depicted and the author who set it all down for future generations?

Textual Evidence

Exegesis is one of the tools that aids in reaching an understanding of the content of a passage. The science, and sometimes art, of exegesis is not some esoteric exercise beyond the understanding of the layperson or the nonacademic. The term means to interpret the passage using the clear text meaning. Every reader practices this method when introduced to a piece of literature. To understand the message the author wishes to convey, the reader considers the content and context of the work.

Methods developed by exegetes include processes that scrutinize the structure, the evident language, and words that appear to be anachronisms or derivatives from a different language. They would also determine the historical setting found within the text and similarities in style and delivery to other known literature. This type of study helps the scholar surmise whether the author was reporting a historical event or using a composite of events or persons to illustrate a point. Is the piece a work of fiction written for pleasure, or is it a parable used to convey a philosophical or theological point? Does the text derive from an eyewitness account, or is it an interpretation of a shared experience?

Understanding the words used or the structure of the prose or poetry also reveals something about the original author: where did they live, what was their cultural background, and what pool of knowledge was available as a resource? Imagine how an indigenous person might have described the first train they saw. Without knowing something about the times the author lived in while telling a story, there may be difficulty recognizing an iron horse within a vision of a fantastical myth about a fire-breathing monster. Even the reference to an iron horse may be a lost comparison after a few more generations of high-speed trains.

Hermeneutics is the study of the principles of interpretations using theories, methods, exegesis, and etymology. Etymology is a field that looks for word origins. Neither exegesis nor hermeneutics is an attack on Scripture. Each brings a different set of tools to help better understand who wrote the passage, why the author wrote it, and what the intended message may be.

Chapter 3 looks more closely at the linguistic structure of Job; however, an overview of the history of the Hebrew language can help place the events portrayed and the authorship of the book. Research into the history of a family of languages can be daunting, especially when there are borrowed words or parallel developments from a shared mother tongue. The *Jewish Encyclopedia* indicates that Hebrew (as a dialect or derivative of Canaanitish) was in use by 3000 BCE.[1] Initially, the Canaanite languages

---

1. Toy and Levias, "Hebrew Language."

A Bit of Exegesis

developed from a very ancient Semitic root. Hebrew is related to Ugarit and Phoenician (the languages of peoples located on the eastern shores of the Mediterranean). Another language with Canaanite heritage used frequently by the Semitic peoples is Aramaic. Aramaic is the original language of portions of the biblical text, and there are elements of Aramaic in Hebrew. Therefore, knowledge of Aramaic assists scholars with the interpretation of Scripture and original word meanings.

The development of Classical Hebrew (or pre-exilic) occurred from approximately 1500 to 1000 BCE. During the Babylonian exile in the sixth century BCE, Aramaic, as the language of the empire, became a stronger influence. Scripture notes that Nehemiah was frustrated that so few of the returning Jews knew Hebrew (Neh 23:24). A post-classical version of Hebrew became archaic and fell out of common use after the destruction of the second temple in 70 CE.

Modern spoken Hebrew is a derivative of Classical Hebrew. Due to spelling and usage changes, the older version of any language is not always easy to understand. To illustrate this issue, compare modern English to the English used in a 1611 version of the King James Bible. Even with a relatively short historical separation, changes in usage, spelling, and meanings make it difficult for the modern reader to be sure of the content or intended meaning.

Dating the language used in the book of Job helps to clarify whether the book is a translation from an Arabic or Aramaic original. Eduard Kutscher investigates the usage of Aramaic in Scripture in his work titled *A History of the Hebrew Language.*[2] He notes that Aramaic contributes to the Hebrew in the book, but there are no indications that anything other than Hebrew was the original language of Job. Edward Greenstein wrote an article on the poetic motives of peppering dialogues with Aramaic called "The Language of Job and Its Poetic Function."[3] In personal correspondence, Greenstein stresses that the original language of Job was, indeed, Hebrew. He further clarifies that

> it was a highly literary use of Hebrew, and the occasional awkwardness of its use, in Job, probably stems from the author's being a native Aramaic speaker, not a Hebrew speaker. His knowledge of Hebrew was broad and deep—but it does not always flow; it has an artificial feel to it very often.[4]

Gary A. Rendsburg takes the position that the book's original language is Hebrew and that the author used expressions from Aramaic to authenticate his characters.[5] S. A. Kaufman, a linguist with expertise in the Semitic languages, believed that the

---

2. Kutscher, *Hebrew Language.*
3. Greenstein, "Language of Job," 651–66.
4. Edward Greenstein, personal correspondence with the author, quoted with permission.
5. Rendsburg, "Linguistic Variation."

original language of the book was a Trans-Jordanian[6] version of Hebrew.[7] Rendsburg takes the position that the book of Job was originally written in Hebrew to address an Israelite audience. He quotes Lynda Hungerford, who wrote that any author who wishes to keep a reader involved might use idioms, which would represent the speech of a character.[8] Rendsburg and Kaufman published later than Kutscher and (in the opinion of Greenstein) misuse the notion of *style switching*. Greenstein, who has recently completed a new translation of Job, sees the usage of Aramaic as a natural occurrence within the development of the characters, a vehicle to add flavor and context.

The composition of the text can also help scholars address the issue of possible interpolations within the text. An interpolation is an addition by the author, a later scribe, or a compiler after the original publication of a work. A case in point is the contribution of Elihu. Elihu intrudes at the last minute, falls silent again just as quickly, and has an ambiguous heritage. His speech is a condemnation of Job and his companions, and yet he reiterates some of the same themes. Not only does his contribution seem to truncate Bildad's last speech, Zophar is missing from the third round of debate. Elihu is missing from the epilogue, where God doles out rewards and recriminations. If Elihu's defense of the divine right of God to punish as he and only he sees fit is right, then it appears God would at least mention him in the closing comments. From another perspective, the medieval Jewish philosophers saw Elihu's speech as the main point of the book. As stark as this dialog is, the structure supports Elihu's contribution as part of the original work or as added by the same author after receiving some feedback.

There are several themes in Job echoed in Psalms and Proverbs. Compare Job 28:28 with Proverbs 1:7; 9:10; and Psalms 111:10.

> He said to man, "See! Fear of the Lord is wisdom; To shun evil is understanding." (Job 28:28)

> The fear of the Lord is the beginning of knowledge; Fools despise wisdom and discipline. (Proverbs 1:7)

> The beginning of wisdom is fear of the Lord; and knowledge of the Holy One is understanding. (Proverbs 9:10)

> The beginning of wisdom is the fear of the Lord; all who practice it gain sound understanding. (Psalms 111:10)

The Hebrew is nearly identical in some of the passages. The question is which text came first?

---

6. The geographic area, not the modern country.
7. Kaufman, "Aramaic," 114–30.
8. Hungerford, "Dialect Representation," 3–15.

A Bit of Exegesis

There are also strong cross-textual references to Deuteronomy. Compare Deuteronomy 28:31–33 with Job 1:13–19. Deuteronomy lists the types of curses that will occur for disobedience, and Job echoes those curses.

> Your ox shall be slaughtered before your eyes, but you shall not eat of it; your ass shall be seized in front of you, and it shall not be returned to you; your flock shall be delivered to your enemies, with none to help you. Your sons and daughters shall be delivered to another people, while you look on; and your eyes shall strain for them constantly, but you shall be helpless. A people you do not know shall eat up the produce of your soil and all your gains; you shall be abused and downtrodden continually, until you are driven mad by what your eyes behold. (Deuteronomy 28:31–34)

> One day, as his sons and daughters were eating and drinking wine in the house of their eldest brother, a messenger came to Job and said, "The oxen were plowing and the she-asses were grazing alongside them when Sabeans attacked them and carried them off; and put the boys to the sword; I alone have escaped to tell you." This one was still speaking when another came and said, "God's fire fell from heaven, took hold of the sheep and the boys, and burned them up; I alone have escaped to tell you." This one was still speaking when another came and said, "A Chaldean formation of three columns made a raid on the camels and carried them off and put the boys to the sword; I alone have escaped to tell you." This one was still speaking when another came and said, "Your sons and daughters were eating and drinking wine in the house of their eldest brother when suddenly a mighty wind came from the wilderness. It struck the four corners of the house so that it collapsed upon the young people and they died; I alone have escaped to tell you." (Job 1:13–19)

Compare Deuteronomy 28:37, "You shall be a consternation, a proverb, and a byword among all the peoples," with Job 17:6, "He made me a byword among people." Given this symmetry, understanding the origins and dating of the book of Deuteronomy is a matter of importance. Does the vision of punishment and reward in Deuteronomy take a central role in the arguments presented in Job? Does this approach somehow limit the message to the nation of Israel, or is it still a universal message? Alternately, is the author retelling the story to tease out a different answer to suffering? Is the writer seeking an answer that looks beyond the curses and blessings model of Deuteronomy?

Another question to answer is if the author is invoking the promises of Deuteronomy to lay the foundation for Job's challenge. In Job's view, he adhered to the commands of God and has every reason to expect the promised blessings. Why then is he cursed? If the blessings and curses promised in Deuteronomy are accurate, Job's companions have reason to suspect that Job has broken the covenant. Putting Job in the context of the ancient covenant, as defined in Deuteronomy, might help broaden the questions at hand. If adhering to the law produces blessings, why then underserved suffering?

According to the *Jewish Encyclopedia*, tradition and internal evidence indicate that the book of Deuteronomy could be the Teachings found during the reign of Josiah (641–609 BCE), four generations before the conquest by Babylon.[9] Josiah's workers found the book while renovating the temple (2 Kgs 22). Further research reveals that Deuteronomy was a sacred text dating to the reign of Solomon. Jewish tradition and scholarship point to a theory that the book is a part of the scriptural heritage returned to Judah by the Israelites of the northern kingdom when they fled the Assyrian army. The defeat of Israel occurred approximately 740–722 BCE.

There are several textual references which support this conclusion. One is the emphasis on a central place of worship. The Israelites worshiped according to the law set out in Leviticus (although not necessarily continuously) for centuries. Those practices, however, did not dictate a central place of worship, whereas Deuteronomy does. A permanent, central tabernacle did not become part of Hebrew worship until the period between the last judge (Samuel) and the beginning of the age of the monarchy (Saul).

Deuteronomy takes the writings of Exodus, Numbers, and Leviticus and presents the requirements, laws, and obligations with some of the logic behind the whys. Deuteronomy 1 does declare that this is the sermon given by Moses to the nation just before the Israelites entered the promised land and immediately before his death. However, in addition to the issue of a central place of worship, some conundrums lead scholars to the conclusion that even if the teachings of Moses are the source material for the book, the book itself was likely not written by him. Within the book of Deuteronomy, there are references to places, people, and events that did not exist until after the death of Moses. The core of the Jewish faith, the Pentateuch, is typically attributed to Israel's first and most beloved lawgiver (or messenger); however, the book itself tells a different tale.

Christians also see the Pentateuch as coming from the hand of Moses. Several New Testament verses quote passages from Deuteronomy to which Jesus adds, "Moses commanded."[10] Such statements, however, are not a direct endorsement of the belief that Moses penned the manuscript of Deuteronomy. The authority acknowledged by Jesus supports Moses' spiritual direction of the nation and his contribution to the foundation of Hebrew law. Again, Deuteronomy speaks to things that were not in evidence during the generally accepted lifetime of Moses. Most notably is his death and Joshua's rise to power in chapter 34. However, there are also references to the division of the land and the agreements required for the nation to cross into Canaan

---

9. Singer and Lauterbach, "Josiah."

10. Matt 19:7–8 (Deut 24:1–4); Matt 22:24 (Deut 25:5–10); Mark 7:10 (Deut 5:16); Mark 12:19 (Deut 25:5–10); John 8:5 (Deut 22:21–24).

A Bit of Exegesis

and assume ownership of the land. The book ends with "until this day," indicating the writer is recounting something that occurred in the past.[11]

A better understanding of the source material for the Pentateuch requires a brief introduction to the JEDP theory of authorship.[12] The acronym stands for Jahwist, Elohist, Deuteronomy, and Priestly. By studying the most ancient manuscripts available to the modern researcher, and comparing composition and style, scholars have concluded there are four primary contributors to the Torah.

1. The Jahwist contribution includes writings that describe God as Yahweh. These passages include most of Genesis, parts of Exodus, and Numbers. The proposed date of composition or compilation is approximately 850 BCE.

2. The Elohist is a description that comes from names describing God using El or Elohim. The line between the usage of Yahweh vs. Elohim is rather vague. Suggested compilation is around 750 BCE.

3. Deuteronomy, according to scholars of Hebrew texts, appears to be sourced from different material than evidenced for other portions of the Pentateuch. The estimated time of composition is 621 BCE. Some scholars date the original composition during the reign of Solomon (approximately three hundred years earlier). Scholars believe this could be the text rediscovered by Josiah (641–609 BCE).

4. Priestly is used to describe writings that seem to have a different flavor than the rest of the text. The passages attributed to this author (or authors) appear in several places from Genesis 1 to Deuteronomy. Scholars date these contributions to around 500 BCE.[13]

Proponents of JEDP vary on what part Moses played in the formation of these books. Some believe his role was minimal; some postulate that he was responsible for the core philosophy and theology of the books while later authors wrote the text. In general, scholars believe that Moses' wisdom was responsible for the critical elements and theological development of the Pentateuch.

Deuteronomy does stand apart contextually. The earlier books say, "do this," Deuteronomy adds, "because of this." The book also makes promises regarding the consequences of following the law or ignoring it. According to the *Jewish Encyclopedia*, the influence of Deuteronomy is evident upon the writings of the later prophets, such as Amos and Hosea.[14] However, this influence is missing from earlier prophets, such as Joshua, Judges, and Samuel. These are a few of the reasons that Jewish scholars

---

11. Barrick, "Authorship of Deuteronomy."
12. "JEDP Theory."
13. Ezra lived approximately 480–440 BCE. He is the priest credited with the composition of the books of Chronicles, and Scripture notes he was tasked with the preservation of Hebrew texts. Perhaps he influenced the priestly tone of these edits.
14. Jastrow, et al., "Deuteronomy."

associate the book with Josiah's reformation. All the elements presented within Deuteronomy are established by the time of the monarchy, not before.

Another theory in keeping with the research is that a scribe or author compiled the sermons and teachings given by Moses into a book sometime during or near the reign of Solomon. As noted above, the Teachings then found their way to the Northern Kingdom of Israel during the national split. They were then subsequently returned to Judah when the refugees fled the approach of Assyria. The voice used in the book is not that of a political or legal authority; rather, it bears the tone of a prophet or priest.

When Josiah's workers found the Teachings, the king formed a committee which consisted of a scribe, Shaphan, and the high priest, Hilkiah (who could not read the Teachings himself). These two men then sought out a prophetess by the name of Huldah to see what importance these scrolls had for the nation. Inspired men *and* women working together to convey a message (2 Kgs 22).

There are several rigorous studies which focus on the question of authorship of the entire Pentateuch.[15] Internal citations and traditions of both Christians and Jews point to Moses as the author. Jesus refers to the Pentateuch as the Law of Moses. Scriptural references credit the author of Israel's legal, social, and theological structure as Moses. However, establishing Moses as author of the core spiritual truths included in the Pentateuch does not preclude later compilations and works based on the legacy of the Lawgiver. Certainly, the content of these cornerstones of faith is the foundation of the traditions, laws, and experiences of the ancient tribe of Abraham's blood. What scholars are still researching is how that information was recorded, edited, translated, and delivered to modern readers.

Taking time to understand the source of Deuteronomy is an important piece of understanding its consequential influences on later writings. Evidence within the text of Deuteronomy might also lead to conclusions supporting the authorship and date of writing for the book of Job. If a portion of Deuteronomy, which was post-patriarchal by any standards and most likely composed or compiled around 900 BCE, reflects the content within the book of Job, then the authorship of Job must be placed later, whatever the historical context of the original tale may be. Some portions of Old Testament writings went through many periods of compilation, interpretation, and rediscovery. Scripture itself bears this out, as seen in the story of Josiah and his team of renovators and reformers.

---

15. Thomas Hobbes was one of the first to press the issue in 1651. He pointed out several passages that indicated a later composition, such as those referring to Moses' grave, and the reference to Canaanites "then" living in the land (implying they were not at the time of writing). Other scholars such as Baruch Spinoza, Richard Simon, and John Hampden came to the same conclusion. Their works were condemned, and several of them were imprisoned. An attempt was made on Spinoza's life. Jean Astruc developed the original Documentary Hypothesis in 1753. Karl Graf revised the initial work in the mid-nineteenth century, and Julius Wellhausen refined the work. This research was the basis of the JEDP theory.

A BIT OF EXEGESIS

Historical and Cultural Content

The circumstances of the characters within the story of Job can help date the events described in the prologue of the book. The cultural situation describes the desert tribes of the region between the Mediterranean shores and the Mesopotamian valley. Job is the head of a household consisting of his family, servants, and their families. He owns large herds to help in trade and agricultural pursuits (1:14). This description is that of many of the tribal families in biblical times, from Terah through the period of the judges. Job's household was not nomadic, as evidenced by the presence of oxen plowing in the fields.

In the book of Job, the word used for God is El Shaddai, or Lord God Almighty. El or El Shaddai is the name used when God appears before Abraham and forms a covenant with him. According to the *Jewish Encyclopedia*, El Shaddai is the name of God used by the patriarchs (Exod 6:2–3).[16] It also appears in the book of Ruth in Naomi's prayer. The tale of Ruth, set around the time of the judges, deals with a family living in Moab, east of Canaan.

El Shaddai appears in the story of Balaam (Num 24:4). The story of Balaam and his resistance to cursing the Israelites occurs just as the Israelites are nearing the borders of Canaan after their sojourn in Egypt. Of the forty-eight occurrences of this appellation in the Bible, thirty of them are in Job. El Shaddai is a name for God during a time of tribal loyalties and the patriarchs, not the time of Moses and his countrymen. The usage in Ruth indicates that the cousins of the Israelites continued to use the name as late as the period of the judges.

By using this older name of God, the author may also be drawing an image of a personal God, one that conversed with his creation on a personal level and, occasionally, argued with them. This view of God is very different from the portrait of a national God of Israel. The image of El Shaddai is one of an accessible Creator, one who is willing and available to address questions regarding promises, blessings, and curses.

Some authorities use the practice of sacrificial offerings to lean toward a date in the age of the patriarchs. Such references point out that, with Moses, sacrifice moved to the tabernacle and the temple. However, only an Israelite would be welcome at the tabernacle, and, as noted above, a central place of worship did not exist until the formation of the monarchy. Likewise, the position that Job's form of worship limits him historically to an earlier date fails when compared to other passages within Scripture. For instance, Gideon, a judge, made sacrifices before and after his conflicts and did so within the confines of his tribal homeland (Judg 6).

Throughout the period between the Exodus and the monarchy, the dwellers of the Middle East included extended family units living with their livestock and engaging in what agriculture was appropriate for the climate of their homes. The characters, the geography, and the cultural indicators stage the tale within the backdrop of private

---

16. Hirsch, "God."

worship and extended tribal families. The household of tribal leaders included servants required for the successful operation of trade or agriculture and their families.

Another contextual clue used to establish an approximate date for a man called Job derives from a direct poetic reference to the exodus. Job 9:13 reads, "God does not restrain His anger; Under Him Rahab's helpers sink down." Job 26:12 states, "By His power He stilled the sea; By His skill He struck down Rahab." Here, Rahab, in Hebrew lore, is a sea monster like Leviathan, which represents the Red Sea. The Hebrew word used here should not be confused with the Rahab of Jericho fame; the words are different in the Hebrew script. Elsewhere, Rahab represents the political power of Egypt, and the passage in Job is referring to her defeat, placing the authorship of the book, if not the story itself, as occurring post-exodus. The Hebrew word used in Job appears in four other passages in the Old Testament (Ps 87:41; 89:8–100; Isa 30:6–7; 51:9–10). In each of these cases, the Hebrew refers to the harlot Egypt and her destruction. There are also extrabiblical sources that contribute to the understanding of specific historical reference points within the book.

Extrabiblical sources which help define the story or the authorship of Job include such things as animal domestication and metalsmithing. Interestingly, the domestication of camels is a hotly debated topic. Recent news articles in both the popular and the faith media have noted that camels have no place in Genesis since they were not domesticated that early in history. The Research Institute of Wildlife Ecology at Vetmeduni Vienna recently conducted a study testing this theory. Pamela Burger of the institute explained how their project analyzed DNA known to be as much as seven thousand years old derived from wild and early domesticated dromedaries.[17] Their research indicated that camels were first used as domestic animals *over* three thousand years ago in the southeastern Arabian Peninsula. The institute's findings refute earlier studies that placed domestication around 1000 BCE. Neil Asher Silberman and Israel Finkelstein wrote that there was no evidence of camels in the Levant at the time of Job's story, let alone highly developed trade routes.[18] Broader studies, such as those conducted by the Research Institute of Wildlife Ecology, are uncovering a more complex story as the peoples of the Mesopotamia, Egypt, and the Levant competed for resources and knowledge. What is important for this discussion is to understand that the search for historical truth continues, even while such information contributes to increased clarity regarding the message Scripture holds for modern readers.

The art of smelting metal is another development that researchers have used to support a date of authorship for the book of Job. In verse 28:2, Job mentions that "iron is taken from the earth and copper is smelted from ore." Since the development of smelted metals took place at different times in different places, any discussion supporting access to smelted metals is dependent on archaeological evidence within

---

17. "Dromedary Camel Domestication."

18. See Silberman and Finkelstein, *The Bible Unearthed*. Note: The book met with a mixed reception within the community of biblical scholars.

A Bit of Exegesis

the region in question. According to an article posted by the Cambridge University Press,[19] analysis as recent as February of 2016 indicates that iron was produced systematically in the Levant by approximately 1000–800 BCE. As a case in point, the use of alloys might have been part of the turning point in the struggle between the Israelites and the Philistines. The shift in power occurred at the time when the tribes formed a monarchy under the leadership of Saul, ca. 1000–950 BCE. Knowledge of smelting iron was not something that would have been common knowledge at the time of Moses. Consequently, this reference again points to a later date of authorship.

Using the internal evidence of domesticated camels and metalsmithing does not help to confirm or deny a claim of historicity or provide a date of authorship. With the mention of iron and smelted metals, either the author is using an anachronistic reference, or he is placing the original tale somewhere during the time of the judges or the early years of the Israelite monarchy. The same is true regarding the domestication of camels, which current research sets at some time before three thousand years ago in this part of the Middle East.

Assessing these details and understanding the source of the "many scholars believe" claims is part of rebuilding the story. Researching the roots of a position enables the reader to delineate between tradition and a supportable interpretation. In the end, collecting these clues about the story and the text will help retell the story for the audience of the original author of the book of Job, and modern readers in search of the same answers.

---

19. Yahalom-Mack and Eliyahu-Behar, "Transition from Bronze to Iron," 285–305.

Chapter 3

The Language, the Author, the Date

Wisdom Poetry at Its Best

THERE IS, AS IN all things scriptural, disagreement regarding how to interpret the different styles of writing in the book of Job. Some scholars believe that the book derives from at least two sources, one being an ancient folktale and another the writings of a different author who created the poetic dialogues.[1] There are also conflicting opinions regarding the composition of the poetic passages, such as whether the present text represents the full original or if there is some later revision or addition. As noted above, there is disagreement regarding Elihu's speech. One opinion is that his sudden appearance and disappearance is a contribution by a later scribe concerned about the clarity of the message. His speech does interrupt the symmetry of the earlier dialogues.

The conclusion in this book is that one author wrote the book of Job, an opinion supported by the work of Edward Greenstein.[2] The difference in format between the folktale and the poem is analogous to a format employed in classical literature. As in Greek plays and many operas or staged plays, there is an opening narrative, which provides an outline of the events. Within that outline, the author provides important information to the audience that the characters do not know.

This man, Job, is blameless and righteous before God, and yet he loses all his possessions, his family, and his health. The prelude is followed by three rounds of poetic dialogues between the various characters, with the final round interrupted by the discourse of a new partner in the debate. Lastly, there are two discourses delivered by God to which Job responds. The book closes with another narrative describing Job's return to good fortune.

The bulk of the book is in poetic form. One of the features of Hebrew poetry is that it follows patterns of thought rhymes, rather than word rhymes or meter

---

1. Ehrman, *God's Problem*, 162–4.
2. Greenstein recently completed *Job: A New Translation*, published by Yale University Press.

patterns.[3] The analysis of the poetic structure of the passages found in Job, Psalms, and the Song of Solomon requires a firm grasp of the language and the culture. For scholars that focus on wisdom literature, the poetry within the book of Job reveals an author who understands the use of several languages and uses that skill to draw an indelible word-picture.

The author of Job uses Aramaic language components. This technique was not merely a tool of characterization, or "flavoring." R. J. Ratner suggests that the authors of biblical texts would use paired synonyms to provide variety as they emphasized key elements with repetition.[4] Repetition in poetry can provide a subtle, potent form of writing that helps develop a thought through varied aspects of the same concept. Like light through a prism, the varied wording can bring out innuendos and tease out philosophical and theological ideas to push the reader to think rather than to accept packaged answers. One of the reasons scholars believe the original language of the book is Hebrew is that it is a classic example of the style seen in Hebrew wisdom literature and poetry. For example, the author develops characters and the setting with Aramaic words and phrases. Rendsburg cites Job 9:9 as an example. The words used by Job for the constellations of Orion and the Bears are Aramaic. However, Hebrew words are used in Job 38:32 when God is speaking.[5]

For all Job's beauty, it is difficult to translate. For instance, the King James Version translates 36:33 as "The noise of it showeth concerning it; the cattle also concerning the vapor." The *Tanakh* translates this verse as "Its noise tells of Him. The kindling of anger against iniquity." The translators of the *Tanakh* add a footnote indicating that the last phrase is of uncertain meaning. A phrase that is nonsensical in one translation can offer clues to intention or provide poetic iteration when seen from a different linguistic view.

The structure of the poem is a compendium of ancient Hebrew philosophies. Scholars in this field believe the book was written originally by a learned individual, living in the hub of an active trading culture, or with access to the records of foreign neighbors. These layers within layers may have been the source of the medieval thought that Job addresses two (or more) audiences. Philosophers such as Maimonides believed that the plain text of the book speaks to the general masses who must be content with their lot. The deeper and more intricate language was for those initiated into the metaphysical sciences. In Gregory the Great's *Morals on the Book of Job*, section 4, he writes, "[The divine word] is, so to speak, like a river which is both deep and shallow, in which a lamb can walk and an elephant must swim" (540–604 CE).[6]

---

3. Poetic rhyme is a pattern of rhyming words at the end of each line, while meter is the pattern of syllables which are alternately stressed/unstressed. For instance: *He* knows *she* will *and* you *can* tell. (Iambic tetrameter).

4. Ratner, "Morphological Variation," 143–59.

5. Rendsburg, "Linguistic Variation," 178–83.

6. Simonetti and Conti, *Job*, xxiv.

Part I—Nuts and Bolts

Job has a greater diversity of forms and foreign words than any other book of the Bible, which is yet another reason that there is still debate regarding the original language used by the author. However, the book of Job shows clear evidence of an author whose use of Hebrew is artistic and rich in its presentation. The style did not require additional languages; the author's command of the Hebrew was more than equal to the task. Consequently, his use of foreign words and phrases was likely a product of the art rather than a carry-over from another language.

Another theory is that the language of Job is a dialect of Hebrew influenced by Aramaic and Canaanitic. Edward Greenstein of the Bar Ilan University in Tel Aviv thinks this proposal is highly unlikely. The influence of foreign languages is not casual; each instance is deliberate and matched with its Hebrew counterpart as an artistic emphasis to convey meaning. Greenstein uses the following example from Job 3:8, "May they execrate it—those who curse Yamm / The ones who are equipped, who curse Leviathan."[7] Job, in this passage, is cursing the day of his birth. Greenstein states that using the Canaanite sea-god Yamm in conjunction with Leviathan in a linguistic twist becomes, "May that night be execrated by the demons whose strength is sufficient to curse the dreaded Yamm/Leviathan; *and* may that night be cursed, eliminated, as all nights are, by the light of day."[8] Understanding the nuances developed in the sounds and meanings of the words adds a richness lost in translation.

The poetic style of the writer also provides clues regarding the status of Elihu. If Elihu is an interloper in structure as well as in speech, this would clearly show as a change in the style of the writing. Greenstein supports the theory that the Elihu passages were added, but most likely by the same author. The style and skill remain similar, if less elegant. Therefore, Greenstein is certain that the Elihu discourses came from the same hand, even if added after, perhaps, receiving community critiques. From personal correspondence:

> There is no major shift in poetics or linguistic use, however there are some subtle differences. Elihu is more repetitive, more verbose, and less brilliant than the other speakers. He has a few linguistic ticks that distinguish him from the other speakers as well.[9]

The author of Job uses Aramaic colloquialisms classified under two specific instances:

1. When the term occurs beside a known Hebrew synonym.
2. When the word appears in Aramaic texts of a concurrent period.

This clue leads scholars such as Greenstein to place the actual composition of the poem in the Persian period, ca. 400 BCE. Persian texts of the period frequently used

---

7. Greenstein. "Language of Job," 651–66.
8. Greenstein. "Language of Job," 651–66.
9. Edward Greenstein, personal correspondence with the author, quoted with permission.

such Aramaic linguistics. The author also uses words considered Aramaic which may prove to be Hebrew. Again, the writer of Job seems to weave the languages together deliberately by placing the Aramaic in direct contrast to the Hebrew while using the native language of his characters to set the scene for the reader. This evidence points to a conclusion that the book was written primarily for the serious student of Hebrew theology.

The Dead Sea Scrolls include fragments of the book of Job. The passages from the Dead Sea Scrolls, which date from around 200 BCE, show evidence of having originated in a very ancient form of Hebrew script dating to the tenth through the fifth century BCE (which would include some portion of the era of the judges). The scrolls also include an Aramaic translation dated around 100 BCE. The archeological record demonstrates that the story of Job was an ancient and treasured tale, making it an ideal cultural foundation for a message an author in later times wished to convey.

These literary tools allowed the author to create a culturally based backstory using language rather than descriptions of location or nationality. The intended reader would recognize both the legend and the setting, just as a modern reader would recognize a French or Spanish accent or the cultural atmosphere of Venice or New Orleans. This use of language may also point to the intended audience of the work. Scripture indicates that Ezra was distressed that so many of the returning remnant could not speak the Hebrew tongue. Had Babylon made the people cosmopolitan in their speech, more familiar with mixed references in the languages of many nations spoken within a large empire? Or is this author writing for a specific audience that has the skill to interpret his work and to think deeply about the ideas presented?

Who Wrote the Book of Job?

The Talmud, a body of commentary codified in the late fifth century CE, holds that Moses wrote the book of Job. The philosophical nature of the poem, the knowledge of ancient lore regarding the presence and purpose of evil, as well as the treatment of natural science within the poem all indicate a well-educated author. Such a resume would suggest the possibility of a scribe or a priest appointed to, or educated within, the royal courts of the ancient Middle East. Scripture provides biographical support for the idea that Moses was the author. Moses was certainly familiar with the philosophical arguments presented in the poem. There is also some evidence he had the education required in the natural sciences. Some of the views expressed may echo his growth during his years in Midian. The problem here, of course, is that the legend itself was determined to have occurred after the exodus and during the age of Israel's judges. Thus, the authorship cannot predate this period. So, if not Moses, then who?

The book provides no clues. Other traditional opinions place the poem sometime before Solomon's reign, during the time of Jacob, or during the time of the Persian king, Ahasuerus, mentioned in the book of Esther. In some cases, commentators cited in this book noted that Job is vague as to time and place, which provides some support that the source was a document in another language. However, the analysis of the internal linguistics examined above leads to the conclusion that Hebrew was the original language of the poem.

There are many segments of Scripture that are powerful and ageless yet bear no clues regarding the author. For the book of Job, the content and linguistic evidence might lead to possibilities. The author is comfortable with multiple languages and is well-versed in theology, philosophy, and the natural sciences. Several references within the text resonate with passages in Deuteronomy, Psalms, and Proverbs. Determining a relationship among these books may help define the order of authorship. That knowledge will lead to a possible time of authorship, even if the identity remains unknown.

Part of what Job addresses is what constitutes behavior subject to retribution and what sort of relief should be expected based on a life of devotion. Job also addresses the consequences of having a direct relationship with a sovereign deity. The book focuses on human suffering and how individuals respond to the consequences of suffering. The characters debate what protections or mediation humanity should expect from God. It is a reflective piece written to convey a deeper understanding of the action of evil or evil things in the world. Also, that understanding may include the activity of something called providence. Providence is defined as the protective care of God or of nature as a spiritual power.

Scholars note that the book deliberately places the story outside of Israel with characters who are not part of the covenant. Early Christian commentators see this as foreshadowing the Christian faith. They believe that this is an acknowledgment that salvation is not limited to a specific group or creed, but that it applies to any who choose to commit to God as defined within Judeo-Christian heritage. In the end, it may have been the use of a well-known legend from the early history of the Israelites to drive home a message without pointing fingers and putting the audience on the defensive.

A rather large portion of literature does just that: it takes a situation and puts it into a setting that is slightly different in time or place. Science fiction and fantasy writers do this frequently by creating a world or scenario they believe is a possible result of current socioeconomic practices. Once in that world, they create a story that highlights unintended consequences of policies and ideologies. Satire can also take a situation and push the outcome to some unacceptable conclusion to shock the reader into rethinking their position. "The Lottery" by Shirley Jackson and "A Modest Proposal" by Jonathan Swift are two examples of this technique. These are all illustrations of how authors can work through the moral or ethical points they wish to make in hopes that the reader will be able to take the lessons learned by the characters and apply those lessons to challenges faced in life. The poem could also be the musings of a

The Language, the Author, the Date

weary and saddened leader or spiritual scribe or priest, one looking for answers which would lead a people back to their spiritual roots.

The academic literature in this field suggests that determining the author's identity is difficult enough when a claim is made in antiquity and within the relevant passage or book. Speculating on the authorship when no such claim exists is virtually futile. However, leaving the question unaddressed is not helpful if the goal is to determine if the author intended to retell a story to convey new information, or reinforce existing doctrine. With Moses eliminated as a candidate due to the date of composition, a priest of the post-exilic period, perhaps Ezra, could be a consideration. According to Greenstein, Ezra is an unlikely author of an intensely poetic wisdom book.[10] This assessment is in part due to a comparison of writings attributed to Ezra.

There are reasons, however, to see Ezra's writing as an influence even if he is not an actual candidate for authorship. The style, content, and language of the book places the composition of the book somewhere in the middle of the Persian period. Ezra lived approximately 536–458 BCE. He was a prominent leader in one or more of the migrations of the remnants of Judah returning from Babylon to Judea. He is considered an accomplished scribe and may have been a high priest. The *Jewish Encyclopedia* credits him as the author of Chronicles, the book that bears his name, and as a potential source for input on the book of Nehemiah. Ezra is considered the second lawgiver (Moses being the undisputed first).[11]

Nehemiah was the practical organizer, and it was his task to raise the walls of Jerusalem and restore the temple complex. Ezra was the spiritual leader whose focus was to return the population to the law as given by God through Moses. In his enthusiasm for his quest, he initiated draconian requirements, including an effort to rid the population of mixed marriages. For Ezra, this was not an ethnic issue. He saw it as the only course of action available to cleanse his people from the influence of foreign gods.

Ezra was a keeper and preacher of the law. He was well equipped to preserve the prophets and the writings and to create a compilation of Israel's history based on the records preserved by the exiles. He had access to the history of his people and that of the empires of the ancient Middle East. Scripture describes how torn and discouraged he was by the apostasy of his people. During his years in Babylon, he wrote from his heart describing the misery of the diaspora.

The apocryphal book of 4 Esdras (sometimes referred to as 2 Esdras) records some aspects of his life. This book describes the seven visions he received before he left Babylon. Included in the seventh is the restoration of the writings of Israel. In that vision, God orders Ezra to compile and record all the known Scriptures of Israel. Some of these writings would be publicly distributed, while some would remain hidden or preserved for the wise alone.

10. Edward Greenstein, personal correspondence with the author, quoted with permission.
11. Jacobs, et al. "Ezra, Book of."

Throughout the text of the apocryphal writings, Ezra tries to console himself regarding the suffering of his people. He struggles with questions of the origin of suffering, and why there is evil in the world at all. How is it that an all-knowing and benevolent God could create humanity to suffer or do wrong? Why are humans given a mind to reason with that makes them conscious of these things? He concludes that a final resolution to these conundrums will not be known until some future time, in part because he remains certain of God's justice.

Ezra's visions refer to end-time scenarios when humanity's never-ending questions are answered. Each vision is rich in imagery familiar from Daniel and Ezekiel. As with Ezra's conclusion, commentators throughout history have determined that Job does not receive an answer. The prevailing analysis is that Job must wait for his answer, that it will only be available when his Redeemer stands upon the earth and the feast of Leviathan is made ready.

Ezra, as noted, fails as a candidate for authorship of Job. Based on style and content, academic literature supports a date of composition at approximately 400 BCE or some fifty years after Ezra laments the difficulty of returning his flock to the fold. Thus, lacking a name to assign to the author, Greenstein describes him as

> a brilliant poet living in Jerusalem (probably) around 400 BCE, with a deep familiarity with earlier Hebrew literature, whose Hebrew was extensive but book-learned more than native, who circulated his work within a small circle until the book became expanded and mellowed, by the addition of the Elihu chapters, at which time it became more widely copied and read.[12]

Perhaps this Persian-period scholar did have access to the writings of Ezra as he crafted an exquisite piece of wisdom literature. In addition to a thorough knowledge of Hebrew tradition and literature, the author had access to the leading thinkers of the age. Chapter 21 develops a view of the world in which this scholar lived and wrote. Was he influenced not only by Hebrew literature but also by the accumulated knowledge of an empire and the growing knowledge of Greek philosophers? Is his message buried in the juxtaposition of the old and the new?

The remaining issue is to reconcile the discrepancy between the suggested timing of the ancient tales of an Edomite chieftain and the style, language, and knowledge of a scholar living around 400 BCE.

Dating—A Conclusion

Several points of view are analyzed here regarding the dating of the story of Job and the composition of the book that tells his story. Scholars vary widely in their estimates on both issues.

---

12. Edward Greenstein, personal correspondence with the author, quoted with permission.

The Language, the Author, the Date

The events, characters, and cultural setting of the backstory place it within the historical context of the leadership of Israel's regional and tribal judges. The poem makes clear references to the exodus. The descriptions of the religious, civic, and cultural traditions of the main characters reflect the period of the patriarchs as well as the period of the judges. The internal evidence of people, places, technology, and themes excludes the period of the patriarchs and leans more toward the culture of Israel's judges.

There are substantial cross-references to the books of Psalms, Proverbs, and Deuteronomy. Either an original Job influences these passages or this telling of Job's story was constructed using the philosophy and theology presented in these sources. As noted, the content of Deuteronomy strongly indicates a composition date near the beginning of the monarchy. Scholars note that the influence of Deuteronomy shows in later prophetic books, while it is lacking in the writings of earlier prophets. As noted, the *Jewish Encyclopedia* supports the conclusion that Deuteronomy was the Book of Law recovered and codified by Josiah around 647–609 BCE.[13] Tradition and scholarship hold that the original document found by Josiah's team was an ancient script returned to Judah by refugees of the Assyrian attacks on the northern kingdom of Israel in 740–722 BCE. Similarly, Psalms and Proverbs, which are considered the work of several authors, are thought to be primarily written by David and Solomon ca. 1000–900 BCE.

In addition to a shared philosophy and theology among these books, much of what Job says himself appears to agree with Ezra's meditations as he struggles with the return to Jewish traditions and faith.

The accumulation of these factors contributed to the process of dating the composition of the book of Job, and the evidence strongly suggests a date during the period of the Persian Empire. As early as the 1940s, Robert Pfeiffer suggested a date of 600 BCE or during the closing years of the Babylonian captivity.[14] He proposes that the author restored the book during the migrations of the Jewish people back to Judea. Other linguistic scholars see a later date, one closer to 400 BCE, and after the remnant of the Israelites had returned to Judea by edict of the Persian king.

Increasingly, scholars lean toward authorship ca. 400 BCE. The poem did not become part of the Hebrew canon until early in the Current Era. The canon of Hebrew Scriptures began to take shape in 400 BCE with the books of the Law, followed in 200 BCE with the Prophets. The Writings,[15] which included the poetic wisdom books, some prophecies, and some stories from the periods of exile, were added as the value of each was recognized. This process occurred from 90 CE through the second century

---

13. Jastrow et al., "Deuteronomy."
14. Pfeiffer, *Introduction*, 678–83.
15. The *Ketuvim*, which includes Psalms, Proverbs, Job, Song of Solomon, Ruth, Lamentations, Ecclesiastes, Esther, Daniel, Ezra, Nehemiah, and 1 and 2 Chronicles.

CE. The selection of the books called the Writings was less rigorous and depended somewhat on their popularity and usefulness for development of the faith.

Given this evidence, is the Job that survives today a rewrite of the original legend, as might be evidenced by the fragments found at Qumran? Such a theory would explain the reference to Job in Ezekiel, written around 593–571 BCE, a full century or so before Ezra. The reference in Ezekiel describes Job as a righteous person and does not echo any content within the book of Job.

There are still some sources (including rabbinic tradition, and some of the commentators quoted in this book) that support Moses as the author of the book of Job.[16] In this view, the book is a personal history of a man from the time of the patriarchs, and it explains the transition of the God of Israel from the tribal God (El Shaddai) into a national God (Yahweh, or I Am). Commentators see the various positions argued by Job's friends as representative of the doctrines prevalent at the time; and that the poetic structure was a way of working through these philosophies to arrive at a cohesive theology of the sovereignty of God. The internal evidence of the book does not bear this out. Based on the work of scholars such as those referenced in this book, the book of Job was written around 400 BCE.

With the evidence presented here, the conclusion is that Job is a dramatic presentation of a story that could have a historical basis in events that occurred sometime during the period of the judges and which has more ancient roots updated by the author to a recognized historical period. This story is about a community leader reduced to nothing, only to find his way back to restoration and prosperity. The lessons learned and the message provided by this ancient tale became part of the literature of the remnant of Israel living in Judea.

In a moment of need and transition, a well-educated and devoted follower of the God of Israel wove the pieces of the tale of Job, the songs of the nation, and the sermons of its beloved spiritual founder into a compelling and memorable wisdom poem. The debates surrounding the dating of the work stem from this combination of an ancient tale and a later, poetic application of the events.

The vehicles of poetry and drama give the message endurance. The human mind remembers things that are set to poetry or music longer, and with more feeling, than short stories or documentaries. Such a format is particularly useful when debating an ideology, theology, or philosophy. The Greeks understood this concept well, often using the vehicles of stage or poetry to convey their philosophy to a general audience.

Now the story has been rebuilt from the roots. For purposes of this book, these are the conclusions used to interpret the legend of Job. The book was written in Hebrew ca. 400 BCE by a scholar debating the issues of suffering and Providence. The selection of the backstory and the setting of the discourses are crucial to the author's message. Since the author began with an ancient tale, the elements of that story must have a purpose. What lessons does the author see in Job's trials? Perhaps retelling the

---

16. Halley, *Halley's Bible Handbook*, 241.

legend in such a manner leads the reader to leave behind the presumption of crime and punishment as the answer to all suffering. Perhaps the author is leading Job on a quest to find a new vision of the cause and mitigation of evil and its consequences.

Chapter 4

What Happened

Whether based on a historical tale or not, the legend of Job is a story staged in a culture and at a point in time that is familiar to a Jewish population. Further, the author of the book of Job wrote the poem at some point after the remnant of the Jews returned from Babylonian captivity. The priesthood, including a passionate Ezra, worked hard to bring the people back into the faith and traditions of their predecessors. However, no matter how hard the people try, the glories of the distant past do not return. What could be wrong?

If the theological and philosophical debate articulated in the book of Job comes from a period after the Babylonian captivity, then the focus of the book could be a reexamination of the doctrine and dogma established by Hebrew Scriptures. The author, who is a scholar familiar with the language and the history, creates a thought experiment.

Job, by all definitions, is following all the requirements established in Deuteronomy. He is above reproach and has every reason to believe he should receive the blessings promised. For reasons unknown to him, disaster strikes, and he loses everything that he knows and loves. Fellow men of stature rush to his side and begin their vigil by showing deep empathy. As soon as Job begins to speak, they quickly turn on him for daring to challenge the justice of his fate. A large portion of the poetic discourses are an examination of how and why good people should suffer, let alone to the extent Job is facing.

For several reasons, the degree and nature of Job's suffering is part of the message. One of the ways humans respond to a tragedy is to deflect the needs of the victim by talking about themselves. The same thing may have happened to them or someone they know. There may be an effort to diminish the impact of the current event or to come up with an outcome that could have been worse. The author of Job restricts this argument by making sure there is not much more, if anything, for his protagonist to lose. Psychoanalyzing Job, a man of legend, is problematic at best. However, to understand suffering from a place that not all individuals experience, investigating modern insights in human psychology can help analyze Job's recorded experiences. In this chapter, the psychological and medical literature contributes to a picture of how suffering affects or influences an individual. As part of retelling the story, the experiences of Job and his companions need to resonate with a contemporary audience. The following research and conclusions come with a warning label. The study of what causes a person to respond to life's events in any specific, predictable manner is not an exact science. Researchers in this field have only begun to scratch the surface of how the brain functions. There is tension between the predisposition created by a person's brain chemistry and what that person is capable of once they choose agency. A crucial part of understanding an individual's response is the need to keep that tension in mind.

The prologue of the book of Job provides an assessment of Job's character. He is blameless and upright. He fears God and shuns evil. He constantly prays and sacrifices for his children on the off chance they may have sinned by omission or commission. In Job 4:3–4, Eliphaz says that Job is always there to support those in need. In chapter 29, Job's portrayal shows a community leader, a deliverer of justice, and a helper of those in need. Nobles and elders respect him and acknowledge him whenever he is present. Job's companions are aware of his reputation; they are not privy to God's assessment of his life.

Within the debate, as Job's friends seek some cause behind his suffering, his reputation becomes a liability. In their need to find cause, they suggest that he has ulterior motives in the practice of his fine deeds. Desperate for a justification for Job's afflictions, they press home the accusation that perhaps his heart was impure. In Job 4, Eliphaz enumerates the contributions that Job made to his community and uses his accomplishments to challenge him now that he suffers. Job's companions are certain that if the heart is right, there is an expectation of promised blessings. Should not Job's piety instill confidence, and his blameless ways provide hope? To Eliphaz, Job needs to weed out whatever his transgression is. Once he does, everything will be made whole. Job becomes a byword (17:6; 30:9) and the fame of his destruction travels faster than that of his goodness. In modern parlance, if it bleeds, it leads. Also, in the contemporary world, the victim is the first to be scrutinized and often blamed for whatever catastrophe occurs.

God, however, declares Job blameless. For the reader, there is no room for doubt. Whatever Job's companions may think or reason, the audience knows that Job is innocent. By providing the information that Job's innocence is not in question, the author of Job is pushing his readers to move beyond the old dogma of crime and punishment and to arrive at conclusions that better fit the world as it is. Suffering occurs regardless of how moral and ethical the person may be. There are occasions when suffering is beyond all understanding.

Part I—Nuts and Bolts

In the opening chapters, the book of Job describes several events instigated by Satan, with the permission of God, to test Job's faith. Job first receives news of the destruction of his agricultural holdings. Some marauder has stolen his plowing oxen and grazing asses and murdered all his servants (save one). Before this report is complete, another lone survivor bursts on the scene to announce that fire has fallen from heaven, destroying all the sheep and the servants tending them. Then yet another messenger arrives to announce that the Chaldeans raided his herds and carried off his camels, murdering the servants in the process. The fourth messenger arrives to tell Job that a storm has crushed the house where his children were celebrating.

Distraught and bereaved, Job tears his clothes, cuts off his hair and falls to the ground to worship God, proclaiming, "Naked came I out of my mother's womb, and naked shall I return there; the Lord has given, and the Lord has taken away; blessed be the name of the Lord" (Job 1:21).

All these things are insufficient to bring Job to the point of cursing God. Next, Job is afflicted with an unknown disease that causes him to break out with boils. He dispatches himself to the ash heaps outside of the city gates with only the clothes on his back and some broken pottery to scratch the sores. His final insult occurs when his wife suggests that he curse God and die. He sends her away, refusing to acknowledge that he should somehow accept only good from God and not evil. At this point, his companions arrive weeping and tearing their clothes. Seeing his great need and feeling unable to speak, they sit with him in silence for seven days.

Following, in intricate poetic form, is a debate among Job and his visitors, a call for divine justice from Job, and an answering discourse from God. As the book concludes, God instructs Job's three companions to supply Job with sacrifices that he may offer on their behalf. God declares, "Job spoke rightly" (42:7).

Wealth and health restored, Job lives for many more years, and enjoys the presence of more children and several generations of offspring. As he regains his wealth, he regains the support of his relatives and their increased assistance. They remain anonymous and absent throughout the rest of the tale. He also chooses to make provision for his daughters as well as his sons.

The process of taking the circumstances of an ancient legend and recreating them in a timeless and universal setting requires seeing these events in general terms. Rather than sheep, oxen, and slaves, the view should shift to the *types of loss* depicted in the passage. The story provides five specific areas of attack on Job's emotional and spiritual stability. These are the loss of a child, acts of violence, bankruptcy, disease, and natural disaster. Further, the passage alludes to the stresses placed on marital partners caught up in such disasters. Although one might add starvation, epidemics, and personal violence such as assault and rape, there is little left that might define suffering. Even so, if the message of Job is to provide an answer for suffering, that answer must be useful regardless of the depth of despair.

What Happened

What drives a human to despair? In general, the human brain, nervous system, and body respond in stages when presented with a stressful situation. Psychologists describe three stages: alarm, resistance, and exhaustion. The person under stress might not pass through all three stages, or they may experience different outcomes dependent on cultural and personal background experiences.

Alarm induces a fight or flight response. At this first level, the response to a frightening event is to intuitively and, if possible, logically determine the chances of survival. If the odds appear reasonable or represent value worth the cost (such as defense of a child), the individual will choose to stand and fight. If the outcome is too risky, too ambivalent, or too costly, an individual may decide that the better part of valor is to run for it. When an individual fails to attain a resolution at the first level, resistance occurs. As the issue escalates, a person's energy levels weaken. Resistance is characterized by a continued desire to fight back or to find a satisfactory resolution.

If the situation does not change during the second level, or the person does not find an acceptable path of resolution, the third stage, exhaustion, occurs. Once stress reaches this level, remaining in control becomes more difficult. The body's response is the loss of mental equilibrium, which causes physical health deterioration: the loss of health results in problems such as excessive blood pressure, ulcers, and other debilitating mental and physical diseases.

In recent times, psychiatry has defined a condition known as Post Traumatic Stress Syndrome (PTSS). PTSS (or PTSD) is characterized by pathological anxiety, which is usually triggered by an event or situation which the brain sees as a recurrence of the traumatic event. When, for instance, a veteran of a foreign war watches a fireworks show, the tracers, bombs, and gunshots of the battlefield may suddenly be far more real than the display everyone else is enjoying. The same can occur with any severely traumatic event, such as a rape victim finding themselves in a similar circumstance, or hearing a specific tone in a voice.

Fight, flight, and freeze responses are an alternative and developing view of the response to trauma. This view considers the element of self-preservation in the choice to flee or freeze. Such a response is a different form of fight. A woman's instincts may direct her to execute evasive actions if she feels someone is following her. Such a reaction is more often defined as self-preserving defense and not a flight response.[1]

What does psychiatry or psychology have to do with Scripture? Quite a bit. Some parts of Scripture laboriously describe how the human spirit might deal with the impacts of life's stresses, both common and rare. Job's experiences will teach nothing if they cannot be made relevant to current times. Analyzing how such events can drive an individual to the very limits of mental and physical strength reveals why Job responds as he does, and why God replies as he does. Job perseveres. He stands on his record and demands an answer. And God responds.

---

1. "Fight, Flight, Freeze Responses."

Part I—Nuts and Bolts

The first catastrophes communicated to Job follow in rapid succession as reports come in that plunderers have stolen his livestock, murdered his servants, and destroyed his crops.

A sudden loss of this magnitude is the kind of trauma linked to a response of PTSS. Such traumatic events can occur suddenly and swiftly and be over just as quickly. For instance, among the varied responses to the attacks on the World Trade Center on September 11, 2001, PTSS, or similar trauma, was part of the aftermath. How each person in the United States and around the world was most likely to respond is based on many contributing factors, including personal history, nearness to someone affected, and interpretation of global politics and terrorism. On that sunny September morning, few of us understood who had perpetrated the attack or what they intended next. Although human instincts are usually quite good (when we choose to listen), with no direct experience to support our choices, such an event can become a shared trauma with multiple and varied responses. Most likely, we will never know the total cost in lives lost or damaged by that event. For citizens of the United States, as well as other countries whose citizens were lost or injured, much of life as they knew it changed in a few short minutes on a bright September morning. Something similar happened in the life of Job when his way of life disintegrated in a day. He lost his wealth, his children, those that helped him maintain that way of life, and his health in quick succession.

Without time to process the loss or to recover from the news of raiding parties, Job learns of a natural disaster that destroys his flocks. One Jewish philosopher[2] uses the "rain of fire from heaven" as a reason for calling the whole affair an allegory. Science tells us that fire does indeed fall from heaven. Perhaps the mention of an event not commonly known echoes some ancient historical context. Whatever the source, the response to a natural disaster is unique. Some people, such as first responders, rush in and help the injured and recover the dead, while others are focused on self-preservation. Self-preservation is not a bad response, especially if an individual is responsible for other lives. However, responding effectively to natural events can be daunting.

In recent history, populations have experienced devastation in the wake of natural causes on a regional basis. The Christmas tsunami in 2004 impacted several countries bordering the Indian Ocean. In modern times, large swaths of land have suffered damage from earthquakes, volcanoes, hurricanes, tsunamis, floods, and forest fires. Always, the devastation is personal and shared. It changes and destroys lives sometimes to the point that those affected never recover. However, survivors do climb out of the rubble and vow to build again—to live again.

---

2. Zerahiah Hen, a Spanish-Jewish physician, philosopher, translator, and Hebraist living ca. 1277–1290 CE. His thoughts are found in chapter 10.

The next messenger to arrive on the scene informs Job that all his children died in yet another natural disaster. There is no aggressor to blame, no way to avenge an attack or criminal assault, no one to hold accountable.

The experience of losing a child is like none other and can cause the full spectrum of response from denial to utter devastation. Sometimes it helps if there are other children to nurture and protect, individuals whose basic survival depends on those devastated to keep fighting in a world gone mad. However, nothing can make up for the loss of a child. Nothing. To assume that Job's new, post-catastrophe family can somehow heal that breach is ludicrous at best and inexcusably cruel at worst.

In most circumstances, friends, family, a faith-family, or coworkers, will step in to help support those who have suffered the loss of a loved one, especially a child. Volunteers handle household matters, transportation, food service, and sometimes provide a buffer against the media. To most observers, descending on grieving parents with accusations that they must have done something wrong is ghoulish. For others, such a loss furthers an agenda. During the aftermath of the shooting at Sandy Hook in Newtown, Connecticut (December 2012), several strangers traveled to the town to create a human shield to protect the wounded and suffering from those who wished to make a statement on the backs of grieving parents and family members. In our country, the response to such events is usually two-fold. Some decry the loss and vow to do something to prevent further harm. Then some attack the victims and their families, often seeking a way to deflect the conversation or to prove complicity in some plot to take away rights or freedoms. Recently, those same families have filed court cases to stop the spread of conspiracy theories and misinformation regarding their loss. Sadly, the number of victims continues to grow as survivors of these kinds of events take their own lives in hopes of ending their pain.

Job suffers similar pain as his companions begin to conclude that the whole affair is his fault. There are no church, synagogue, or neighborhood suppers; there are no comforting arms. No friend or family member offers to help Job and his wife in their great need, nor does anyone pause to offer help in burying the dead. The best his companions had to offer is seven days of silence. After showing the respect due to Job in a period of mourning, the companions begin the process of blaming the victim. The same response often occurs in catastrophic events in the modern world. Find a way to blame the victims. Why wasn't there more security? Why was she in that place at that time? Why was she wearing those clothes? Why was she drinking? There are a thousand excuses offered that tell victims they are lying or that the tragedy visited on their life is all their own doing. In the end, proving that the victim is the cause of all their suffering reduces or eliminates the obligation to help. Perhaps this misplaced choice of cause and effect also protects us from seeing that, given different circumstances, the trauma could have been ours.

For Job, his life and family are in pieces around him. In such circumstances, it is not uncommon for financial difficulties to follow. Scripture does not address the subject of bankruptcy directly. Concepts of property and industry were not the same in ancient times. Wealth was measured in stock (animals), in servants, in levels of production, and in lands owned or managed. However, the loss of a stable livelihood and wealth in any age constitutes what we now call bankruptcy. Job, and what remained of his family, were destitute, without a source of support and without much hope of rebuilding.

Bankruptcy can draw a radically different response from friends and acquaintances than the death of a loved one. Depending on the economic atmosphere at the time, as well as the experiences of the people involved, financial ruin of a close friend or family member may cause those closest to the family to withdraw or avoid contact. The sight of a homeless person, a family member in financial need, or a friend that has lost a business will sometimes drive the comforters away. Perhaps family and friends fear initial involvement because the depth of need cannot be determined. Perhaps those who know the victim may suffer apprehension that their resources are insufficient and the burden may destabilize their finances. Perhaps the response has more to do with the thought that "but for the grace of God, there go I."

Job's response is, "In the thought of the complacent there is contempt for calamity" (12:5); and, "If I speak, my pain will not be relieved, / And if I do not—what have I lost?" (16:6). Lost in his agony, Job cries out for justice and refuses to curse God. The author of Job makes it clear that Job believes that the source of his misery comes from God and no other. Even so, Job maintains faith that there are answers, answers his companions do not know.

Job, financially crushed and bereaved, falls ill. Job's illness is Satan's last assault against his integrity. Sudden and debilitating disease is another high-scoring event on psychological stress charts. Although cancer is not the death sentence it once was, a diagnosis of cancer, or any other terminal or chronic disease, often tests the faith and emotional strength of an individual and their family. Telling the patient or the family that these things happen according to some plan, or that they must try harder, or pray more, causes far more harm than good. Job's illness is the final blow that sends him to the ash heaps on the outskirts of his town. Here he sits and contemplates the fate of humanity. Still, he refuses to curse God.

Enter Job's wife. In later chapters, there are several differing opinions regarding the part Job's wife plays. Some scholars see her as an instrument of Satan, while some see her as a bereaved mother who is beyond her endurance limit. Given the strong cultural foundation of the passage, perhaps there is further meaning beyond the bare declaration to curse God and die. Job's response to her is, "You talk as any shameless woman might talk! Should we accept only good from God and not accept evil?" (2:10)

Why would this bereaved woman be so willing to see her husband die, leaving her in bankruptcy and destitution? Job cared for his wife or at least took his commitment to her as unbending. In 31:1, he states that he has made a covenant with his eyes and sees no reason to think on another woman. She does not appear in the tale after chapter 2. However, there is no evidence that Job set her aside upon his restoration. References in the Qur'an[3] also support the idea that he kept her as his wife. Is his wife's condemnation of Job and his integrity just one more burden for Job to bear?

Hebrew law was, in some ways, far more advanced than that of its neighbors, including the protection of the right of women to inherit under specific circumstances. There were several requirements, and the law did change throughout history. The *Jewish Encyclopedia* addresses the rights of the widow under Hebrew law.[4] In the event of the death of a husband, a widow, unless she remarried, had first claim against the couple's assets for her support. Creditors could not attach the estate with a superior claim. If Job dies, his wife can preserve whatever remains of their wealth and have some hope of continued support. While he remains alive, the creditors have a claim against their assets.

Is Job calling her a foolish woman because she lacks the faith to stand with her husband and see the situation to its end? Job's position is that if God chooses to strike him dead, then so be it. The incentive to do so will not emanate from his lips. Perhaps the author is using this pressure as inspiration for Job to ensure his daughters receive a separate inheritance. Was this part of the ancient tale, an admonition of the poet, or both?

Job's wife sees only death and destruction. In the deepest well of agony, she seeks out her husband, perhaps hoping he has survived, surely hoping for comfort. She finds him afflicted with a horrible disease. Confronted with a world gone mad, she revolts against his stoic, unsatisfying responses. She does not, however, accuse him of wrongdoing. Whatever her role has been throughout history, her challenge to Job stands as a precursor to his demand for justice. At the moment she confronts him, her stance shows no interest in justice; her statement is far more direct. Curse God and be done with it. To her, there is no safety in his care, no promise of providential action. Job's wife presents more than a footnote to the story, more than just one more stumbling block placed in her husband's path. She vocalizes what many individuals face when suffering strikes without reason, without a discernable cause—the inability to reconcile a loving creator with the inexplicable devastation so evident in life. Her voice is the first to cry out against the injustice, though she has no patience to seek it. Job rejects her proposed resolution. However, perhaps he begins to think on her deep need for answers.

Job is just where the author wants him: broken, disillusioned, abandoned, yet still standing on his integrity. An integrity that even his grieving wife acknowledges. His wife may see his virtue; however, his companions seem determined to call his bluff.

---

3. The spelling of the Holy Scriptures of Islam tends to include Koran, Qu'ran, Quran, and the usage in this text of Qur'an. The format was chosen after researching Muslim sources for preferred spelling.

4. Dembitz, "Widow."

Part I—Nuts and Bolts

When dealing with suffering in this world, it is crucial to understand where the victim is emotionally, mentally, and spiritually. Humanity is both blessed and cursed with the gift of empathy. Too often, the fear of feeling too much puts a wall between the sufferer and those who have the means to help. Like Job's companions, the easy path is to bypass that pain and victimize the victim. One of the critical points this book intends to demonstrate is that offering only prayers, remaining silent, walking away, or blaming the victim, are not acceptable courses of action. Understanding Job in a different light unveils the possibility of becoming an active force for good. Accomplishing this goal requires clarity regarding the factors contributing to any specific case of suffering.

To be effective in the mitigation of suffering, one must answer three basic questions regarding the factors that create suffering.

1. Is the root of the suffering due to a discernible action within the laws of nature, such as volcanoes or earthquakes?

2. Is the suffering due to personal choices within control of the individual, such as smoking or substance abuse? If a bad choice is the factor, can the tension between a biological influence and the individual's agency be resolved successfully?

3. Is the obvious cause of the suffering due to the nature of violence and how it operates in the world? Is this individual suffering due to acts of violence over which they have no control?

Job's companions never come to understand these issues; their only focus is on dogma, tradition, and the wisdom of their elders. Without regard to how right their views might be in the correct circumstances, as counselors to Job they fail miserably. Before that failure can be analyzed and used to develop a more productive course of action, a brief course in the building blocks used by ancient and modern scholars, commentators, philosophers, and theologians will be helpful. The next chapter builds a toolbox of terms and basic philosophies used in discussions about Job, suffering, and the action of Providence. First, one must learn the historical versions of the story; then, a new story unfolds in light of the author's contributions to the theology and philosophy of his time.

Chapter 5

Building a Toolbox

THE STATED PURPOSE OF this book is to retell the story of Job by stripping away centuries of interpretive packing and see if there is a practical answer to suffering. Changing one's perceptions requires an understanding of the sources of preexisting conclusions. An academic would quickly recognize the philosophy of Aristotle or Plato in the dissertations of a Jewish philosopher; a lay student of Scripture may not. That academic, however, may not recognize the Islamic influence in the same writings. A Christian minister seeking guidance for compassionate support of a church member may be oblivious to such an influence. If the goal is to retell the story, then the influences which directed early church doctrine on suffering and Providence need to be understood within context. Such is the purpose of this somewhat brief journey into terminology and philosophy.

A grasp of the language and terminology used in source material provides depth to understanding and reduces the opportunity to misinterpret a theme or reject a new idea without forethought. A common error is to assume familiarity with a definition when usage of the term may be different from the reader's previous experience. For instance, the word *cultic* may be a derogatory label in common vernacular, but when used in archeology or anthropology, it merely means that the site or practice has religious connotations. The application of the term carries no value judgment about the validity of the implied religion. Time invested in understanding the language used improves the chances of learning something meaningful. Thus, here is a toolbox to aid in that understanding.

Allegory is a term used frequently in biblical studies, often rather loosely, especially when the message is difficult to understand or if the clearest interpretation does not fit well within a commentator's established worldview. An allegory is a type of analogy that uses a story, a poem, or a picture to convey a moral or political meaning. That is, an allegory is a symbol in artistic form. Sometimes authors use an allegory to create a visual picture of an abstract concept, such as a grandfather and a baby for the turn of the year. However, the reader must understand both the symbolic nature of the story and its relationship to the reality the symbolism explains. Is there, for instance, a true analogy between the thing or idea one knows and the thing or idea one is attempting to understand?

An analogy can take several forms; however, the goal is to provide a statement that most closely correlates the thing known with the thing not known. For instance: such statements as "Saint Cyr is to the Army of France as West Point is to the Army of the United States," or "Electrons are to the nucleus of an atom as planets are to the sun," compare something the reader may know with a similar thing the reader does not know.

If the commentator defines a passage as allegory, the reader should test the relationships between the image revealed and the reality they are attempting to understand. Does the analogy provided by that interpretation make sense? Further, analogies can only have meaning if the elements of the story have a foundation in human experience.

For instance, one favored use of allegory by early church fathers was the Song of Solomon. In many commentaries, the Song becomes a representation of the relationship between Christ and the church. Some will go so far as to adamantly deny it is a tale of human love and passion. If the point is to illustrate the passion that Christ has for his bride, then what lesson is learned if the passion of two people in disparate social positions is not acknowledged? How can we learn anything from an analogy if the basis of the comparison is incomplete or denies an individual's basic character and needs? This concept is important when reading doctrinal literature. Is the writer trying to patch together an interpretation that avoids a conclusion not derived from a simple reading of the text?

In addition to allegory and analogy, there are other strategies to connect known information to new information. One of those strategies is *anthropomorphic* comparison. Anthropomorphism is the practice of attributing human traits to animals, inanimate objects, and even gods. Fables and myths weave images of human-like creatures that represent natural causes and effects. People often personify instruments and conveyances. Sometimes this comparison can be useful by building a picture of an abstract concept. Examples might include the scriptural reference to God as a father, or as having benevolence and compassion. Such comparisons may be helpful or may conversely remind one who suffers of a relationship that was void of benevolence or compassion. There are times when using an anthropomorphic comparison can confuse or result in a fallacy of logic. If God is like a compassionate father, then how can he be so destructive?

The book of Job also requires a brief introduction to philosophy and theology. The book presents a detailed debate on different types of providence or different views of what sorts of influence a supreme being may have or want over human activity. A dictionary would describe providence as guidance or care coming from a divine source. Most often, the term describes God (or nature) in the role of a power that sustains and guides us. Providence can also define a quality of our state of being, which is a definition used both implicitly and explicitly by medieval philosophers. The coming chapters explore more specific details of the types of providence represented in Job and the impact of each school of thought.

The subject of providence is crucial to such a study. How to define it and how it might operate in the world are two of the dividing issues amongst the various belief systems developed throughout the history of humanity. Why? How important is it to a believer whether there is an ultimate power looking out for individual health and safety? Is there a power that listens to a plea for help and that actively intervenes to assuage suffering? Is there someone there to answer prayer?

Providence also addresses the issue of how much control God has over the day-to-day events in a person's life. Does he permit wars, famine, and disease? If God is omnipotent and omniscient, why does suffering go on? What an individual's outlook is regarding the existence of suffering and what one should expect from God in the face of suffering is key to how an individual can or will respond when assailed with unexpected circumstances. Assigning responsibility for suffering makes for some interesting dialogue within the book of Job and in the commentaries about the book.

Although *theodicy* is a concept established by commentators in the early centuries of the Common Era, it was the German philosopher Gottfried Leibniz who coined the term.[1] Some philosophers consider Job a definitive exemplification of the term, while others believe theodicy is an idea that lacks any substance. The concept of theodicy is an exploration of how one vindicates divine goodness in the face of evil. Leibniz addresses the problems of suffering and evil in several of his essays and concludes that evil exists in the world because God saw the need to permit humanity to possess free will. Keep in mind that the authors of Scripture, and a large majority of their contemporaries, did not need to prove the existence of God. There was no doubt regarding the existence of one God or many. The problem was working out how to understand divine action and how to relate to divine beings.

The Western European Enlightenment philosophers of the seventeenth and eighteenth centuries challenged the previous acceptance that all things work to the good. These scholars and theologians were interested in the attempt to reconcile the existence of evil in the world with a belief in a God that is all-loving, all-powerful, and all-knowing. Many believers in a supreme being who creates and controls become rather preoccupied with this paradox. Some philosophers, such as Augustine,[2] solve the conundrum by stating that evil does not exist except as a corruption of good, and, therefore, only occurs due to the free will of mortal beings and angels. Based on this line of thought and twist of mental gymnastics, evil exists as a punishment for sin.

---

1. Leibniz, *Theodicy*.

2. A Roman African theologian and church father. He lived 354–430 CE and was a major contributor to early church doctrine. See chapter 7.

Part I—Nuts and Bolts

Irenaeus[3] suggested that human suffering exists for the development of character. In other words, humans are created imperfect, and suffering helps an individual attain some level of moral perfection. Thus, theodicy is the search for some balance or untangling of the paradox. A similar term, *cosmodicy*, is the philosophical attempt to justify that the universe is good even though evil and suffering exist.

Understanding the bedrock of doctrines on suffering requires more than terminology. Throughout the centuries of interpreting Job, many commentators relied on antecedent philosophical thought. Knowing which influences guided these authors may help analyze their conclusions more effectively. There is clear evidence of the contributions that the Greeks, Muslims, and early conflicting Christian doctrines made to the literature on suffering. Knowing the source of a conclusion, the DNA of the analysis is part of retelling the story. Where did it come from, and what precepts did the proponents wish to teach?

Plato, living in ca. 428–347 BCE, is considered a pillar of Western philosophy. He and his followers separated the invisible world (the source of all things) and the phenomenal world (that which is seen). Platonists looked for a source of life which could not be known by reasoning. Their position was that humans are only a part of the whole and, therefore, unable to conceive of what the whole might be. Nor would Platonists assign moral attributes to the original force, because this would put limitations on something that had none. As shown later, many paradoxes in theology and philosophy occur when attempting to describe an infinite entity in finite terms.

Platonists admire the beauty and wonder of the phenomenal (physical) world. They believe that the world is naturally beautiful unless it is not in harmony with the soul. When conflict arises, matter loses form and becomes evil. The goal is to bring the soul into harmony with the source; then the material world will find greater harmony with the metaphysical world. For Platonists, the highest goal of an individual is to seek harmony to attain right living. If a person can learn these things, then the soul will be happy. Aristotle, however, emphasized learning and wisdom as the path to happiness and fulfillment.[4]

This search for a life in harmony with nature is strongly represented in Far Eastern traditions, as well as in some pagan practices. These systems of belief emphasize the need for an individual to find a balance within creation to achieve their highest potential—thereby reducing if not eliminating suffering.

Aristotle was born in 384 BCE in a small town in Thrace, Greece. At age seventeen, he was sent to Athens to study under Plato, the student of Socrates. Because of his fundamental differences with Platonic philosophy, he did not remain as a teacher at the Academy when Plato died. He traveled for some years and then returned to Macedonia and became a tutor for young Alexander (not yet Great). Aristotle's

---

3. A Greek bishop recognized as a church father living ca. 130–202 CE in the south of France. See chapter 8.

4. Copleston, *History of Philosophy*, 242.

writings spanned a variety of subjects including logic, metaphysics, mathematics, physics, biology, botany, ethics, politics, agriculture, medicine, dance, and theater. Cicero, a Roman philosopher and defender of the republic as a lawyer and political theorist, considered Aristotle's writings to be "a river of gold." There is some confusion regarding the authorship of some of the works that carry his name. As in many cases of ancient thinkers, some works could be compilations and commentaries by other individuals.

Aristotle's works on mind and philosophy provide the background to important concepts used by later interpreters of Job and the part suffering plays in the world. For instance, the thoughts he developed in *On Soul* contribute to the metaphysics of early Jewish philosophers. Although his writings are still a subject of debate, the simplest interpretation of his work in this area is that all things that have life have a soul. Soul is the mover of the living body and the reason behind the actions of a mind. As an illustration, Aristotle uses the process of stamping a piece of wax with the imprint of a seal. The wax changes shape without taking on the material or separate characteristics of the seal.[5] The soul is not a body; it is that essence which gives the body life, through which things become known, and by which the living act.

Much of the commentary and interpretation of how and why people suffer and how they should respond develops from the concept that the soul, the part that animates the body and gives it life, resides in the body yet is not of the body. Aristotle, unlike his predecessors, believes that discussions of the soul cannot take place without consideration of the body. Throughout his works, he emphasizes that the body and the soul depend on each other for existence.[6]

He develops this concept with the use of *faculties* or *parts*, which he correlates to the stages of biological development. Aristotle theorizes that the human soul is composed of three elements, two of which are present in simpler life forms. The elements are irrational, irrational and rational together, and purely rational. The first and most basic, irrational alone, is rooted in mere survival. One must eat, have reasonable covering and shelter, and be relatively safe from danger. Aristotle called this *nutritional virtue*, a faculty of life, the soul found in vegetation and non-sentient life forms.[7]

The second faculty, irrational and rational together, is more complex and consists of emotions, feelings, and desires. Humans share this awareness with animals. In this case, virtue arises when the human exercises control of desires and feelings with rational thought and cultural limits. Moral rightness occurs when the person successfully develops the control of urges with the use of reason. Such is the essence of *moral virtue*.

---

5. Aristotle, *On Soul*, 48.
6. Kiernan, *Aristotle Dictionary*, 459–63.
7. "Sentience" is defined as the ability to perceive and respond to sensations of whatever kind. Modern interpretations of what constitutes a sentient being have developed considerably beyond Aristotle's philosophy.

Part I—Nuts and Bolts

The ability to be rational in thought and deed is the third element, and that which makes life human. Aristotle writes that this element allows humans to realize true happiness and—as theorized by some of the philosophers cited later in this book—perhaps survives the death of the body. Aristotelian thinkers consider mastery of this third element to be *intellectual virtue*. Aristotle and many of his later followers did not believe that intellectual virtue is universal.[8] According to Aristotelians, although all people by nature desire to know (metaphysics), individuals possess varying degrees of understanding. Some have mere experience, while some learn to apply that experience to different situations. If an individual can apply what experience has taught them, they can obtain wisdom.[9]

The influence of Gnosticism is also evident in the commentaries written by the medieval Jewish philosophers. Gnostic tenets may have developed from earlier Jewish mysticism with contributions from other ancient faiths. A well-known surviving record of gnostic beliefs is the Nag Hammadi Library. The library consists of scrolls found in the town of the same name in Upper Egypt in 1945. They are a Coptic translation of early Christian and gnostic testaments and gospels. Gnostic beliefs varied depending on the location and historical traditions held by each group. For the most part, they followed a creed that demanded constant study and discussion. Gnostic comes from the root *gnosis*, which means knowledge, primarily in spiritual mysteries. Many Gnostics also believed that matter was evil and that the Old Testament God was an evil demiurge that created a wicked world. To set the human soul free from the trap of a material and wicked world, one must study and grow in knowledge (*gnosis*).

Another source of information regarding the gnostic sects is the adversarial writings of the early church fathers. During the first centuries of the Common Era, the newly minted Christian faith struggled to define orthodoxy. Some of the most influential leaders of the time decreed all things gnostic a heresy and did everything in their power to destroy the various sects and their writings.

Heresy is not intrinsically an evil thing. The word comes from the Greek *hairesis*, which means to choose an answer or a result for oneself. At its root, it is the process of examining different ideas and then choosing among them. *Orthodoxy* means right, true, or straight. History controlled these definitions and, eventually, orthodoxy could have a dubious relationship with right thinking. In the end, stronger organizational skills and the development of a hierarchy established the orthodox church, and the many competing sects of early Christian thought disappeared or retreated into the relative protection of anonymity.

Irenaeus described the Gnostics as a people constantly in search of new ideas that reshaped their beliefs.[10] With each new convert came a claim of discovering some hidden truth that no one had thought of before. He felt it difficult to define what their

8. Humphreys, "Aristotle."
9. Copleston, *A History of Philosophy*, 30–31.
10. See Irenaeus, *Against Heresies*.

creed was because of this constant search for truth. The most prevalent tenet for which the orthodox could not forgive them was the point of view that Jesus was a divine being sent from the higher God to inform those trapped in this world of their true nature and origin. In other words, Jesus was not coequal with God, and there was a higher god apart from the one described in Old Testament literature.

In the early centuries of the Christian church, many devoted followers understood that wisdom and enlightenment came from inner reflection. This need to seek inner revelation was an impetus for the advent of monasteries and convents. So why was the pursuit of knowledge (*gnosis*) so abhorrent in the eyes of the church? In part because of the broad spectrum of beliefs that claimed the title, as well as some of the rituals that attached to the practice of a faith steeped in spiritual mysteries and visions of superiority. Importantly, the creed that this world was inherently evil and created by some subordinate being did not fit well within the prevailing church doctrine.

Throughout the initial development and institutionalization of orthodoxy, church organizers held the position that the only path between man and God is through the church and the church's interpretation of Scripture. The Gnostics were adamant that this was not true. With all their differences, one belief was common among the gnostic sects: the relationship between humanity and its gods was direct and unique to each believer.

Another point of major contention was that increasing institutionalization in the church contributed to the belief that what separated humanity from God was sin. Gnostics, however, believed that what separated humanity from God was ignorance. The focus was on acquiring knowledge, and in that way, an individual could control impulses and feelings. This idea was closer to the writings of the Greek philosophers than to those of the church fathers. For these reasons, the church chose to quash the writings and practices of the gnostic communities as heresy and a crime against God.

The creed developed by the Gnostics contained two main points of interest relevant to this retelling of Job. First, matter is evil and is the source of decay and destruction. Valentinus (ca. 150 CE), a supporter of the gnostic viewpoint, indicated that the world was born out of suffering and used the Greek form (*pathos*) to indicate a passive recipient and not an initiator. In this view, suffering was inherent in this creation. However, Valentinus wrote that suffering was not a result of sin, original or otherwise. What constitutes sin and any expected consequences that must be faced is a crucial piece in the discussion on suffering and whether God, in whatever form, initiates evil.

Second, Gnostics believe in the acquisition of knowledge, so without knowledge, one is consigned to oblivion throughout eternity. Without the acquisition of knowledge, one could not experience fulfillment. In this view, nonexistence is the equivalent of eternal damnation. Knowledge is the basis of not only salvation and the only hope for eternal life; it is also the path to dealing with suffering and deprivation in this life.[11]

---

11. For a rather interesting description of the shared theology of the various groups, see The Gnostic Society Library, http://www.gnosis.org/library.html.

Part I—Nuts and Bolts

Finally, this book uses the term *Kabbalah*, which is a tradition that may predate religious practice as it is known today. Kabbalah is an esoteric teaching that attempts to explain the relationship between the creator and creation. The philosophy contained in the compiled writings is an integral part of ancient Judaism and considered a cipher key to Hebrew Scriptures and rabbinic tradition. These teachings could be the root of Jewish festivals and rituals. The practice of Kabbalah seeks to define the nature of the universe and its inhabitants.

For the student of the Kabbalah, there is no evil. The notions of sin, depredation, and suffering are a direct result of humanity losing affinity with the Creator. The more in alignment with the beneficial force of the universe a student becomes, the nearer they approach fulfillment. A Kabbalist would embrace suffering as the tool by which the Creator helps one break away from egoism to become more in tune with the universe and the Creator's vision for humanity.

This brief introduction provides definitions and background to help the reader analyze and test the arguments presented in this book. These are the tools used to retell the story of Job and to determine if there is a different message, something overlooked, which may be a combination of elements previously explored. Each conclusion, each encrusted doctrine, will be examined under the light of humanity's experience. If Scripture is to speak, it must speak from within the experience of a mortal being. Can a retelling show that the author of Job wished to revisit the application of the crime and punishment system of blessings and curses? Can a retelling show that the author of Job saw in Scripture a reason to break away from blaming people for circumstances not understood and that there may be causes of suffering not related to sin? Can a retelling show that this author believed in a world that demands active participation in the mitigation of suffering, wherever it may occur?

Part II—Theodicy and Philosophy

Chapter 6

The Study of Why

WHY STUDY THE HISTORY of interpretations and commentary on the book of Job? Because this body of scriptural scholarship has formed the basis of how many people see suffering in themselves and others, even if they have no faith tradition of their own. In John 9:1–12, an incident is recorded where Jesus heals a man blind from birth. His disciples wish to know who sinned to cause the man to suffer. Jesus replies, "No one." We continue to give the disciple's response in modern life. If someone is poor, they must be lazy. If there is a catastrophe, God is displeased. These are some of the reasons it is so important to retell the story—is a perspective missed or lost in translation? If a doctrine is formed based on faulty logic, then that doctrine should be revisited and analyzed in a new light.

One example of this concept is the story of Galileo Galilei. In this modern world, scientists (amateur and professional) often point out the clashes in history between science and religion. They contend that this conflict held back the development of science and the progress of our species. When Galileo Galilei stood before the Church of Rome to present his findings that the earth traveled on a heliocentric path, he was not denying his faith. What he challenged was the cosmology of Greek philosophers whose ideas the church had adopted. One wonders why the thoughts of the Greeks, whose commitments to the divine were varied and often somewhat ambiguous, were preferred over the findings of one of their own, a man educated within the Catholic system. Galileo's argument was not with the church, but rather with established dogma. He wrote a letter to the Dowager Grand Duchess Christina that passionately argued for church and science. He explained that he did not doubt the church's authority over the soul. However, when it came to science, we must rely on our God-given ability to observe and grow to understand the truth of the world we live in.

There are passages within Scripture that appear to support an earth-centric cosmos. In Joshua 10, Israel's defeat of the five kings of the Amorites becomes possible due to an extra-long day. The context implies that it was not just a figure of speech.

Part II—Theodicy and Philosophy

That is, the sun setting and rising did not occur as expected. This passage in Joshua was one of those used to refute Galileo's proposition. However, there are many events in Scripture that have no explanation using known processes, such as turning water into wine. Scripture is not and was never meant to be a science handbook. The mistake of the church in Galileo's time was to choose doctrine over knowledge. This attitude persisted even though many brilliant scientists on the leading edge of our understanding of the universe were people of faith who believed that to grow in knowledge of the creation was to grow in knowledge of God. The book of Job supports this process by offering an alternative cosmic view in Job 26:7: "He it is who stretched out Zaphon[1] over chaos, / Who suspended earth over emptiness." Galileo was not the first to see the orbits of planets.

Science itself suffers from dogmatic wars and the resistance to change. Therefore, considering the context, the resources, and the technology available is critical. Additional insights can lead to a different interpretation of the same set of observations. Scientists use a methodology to correct the misconceptions of the past. Each theory is put to the test repeatedly, with the expectation of predictable results. Such revisions can take months or years, eventually resolving the controversy and bringing new enlightenment. This lesson also applies to Scriptural studies: know the context of the information and determine what conclusions are possible given the nature of humanity and the universe it inhabits. Scripture demands that we observe, that we learn, that we grow in understanding.

That is the goal of the next several chapters—to obtain some understanding of the roots of the interpretations of Job's story and determine if a different story can take shape. What is important to understand is where closely held beliefs come from and why those beliefs constitute a truth as understood by the reader.

The first step is to become familiar with some key points in the philosophies of each of Job's companions. Many of the writings of the early church fathers and Jewish philosophers referred to sects and philosophies that were prevalent in their own time. As with Scripture, these authors used images known to their immediate audience. If the reader is attempting to gain perspective on the vast spectrum of thought regarding Job's trials, suffering, or the question of providence, the research must begin with something basic using generic terms and interpretations.

Scripture, being what it is, does not contain accidental references. If an author chooses a person, nation, geographical location, trade, or profession for a passage, that representation brings with it a cascade of related interpretive aspects. Perhaps a familiar example is the parable of the good Samaritan. In this story, Jesus uses characters thought of either as superior, untouchable, or inferior to the audience. The question illustrated was "Who is my neighbor?" The answer given was "Every one of these."[2]

---

1. Zaphon is both a god and a place, both related to the Red Sea. The meaning is discussed in rabbinic literature with references to the exodus.
2. Luke 10:25–37.

The representatives in Job's tale include individuals from related tribes, all of which claimed Abrahamic heritage. The implication throughout the story and the poem is that all participants are adherents of a monotheistic faith—specifically, a belief in El Shaddai. From historical records and some biblical references, people living in the Middle East during the time described lived in large, extended-family groups. These family groupings included servants, slaves, and workers, along with their associated family members. In Genesis 14, Abraham raised an army of 318 trained men "born of his house" to recapture Lot and the wealth of Sodom and Gomorrah. Such references help define what such a tribal affiliation would look like and the number of people who might be dependent on the head of household. Scholars consider the tribal identities that form the structure of the book of Job as representative of the religious and philosophical thoughts of Hebrew and Arabic peoples of the time with good reason. These thoughts and ideas—as interpreted, argued, and defended throughout the ages—served to highlight specific points. The assumption that each of Job's companions represents some specific philosophy or doctrine is part of the interpretive literature regardless of time, place, or faith affiliation.

Eliphaz—the son of Esau (Job chapters 4, 5, 15, and 22)

With a conflict that began over a birthright, the nations of Edom and Israel maintained a relationship that was sometimes tolerant, sometimes stormy, and sometimes mutually protective. Though the brothers themselves reconciled on Jacob's return to Canaan, the two nations barely tolerated each other throughout their history. Edom denied passage to the tribes of Israel on their return from Egypt. The Maccabees (a Jewish family of priests) pressed the Edomites to convert to Judaism under threat of the sword. Rome set an Edomite on the throne of Judea at the time of Jesus, causing much of the political intrigue of the time.

Nevertheless, regardless of their contentious relationship, Israel and Edom still recognized brotherhood in faith and blood. As a descendant of Esau, Eliphaz represents tradition, the ancient ways, and law as given to Abraham before there was a nation of Israel. During the sixth century CE, an Arabic movement to return to the faith of Abraham was the spark that became Islam.[3]

To support his position that God is not arbitrary, Eliphaz goes through great lengths to suggest that Job must have done something wrong. He is quick to point out that Job has always been a do-gooder. Why, then, should there be such an issue now? Certainly, the whole problem of Job's suffering will resolve if he changes his attitude. The tormented man before him does not have all the answers. Perhaps his charity was all show and not a true commitment to help individuals within the community. The

---

3. See chapter 14, "Ayyub–Prophet of Patience."

promise from deep in the past is that if one is obedient, God will bless him. Job must have done something wrong.

Eliphaz insists that if God required restitution of the angels, why then would he not require as much of man who is born to sin?[4] Job should repent of his hidden sin and not reject the discipline of the Almighty. This companion even tries to convince Job that the wicked live in constant terror of the Almighty, which they do not. In contrast, he also points out that a righteous life cannot mean much to God. What real contribution can a mortal be to the universe? God is so beyond humanity that day-to-day lives are just not that important to him. Therefore, Job should accept his plight, confess to whatever, and then maybe he can be returned to his previous place of privilege.

There are many contradictions inherent in this argument, not the least of which is, if there is no hope of meeting the standards of a God who doesn't have time for humanity, then why should an individual be punished for sins that they may not recognize? Eliphaz, just as many thinkers over the centuries have tried, cannot have it both ways. Determining that God is interested in punishing or rewarding individuals based on all the minutiae of their lives, and yet is so far above humans that they cannot begin to fathom what it is he expects, is a logical conundrum if not an outright fallacy. The argument is a non sequitur[5] since it attempts to create a logical connection between mutually exclusive conditions. However, Eliphaz's arguments may have value once the perspective is changed.

Bildad—the son of Keturah (Job chapters 8, 18, and 25)

Bildad, the representative from the clans of Keturah, has a slightly different point of view. He feels that God would not reject the pleas of the righteous, nor would God oppress a good person. If Job is ignorant of his specific sin, he should seek the accumulated wisdom of the past. Surely the writings of the ancients can shed some light on the situation. Bildad represents the tradition that all things can resolve with reason and study. Therefore, wisdom and reason must dictate God's actions. Bildad would have made an excellent Greek.

To reinforce his argument, Bildad urges Job to listen to the counsel of his friends. Job should realize that the workings of the universe will not alter their course to accommodate Job. According to Bildad, man himself is not worthy to present himself before God; therefore, he should seek the ancient wisdom and use reason to solve his mysteries. Job, of course, insists on taking his case directly to God.

Bildad presses the case that if Job is a good man, then he will be restored. Only the wicked perish without hope, and when they do, all look on the destruction and remark that they must not have truly known God. Again, a companion of Job tries

---

4. Job 4:18; 15:15.
5. Latin for "does not follow."

to reassure him by making a point that simply does not manifest in life. People who perpetrate acts generally thought to be wrong or sinful do not always give thought to consequences. Even if such individuals acknowledge there are consequences, they often believe they will not be subject to them. How people respond to acts considered evil or abhorrent is dependent on the social and political climate of the time. There are always those who want to see the evildoer punished and those who do not seem to understand why anyone should face consequences for their actions whatever they may be.

However, maybe Bildad does have a piece of the puzzle, some piece of the truth once seen in the right perspective or given correct circumstantial application.

Zophar—the son of Benjamin (Job chapters 11 and 20)

Zophar represents a point of view which relies on established authority. He believes that the nature and attributes of God are beyond reason and experience. For him, those in authority teach moral truths through revelation; they cannot be reasoned out.

Zophar tells Job to be still and listen to the wisdom of his friends. In response to Job's demand that God answer his challenge, Zophar proclaims that talking does not make a man right, advice he seems more willing to give than take. If God would condescend to speak to Job, he would point out that Job has overlooked something in his life that needs attention. According to this friend, Job is not in any position to know the transgression he committed or even the nature of God. The world would be right again if Job will submit by repenting for any unknown sins. Zophar repeats the illogical argument that individuals can be held accountable for a standard which they do not know and cannot understand.

Even Zophar chooses to believe that the happiness of the wicked is fleeting. Wicked persons find destruction when they least expect it. Whether he means this as reassurance that Job can look forward to future happiness, or as a pronouncement that Job is getting what he deserves is not clear.

Does Zophar's view offer something of value? Are there things that must be accepted on prior authority, even if the source of that authority is not clear? Can the authority of one person or organization be effectively tested against that of another? If this were an easy question, there would not be multiple denominations, each of which all call themselves Christian. The same situation, to a lesser extent, exists in the Muslim and Jewish faiths. Part of the goal of this book is to show that which authority is acceptable to an individual depends on how much effort a person puts into learning, researching, and testing the information found. Does the source make sense based on what was previously known? Does the conclusion look reasonable, given the individual's understanding of life in general or the issue at hand in particular?

Part II—Theodicy and Philosophy

Elihu—presumably the son of Nahor, with mention of Gad and Ram (Job chapters 32:6—37:24)

Elihu is the angry young man. He is quite perturbed that, in his opinion, he has not seen any gems of wisdom from these gray-hairs of the tribes. Wisdom, then, must come from God and has little to do with how aged one might be. The champion of the text in the eyes of the Aristotelian philosophers, Elihu proposes that Job may be looking for God's voice in all the wrong places. Perhaps, he feels, now is the time for a touch of reality.

He is emphatic that God can do no wrong and that he dispenses justice according to the actions of an individual. God alone can ransom a mortal. In Elihu's opinion, there are no grounds on which to challenge the authority upon whom humanity's very existence depends. Elihu justifies his Maker, a Maker he feels needs no justification.

Elihu is quick to emphasize the confusion in Job's argument that his life should be a testimony against his suffering. Simultaneously, he denies that there is any profit in living a moral life. Logic, however, rarely visits in suffering. Elihu, in his tender age, seems unaware of a need in the believer to know God. However, he adds wisdom to the argument by pointing out that God speaks in several ways to warn and guide those who seek him. As many of the commentators examined in this book note, Elihu argues that providence is the action of an individual learning to be ever mindful of the world and the actions of others so that they can be prepared to respond to dangers and warning signals. He believes that the avenues for these warnings and messages exist in dreams and visions.

He ends his argument with an emphasis on the greatness and vastness of the Creator, the mover of all nature. God, to Elihu, is a universal logician, perfect in action, all-knowing, and just, all without being in touch with humanity's frailty, feeling, hurt, or uncertainty. This concept delivers a large blow to the school of a personal God.

For all his bluster, Elihu makes a valid point. For the individual who listens, there are many warnings available to guide the way. Humanity's instincts are highly developed, even if often ignored. If a situation or a person causes an uncomfortable feeling, there may be an excellent reason that is so. If sleep is bothered with a repeated theme, a dream interpreter is not required to know that something is causing a sense of worry. In such cases, it is advisable to look for resolutions or possible dangers. Even here, then, are pieces that may fit the puzzle, things that will help complete the picture of the message the author of Job is trying to convey.

Employing the Basics

These are the central themes used in much of the literature about Job. Philosophers and theologians of the first fifteen to sixteen hundred years of the Common Era used these ideas to build their interpretations and defend their points of view.

Islamic philosophical traditions are prevalent in the writings of this period. Many of the scholars of Job and related subjects lived in cities or university towns built, staffed, and maintained by the Arabs. During those periods, and in those places where the Islamic rulers were tolerant, societies grew strong with economic and spiritual health. There were resources to devote time to the pursuit of wisdom from all over the world. There is much in common among the three Abrahamic traditions. The difference lies in how the information is applied.

The body of work that interprets or refers to the Job and his suffering is extensive. The authors investigated in the next four chapters lived and worked from ca. 180–1480 CE. The timeline places the authors within the context of their time and the political influences of their day. The chart will also help locate where each man lived and worked.

The authors are presented in four groups to help demonstrate the contrasting and correlating views of Job which form the foundation of modern interpretations. These four groups are the pillars of Christian thought, the fathers who contributed to the philosophy of suffering in the Christian church, the conservative Jewish philosophers, and the Jewish Aristotelians.

PART II—THEODICY AND PHILOSOPHY

Chart 3

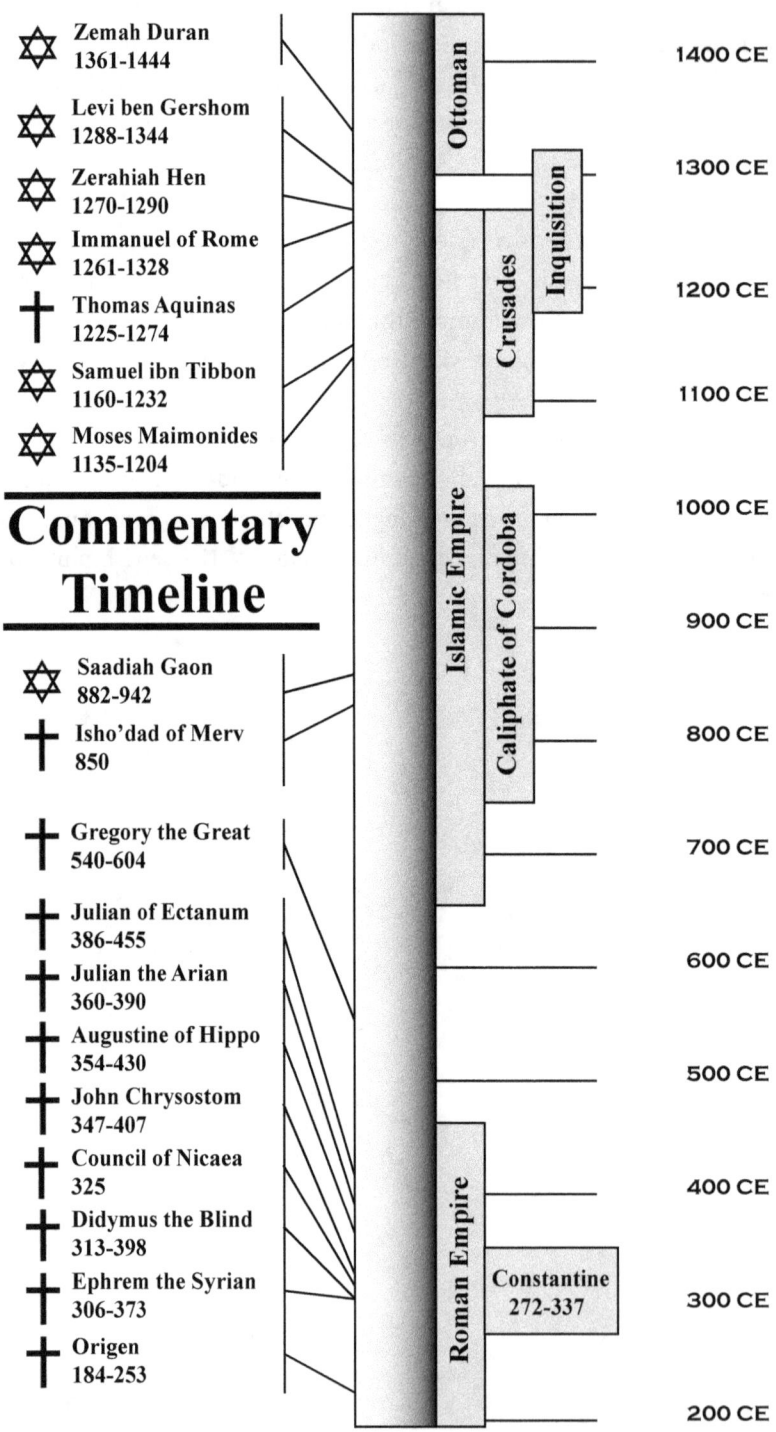

Commentary Timeline

✡ Zemah Duran 1361-1444
✡ Levi ben Gershom 1288-1344
✡ Zerahiah Hen 1270-1290
✡ Immanuel of Rome 1261-1328
✝ Thomas Aquinas 1225-1274
✡ Samuel ibn Tibbon 1160-1232
✡ Moses Maimonides 1135-1204

✡ Saadiah Gaon 882-942
✝ Isho'dad of Merv 850
✝ Gregory the Great 540-604
✝ Julian of Ectanum 386-455
✝ Julian the Arian 360-390
✝ Augustine of Hippo 354-430
✝ John Chrysostom 347-407
✝ Council of Nicaea 325
✝ Didymus the Blind 313-398
✝ Ephrem the Syrian 306-373
✝ Origen 184-253

Timeline bands: Ottoman, Inquisition, Crusades, Islamic Empire, Caliphate of Cordoba, Roman Empire, Constantine 272-337

1400 CE
1300 CE
1200 CE
1100 CE
1000 CE
900 CE
800 CE
700 CE
600 CE
500 CE
400 CE
300 CE
200 CE

Chapter 7

The Pillars of Early Christian Thought

THE BIRTH OF THE Christian church was a rather messy affair: conflicting philosophies, theologies, dogmas, and legal requirements made for heated battles for centuries. For instance, Europe suffered a series of wars from ca. 1500 to the early 1700s. One of these conflicts was the Thirty Years' War (1618–1648) between Catholic and Protestant factions vying for supremacy.[1] Sparked by the new Roman emperor, Ferdinand II, the conflict began as an effort to convert the population to Roman Catholicism by the sword. In the end, it was about land and political power. The advent of the printed word granted the person on the street greater access to religious literature and added volumes to the search for consensus. Some of the conflicting views are now lost or survive only in fragments. Even today, denominations spring up over the smallest of differences in doctrinal interpretation. The formative years of the church and the later Protestant Reformation provided a stimulating background to commentaries that address suffering, punishment, and providence.

In the first few centuries of the Common Era, Christian commentators did not show much interest in the book of Job. Origen, an early Christian scholar and theologian living in Alexandria (ca. 184–254 CE), was the first to write more than passing references. Near the latter part of the fourth century, Christian philosophers and theologians began to focus on Job. The foundation of Christian thinking on the book begins with the insights of two men familiar to many students of biblical and theological studies: Augustine of Hippo and Thomas Aquinas. The works of these two men form the pillars of Christian philosophical and theological thought. Nearly nine centuries separated these theologians and they wrote from different historical backgrounds and cultural influences. Both devoted much of their contemplation to the operations of the mind, emotions, and spirit.

As a foundational contributor to the development of Christian theology, Augustine brings understanding to questions of suffering and providence that help form a

---

1. See Wedgwood, *Thirty Years War*.

basis of later interpretations. He wrote at the beginning of this period, in the early fifth century. He was not among those who devoted special attention to the life of Job or the teachings of the book. For these reasons, the analysis of the contribution of Augustine focuses on the issues raised within the book of Job rather than on the book itself.

Augustine of Hippo

Augustine (354–430 CE) was a Latin philosopher and theologian who lived in Hippo, a Roman province located in present-day Algeria.[2] Early in his life, he was an adherent of a gnostic sect, the Manichaeans, and studied the Neoplatonic philosopher Plotinus. After he converted to Christianity, this background influenced his philosophy and theology. He believed that the grace of Christ was the fount of freedom, and he codified the concepts of original sin and just war. The Roman Catholic, Eastern Orthodox, and many Protestant sects revere Augustine as a father of the faith.

The writings of Augustine consist of essays grouped under general headings. Rather than being structured as commentaries on specific scriptural passages, he addresses the events and philosophical arguments of his time. In contrast to the Jewish Aristotelians introduced later, he follows a school of thought known as Neoplatonism.

In *The City of God*, chapter 8, Augustine comments on the question of why good and evil events seem to fall on good and evil men indiscriminately. After describing the bounty of God, Augustine determines that how the individual responds to that bounty contributes to determining the soul's eternal home. From the text,

> For though some of these men, taking thought of this, repent of their wickedness and reform, some, as the apostle says, "despising the riches of His goodness and long-suffering, after their hardness and impenitent heart, treasure up unto themselves wrath against the day of wrath and revelation of the righteous judgment of God, who will render to every man according to his deeds:" nevertheless does the patience of God still invite the wicked to repentance, even as the scourge of God educates the good to patience.[3]

Augustine answers the question of why the wicked prosper by pointing out that nature's bounty as well as its devastation affect both the good and the evil. Job's cry of "the Lord giveth, and the Lord taketh away" (Job 1:21) is echoed in this passage. Augustine is a realist and sees the world more as it is than as we would wish. From later in the same chapter:

> But as for the good things of this life, and its ills, God has willed that these should be common to both; that we might not too eagerly covet the things

---

2. See maps at the end of chapter 8.
3. Augustine, *City of God*, 29.

which wicked men are seen equally to enjoy, nor shrink with an unseemly fear from the ills which even good men often suffer.[4]

From this perspective, the point of suffering is not so much why something happens, but the way a person learns to deal with the suffering. From the same chapter, he writes that,

> The same fire causes gold to glow brightly, and chaff to smoke; . . . as the lees are not mixed with the oil, though squeezed out of the vat by the same pressure, so the same violence of affliction proves, purges, clarifies the good, but damns, ruins, exterminates the wicked. . . . So material a difference does it make, not what ills are suffered, but what kind of man suffers them. For, stirred up with the same movement, mud exhales a horrible stench, and ointment emits a fragrant odor.[5]

Job, for Augustine, would be a man of mettle. The firing of adversity brought out his deep and enduring commitment to his God, even if it was difficult for him to understand that those who were wicked could prosper while he faced utter destruction. There is no need for Job's friends to come up with convoluted explanations of how the wicked lived in terror or feared their destruction. For Augustine, the point is the way individuals handle trials and tribulations. Do they do so by strengthening themselves and those around them? Supporting the suffering individual by providing tools to gain the most from the situation is a practical approach with merit. By focusing on healing, the need to search for cause and effect is less urgent unless there exists a cause with a direct impact on healing and moving forward.

As the author of the church's concept of original sin, Augustine believes that no man is blameless before God. He sees providence as guided by punishment and reward. In book I, chapter 9 of *The City of God*, he teaches that God punishes the good with the bad, not because they are equally wicked, but because they learned to love the present life rather than counting it cheap.[6] The phrase "they lost everything" holds no power for Augustine. His question is, have they lost "their faith, their godliness, the possessions of the hidden man of the heart, which in the sight of God are of great price?"[7]

Anyone who has suffered great loss would consider this interpretation impractical. However, Augustine is addressing the trials of Christians throughout Europe as the Roman Empire falls to the invading hordes. He devotes nearly four of the books in *The City of God* to the history of Rome, its treatment of others, and the testing of its policies in defeat. How and why people suffer physically, spiritually, and emotionally took up great portions of his thoughts on Christian theology.

4. Augustine, *City of God*, 29.
5. Augustine, *City of God*, 30.
6. Augustine, *City of God*, 32.
7. Augustine, *City of God*, 33.

Augustine also writes that the believer is responsible for seeking guidance and avoiding harm's way when and if possible. Much later in *The City of God*, volume II, chapter 22, Augustine discusses the intrinsic good or evil properties of aspects of creation. He does not follow his gnostic roots with this interpretation. He does not view matter as a source of evil or deprivation. After providing a list of things that can be bad or good, depending on application, he states,

> Divine providence admonishes us not foolishly to vituperate [censure or berate] things, but to investigate their utility with care; and, where our mental capacity of infirmity is at fault, to believe that there is a utility, though hidden, as we have experienced that there were other things which we all but failed to discover.[8]

All things, to Augustine, have their place in the knowledge of God, some great, some small, each in its proper place and each within its proper use.

Even though Augustine does not directly address Job, his writings provide a rich resource for guidance on suffering. He believes that good and evil befall the wicked and the righteous equally and that the judgment of God comes from the way the believer responds. All have sinned, and all are subject to some form of punishment as well as reward. Sometimes, the trials in this life lead the believer to appreciate the life beyond. He believes that the loss of worldly possessions is meaningless so long as the sufferer does not lose faith in God.

These basic ideas contributed to the interpretations of Job in later years. What is interesting is that even though Augustine does not address the book directly, his thoughts are more compatible with the speeches from God than those of many later commentators. His writings appear influenced by the large portions of Job devoted to the balance of nature and the functions of the universe. For Augustine, nothing in creation is intrinsically good or evil. Humanity is only part of creation, which can be either good or evil. The individual's response to both the bounty and the devastation of life is what determines their character and any possible rewards. Attitudes and circumstance changed substantially over the next eight hundred years. Consequently, Aquinas provides a different perspective and a finer focus on the book of Job itself.

Thomas Aquinas

Thomas Aquinas lived approximately eight hundred years after Augustine (1225–1274 CE). The face of Europe had changed. The old Roman Empire was gone, and the Catholic Church was well established as a political and religious power on the European continent and beyond. The Mongols were conquering the Caliphate of Baghdad (1258) and invading Eastern Europe (ca. 1222–1242), and the Caliphate of Córdoba was a thing of the past (1031). Thomas Aquinas, writing and teaching at the University

---

8. Augustine, *City of God*, 503.

of Paris, lived during a time of peace and relative prosperity in Western Europe under the reigns of Kings Louis VIII and IX. The church granted Louis IX sainthood for his contributions to the expansion and protection of the church and the faith.

Aquinas was the son of a nobleman of Naples. He was an Italian Dominican priest recognized for his influence as a philosopher and a theologian. He established a tradition of scholastics, and his works include commentary on natural theology, natural law, metaphysics, and political theory.

In the prologue of Thomas Aquinas's *Commentary on Job*, he writes,

> Therefore after the majority of men asserted the opinion that natural things did not happen by chance but by providence because of the order which clearly appears in them, a doubt emerged among most men about the acts of man as to whether human affairs evolved by chance, or were governed by some kind of providence or higher ordering. This doubt was fed especially because there is no sure order apparent in human events. For good things do not always befall the good, nor evil things the wicked . . . This fact then especially moved the hearts of men to hold the opinion that human affairs are not governed by divine providence. Some said that human affairs proceed by chance except to the extent that they are ruled by human providence and counsel, others attributed their outcome to a fatalism ruled by the heavens.[9]

The actual discourse on Job is quite lengthy. Many of his thoughts resonated with the conclusions brought out in this text. In the main, to be held accountable to a code, one should have the means and the methods to learn what the code is and the ability to understand what the code implies. A rational mind requires a rational answer. Aquinas brought clarity and immediacy to the piles of interpretative literature that had accumulated before him.

Every bit as applicable today as the day he wrote it, Aquinas begins his commentary by addressing the thought that if there is no apparent order, then there is no One who orders. However, he goes on in his prologue to discard this line of thought as a path to perdition. If each man feels free to follow his own needs and wants without fear or love of God, then it should be easy to see how quickly vice would fill world. Aquinas believes firmly that the whole purpose of the book of Job, including its very placement in the canon, is to "show that human affairs are ruled by divine providence using probable arguments." He goes on to further support Job: "But that the just are afflicted without cause seems to undermine the foundation of Providence. Thus the varied and grave afflictions of a specific just man called Job, perfect in every virtue, are proposed as a kind of theme."[10]

Aquinas is a literalist and sees the book of Job as a report of actual events. He emphasizes Job's innocence, wealth, and family. While commenting on the conversations

---

9. Aquinas, *Commentary*, 6.
10. Aquinas, *Commentary*, 7.

between God and Satan, he clarifies the need for God to ask Satan where he has been by defining two ways in which God speaks. The first is in the eternal sense, an interior concept of the heart—for instance, when God spoke the world into existence. The second way is God's direct speech to a mortal being by speaking in time and with a manner known to the subject.

Aquinas sees God's act of speaking to Satan in the eternal sense. He explains that God speaks directly through the senses or visions. In other words, he is not proposing that there was a physical confrontation between two entities, one being God and one Satan; he describes a situation in which information becomes known between the parties by God himself. He also indicates that Satan doesn't provide God with new information. His input is only required to make him aware or remind him of what God already knows. Aside from this analysis, the prologue to the story introduces key points for the audience, with or without some direct communication between God and Satan.

Aquinas wrote in a derisive manner concerning women, declaring them imperfect and outright useless except for the delivery of male heirs.[11] However, once the reader filters out Aquinas's medieval ideas regarding the subjugation of women to men, there is much to learn from his commentary. In analyzing the text, Aquinas uses the ancient vision of a layered universe, one layer being the things that belong to earth and the other being things that belong to heaven. In this version, Satan may not have initially noticed Job because Job's mind, being constantly on God, placed him closer to heaven than earth. Therefore, God must point him out since Satan could not see him without divine assistance.

Aquinas, unlike Augustine, sees Job as suffering real loss, although he defines that loss with some moderation. He alludes to the philosophy of the Aristotelians and Augustine's *City of God* by saying that the goods of a man are truly exterior and that the loss of such by a wise man only makes him moderately sad.[12] However, this theory makes no sense within the context of the book. The attacks on Job were direct attacks made to illustrate a point. If Job was in such an elevated spiritual state that the losses would not affect him, then why the waste of life and property?

Aquinas analyzes Job's reactions. He notes that, initially, the man is subdued and appears to be accepting the fate that befalls him. Aquinas believes that Job looks at the first incidents as causing the loss of mere possessions. He notes that Job believes that all things come from God and that God is at liberty to take them back should he choose. Job may have viewed material goods in this manner. However, it is doubtful he would feel the same way about the loss of human life. The loss of any life, even the life of a servant, would have been a loss that wounded Job's sense of justice deeply; at least, his reactions in the prologue indicate that he was deeply affected by the wholesale destruction of his servants and his livestock.

11. Aquinas, *Commentary*, 11.
12. Aquinas, *Commentary*, 34.

While reading Aquinas's thoughts on the depth of Job's losses, it is important to remember the cultural and social structures of his time. In addition to his notions on the status of women, his commentary also drives a wedge between Job and his servants by indicating they are disobedient and restive. Job 19 speaks to the treatment Job is receiving from family and friends since his misfortunes. He also laments that his former tenants no longer recognize him, and his servants will not respond. Aquinas sees this passage from the perspective of the class structure of his time and seems to ignore the pain Job experiences when first hearing of the destruction and the loyalty of those who escape to warn him. The process of this retelling of Job is to analyze the context of the original tale and to look objectively at the context of later commentary. Men such as Aquinas made substantial contributions to the doctrines of the modern church. The theology of the Christian faith is richer for the insights provided by such men; however, it is crucial to interpret their contributions within context of their life and times.

Aquinas classifies possessions into three categories: the soul, the body, and exterior things. The body exists for the sake of the soul, and the external things exist for the sake of both body and soul. He sees Job's trial as God's will to allow Job to suffer such tremendous loss to prove that Job is a good and faithful servant and not dependent upon good fortune to trust and love his God. There is no doubt in the mind of Aquinas that the events would not have occurred without explicit divine will.

Remembering Aquinas's thoughts on women, we see him say that Satan left Job's wife to tempt him in the same way as Eve tempted Adam. The translation of Scripture used in Aquinas's commentary reads, "Do you still hold fast your simplicity?"[13] This transcription provides quite a different understanding than the Hebrew rendition, "integrity."[14] Aquinas's text also interprets the last part of the exchange as "Bless God and die." He makes it clear that he sees Job's wife as the temptress, insisting that if Job continues on the path he has chosen, then all will be lost.

As with most interpreters of the poem, Aquinas sees Job's companions as more hindrance than solace. Of course, if they had been on their best behavior, much of the message would be lost. Job's visitors agreed with Job that both natural things and the affairs of men were subject to Divine Providence. The differences in their beliefs arise when they become insistent (in the various manners of their approaches) that the only possible answer is that God rewards individuals for good and punishes them for evil. There can be no cause for calamity other than as a result of the commission of an infraction or the omission of some required deed. Aquinas sees the visitors' mistake as assuming that God used temporal goods for reward or punishment, whereas Job sees reward and punishment as a future thing. The visitors do show concern about Job's

---

13. Aquinas, *Commentary*, 44.

14. Note: It is beneficial to read through the source material to see the differences that exist between the translation that Aquinas used for his work and modern translations of the same passages. "Integrity" is the word used in Job 2:9 in the *Tanakh*.

tragedies and offer comfort in their companionable silence. The situation only goes awry when Job begins his lament. Then the atmosphere of support melts away, and his erstwhile friends become adversarial.

Aquinas focuses on Job's responses and what is proper in the service of God. He notes that the Stoics felt there was no place in a wise man for sorrow.[15] However, Aristotelians felt that a wise man did experience emotions, moderated by reason. Aquinas arrives at the same conclusion and determines that a wise man would not permit unseemly reactions. After all, Christ exhibited sorrow, and who could be wiser or more virtuous? In these thoughts, Aquinas glimpses the findings of modern science. The mind does indeed create agency and, when rational, can and does moderate the emotional centers of the brain.

What is most interesting about this treatise is that Aquinas looks very closely at Job's dilemma. He at no time accuses God of being unjust. He knows that the creature cannot presume to be justified in comparison to the Creator. Job's question is not an accusation; it is a quest for knowledge. He does not resist; he seeks the path to correct obedience. Aquinas believes that no man can have peace with God through resistance. Peace will only come through obedience and humility.

The dilemma, then, is that destruction comes to both the innocent and the wicked. Aquinas might summarize Job's point of view as "If God is going to afflict you anyway, then make it quick and relatively painless and get it over with." Unable to explain why there appears to be no consistency regarding what befalls whom, he concludes that the earth is given over to evil. Job declares, "He covers the faces of his judges" (9:24), as if ensuring that there is no witness to the conflict caused by evil influences.

Aquinas finds this answer unsatisfactory because Job cannot relinquish the belief that God is in control. Job's heart weeps because, as hard as he tries, he cannot determine the source of his condemnation. Aquinas makes the point quite clearly: "Man must know the cause of his punishment, either to correct himself or to endure the trials with more patience."[16] I couldn't agree more.

Aquinas suffers with Job in his mental exercise of finding a reason for his fate and that of innocent persons everywhere. Believing God to be the ultimate author of all, he looks for ways in which his fellow humans punish each other.[17] Perhaps there is some answer there.

He describes two ways in which he believes humanity punishes the innocent. One is through malice, which does not fit the preferred picture of a creator, and the second is the effort to seek truth through torture, also not a particularly palatable vision. Neither approach makes any sense if one is to believe that God created humanity.

---

15. Aquinas, *Commentary*, 48.
16. Aquinas, *Commentary*, 170.
17. Aquinas, *Commentary*, 170–71.

If people are the work of his hands, then an agenda destined to destroy that very creation would be counterintuitive.

Finding himself in another blind alley, Job, with the help of Aquinas, seeks his answer elsewhere. Aquinas formulates a logical conclusion that if a believer commits a sin requiring punishment, then the punishment should follow the sin. Since Job has been living in much the same manner for many years and nothing has happened, then why is he suddenly under attack? If there were no adverse consequences in the past, and he made no changes, then why now? After all, not only has he lost everything dear to him, including his health and the support of his spouse, his closest friends are adding salt to his wounds. Even though they make a pretense of defending the justice of God, they do so by attacking Job and accusing him of failing—if not in outright sin, then by doing the right thing for the wrong reasons.

Having analyzed the options, Aquinas draws a few conclusions. The cause of Job's trial is not an unjust deity who rules the earth, nor a God who persecutes based on a pretense, nor a God who has found an unobtrusive fault in his servant, nor a God who enjoys inflicting punishment. If Aquinas is to believe that God is just, then he must find a way to balance the scales. To do this, he must assume that all things will be made right in a life beyond the grave. Job and Aquinas must find a way to believe there will be a time when the innocent suffer no more, and the wicked are banished. Aquinas thus solves the problem by pushing the resolution into some elsewhen.

Contemplating this option, he introduces a discussion on the nature of law. He discerns that mortal law looks to "certain universal things which happen in the majority of cases because those who frame them were not able to consider every single case."[18] The discretion of the judge (and jury) ruling on each case is left to interpret the law based on the circumstances. Therefore, an individual can be judged innocent or guilty by degrees rather than absolutes. Divine law, however, has no such gray area. Divine code is a law authored by a Sovereign who *does* know every single case.

Aquinas returns to the argument of Eliphaz, writing,

> Since then man cannot attain the divine law itself as though investigating things hidden in the wisdom of God, and consequently cannot understand its complexity, he sometimes does not think he is acting against the law of God when in fact he is, or he thinks he is sinning a little when he is sinning a lot.[19]

The problem is, of course, how can God hold one accountable for fulfilling a law that is not understood and cannot be comprehended? What justice is there in that?

The deeper the debate between Job and his companions, the more his visitors exhibit fear and apprehension. If this group of men, considered wise leaders in their communities, cannot resolve this issue, then it appears possible that the same calamity could beset them at any time. The visitors must find a way to blame some hidden

---

18. Aquinas, *Commentary*, 188.
19. Aquinas, *Commentary*, 188.

issue in Job's past. If his visitors cannot blame Job for this catastrophe, then anybody or nobody can be blamed. In other words, they, too, could lose it all. Either case is intolerable to an ordered mind. Perhaps Job is not getting all he does deserve. God, after all, knows all things regarding the vanity of man. If Job will repent, then everything will be fine, and everyone can go home.

Aquinas points out that Job does not entirely discount the arguments presented by his friends. Job is knowledgeable of these principles and the doctrine that they represent. Still, Job cannot reconcile the attack on his life and his person with the conduct of that life. Job wishes an audience with the Almighty, not to question his justice, but to question what he perceives as the errors of his companions' conclusions. If his friends are right, then God is unjust for punishing Job, who is without blame. Job is taking them to task for making him the brunt of an unsolvable riddle, for believing that God passes out rewards and punishments in this life only and, therefore, Job has sinned. Aquinas feels that Job is pointing out that they worship a perverse view of dogma, mostly to still their quivering hearts. Whom do they worship—God or their doctrines? As ancient as this poem is, this question could not be any timelier. Do we worship our creed, or doctrine, more than we worship God?

In the words of Aquinas himself, "Men often propose some things as capable of being proved, although they are false: but when they do not know how to defend them or prove them convincingly they show their ignorance when they speak."[20]

Job's friends find themselves caught in this dilemma. Consequently, Aquinas quotes Job as saying,

> "Would that you were silent so that people would think you were wise men." Because the very fact that you defend and prove false dogmas unfittingly, shows that you are foolish. So, since you propose false dogmas and you take unsuitable means to prove them, you are in need of correction. This is what he concludes, saying then, "Listen, then, to my correction," by which I will correct your process of reasoning, "and hear the judgment of my lips," with which I will condemn your false dogmas.[21]

Aquinas sees this as a key point in his commentary. He stands with Job in taking issue with an argument that requires that some unknown crimes must be attributed to the innocent to support the justice of God. He makes it clear that Job is accusing his friends openly, asking them if they dare to judge in God's place. Unlike God, who sees all, they only have their expectations. Job, then, is adamant that God does not need a lie to prove his justice, so this cannot be the answer. There is no reason to wonder at God's response to the contributions of Eliphaz, Bildad, and Zophar. In the words of God, they have "darken[ed] counsel with words without knowledge" (Job 38:2).

---

20. Aquinas, *Commentary*, 211.
21. Aquinas, *Commentary*, 211.

Returning to Job's line of inquiry, he asks the only source who can answer his challenge: God. Job's companions have accused him of many things, among them impatience and ostentation. However, Job, in the eyes of Aquinas, remains firm in the knowledge that his Creator has not changed. There is no one else that has the answer; thus: he whom God finds innocent is he who speaks the truth. On this basis, Job feels confident in saying that if judged, he will be found just (Job 23:10).

In chapter 13 of the book of Job, Job utters several rhetorical questions to illustrate the contrasts inherent between the Creator and his creation. Aquinas sees this speech as pure irony; as a collection of superficial arguments intended to excuse the actions of God. For instance, in Job 13:24 Job asks, "Why do you hide your face and think of me as your enemy?" Aquinas asks if the creature carries enough power to rise to the level of an enemy of the Creator. Job asks, "Do you show your power against the leaf which is driven by the wind?" (13:25). Aquinas inquires whether it is necessary to destroy a man to prove that the Creator has power over him. Aquinas then asks if Job is paying for the sins of his youth. Job asks, "Do you break a dry stalk? / Do you write bitter things against me, / and do you want to consume me for the sins of my youth?" (13:25–26). If this is the case, then the punishment is rather tardy and not delivered in a way to correct a lifetime of error.

Both Job and Aquinas ponder the question, "Would God chase down every small and insignificant act if it perishes at death?" Is it, they ask, reasonable to expect that such minutiae occupy the Creator of the universe? In Job's words, people are weak, born of women, live a short time, and face many sorrows. Why would a sovereign deity be interested in the day-to-day frailties of such a creature? The things that people can glory in pass quickly, such as the beauty of youth and fame, which can be like a passing wind. Power and strength can also fail. Job knows that there is evidence that someone, somewhere cares. Humanity has developed laws and precepts, rewards and punishments to create order in society. If the rational mind perceives this requirement for order, why is it so difficult to discover a greater universal order, one that explains why suffering occurs and what one should do when it does?

Aquinas believes that Job concludes that the only possible reason every infraction in this life is sought out and cleansed is that there is another life where actions taken while living multiply. Much is forgiven to balance what has happened with what will be.

Job reminds us nature itself decays. Mountains wear down, rocks are displaced, weather and catastrophes change the earth. Everything becomes corrupt through violence or nature. Job asks if God will then destroy man in the same way (Job 14:18–22).

Aquinas believes that only the body is subject to this end. He sees, in humanity, a difference in the mind. Humanity has developed the ability to reason, to gain knowledge, and to make choices. The mind is not a thing which fails through corruption unless the individual so chooses. Aquinas sees this as the question Job has put to God. Although a creature of nature, humanity has the capacity for agency, the ability to

Part II—Theodicy and Philosophy

reason and make a moral choice. Would God grant free will and the power to change the future and then arbitrarily negate the results of these gifts? Does God bestow intellectual knowledge without a productive, creative purpose? Aquinas sees the gifts of reason and intellect as evidence that there is immortality, and not just the immortality found through the lives of one's offspring.

Job and his companions come to an impasse. They refuse to believe that he is blameless, and Job refuses to admit guilt, which, if done falsely, would be a sin in and of itself. Job makes it clear that he doesn't expect them to have the answers. The only source of truth is God. They believe that the very act of demanding answers from God is blasphemy. Perhaps as a way of separating himself from his companions and refocusing his attention on God, Job delivers his Ode to Wisdom (Job 28).[22] He describes all the wonders of creation, as he knows them. He explores life itself, the power of evil, the beauty and mystery of the physical world. He despairs, seemingly unable to find a satisfactory answer to his dilemma in heaven or earth.

Aquinas, as did many of the Jewish philosophers, sees the arguments of Elihu as the deeper message. His input is not the whole answer, even though many commentators see his words as a clarification of what Job's companions have been attempting to say. Elihu thinks that they have all fallen silent because they think Job has proved his righteousness, or that there is no hope in convincing Job there is something he must confess.

Elihu expands on the recorded commentary of Job himself to make his point. He affirms that no one is pure and without error, that Job is unforgivably arrogant to call God his enemy, and that he has presumed that God has taken away his ability to mount a just defense.

The angry young man of the encounter is incensed that Job presumes to argue with God. Job never says he wants to argue with God. What he wants is an opportunity to learn from God. He never stops asking "why." Job believes there is a reason, a definitive answer to his suffering. Elihu turns the argument on its head. He determines that God speaks once, in visions, in dreams, and through natural reason. When necessary, he may speak through illness or death (as a last resort). There should be no need to discuss the issue further or to challenge God. These are the accepted and established means by which God corrects and disciplines the individual. This angry young man believes that, by Job's testimony, he has received communication through all available channels: natural reason, dreams, and illness. He sees the recent events as acts to guide Job to correction, not as punishment, *per se*.

Aquinas then looks at Elihu's angels. He sees the angels as intercessors to the throne of God. Since he believes that Job does not have direct access to the throne, the

---

22. It should be noted here that both Greenstein and David Clines see Job 28 as the misplaced conclusion of Elihu's speeches. Greenstein also states that scholars regard Job 28 as an autonomous poem and not an expression of Job's point of view. Whatever the source of this passage, the poem does indicate a point when Job draws away from his companions and focuses on the conversation between himself and God.

angels must speak for him. Elihu assures his reluctant audience that there are enough to go around. These messengers are the mediators between God and men, and they propose the justice of man to God and help mortals obtain their desires.[23] Intercessory prayer is something the modern Christian would find familiar. Prayers directed to angels and saints must include sincere repentance. Elihu returns to the same theme as Job's friends: Job needs forgiveness for something. He points out that God might send warnings multiple times to reach a soul, to bring the heart back to a true course.

After adding something of merit to the conversation, Elihu goes on the attack. In his effort to show his great wisdom, he manages to misquote Job on several issues. He says that Job has declared that God is wrong in punishing him. Job never does this. He only asks why. Elihu says God must be just because there is no other. If God is not just, then there is no justice. Job agrees with this statement. He also attempts an argument from the point of view that God withholds his hand from all men. Scripture indicates this is not always the case. Elihu is creating a conundrum by saying that God is just because he does not destroy all that justly deserve it. Withholding punishment when punishment is due is mercy, not justice.

His argument continues to spiral out of control when he decides that Job lacks the understanding to reason with him. He assumes that Job has blasphemed by declaring himself more just than God. He turns his back on Job as unworthy of discourse and offers his thoughts to prudent men, which, by his estimate, are not present. Aquinas points out repeatedly that Elihu begins to reiterate the arguments of the others with greater force (and arrogance). For him, people's lives are too small to be of great concern to God, yet the only justice in the world comes from God. If things are going wrong in life, then the sufferer needs to get right with God. The one who appears to be the king of verbosity accuses the victim of being too wordy. Keeping with the ironic theme of Job's initial companions, Elihu wishes to point out that human lives are too insignificant for the attention of the Creator of the universe, and yet said Creator is forever looking for the smallest infraction on the part of his creatures.

Aquinas begins the final analysis with this:

> After the discussion of Job and his friends about divine providence took place, Eliud [Elihu] had assumed to himself the office of determining the answer, contradicting Job in some things and his friends in others. But because human wisdom is not sufficient to understand the truth of divine providence, it was necessary that this disrepute should be determined by divine authority.[24]

Aquinas sees the answer to suffering and providence as evident in the acts of nature and the control of evil. He gives some credit to Job's companions for thinking rightly about many things. However, he feels they have misapplied their dogma to Job's situation. I would agree.

23. Aquinas, *Commentary*, 429.
24. Aquinas, *Commentary*, 479.

Part II—Theodicy and Philosophy

Augustine and Aquinas reach deeply into the experience of their time to attempt to resolve Job's dilemma. Their interpretations form a backdrop for the discussion without reaching a completely satisfactory answer. Perhaps there is something in the writings of other church fathers that will help in the search for an answer. Throughout the period between the lives of Augustine and Aquinas, the men who formed early Christian thought wrote volumes about Job and his trials. The question is whether these writings contributed to the theological thought of the church, or whether they were primarily homilies and sermons for the flock.

Chapter 8

Philosophy or Homily?

EVEN AFTER TWO MILLENNIA, there is no consensus on what it means to be a Christian. In the early centuries of the church, as it endeavored to define some form of orthodoxy, many schools of thought were actively suppressed and maligned. The attacks on the doctrine of some sects were not entirely born of malicious intent. To survive as a faith in the ancient world, the leaders had to develop a cohesive doctrine and a hierarchy of authority. Initially, groups of believers each had their own beliefs about how Jesus' life related to Hebrew tradition. The surviving literature contains portions of the battles for general acceptance. Although some of these writings survive wholly or in part, others are known only through essays that condemned the content. There are also works attributed to known individuals yet have indications of authorship by someone else using a pseudonym, or that have been translated and preserved in a different tradition. Studying these works can give insights into the development of scriptural interpretation and the theological views that lost in the struggle toward orthodoxy.

The group of men commonly thought of as the church fathers wrote their commentaries during the period of ca. 100–750 CE. As the thoughts and interpretations of Job developed, each group added their own experience, insight, hopes, and fears. This chapter includes selected writings of church fathers who wrote throughout the first eight centuries of the Common Era. By researching the commentaries written on the book of Job, one can begin to understand how the interpretation of the text changed with the ebb and flow of political and religious power as well as the strength of the church. The "Commentary Timeline" introduced in chapter 6, as well as the key and map, "The Church Fathers," which follows this chapter, will place these men within their historical and geographical context.

The primary source for this part of the journey is the sixth volume of the Ancient Christian Commentary on Scripture, *Job*.[1] The book is a compilation of the works of

---

1. Simonetti and Conti, *Job*.

men considered to be fathers of the Christian faith. These writings begin shortly after the last known works of the New Testament canon and continue to 750 CE, approximately a century after the founding of the Islamic faith. These men held a variety of positions within the church and adhered to differing interpretations of revealed truth. However, in contrast to Aquinas and Augustine, their focus, in one way or another, is on Job as a foreshadowing of Christ, the Christian church, and martyrs of the faith.

The authors presented in this chapter were leaders of the Christian communities where they served. Each of them represents some aspect of the developing Christian theology. These theologians, philosophers, and ministers debated the meaning of Scripture and what influence the Hebrew Scriptures should have on the life of a Christian. Many of their perspectives reflect the influence of the cultural environment where they lived and worked. For this reason, the source material groups them together by theological schools of thought:

> The Greek Fathers—Origen, Didymus the Blind, Julian the Arian, and John Chrysostom

> The Latin Fathers—Julian of Eclanum and Gregory the Great

> The Syriac Fathers—Ephrem the Syrian and Isho'dad of Merv

Each commentator's contribution begins with a brief biography followed by the commentator's doctrinal views and a summary of the their thoughts regarding the book of Job. The chapter closes with a synopsis of the most common positions on the key issues as addressed by these authors.

For these authors, the interpretations of the book of Job fell into two basic schools of thought. The Alexandrian School (Egypt) was prone to use allegory, while the Antiochian School (Greek) used a literal, textual interpretation. Allegory can be a powerful tool in the interpretation of Scripture; however, some of the early Christian writers used allegory as a tool to avoid an interpretation when the clear text did not rest easy with the author's specific doctrine.

The differences in doctrinal theory provided a rich background to the interpretation of the story of Job and what the message of the book might be, whether the doctrine survived or not. One sect that lost favor with the increasingly powerful orthodox community was the Arians. This group of Christians suffered from persecution from the empire and the church in Rome. Like Origen, Aetius (the founder of the Anomoean sect of Arian believers)[2] saw the Son of God as subordinate to God the Father and as a created being who was not co-eternal. After four centuries of debate, the church incorporated the word *homoousios* to declare Christ and God as of one substance. Although a formal doctrine on the nature of Christ was of primary

---

2. A follower of the Egyptian monk Arius, who was a bishop of Alexandria. He denied the Trinity but believed in the preexistence of Christ and that the Son was created by the Father. Aetius was a leader in this sect and was called The Atheist by orthodox leaders.

importance for the Council of Nicaea,[3] many other matters of orthodoxy were settled, such as the date for Easter and some administrative issues. A move to enforce celibacy on the clergy failed. After the council completed its work, the emperor exiled Arius, and his works were declared heresy. The four-century-long debate regarding the status of Jesus might be an interesting study for any Christian, as it provides the root of doctrine as known today. *When Jesus Became God* by Richard E. Rubenstein is an excellent starting point for this research.[4]

Origen

Origen (ca. 184–254 CE) was born in Alexandria, Egypt, and spent much of his career there. Based on references to his work, he was a prolific writer, although not much of his original material survives. What portions remain come from a Latin translation compiled by Hilary of Poitiers. Origen believed in a final reconciliation of all creatures, even Satan. As noted, he also saw the Son of God as subordinate (not coequal) to God the Father. For these reasons, the Roman and Eastern Orthodox churches declared him a heretic. Devout, studious, and disillusioned with the laxity he saw forming in the church (especially in Rome), he focused on teaching, comforting the persecuted, and building his school.

There are conflicting reports concerning the details Origen's life. Most of the literature agrees that his father was a martyr during the persecution of Emperor Septimius Severus in 202 CE. Rivalries and differing philosophies put Origen at odds with the bishop of Alexandria, Demetrius. As the differences between the two escalated, Origen felt the need to leave. He found a more receptive community in Caesarea, Palestine. Demetrius contested his ordination by the church in Caesarea and made it impossible for him to return home to Alexandria. Origen became one of Emperor Decius's victims during his purge of Christian believers (ca. 250 CE). Decius believed that Christians brought on a deadly plague because they refused to recognize the divinity of Caesar.

Origen saw Job as a prototype of Christian martyrs. To him, Job was a symbol of those who were righteous yet still suffered tribulation and suffering. He kept to moral interpretations of the book unless he felt the context required allegory.

Didymus the Blind

Didymus (ca. 313–398) was a theologian in the Coptic church of Alexandria. He was a brilliant scholar who compensated for the loss of his sight with an exceptional memory. He studied and taught dialectics and geometry, as well as theology. His commentaries

---

3. The Council of Nicaea took place in 325 CE at the order of Emperor Constantine I. His hope was to solidify the authority of the church and reduce the conflicts within the empire.

4. Rubenstein, *When Jesus Became God*.

include thoughts on the Psalms, Matthew, John, several Old Testament prophets, and the Holy Spirit. There is a clear indication within the fragments of his surviving works that he was loyal to the teachings of Origen.

Although Didymus looked at Job in a literal, moral sense, he made wider use of allegory than the Antiochian commentators did. For instance, he saw the description of Job's children banqueting and partying as a metaphor for brotherly love. His interpretations of this passage centered on moral lessons and Job as a symbol of the righteous exposed to tribulation and suffering. In the verses where Job curses the day he was born, Didymus sees a reference to the belief in the preexistence of the soul. He believed, as did Origen, that the soul entered a body as punishment for a previous fault. Consequently, he sees Job in this passage as speaking for the entirety of the human species in that he wishes he did not have to be born. Job, then, is not cursing the day but the painful events that took place on that day and the event that made it necessary.

Julian the Arian

Who and what Julian was is rather obscure, although some records exist that indicate he was an official in the church ca. 360–390 CE. Scholars know from writings attributed to him that he was an Arian, more specifically, a follower of Aetius and Eunomius, both of whom lived late in the fourth century. He is associated with a group of writings known as Pseudo-Ignatian. Since the Arians were considered heretics, Julian wrote under the cover of a pseudonym, perhaps in hopes that some of his writings might survive. Records indicate that Julian became a bishop in Cyzicus in 360. He lost his post by order of the emperor for preaching the Arian doctrine. Julian would have found some comfort in Job's story, as did many who felt they were righteous and suffered without cause. For Julian, even if Job receives no answer, some comfort can be gained from company, supposing that the company does not add to the pain.

Julian's commentary focused on a literal translation of the book, although he used allegory to temper that literalism. He attributed authorship to Moses and used the Greek Septuagint translation as his biblical reference. He presented the initial conversations between God and Satan in an anthropomorphic form. None of the church fathers attempted to explain the prologue as a conversation between God and Satan. Many of the doctrinal variations of the early church would have considered such an interpretation sacrilegious, if not blasphemous.

John Chrysostom

John Chrysostom was the Archbishop of Constantinople (ca. 347–407). He was born in Antioch to Greco-Syrian parents. Reports on the religious convictions of his parents vary; however, his loyalties were with the Christian church. He taught and studied during the twelve years he served as presbyter in Antioch. In the autumn of 397, he received a promotion to the position of Archbishop of Constantinople. To accept his new position, he had to leave Antioch in secret. He was so popular with the community that the church feared uprisings should his departure be publicly known.

In Constantinople, his popularity was replaced with animosity as he proceeded to turn the city's society inside out. He refused to host the extravagant social gatherings of his predecessors and decreed that the clergy return to their churches and minister to their congregations. He enforced a more ascetic lifestyle for both the clergy and the population. He also developed a system of hospitals for the poor. His time in the city was filled with turmoil, mostly because the aristocracy did not appreciate his sermons against excess. The church authorities exiled Chrysostom around 405. He died in 407 while still attempting to reach a haven.

The Eastern Orthodox and the Roman Church both recognize him as a saint. Although the population of Constantinople rejected his stringent proposals, his reputation as a great speaker, preacher, theologian, and architect of early Christian liturgy remained unblemished.

As to his commentary on the book of Job, he was rigorously literal and moral. Although the book is well-suited to this treatment, there are occasions when he, too, was forced to resort to allegory. Again, there is this problem created when Job curses the day of his birth. In general, he sees Job as both a righteous man facing temptation and as the model of a wise man.

In agreement with many of the early Christian writings, Chrysostom was firm in the belief that God controlled all the events in Job's life. He does not try to sugarcoat the reading of the text that indicates Satan had no power to inflict suffering unless he had leave to do so. Chrysostom uses this premise to teach the suffering Christian to accept whatever trials come into one's life and rest assured that God has ordained it.

Julian of Eclanum

Julian of Eclanum (ca. 386–455) was a commentator who used Jerome's Vulgate[5] as his source, as well as older Latin translations of Scripture. He brings an interesting twist to the interpretation of this book as a leader of the Pelagians. Pelagians believed that the original sin of Adam did not infect the entire human race, and each person still had the capability of choosing between good and evil. Individual accountability put the group in direct opposition to Augustine and his doctrine of original sin. To a Pelagian, everyone was responsible for their choices, and each required pardon through the

---

5. The Vulgate (Latin for "common version") was commissioned by Pope Damasus in 382 CE. Jerome completed his translation of the Gospels by 383. Using the Septuagint as a reference, he also translated portions of the Psalms. During his work, he determined that the Septuagint was unsatisfactory and proceeded to translate the entire Old Testament from Hebrew versions available to him. He completed his work in around 405.

grace of Christ for those choices that were wrong. Consequently, the views expressed regarding the troubles of Job take on a different light.

To Julian and the Pelagians, the concept of law is rational and divine in origin. An unjust God is inconceivable. They reasoned that God would not condemn every human being because of one sin committed by one man, nor would he condemn a finite number of human beings to eternal punishment for the slightest infraction.

In his interpretation of Job, Julian was a literalist. Based on the understanding that each has the power to choose good or evil, he sees Job as perfect proof that virtue is attainable. The trials that he faces are merely temptations that God permits to try Job's resolve to remain faithful. Julian does not see any sin for Job to confess; only a life lived in choices, and a trial formulated to test his moral character and resolve.

Gregory the Great

Pope Gregory I lived from ca. 540 to March 12, 604. Both the Roman and Eastern Orthodox churches acknowledge his sainthood. Anglican and Lutheran churches also recognize him as a saint, where saints are good and faithful servants of God, not pathways to intercession or suitable recipients of devotional offerings.

When Gregory's father died, he converted the family villa in Rome into a monastery dedicated to the apostle Andrew. In 579, the church called upon him to leave his home and serve as the pope. He died fourteen years later. His writings indicate that he would have much preferred to remain at the family estates. In addition to the properties in Rome, Gregory's family held large estates in Sicily.

Gregory's commentary on the book of Job is composed of thirty-five volumes. For Gregory, the scholar of biblical texts should never miss the opportunity to edify the congregation.[6] He is the clearest example of the Alexandrian tradition of allegory. The use of allegory in his writings allowed him to emphasize that every word of Scripture could edify and nourish the believer.[7]

He begins his commentary by dissecting the book of Job using three layers of interpretation: literal events, a collective point of view showing the struggle of the church, and an individual point of view as a guide to Christian behavior and moral growth. Although rigorous in this process at the beginning of the commentary, the latter part of his work focused primarily on moral interpretations.

His allegorical premise is to see Job as a figure of Christ and the church and Job's companions as heretics. He uses Job as a model for the spiritual progress required to persevere in faith through afflictions and tribulations. Gregory finds allegories in every passage. For example, in his discourse that sees Job collectively as the church, Job's children represent the apostles and those of simple faith. In the analysis that views Job

---

6. Simonetti and Conti, *Job*, xxiv.
7. Simonetti and Conti, *Job*, xxiv.

as representative of the individual Christian, the seven sons represent the seven gifts of the Holy Spirit and the three daughters the virtues of faith, hope, and charity.

Comparisons of this nature are allegory run rampant. However interesting it may be to compare the numbers, places, and characters of the Bible or to seek correlations between the Old and New Testaments outside of supported biblical exegesis, the reader can lose touch with the basic underlying message. The point becomes lost in a maze of symbolism if too many layers of ecclesiastical musings smother the hard realities. When symbols take on a life of their own, they are no longer representative of useful information to aid in the navigation of the plain, hard facts of a life lived in the face of untidy reality. Although Christians look to the Old Testament writings of the Hebrew Scriptures as the harbinger of the New Testament Scriptures, it is an insult to the ancient people of God to rip their heritage from its roots and appropriate it for the Christian faith without consideration of the source or context. Denying the Hebrew roots of Scripture while seeking consistency in the message of Scripture from Genesis to Revelation is certain to weaken and distort the communication between Creator and creation.

Ephrem the Syrian

Ephrem (306–373) is a preeminent representative of the Syriac fathers. He was a prolific writer and the author of one of the few complete commentaries that have survived to modern times. He wrote in Syriac, which is also the language of early Christian believers. Scholars value Syriac translations of Hebrew texts because they are the earliest known Christian translations from the original languages.[8] There is some evidence that someone else wrote the commentary on Job included in Ephrem's compiled works as J. S. Assemani translated them in the eighteenth century. Assemani's work is called the *Bibliotheca Orientalis* and is a collection of works from the Syriac church compiled for the Vatican. The style of the work is typically Syrian regardless of who the author may be. Even though there is some question as to whether Ephrem the Syrian wrote all the commentary accredited to him, many scholars agree that the acknowledged text is representative of his thought and style.

The Syriac church brings unique insights to Christian theology. Ephrem himself drew on the influences of Rabbinic Judaism, Greek science and philosophy, and Mesopotamian/Persian mystery symbolism. These sources provided a heritage that had little influence from the Western church. He wrote hundreds of hymns, some of which are still in use today. Translations of his accumulated works include Armenian,

---

8. The Peshitta, a revision of the Old Syriac Gospels, was completed in the fifth century. The Septuagint is credited as a source, as well as Armenian texts. According to the Syriac Orthodox Resources website, the Syriac fathers contributed at least six versions of the New Testament and two versions of the Old Testament. Eberhard Nestle, a contributor to *Hastings' Dictionary of the Bible*, credited them with reaching Lebanon, Egypt, Sinai, Mesopotamia, Armenia, India, and China with their work.

Coptic, Georgian, and Greek. The treatise on Job uses a literal and historical interpretation with some influence from the allegorical point of view.

Ephrem sees Job's three friends as representative of high priests, priests, and prophets. Unlike the Jewish philosophers, the church fathers did not draw comparisons between Job's friends and known doctrinal variations. They were either heretics or representative of members of the hierarchy of leadership within the church. Such a distinction may reflect the struggle of the different factions seeking the crown of orthodoxy. The suffering that enlightened their interpretation of Job was the struggle for the survival of the version of the faith they held as truth.

Isho'dad of Merv

Isho'dad was also a Syrian living around 850. He was ordained the bishop of Hedatta, located on the Tigris River near Mosul in Mesopotamia. Isho'dad was a Nestorian.[9] His works would not have survived if not for extensive quotations by such men as Theodore of Mopsuestia.[10] Isho'dad uses a literal interpretation of the text. He also takes great care to place Job in a historical setting to keep the story in context.

Information on Isho'dad comes mostly from Arabic sources. He worked diligently to bring together the allegorical method of Alexandria with the scientifically founded ideas supported by the Nestorians. For this reason, he is considered a key leader in biblical exegesis in the Eastern church. The Nestorians emphasized a separation between the divine and human nature of Jesus. They also objected to the elevation of Mary to Mother of God. The Roman orthodox leadership considered their doctrine to be heresy. Persecution pushed them further eastward, where they eventually traveled as far as Asia. Although initially quite successful, the Asian church shrank to a few pockets in India. The Nestorian priesthood won modern attention as the caretakers of Shangri-La in the classic *Lost Horizon* by James Hilton.

According to Isho'dad (and others in this group), Job is a model, a perfect representation of how a Christian should behave while suffering from affliction and tribulation. The Syriac fathers see the life of Job as a foreshadowing of Jesus' suffering. When Job speaks out in despair and curses the day of his birth, Isho'dad instructs Christians to avoid offending God even when overwhelmed. He and Chrysostom see Job's desire for death as his desire to reach eternal life, not as a hoped-for end to this one. The theme here is that departure from a corrupt world and deliverance from the travails suffered here is a blessing and not something to fear.

---

9. Nestorius was exiled to Egypt by Emperor Theodosius II in 431. The Assyrian church, however, did not reject Nestorius's teachings, and the doctrine eventually spread to China.

10. Bishop of Mopsuestia, Turkey, from 392–428.

Philosophy or Homily?

Interpretations in General

Each of these men had a different perspective on Christian doctrine. They also had a unique approach to the interpretation of Job. By using varying degrees of allegory and literal translation, they delivered the message they saw as most crucial to their contemporaries. Some, such as John Chrysostom, used every phrase as a basis for instructing the Christian moral life. Some interpreted the book as straightforward instruction on how the faithful should deal with suffering and tribulation in this world. They also drew on the book for guidance in the correct way to lead a Christian life, even though they structured their interpretations around varying doctrinal backgrounds. There is a pronounced difference between each commentator when they provide instructions for how a Christian should respond to a sovereign Creator amid agony.

The Friends and the Angry Young Man

All the commentators mentioned here find themselves conflicted over interpretations of the message delivered by Eliphaz. On the one hand, they are defensive on Job's behalf because they know he is innocent. On the other, they see moral instruction in the words of Eliphaz for members of the church. They are nearly united in viewing Eliphaz as narrow-minded.

Their view of Bildad is comparable. Each commentator looks for some value in Bildad's speeches even as they perceive him as narrow-minded and too focused on the material aspects of the world. Interestingly, there are few exceptions among the fathers when it comes to accounting the rewards and benefits of this world as having no real value.

Zophar is a false accuser and a man full of resentment. Each author uses his words as a basis for moral instruction and a lesson that the righteous must suffer on, regardless of the trials they face.

Elihu, however, fares the worst. The fathers accuse him of eavesdropping on his elders not to learn but to judge. He is arrogant and seeks to twist Job's words. Although each commentator finds points of interest that provide moral lessons, in general they see this participant as brash, unforgiving, and much too full of himself. Chrysostom gives a resounding rebuff by declaring that those who are eager to seek quick agreement are just as dangerous to themselves as those who listen to their declarations.[11] The commentators stand united in feeling that Elihu is much too busy making sure he looks wise, although they grudgingly acknowledge a glimmer of intellectual honesty.

They cannot, however, forgive him for attacking Job. Gregory provides an illustrative sentiment by writing that the arrogant typically believe, even before they speak, that they are full of wonderful things to say; then they fall on their face.[12] The fathers

---

11. Simonetti and Conti, *Job*, 165.
12. Simonetti and Conti, *Job*, 167.

do see Elihu's speech regarding repentance as useful to the believer. Gregory again leads with the thought that believers suffer in three states. First through conversion, then through probation, and lastly through a dread of dissolution. In the end, the process purifies us and sets us free from the suffering that molds us.[13]

The fathers soften toward Elihu near the end of his speech, since he does seem to have a grasp of the true meaning of God's justice; though, he misses the mark on how it might apply to Job. However, even with this begrudged nod of approval, there is a consensus that he is arrogant and brash. They pronounce Elihu correct for his views on the limitation of man's knowledge and the omniscience of God. However, they deem him in error regarding his views on Job's circumstances and what he should or should not do.

Gregory and Chrysostom interpret the debates between Job and his visitors as a representation of the controversies between the Jews, the Christians, and the Gentiles (the rest of humanity). They believe that those filled with pride (Jews and Gentiles) are unable to see the truth because they have imperfect knowledge. As arrogant as this position may seem, if the individual does not honestly believe the doctrine they champion, then cognitive dissonance is sure to follow. It also serves each person well to be open to additional information and a willingness to test that assurance based on new and better-supported evidence. That is, after all, at the core of the mission of this text.

Job's Petition

As Job's suffering and the torment of his purported friends increases, commentators have more trouble interpreting Job's dialogue literally. None of these writers wishes to risk showing Job as having doubted the justice of God. Therefore, his words become the basis of moral lessons, a prophecy of the Christ to come, and the result of the duress caused by unbearable pain and suffering.

When Job strikes back at his friends, the fathers are in full support. They believe Job is justified in his responses to the shallow and misinformed men. There is a definite sense that at some point, these men of varied background and doctrinal faith grow protective of Job. They wish to save him from his suffering without falling into the trap of seeing his words as a cry against God and his divine will.

The passage that strikes Christians most directly as a foreshadowing of Christ is Job's declaration that he knows God will eventually vindicate him. The Hebrew word in Job 19:25 translates in several ways, including "vindicator" (*Tanakh*), "avenger" (New Jerusalem), and "redeemer" (most modern Protestant translations).

From the Jewish perspective, this is a direct claim on a legal right. In Jewish law, there was a kinsman redeemer or someone who redeems a kinsman in time of trouble. The redemption process often required a ransom. There are many references in Psalms

---

13. Simonetti and Conti, *Job*, 169.

that look to Yahweh as the Redeemer of Israel. Job is claiming the right to have his Redeemer stand up for him and vindicate him. The church fathers would have been uncomfortable with Job demanding his rights in the court of heaven. For these men, demanding anything of God, or claiming something as a right in his courts, would have seemed preposterous and profane.

The Problem of Good and Evil

Each, in his way, tries to reassure a Christian reader that God only tests the righteous and is lenient on the sinner. Keeping in mind that the fathers agreed with the visitors on their points, not their application, this is the opposite of what Job's visitors are trying to say. This point of view also does not address reality, as evidenced in the world. Good and evil fall on everyone, everywhere, without differentiation between those considered righteous and those considered evil. Both Augustine and Aquinas are clear on this point.

To support their interpretation of punishment and reward, the church fathers determined that the wicked didn't suffer because God scorned them. Such a rendition seems counter-intuitive if one believes that God loves everyone and wants all to find the path to salvation. How would sinners find a path no one is interested in showing them?

The fathers also believed that God disciplines those he loves. Parents usually do discipline their children. However, a simplistic view that God ignores the sinner and disciplines the righteous may well have the opposite effect from that intended—especially when the righteous have no idea about why such discipline is occurring. Among the analyses found in these writings, this one seems most unsatisfactory and contrary to all I knew and felt about what the Creator is or should be. Even with this perceived gap in understanding, there are points of value within these ancient interpretations. By filtering the thoughts of these men through the lens of their time and faith, the inherent wisdom of their writing can help retell the story in a new way. Part of the mission of this book is to show the way to retelling the whole story, including the breaking down of old notions of what God must be or do. In this way, the world can become coherent and, in part, more predictable.

When God Answers

These commentators interpret the speeches of God through three aspects: theological limitation, pastoral encouragement, and prophetic expectation. The fathers see God's intervention as an expression of divine power. They note that it is Job that God speaks with and not the hypocritical and narrow-minded visitors. They do not view the questions presented by God as challenges to Job's knowledge. God presumably knows the extent of what Job knows. These men determine, based on the form and tone of the questions, that God's quizzes were the best means to convince the audience. Who that audience is and what the message is remain uncertain.

Reiterating points from Job's earlier speeches, God reminds him that the most common of elements formed humanity, yet humans reason. Gregory sees this as evidence that it is difficult for the human mind to comprehend itself, often swelling with pride and a false sense of superiority. Our minds can be obscure, our thoughts hidden.[14] Perhaps. However, over the past several centuries, humanity's accomplishments in philosophy and the sciences can reveal new information about the unfathomable human mind. The discoveries made and the questions left unanswered are an echo of Job's quest. Who and what are we, what can we expect, if anything, from the universe?

The fathers see the use of real and legendary animals (Job 39:1–30) as an allegory for different types of people. In one interpretation, the unicorn's single horn represents faithfulness. (The *Tanakh* translates the Hebrew as "wild ox"). The ostrich represents a hypocrite that doesn't care. The eagle is a representation of Christ.

Most of the fathers see Behemoth as a real creature which is used as a symbol to show that God creates to his purpose and according to his will. As for Leviathan, all the fathers see this creature as a representation of the devil. The legend of Leviathan is the piece best suited to allegory within the Christian doctrine. In Jewish legend, God conquers Leviathan in the end times and serves it up as a feast to the restored Israel. The story is a precursor, or prefiguring, for Christian eschatology.

The Christian Job

Doctrine was not a settled issue in the early centuries of the church, if it ever has been. Since it was a faith originally followed by the people of the street, the merchants, the tradesmen, and the common folk, all matters of doctrine were in flux and constantly debated. At least in part, it was the persecution of the church and the newly faithful that caused the leadership to build the walls of dogma and articles of faith. Among the most hotly contested issues was the nature of Christ. Was he fully divine, fully human, or something of both?[15]

Another fiercely debated topic was whether there was an original sin. Did the actions of one man condemn all of humanity? As the factions warred among themselves, those who saw a need to consolidate became unrelenting in their drive for control of the church. Although, in part, a power struggle forming a cohesive doctrine and faith history was a matter of survival. Once the Roman and Eastern Orthodox churches gained political as well as ecclesiastical strength, the dissenting voices were subdued, driven eastward, or driven underground.

Out of this turmoil came the Christian interest in and interpretation of the life of Job: the persecuted righteous man, full of wisdom, and accepting of the turmoil and

---

14. Simonetti and Conti, *Job*, 195.
15. See Rubenstein, *When Jesus Became God*.

tribulation that raged around him. The book became a basis for moral instruction and upright behavior and an illustration of the promise of a final reward for steadfast belief. The fathers ignored those parts that clearly show Job challenging his Creator and smoothed them over with a bit of allegory or moral homily. Some of the earlier passages were a platform to attack pagan beliefs such as astrology.[16] The fathers also found it necessary to seek a path around Job's clear and desperate cry that he wished he had never been born. Since so much of the original texts are missing, it is difficult to be certain whether some of these writers addressed the more contentious passages.

Those who chose to see Christ and his sufferings in the story of Job are doing neither justice. Jesus of Nazareth, at least in Scripture, does not challenge God or his fate. Jesus does not demand justice from his Creator, although he does occasionally note he would have preferred a different path. There is also no question in Christian minds regarding the guilt or innocence of Jesus. He is the unblemished, the perfect, and the only acceptable sacrifice. Job's place in the story must be substantially changed for his experience to emulate the sacrifice of Jesus.

As the debate progresses, Job is less submissive and more challenging. He is steadfast in presenting the case that he comes to court with clean hands, demanding judgment based on his record. Any direct challenge to God would have been blasphemy to many of the writers in the early church. Some of these men were instrumental in developing a doctrine that all had sinned and were unworthy to look upon the face of God without the shield of his Son. Some, however, were not convinced that the sin of one could condemn the whole race. They all saw in Job a man struggling to reach his spiritual potential and to acknowledge responsibility for his own choices and not those of others.

In the hands of the early church fathers, Job became a long-suffering servant, attendant to his God, and somehow mysteriously submitting to whatever life threw at him. This interpretation finds its way into the literature today. At the very least, I find this position unsatisfactory, if not profane. For, in the end, they are asking the reader to surrender the gift that makes us human, the ability to reason.

If these interpretations inspired no satisfactory answer, is there anything in the developed wisdom of the Jewish philosophers that might be enlightening regarding the universal questions of Job? Did ancient theological and philosophical traditions shed light on the author's intent? As direct heirs to the Hebrew tradition, are there nuances Hebrew scholars can provide? Can they save Job from an arbitrary universe ruled by an unknowable Sovereign?

---

16. There are many articles written on whether the references to the constellations (Job 38:31–33) do show a hint of astrology, or if Job's cursing of the stars on the day of his birth alludes to some astrological context. None of the literature seems to be conclusive; there are ambiguities in the language which prevent a precise interpretation, at least for now.

Part II—Theodicy and Philosophy

Map 3

**The Church Fathers
184 - 1274 CE**

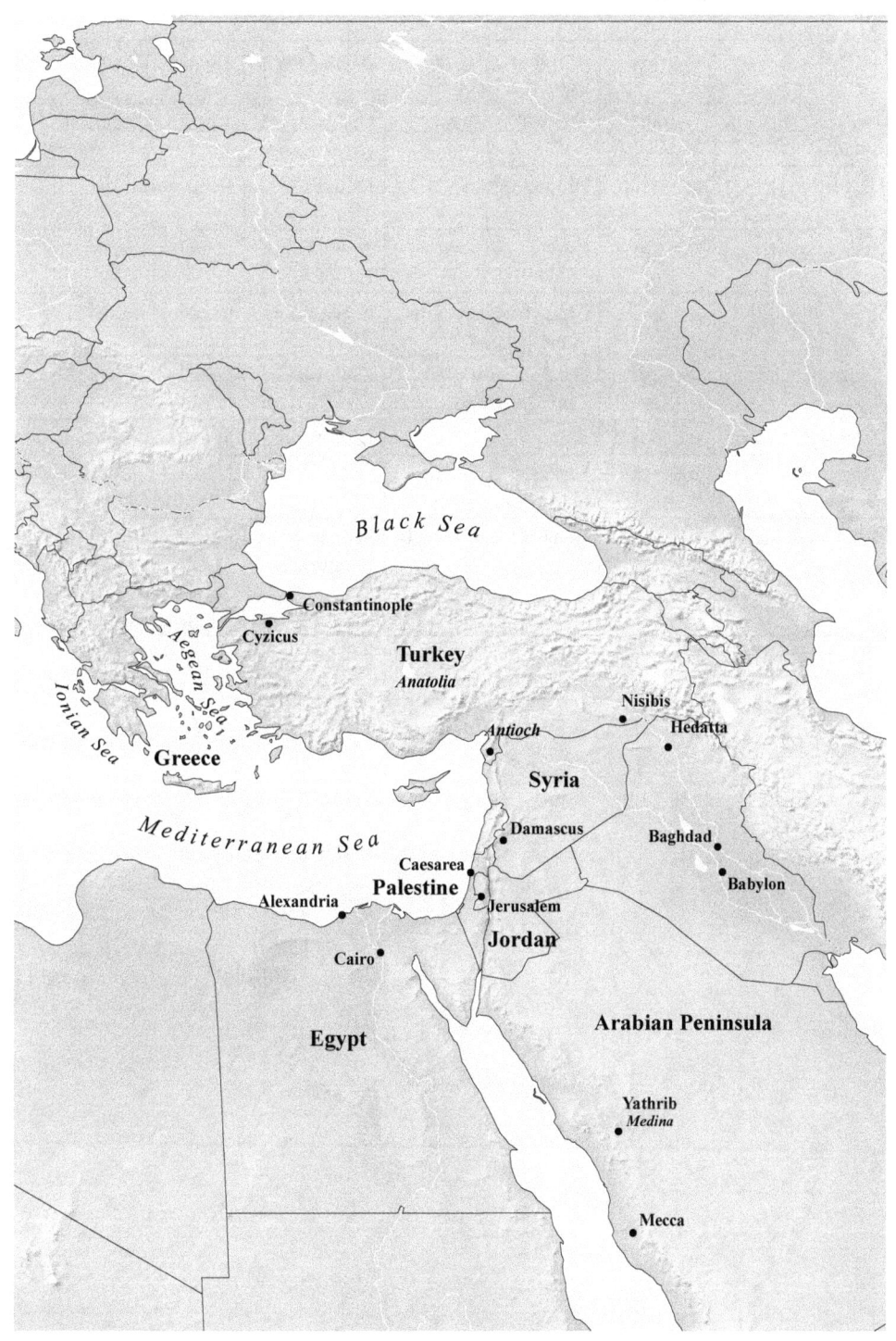

PART II—THEODICY AND PHILOSOPHY

Chart 4: Key to Church Fathers

Origen	184–254	Alexandria, Egypt; Caesarea, Palestine	Arian, Greek Father	Moral & Allegorical
Didymus the Blind	313–398	Alexandria, Egypt	Coptic Arian, Greek Father	Moral & Allegorical
Augustine of Hippo	354–430	Hippo, Algeria	Latin Father	Neoplatonic
Julian the Arian	360–390	Cyzicus, Anatolia (Turkey)	Arian, Greek Father	Literal & Allegorical
John Chrysostom	347–407	Antioch & Constantinople (Turkey)	Greek Father	Literal, Moral, & Allegorical
Julian of Eclanum	386–455	Eclanum near Benevento, Italy	Latin Father	Literal
Gregory the Great	540–604	Rome, Sicily	Latin Father	Moral & Allegorical
Ephrem the Syrian	306–373	Nisibis, Mesopotamia (Nusaybin, Turkey)	Syriac	Literal, Historical, & Allegorical
Isho'dad of Merv	850	Hedatta (Near Mosul)	Syriac (Nestorian)	Literal, Historical, a mix of Allegory and scientifically founded ideas of the Nestorians
Thomas Aquinas	1225–1274	Naples, Italy; Paris, France	Aristotelian	Literal, Historical

Chapter 9

The Conservative Jewish Philosophers

SOURCE MATERIAL FOR THE next two chapters came from a thoroughly researched study by Robert Eisen, *The Book of Job in Medieval Jewish Philosophy*. His study begins with a conservative commentator, Saadiah Gaon, who based his reading of Job on the traditional rabbinic teachings on the Torah and the question of human suffering. Eisen then introduces five Jewish philosophers who completed their commentaries over the following four to five hundred years. Beginning with Maimonides, their writings take a radical and Aristotelian approach. By the early to mid-1350s, commentators such as Levi ben Gershom begin to gravitate back to a conservative point of view. The last of the group, Simon ben Zemah Duran, represents a full return to the rabbinic tradition and conservative interpretations. Thus, although the study is not (and does not purport to be) exhaustive, it is an introduction to the span of Jewish thought on the text from approximately 900–1450 CE. The "Commentary Timeline" found in chapter 6, along with the map "The Jewish Philosophers" and the "Key to the Jewish Philosophers" following chapter 10, all help illustrate the cultural, political, and religious influences experienced by these scholars.

For the purposes of this book, the analysis begins with the conservative thinkers. The following chapter explores the writings of those who based their philosophy on the teachings of Aristotle. Eisen's purpose was to show a progression of thought, while the purpose here is to compare the approaches represented by the conservatives versus the Aristotelians. His structured and methodological analysis is quite instructive in the process of understanding what each of these men contributed. His familiarity with other works by the same authors provided clarity when a specific commentary was not explicit in the discussion on the book of Job itself. The development of these chapters was also dependent on his understanding of the languages of the original authors. Not all the referenced works have an English translation.

In general, these six men believed that the rational human mind could access all truths in all fields of knowledge, including natural science, mathematics, and metaphysics. They firmly believed that all things related to religion, including doctrines, ritual, and the texts themselves, should be interpreted using rationally determined truths. These philosophers borrowed a great deal from the Greek traditions. Arab and Persian scholars such as Al-farabi,[1] Avicenna,[2] and Averroes[3] also influenced these men. For whatever agreement or disparity found among their works, each author sincerely sought the truth within the texts they studied.

Saadiah Gaon

The first Jewish thinker to write a systematic study on Judaism was Saadiah Gaon. He lived from 882–942 CE. He spent the first half of his life in Egypt then traveled extensively throughout Syria and Palestine before settling in Babylon. In 928 CE, he became the head of the Sura Rabbinical Academy. At this time, the Islamic Empire encompassed most of northern Africa, the Levant, Persia, portions of India, the Arabian Peninsula, parts of Central Asia, and most of Spain.

Saadiah's work shows evidence of his interaction with the brilliant thinkers of his age. He lived during the golden age of the Islamic Empire. With the capital in Baghdad, the Abbasids ruled by their interpretation of Islamic philosophy, the premise being that the "ink of a scholar is more holy than the blood of a martyr."[4] The rulers of this period stressed the value of knowledge and invested large portions of state funds to support scholarship and the preservation of ancient works. The heart of the Arab world was an intellectual center for science, philosophy, medicine, and education. There was also an effort to translate the world's entire known knowledge into Arabic. It was a fertile atmosphere for the scholar and the philosopher.

Saadiah's doctrine of choice was that of the Mu'tazilites. The commentators analyzed in these chapters link the doctrine of this Islamic sect to Bildad. The Mu'tazilite philosophy developed early in the history of Islam. They believed that only a member of Muhammad's family could lead the community. They also believed that human reason could develop all aspects of the faith. The name itself means "those who withdraw themselves."

As taught by their leader, Wasil ibn 'Ata, they believed that it was necessary to give a rational explanation of Islamic beliefs. Of their specific doctrines, two were most crucial for this book. One was the unity of God, and the second was divine

---

1. Known to the Arabs as the "Second Master" (after Aristotle), he was a philosopher, logician, musician, and political scientist. Abu Nasr Al-Farabi lived ca. 870–950 CE.

2. A Persian physician and philosopher that was a profound influence on medieval Islamic and Christian philosophy. Avicenna ibn Sina lived ca. 980–1037 CE.

3. Ibn Rushd (Averroes) lived from 1126–1198 CE during a time when philosophy was waning in the Muslim world and igniting in the Western Christian world. He brought renewed attention to the work of the Greeks.

4. This quote is attributed to the Hadiths, or sayings of the Prophet Mohammed. There is some controversy regarding the translation.

justice: God punishes the sinful and rewards the righteous. They also believed that God tests the righteous to give them greater rewards in the future. Saadiah composed his work within this philosophical and cultural environment.

In his writings, Saadiah sees four central issues to understanding the book of Job. These are 1) who is Satan and what does he represent; 2) why does Job suffer if he is truly blameless; 3) what is the real course of the arguments provided; and 4) how does God's speech bear on an answer to Job?

Saadiah spends a great deal of time analyzing the first several verses. He goes into some detail about who comes and goes and when and with whom. In Job 1:6–12 and 2:1–7, Satan interacts with the *beney elohim*[5] or *divine beings* (more literally, the children of God). Saadiah sees these beings as compatriots of Job in the land of Uz. The Hebrew is rendered as "God's beloved" by Saadiah, and he believes they are beloved because they gather to worship. Satan, he feels, is the leader of the group, given the name because he is an enemy of Job. The setup of Job then becomes his enemy's premise that the only reason he glorifies God is that he is so successful. Thus, God gives Satan permission to afflict him.

Saadiah does not believe Satan is a fallen angel. Rabbinic tradition sees angels as created to serve and incapable of rebelling against God's authority. Angels do not have human emotions. Saadiah may have gone to such lengths to get Satan out of the realm of heaven (rebellion or no) to provide a direct argument against the Midrashic, Christian, and Muslim views that Satan was an angelic rebel.

His logic is also a direct attack against dualist doctrines expressed in his period. The philosophy of dualism proposes that the powers of good and evil are the product of two distinct and ultimate first causes. Most monotheistic faiths (not all) adhere to a sovereign creator who has no equals. Perhaps this is part of the reason that the concept of Satan as an adversary to God is so unpalatable. Within the resource material for this book, Saadiah does not address how a mere mortal would have the powers required to carry out the devastation visited on Job, nor does he address the passage that reminds Job that God demands restitution from the angels,[6] therefore why not from man.

On the subject of why Job suffered, Saadiah supports the view that this is an illustration of a providential trial. The nature of this trial appears to take on several forms. For Saadiah, the only explanation is that this is a test for Job, and if he knew it was a test, then the test would no longer serve its purpose. Also, he discusses the conservative position that God may punish the righteous for their few misdeeds so that they may have greater rewards in the future life.

Another aspect of trial defined by Saadiah is something explored in theological and philosophical literature as sufferings of love. The definition of this type of suffering is the belief that God tests righteous persons so that their contemporaries will

---

5. This phrase is also seen as *bene elohim* or *bene[y]'ha-Elohim*. Interpretations vary from sons of God, fallen angels, or simply ministering beings.

6. Job 4:18.

know that God has rightly chosen his favored servants. The believer is not loyal to God solely because he receives rewards from God. Rabbinic literature uses the near-sacrifice of Isaac by Abraham as an illustration of this type of suffering. Saadiah notes that at no point does Job declare God unjust; therefore, a reason must exist for such a trial. Saadiah concludes that Job teaches one must suffer with fortitude and not doubt the justice of God. The believer must submit to whatever calamity presents in life.

As an analysis of the discourse delivered by each of the participants, Saadiah focuses on the speech of Elihu, with the firm conviction that this is the central point of the book. Elihu describes three types of individuals who receive rewards in the afterlife: those who repent of their sins after God chastises them, those who repent of their sins before God makes them suffer, and those who face a test of faith even without sin. Saadiah applies the last option to Job. God kept Job in the dark about the true meaning of the trial because Elihu does not specify which case applies to him. Consequently, God's answer is obscure to preserve the nature of the test. In Saadiah's opinion, Elihu also defends Job by saying that his responses are due to his ignorance. If Job had known the purpose and the outcome of his sufferings, he would have managed with more grace.

Saadiah applies his analysis to the Jews as a people, indicating that if their obedience to the law had given them prosperity, then the world would think they only followed the law to receive rewards. Their suffering indicated this was not the case. He compares this trial to the dialogue of his era when Muslims and Christians argued that the Jews suffered because of their sins while the Jews professed innocence.

This point of view fails in the face of history. Neither Job's friends nor the competing Abrahamic faiths seem particularly impressed with the idea that suffering somehow proves that Job (or the Jews) enjoy a special place of divine favor. Some of the laws given to the Jews carried self-evident rewards in health, stable societies, wealth, and the means to care for those facing challenges. If the Israelites are called to task for anything specific by their prophets, it is their treatment of the poor among them. By the time they tried to rebuild their society as initially intended, the world had changed. The inability to regain the blessings of the past was not punishment as much as it was lost opportunity. Living with the consequences of a lost opportunity is quite a different thing from suffering to prove devotion with or without reward.

Simon ben Zemah Duran

More than four hundred years later, and after the contributions of a transitional philosopher, Gersonides (chapter 10), Jewish thought returned to the conservative point of view. Duran lived from 1361–1444, obtaining a position of respect as a rabbinic authority and a philosopher. Initially, he resided in Majorca, an island in the Mediterranean Sea, which was under Spanish control. He was a member of the upper class and a practicing physician. The crown protected Jews during the reigns of James I and

II of Aragon. By law, they could loan money at interest rates as high as 20 percent, as long as the interest did not exceed the capital. However, as the debt increased, the situation became tenuous. In 1390, Jews could not carry weapons, even in their quarter of the city. In 1391, riots broke out, resulting in the deaths of over three hundred Jews. The rioters also sacked the homes of Christians sheltering them. Duran had to flee the country and found a home in Algiers, where his lifestyle changed dramatically.

The political and religious strife that struck Spain at this period had been building for nearly a half-century. In 1350, a young and inexperienced monarch, Peter I (Peter the Cruel), took the throne of Castile and Leon at the age of sixteen. He surrounded himself with Jewish advisers. The contender, his older half-brother Henry, used his brother's policies about the Jews to inflame his supporters further. After many bloody and lawless years of battle, Henry ascended the throne in 1369 as Henry II. He immediately initiated an extermination order against the Jews throughout the realm, including Aragon. However, not one to waste good talent, King Henry hired some of the most influential Jews of the period to be his fiscal and tax advisers. In this atmosphere, Algiers, still a relatively tolerant Islamic society, looked quite inviting. Duran's only problem was that Algiers was not as advanced as the cultural centers of Baghdad and Babylon. Much of the practice of medicine used superstition rather than the more scientific approach he had learned. Consequently, Duran, with no other source of income, was forced to accept payment for his position as rabbi. As may be expected, his circumstances influenced his interest in the book of Job.

Duran revolts against Aristotelian thought and veers back toward a literalistic interpretation of Scripture and a closer adherence to rabbinic sources. He writes that philosophers wrestle with three types of problems when dealing with the concept of providence: those which can be reasoned (such as the existence of God), those which cannot be reasoned (such as creation), and those which survive reason yet the senses reject (such as providence). He states that his purpose was an effort to collect an anthology of thinkers that looked for the literal meaning of Scripture as well as those who viewed Scripture through allegory and analogy. His initial goal was to accumulate the wisdom he could find and, perhaps, formulate an answer to his aching questions—a mission this current author can well appreciate, although with different outcomes.

Duran's studies helped him compile a thorough analysis of the contributions of previous authors. He used these studies to form some of his own opinions and produce commentary on previous contributions. He believed that the proof of providence lay in God's perfection and God's actions in the world. Providence, he believed, means that God cannot ignore our needs because we are the most exalted of his creation. He sees God's actions in the world as being a force through nature and humanity but not, however, as an agency within individual human lives.

Keeping in mind that his initial training was as a physician, Duran believed that God's creation of the human body, with its many wonders and its capacity for reason, had a purpose. He felt that God provided the commandments to nurture improvement and that the actual evil in the world was far less than one might assume based on the number of people bent on pursuing it. He also discussed the relevance of prophetic warnings and noted that there were at least some instances in which the wicked received their due.

Duran strives for an interpretation that includes some elements of all the commentary that preceded him. His view was that punishment comes directly from God by first intention and not by chance events. In other words, God decides and then executes the action required. He explains some situations where people are somehow protected from the vagaries of life by referring to Nahmanides's[7] theory of hidden miracles, or events in which individuals are rescued from harm when Providence acts in concert with natural laws.

Duran's take on Satan is somewhat ambiguous. On the one hand, he supports the rabbinic view. In this case, Satan is not a fallen angel; he is the vehicle by which God punishes those who sin. Consequently, Satan's actions are under the control of God himself, and he can do nothing God does not allow. In Hebrew tradition, the name Satan means "hinderer" (or "adversary"). He hinders progress such that the believer is tested and learns how to pass the ethical and moral tests of this world.

This approach also tempers his view of providence. He takes a broader view compared to some of the historical contributors to rabbinic literature by noting that the processes of nature are not selective. The rain falls on the wicked as well as the righteous, and actual severe calamities are not that frequent. With this thought, Duran brings out some of the lessons buried in God's speech.

The question of whether providence exists only arises in individual circumstances. In his analysis, a calamity or instance of suffering is only a misfortune if a righteous individual seems to be the target. He also points out that one must know the circumstances of the individual to determine whether an event or situation causes actual suffering. For instance, some might consider the rise to middle class a blessing. Conversely, a nobleman might consider the loss of status and reduction to such circumstances a catastrophe.

Duran devotes much thought to distilling several specific reasons why an individual might suffer. Some of them he gleans from his survey of available literature, and some are his assessment of the subject.

1. Suffering can come from a natural process of creation and corruption, or the functions of the world as we know it. These cases do not target any specific person. Disasters such as storms, flooding, or volcanoes come to mind. Duran's thoughts here show attention to the passages attributed to God, which does have bearing on the subject at hand. Many actions which take place in the world are

---

7. A Spanish Talmudist, Kabbalist, and biblical commentator living 1194–1270 in Girona, Spain. Rabbi Moshe ben Nahman was influential in the development of the Codes of Jewish Law.

not direct assaults on an individual or a specific community; they are functions of the universe in which we live.

2. God might punish the righteous for small evils so that they can enjoy eternity more deeply. Whatever comfort such a thought might bring to the sufferer, it seems unlikely that persistent punishment for small infractions would encourage the human soul to seek a greater goal. Studies into the psychology of instruction indicate that punishing for infractions can result in better performance, and praise can result in a performance less than optimal. Subject to individual influences of life in general, what is happening in such cases is not a result of cause and effect but is rather a regression to the mean.[8] Everyone tends to find a personal level of mean. Screaming at the student or offering praise is more a function of the individual personality than a general code of practice. In training for highly specialized careers, some individuals excel, and some are not suited. Those that fail are not necessarily less than those that succeed. There may be a better fit for their specific talents and personality. Challenging the righteous to suffer more in this life to gain some undefined reward in the next is not born out as a successful strategy in human psychology.

3. God subjects the righteous to divine tests to achieve extra rewards in this life or the next. Duran does not support this view. He rejects the idea that God would cause the innocent to suffer. For this reason, he leans toward the explanation of accidental sins. Based on an unavailable source, he uses an instance in Abraham's life, where he sins by not offering a sacrifice to God during the celebration of Isaac's birth.[9] Duran insists that at least in this case, Satan's accusations have merit. However, it is humanly impossible to accurately record every instance of life so that when the punishment comes the deed that causes it is known. Job's cry is precisely this issue. He has been righteous and has every right to claim the blessing promised, yet he suffers.

4. The current suffering may not be truly evil and may bear beneficial fruit in some future time. The position that today's suffering helps create a better future is known as redemptive suffering in modern parlance. To some extent, this does have a valid place in the discussion of suffering and providence. Sometimes the event that causes the suffering opens the way for a greater good or a beneficial change in course.

5. Suffering can be a result of the sins of the ancestors. Some readers will shudder at this phrase. However, there are repercussions in later generations for actions taken by an earlier generation. For instance, one might think about the sickness caused in communities due to years of environmental abuse. In these cases,

---

8. Kahneman, *Thinking Fast and Slow*, 175.

9. Genesis 21 is silent on the matter of sacrifice, given or forgotten. It does refer to the feast day for Isaac's circumcision and the exile of Hagar and Ismael.

Part II—Theodicy and Philosophy

residents often face the choice between a livelihood and an unknown future result. It is a tough decision; however, it is crucial to understand the options before a community chooses to mortgage its future. Can we blame God when the consequences are a natural and foreseeable result of our choices?

6. Finally, Duran writes that suffering can occur because God makes no distinctions, and the righteous and the wicked both suffer. Abraham had this argument with his visitors who stopped on their way to destroy Sodom and Gomorrah. There is also a reference in Ezekiel that even the righteousness of Job was not enough to save his countrymen.[10] The carnage visited on Job's servants and family was devastating. Many lost their lives when Job's fortunes failed. In December of 2004, millions living on the shores of the Indian Ocean died in a tsunami. In August of 2005, Hurricane Katrina battered the southern coast of the United States, killing over a thousand people and causing over $108 billion in damages. Whether we can describe such wide-scale destruction as punishment for anyone, good or evil, is debatable. As a point of fact, a good portion of humanity would consider the idea reprehensible.

Perhaps, at least in part due to his more detailed analysis of the types of suffering an individual can endure, Duran spends more time than most looking at the character of Job himself. He believes Job to be a historical figure and cites some of the same sources as were called out in Part I of this book. Duran follows the rabbinic tradition that Job was a non-Jew who lived before or around the time of the patriarchs and that he was a descendant of Esau.

He also assumes that Job's friends are the descendants of Abraham. The rabbinic tradition indicates there was a much older tradition of the writings which existed before the events at Mount Sinai. These writings consisted of knowledge shared among the tribes related to Abraham and other members of his father's family. This tradition could have shaped Job and developed his ethical and moral standards. Duran concludes that Job is a moral and ethical person and that his perplexity has more to do with the severity of his trials than with the fact that he is suffering at all.

In his quest to research the philosophies and arguments that had developed through the ages, Duran also looks to the Kabbalah to test some of the more esoteric interpretations of his predecessors. As representative of the Kabbalist view, he explores the premise that the righteous might suffer to redeem their souls from errors in past lives. Nahmanides supports this philosophy, and he uses it frequently in his biblical commentary to explain situations such as Job's. For these scholars, Elihu is saying that Job's suffering is due to sins in a past life. Duran indicates in his writings that he does agree with Nahmanides's interpretation that dreams and night visions are an instrument of Providence. However, he again shows his conservative roots by returning to

---

10. Ezek 14:14.

Saadiah's belief that the answer to undeserved suffering lies within the circumstances of the current life or looks forward to a future world.

Several philosophers (and not just those with mystic leanings) see Job's dreams as a warning of coming troubles (Job 3:25–26). As a further about-face from the Aristotelians, Duran returns to Saadiah's conclusion that the protective angel in Elihu's speech is a symbol of good deeds, which protect against harm. Perhaps this is a vindication of Job's plea that his past contributions should provide a basis for mercy. Perhaps it is Job's good deeds that provide the hedge referred to in 1:10.

Duran disagrees with the view of Maimonides and Gersonides[11] that the stars influence human events. This topic becomes a matter of debate due to the passage where Job curses the day he was born.[12] Another allusion often translated with a more mystical approach is in Job 38:31, where God asks Job if he can "bind the sweet influences of Pleiades, or loose the bands of Orion."

Duran also contradicts the Kabbalists and Aristotelians regarding how much God knows about the particulars of people's lives, and if so, whether he is then ultimately interested in the outcome of those specific lives. His writings indicate that he does believe in the operation of personal providence. Therefore, life's trials are not due to the course of the stars or some general happenstance, rather the personal attention of a Creator. However, this still presents the conundrum of a desire for a personalized action of Providence when the historical record proves that calamities fall on the wicked and righteous alike. This unresolved dissonance is part of what lies at the heart of the debate on undeserved suffering.

Duran sees the debate between Job and his friends as an escalation of dialogue that grows in tension with each round. Initially, Job's friends indicate that God is just. Therefore, Job must be suffering because of something he did. When he protests the severity of his suffering, they become convinced he must have done something truly evil. Duran agrees with Job's visitors in that he can see no answer to the question other than there was sin somewhere. He relies on tradition to support his conclusion that this is the meaning of Job's trial. By referencing Deuteronomy 8:16[13] and the Babylonian Talmud,[14] Duran is certain that suffering is either the consequence of a test or the result of sin.

Duran cannot get past the conviction that no one is guiltless; and, therefore, suffering is always due to something done wrong—or some right thing left undone—in this present life. Using his own life as an example, Duran feels that the error can sometimes stem from a complacency that grows when a privileged position leads to neglecting to honor God in the ways deemed appropriate. Thus, God punishes the oversight as well as the overt act.

11. Chapter 10.
12. Job 3:1–9.
13. The reference reports that God gave the Israelites manna in order to humble and test them.
14. b.Šabb. 55a; 55b, https://www.sefaria.org/Shabbat.55a.8?lang=bi&with=all&lang2=en.

Part II—Theodicy and Philosophy

Once Duran establishes that there must be something worthy of punishment or correction in Job's life, he addresses God's condemnation of Job's friends. Although he is certain there is grounds for punishment somewhere in Job's life, he condemns the visitors for arriving at the same conclusion. In their attempt to appear wise and pious, they try to prove Job wicked so that they can protect or justify God. Job, however, remains sincere in his search for truth regardless of what his perceptions might have been before his life changed so dramatically.

As an example of a return to the conservative perspective, Duran's writings attempt to combine some of the attributes of the ancient rabbinic and Kabbalistic thoughts with those of the more esoteric and Aristotelian approaches of his immediate predecessors. He dismisses the position of Maimonides and Gersonides that providence is dependent on the perfection of the intellect. He believes the human soul calls on Providence for the protection of humanity. Although Duran settles on the conservative views of the rabbis and their picture of rewards and punishments, he weaves the conclusions of the mystic scholars throughout his commentaries, perhaps to find comfort in his circumstances.

These two philosophers provide a theme seen in many of the interpretations of the book of Job. God punishes or tests those he loves, and it is sometimes difficult to determine which purpose drives any specific event. They believe that we cannot always know why God disciplines us. As a response to suffering of any type, this is one of the most unsatisfactory answers found in the relevant literature. There is great value found in these descriptions of suffering and the analyses of how different events influence different individuals. However, the image of a God that hunts down every small transgression to weed such terrible things out of the life of the believer does not fit into my perception of the Creator of the cosmos, nor do arbitrary tests of character appear to be beneficial to overall spiritual health. The belief that suffering is always a punishment, or a test of character, permeates commentary on Job. It is a conclusion rejected in varying degrees for centuries. There must be something more within the book of Job or supporting Scripture that helps unravel the conundrums presented here.

This chapter describes the conservative views, which include a literal interpretation and use of the plain text of Scripture to seek a meaning. The next chapter is an analysis of the philosophy of the Aristotelians. Their path to understanding was that of allegory and imagery. Here the tale of Job becomes a parable used to explain things not apparent in a superficial examination.

Chapter 10

The Aristotelians

RABBINIC AND CONSERVATIVE AUTHORS favored the literal interpretation of the book of Job. However, they confronted the same conundrum as Job and the conservative Christian theologians: what is the source of undeserved suffering? Since the literal interpretation creates a paradox, there were Jewish philosophers that, like their Christian counterparts, concluded that an allegorical interpretation was the only way to understand Job. Rooted deeply in the philosophy of Aristotle, the medieval thinkers saw esoteric and exoteric truths revealed within the story.

Aristotle and his followers believed that humans were a composite of a material body and an active intellect. Although both were required to be human, the intellect is resident in, not part of, the body (chapter 5). Aristotle also introduced three types or stages of virtue: nutritional, moral, and intellectual. These ideas developed as an interpretive tool for Jewish biblical philosophy. Moses Maimonides was a substantial contributor to Western philosophical thought and the most influential of those philosophers with an allegorical perspective.

Moses Maimonides

Moses Maimonides was born in 1135 in Córdoba, Spain. His ancestry includes a long line of rabbinic teachers and judges, a heritage running deep in the history of Arabic Spain. During the tenth century CE, the Caliphate of Córdoba enjoyed a pre-Renaissance and diverse culture. Córdoba was home to a populace that was largely literate, well-fed, and living comfortably regardless of social station or faith. The city and the towns, villages, and farms surrounding the city were a center for Arabic, Christian, and Jewish intellectual pursuits. Once the Almoravid[1] movement of Islam conquered

---

1. A Muslim Berber people that established their reign in Morocco, Algeria, and Spain in the eleventh century.

Córdoba, the tolerance of the tenth century evaporated. The Maimonides family found it expedient to seek a self-imposed exile.

After staying in Fez, Morocco, for a brief time, Maimonides's family traveled through Palestine to a home in Cairo. Maimonides died in Cairo in 1204. He is seen as the father of medieval Jewish philosophy and as a leading contributor to Western philosophy in general. Among his most important contributions are commentaries on the Mishnah, the Torah, and his exoteric and esoteric philosophies in a work entitled *The Guide for the Perplexed* (1185–1190).

The prominent thinkers of Islam influenced Maimonides. He rationalized Jewish thoughts and tenets by subjecting them to rigorous philosophical methodology. Such projects also happened within the philosophical circles of Islam and Christianity. Later translated into Hebrew, Maimonides originally wrote his works in Arabic. The first translator of his works was Samuel ibn Tibbon, a resident of Provence, France, and a much younger contemporary. In addition to his translation of Maimonides, ibn Tibbon added his thoughts to the subject of Job and his trials.

Maimonides wrote for two audiences. He felt that Scripture had an overt meaning suitable for what he called the masses. He also wrote for those he considered the philosophically elite who were better able to understand esoteric concepts. Throughout his commentaries, he develops the idea that Aristotle's moral virtue was the highest form of perfection achievable by the uninformed masses. For Maimonides, however, those who could conquer philosophical thought and attain intellectual virtue must achieve more.

For this reason, he approaches each question with a double-edged sword directed toward two different audiences. First, he sees the clear text of Scripture as written for those who are unlearned or unenlightened and who must learn to accept life events as providence. Second, there are deeper meanings in Scripture for those who are enlightened and require direction to achieve the eternal promises of the active intellect.

Maimonides taught that one should not attempt to understand metaphysics (religion and philosophy) until one had conquered the sciences. Among other tenets of the philosophy of Aristotle, he agreed that only those individuals who attained intellectual virtue had the promise of immortality. His understanding of the writings of Aristotle contributed in many ways to the development of his work *The Guide for the Perplexed*. The philosophers who followed him depended, in large measure, on this groundwork to blend Aristotelian and Jewish philosophy.

Maimonides departs from the conservative interpretation of the book of Job in several ways, beginning with the question of who and what Satan represents. He sees Satan as a symbol of a negative and harmful force in the natural world. For him, Satan is the personification of privation or the absence of natural form, the source of decay and corruption. Maimonides is adamant that God does not produce evil as an intention; rather, evil is a by-product of creating a material world. Evil is present because matter exists, and matter always brings privation and decay. The concept of matter as evil is evidence of the possible influence of the Gnostics or the even more ancient writings that inspired the gnostic creed. Since Maimonides draws attention to the two different methods of Satan's entry into the conversation, he is emphasizing both a privation (Job's imperfect understanding) and matter, or harmful chance occurrences.

Maimonides pays specific attention to the actual events in Job's life. His premise is that the adept can control responses to these disasters if not the causes themselves. He describes three categories of evil and correlates these with what happened to Job. First is a group of afflictions that include natural disasters and matter.[2] One should consider such events as mere changes in the elements of the universe.[3] He combines the things that occur due to natural disasters and things that occur as a function of the presence of matter into one of the causes for suffering. Observing nature leads to the same conclusion. Humanity, as of yet, cannot directly control earthquakes, volcanoes, or other natural disasters. (Although recent science has provided clear indications that human activity does influence these occurrences.) Also, control over the natural deterioration intrinsic to nature's process is limited.

The second form of evil described by Maimonides relates to human violence. These are acts perpetrated by the thoughts and choices of individuals. There are means to mitigate the results of violence, and there are choices that might influence the future actions of others. However, the subject of such violence is not always able to control the action or the outcome. This conclusion also has merit. Horrible things happen to good people because of others who have little or no respect for life or property. Leibniz's free will philosophy further develops this argument.[4]

In the last group of evils, Maimonides includes those that are self-inflicted. He believes that people bear the burden of their difficulties because they do damage to body and soul through immoderation. Although this thought does not fit the characterization of Job, the results of excesses of all kinds are evident throughout history. Immoderation can include habits that are obvious detriments to health, such as smoking or excessive drinking, or the omission of healthy habits causing slow and insidious damage to physical existence. There are some things initiated by the sufferer in full knowledge of the consequences. Blaming God for not protecting the individual against the results of personal choices seems inappropriate at best.

After Maimonides defines the parameters of suffering, he presents five theories of providence and links each interpretation with a participant in the story. These five theories may overlap in subtle ways.

Aristotle: A preeminent Greek philosopher that believed God exercises providence over things that are stable and permanent. He felt that providence was general within nature as a whole. That is, it operates on species or environments without

---

2. Maimonides, *Guide for the Perplexed*, 3:12.
3. Maimonides, *Guide for the Perplexed*, 3:12.
4. Gottfried Wilhelm Leibniz was a German mathematician and philosopher who lived from 1646–1716.

interacting on a personal level. In the debates that occur between Job and his friends, Maimonides sees Job as a representative of this point of view.

Ash'arite: An Islamic sect that looks to tradition and authority for interpretation of divine activity in the world. The sect developed through the followers of Abu al-Hasan al-Ash'ari beginning in ca. 936 CE. The Ash'arites believed that the nature and attributes of God were beyond human reasoning and experience and that knowing God can only occur through revelation. This Muslim philosophy became what we understand as orthodox Islam or Sunni. These followers believe in the freedom of intention and that humanity was not capable of creating anything in the material world. According to this sect, God teaches moral truths by revelation, and then they are handed down by authority. That is, individuals cannot reason out moral truths. Zophar is the defender of the arbitrary and unknowable will of God.

Mu'tazilite: This Islamic sect grew from the supporters of Muhammad's family as the rightful leaders of the early community. They believed that the directives of God were discernible through reason. Their doctrine posits that wisdom dictates all of God's actions and that the righteous who suffer will gain greater rewards in the world to come. Maimonides's choice for this philosophy is Bildad.

Rabbinic tradition: This is the study of the Torah and the ancient traditions and learnings of the rabbis. In this arena, reward and punishment occur according to divine law and for no other reason. Good fortune is always a reward, and suffering is always a punishment for sin. Maimonides uses Job's friend Eliphaz as defender of this point of view.

Maimonides, however, spends most of his effort interpreting Elihu's message and considers it pivotal to the entire book. Maimonides teaches that the natural order consists of benevolent and harmful processes and equates Elihu's angels with natural forces that can preserve the soul from the brink of death. These forces can be such things as advantages gained by advanced intellect, beneficial natural causes, prophecy, or divination.

There are also forces of privation, which are destructive and can be caused by violent weather, disease, or warfare. Maimonides interprets Elihu's warning that these angels can only save man "two or three times" (33:29) to mean that privation does eventually win. Life does not go on forever. Maimonides takes the absence of a rebuke from God as approval of Elihu's conclusions. He interprets God's comment that Job has learned all that a man can comprehend as acknowledgment of Elihu's position. Natural processes can be either good or bad, and the description of the process is the best explanation man can hope for in how God governs the world.

As the leader of the Aristotelians, Maimonides believes that Job does come to an understanding of the right way to view suffering. In other words, Job attains intellectual virtue as a result of his trials. The highest form of devotion to God is when a person has achieved such a close intellectual and emotional connection with God that they are in constant contemplation of him, even while going about the duties required of a person living in the world. In Maimonides's mind, this type of relationship defines a Providence that teaches a person psychological immunity to suffering. The cares of this world do not affect this kind of person at the deepest levels. As explained by Eisen, Maimonides is teaching that the experience of life itself denies the existence of true providence (bad things happen to good people). Therefore, the only conclusion left is that we must break our attachment to physical and material well-being. To attain favor, one must detach themselves from these earthly concerns.[5]

Maimonides teaches that an individual with a developed intellect, such as a person with the rational mind of Aristotle, is better prepared to be open to individual providence. Such a person has a better understanding of possible future events and is better able to avoid harm.

Moreover, the better developed the intellect, the easier to achieve moral virtue, which leads to better overall health and well-being. In Maimonides's view, Job learns that intellectual perfection—the ability to concentrate on God while conducting one's worldly affairs—allows a person to develop a resistance to suffering. The proposal is that this state of being allows a person to achieve the ability to become impervious to physical affliction. One uses mental tools to mitigate the impact of suffering caused by unavoidable events. At least one can hope. Although knowledge is a key to avoiding disaster, developing a shell against suffering could make a person so heavenly minded, they are of no earthly good.[6] Sharing a burden takes knowing something about that burden, and that requires the experience of suffering to develop a true sense of empathy.

Maimonides argues for the impersonal God of Aristotle and places the ability to tap into the divine in the individual's hands. He believes that the more time one invests in the intellect, the closer to God one becomes, and then this relationship can be used to make better decisions than others might make. He also notes that although Job appears morally virtuous, the prologue does not mention the attribute of knowledge. To Maimonides, Job somehow believes that happiness springs from things such as wealth, family, and good health. Job only comes to realize later that all his possession are objects of little more value than ashes. By testing Job, God teaches him that true happiness is the immortality imparted by intellectual virtue. Job's test helps him develop his intellect so that he can find eternal existence. In the mind of an Aristotelian, the intellect is the only thing that survives this life. There were several centuries of interpretation based on this contribution. Many of the medieval religious philosophers wrote to expand or refute these conclusions specifically.

---

5. Eisen, *Medieval Jewish Philosophy*, 68.

6. The quote "Some people are so heavenly minded that they are no earthly good" is usually attributed to Oliver Wendell Holmes, Sr., a physician and poet and the father of a Supreme Court justice.

Part II—Theodicy and Philosophy
Samuel ibn Tibbon

Ibn Tibbon lived and worked in Provence, France, around 1160–1232. He was the first to translate Maimonides's *Guide for the Perplexed*. He was also the first to produce a Hebrew version of works by Aristotle and Averroes.[7] Ibn Tibbon's commentaries contributed to the philosophical-exegetical discussions in Italy, Byzantium, and Spain. The communities of Beziers, Carcassonne, Narbonne, Lunel, Montpellier, Arles, and (ibn Tibbon's birthplace) Marseilles, were home to many of the period's brightest minds in all fields of study. This society of scholars contributed to the literature that combined traditional learning in biblical and rabbinic works with the disciplines of science, philosophy, Hebrew grammar, and mysticism. Ibn Tibbon was one of many scholars of Provence who borrowed from the Arabic philosophers and translated Arabic works into Hebrew.

Ibn Tibbon's work focuses on Elihu's position on providence and spends some time developing the differences between the two appearances of Satan. To support his commentary, he draws much of his inspiration from Psalm 73. Here the psalmist, Asaph, looks on the success of the wicked in comparison to his lot in life and wonders why one serves God. Then Asaph enters the sanctuary and understands that the wicked are brought high only to fall further and that the only comfort is in nearness to God.

For ibn Tibbon, the two speeches of Satan are tools to draw out two types of suffering. These are the things that happen to a person's belongings and family and the things that happen to one's own body. He teaches that the suffering caused by the loss of possessions, or even one's children, constitutes suffering of the righteous. These things can happen by chance occurrence. In his opinion, true suffering only occurs when it targets the individual. He believes that the book of Job is about this very personal type of suffering.

In ibn Tibbon's view, Job 33 is the key to the book and the message. To him, Elihu refutes Job's misquoted claim that suffering without sin is divine injustice. He writes that one should not believe God brings suffering on those who have not sinned and who have acted according to his will. The blame for suffering belongs to Satan. Ibn Tibbon does not see Satan as a being, but rather as a representation of the natural causes which afflict man because he is composed of matter. This philosopher postulates that God is just even if he does not preserve that which has no permanence.

He also emphasizes Elihu's reference to providence in the form of prophecy. Those who are sufficiently enlightened can use prophecy to be forewarned of harmful events and, therefore, avoid them, at least to some extent. Ibn Tibbon sees prophetic providence as a process by which God perceives what is happening and shares that knowledge with the enlightened through their relationship with God.

---

7. Averroes is the Latin name for Ibn Rushd. He lived in Córdoba, Spain, from 1126–1198. Averroes was an influential Islamic religious philosopher who integrated Islamic traditions with ancient Greek thought. His works include a series of commentaries on Aristotle's works and on Plato's *Republic*. His writings were influential in both the Islamic Empire and Europe.

Ibn Tibbon also suggests that a second type of providential communication exists when an event occurs by chance. God might speak to the individual through night visions and by way of suffering; however, Satan, as a type of matter, is the cause. He affirms Maimonides's position that providence operates on nature as a whole and that there is no individual providence that guards the individual's well-being.

Immanuel of Rome

Immanuel was an Italian-Jewish scholar and satirical poet living around 1261–1328. He was a member of a prominent family and held respected positions within the Jewish community. In addition to biblical and Talmudic studies, he devoted time to mathematics, astronomy, medicine, and the philosophies of Islam and Christianity. Verse, however, was his first love, and he was quite gifted at its composition. Due to circumstances not described in the source material, he lost his entire fortune and wandered the country friendless and penniless until a friend in Fermo, Italy, took him in and provided for his old age.

Immanuel, although influenced by ibn Tibbon, saw the function of providence differently. He believed that providence consisted of immortality of the intellect and protection from physical harm in this world. He takes a traditional view contrary to ibn Tibbon's that prophecy and divination warn an individual, which will, in turn, cause them to repent to defer suffering.

When commenting on Elihu's angel, Immanuel writes that it might be a representation of a person's good deeds, which can mitigate a deserved punishment (also an interpretation from the Talmud).[8] For him, the angel represents the human intellect, which is a person's only salvation and the only thing that lives beyond the grave.

As a representative of the earlier interpreters of ibn Tibbon's works, Immanuel also deals with the difficulty that Elihu tends to overlap Bildad and his Mu'tazilite philosophy: suffering helps an individual gain merit for a better afterlife. Immanuel goes against the previous position that rewards only present themselves in the afterlife. He insists rewards exist in the current life. One must wonder if his views changed when his fortunes changed so drastically.

Zerahiah Hen

Zerahiah Hen, born in either Barcelona or Toledo, became a Spanish-Jewish physician, philosopher, translator, and Hebraist. Arabic was his language of birth, and much of his work was the translation of important works from Arabic into Hebrew.

---

8. The Talmud is a work that is studied, not necessarily read. It is an accumulation of civil and ceremonial law. It also is a collection of legends which comprise the Mishnah and the Gemara. There are two versions of the Talmud: the Babylonian Talmud from around the fifth century CE and an earlier Palestinian or Jerusalem version.

Part II—Theodicy and Philosophy

Rather than a direct record of his life, researchers depend on the dating of his works to place him in historical context. Historians conclude that he wrote between 1277 and 1290. He taught the philosophy of Maimonides while living in Rome. Only parts of his commentaries survive, as well as some record of his correspondence with Hillel of Verona[9] and Judah ben Solomon.[10] Zerahiah is the first Jewish philosopher to use the tools of exegesis to support his belief that the book of Job is allegory and lacks any historicity at all. His analysis provides the basis for his conclusions regarding the lessons of the passage. His commentary includes insights into Hebrew wisdom literature.

First, Zerahiah cites the lack of historical detail and the absence of dates. This observation is in counterpoint to much of the literature of the Old Testament, which includes genealogies, references to relevant events, rulers, and empires. Zerahiah sees the lack of dating as a clue that the author of Job intended the piece as an allegory.

Evidence presented earlier in this book indicated that the actual writing of the book of Job occurred much later than any events that may have inspired it. Consequently, the primary purpose of Job is not to record a historical account of past events. The author chose to use a well-known legend as a means by which he could convey his intended thoughts. Based on this information, an allegorical interpretation becomes a good option: a parable developed using reference points familiar to the target audience, and from which we understand deeper abstract thoughts.

Zerahiah believes that the names of places and persons are contrived. For instance, Job's name, Iyyov, is related to the Hebrew word for enemy. Zerahiah thinks this reflects a situation where God despises Job, and that he is despised by the forces of nature and by all those around him. Job, however, is not despised of God.

In contrast to his depiction of the disparaged Job, Zerahiah's treatise also focuses on the exemplary description of Job, which the philosopher believes depicts a fantasy hero, for no one could be that good. He emphasizes this point with references to the repetitive uses of the number ten, which is the number of good luck and power in Hebrew lore. In his opinion, the device makes it blatantly evident it is meant as allegory since real-life scenarios rarely come in neat groups divisible by the number ten. However, the poet's use of this vehicle to paint the picture of the perfect world may not eliminate the possibility of a historical basis. Rather, the artist may have used such symmetry to incorporate Hebrew imagery and symbology, which further set the stage for the events about to happen. Things were perfect—and then they were not.

Zerahiah also points out that there are many unusual events. He agrees that much of the activity is believable yet stops short of accepting "fire from the sky" (1:16). In his mind, this is also a key to the enlightened that this book is allegory even though

---

9. Hillel of Verona was a physician, Talmudic scholar, and philosopher whose rabbinic family came from Verona, Italy. He himself resided in Naples and Capua and is thought to have lived from ca. 1220–1295.

10. Judah ben Solomon was a Spanish-Jewish philosopher who lived from ca. 1215–1274. He was an astronomer and mathematician and author of Midrash ha-Hokmah, a Hebrew encyclopedia.

the unlearned masses would most certainly believe such an event possible. He further states that the ending of the story is an overstatement and a balm to those same masses.

Unlike his predecessors, Zerahiah additionally considered the literary structure and style of the dialogue. Previously, Maimonides postulated that there were twenty-six premises needed to prove God's existence. Based on Maimonides teachings, Zerahiah subdivided the poem into twenty-six speeches. He also cites the uniform style of dialog and points out there are no differences in the delivery between the participants. Thus, it cannot be a true story because different people would not speak in the same manner. Here Zerahiah is looking for the voice of the participants, not the voice of the author. The author did identify his characters by using Aramaic references within the debate and Hebrew usages for God's speeches. Zerahiah believes that Moses wrote the book but that Moses did not acknowledge authorship because he based it on his wisdom and not divine inspiration.

Zerahiah, like others in this group, is very uncomfortable with the anthropomorphic representations of God and Satan. As an example, he sees no reason why God would need to ask Satan where he has been. Well, true, but then it is difficult to convey a thought process or exchange of ideas in a dramatic or poetic presentation without the vehicle of dialog of some kind. Scripture often attributes human qualities to God, even when such anthropomorphisms would be meaningless in actual practice. Whether there is an actual exchange of this sort between two entities that results in the ensuing events is immaterial. The prologue gives the reader details they would not otherwise have. Job is blameless, and a devout worshiper, yet that is not enough to avoid the suffering of this world.

Zerahiah looks at the character of Satan as a type of a philosophical argument, an archetype of evil inclinations. In correspondence with another philosopher, Judah ben Solomon, Zerahiah expands on this notion by indicating that the divine beings are representatives of natural forms, and Satan is representative of matter. In his commentary on Maimonides's *Guide for the Perplexed*, Zerahiah interprets the prologue as an allegory describing the inclinations of good and evil. For Zerahiah, the book of Job is a folk tale for the uninformed and a metaphysical guide to spiritual maturity for the enlightened.

Levi ben Gershom (Gersonides)

As is the case with many of these men, the dates for the life of Gersonides are an approximation. Most authorities place him as living from 1288–1344. He, too, lived in the philosophical and scientific center of Provence. He was a well-respected philosopher and exegete and made substantial contributions to astronomy and mathematics. Although he does not appear to have held a rabbinical post, he was a recognized authority on the Talmud, Jewish law, tradition, and biblical law. His major contribution to philosophy was a work entitled *Wars of the Lord*, which contained a section on Job. He completed a separate commentary on Job in 1325.

The methodology used by Gersonides was that of a teacher. First, he would explain terms; then he would explain the content; then he would talk about what it all meant. In this manner, he constructed a bridge from the Aristotelian school of thought back toward the traditional teachings of rabbinic literature. He concluded that Job deals with individual providence in support of the Torah, and he assumes that Moses was the author. Primarily, Gersonides held to a philosophy that *sublunar* species, those that inhabit this world, experience a general providence, not an individual Providence. He believes this is the lesson that Job finally learns.

He also postulates that there might be a form of individual providence, in which case God would issue punishments and rewards based on personal conduct. Job's friends introduce the three ways in which this type of providence can manifest. Eliphaz explains that some good and bad things are a result of punishment and reward. However, some are a result of other causes, such as ignorance. Bildad's position is that good and bad things are always a result of punishment and reward, and so if it looks unjust, then the bigger picture is unclear. The last approach is represented by Zophar, which is that good and bad things always happen because of punishment or reward, even though it may not appear so to an individual since they lack the omniscience of God. Sometimes the suffering occurs to push individuals to their highest potential, which God, in his wisdom, knows better than the sufferer. This last observation Gersonides derives from the speeches of Elihu. Here he presents the somewhat inexplicable idea that some persons experience individual providence while, for whatever reason, others do not.

For this philosopher, it is important to understand the two sources of evil to understand the lessons of Job. One source is the existence of matter, which is responsible for ill health and bad conduct. In Gersonides's opinion, matter is also responsible for evil created through violence perpetrated by others.

The second source of evil comes from chance events and natural occurrences. Chance events are not evil because, according to Gersonides, no evil can come from God. They are just a product of living in a world of matter. Dreams and visions provide opportunities to mitigate or prevent harmful events. Gersonides supports the conclusion of Maimonides that development of the active intellect is the only measure of good or evil.

From this, Gersonides goes on to show that Job, at some point, learns that individual providence does not exist. At first, he curses the day of his birth and Eisen interprets Gersonides as believing that Job believes the stars determine all events, making them ultimately responsible for Job's trials.[11] Gersonides does not, however, lose his firm conviction that the soul is immortal.

---

11. Eisen, *Medieval Jewish Philosophy*, 150.

Gersonides uses Elihu's words to explain his view on providence. Job suffered because he didn't consider his influence on others. People would not see a purpose in worshiping God if there was no punishment-reward system. Also, without the evils in the world, there would be no motive to strive for intellectual perfection. As with all of the Aristotelians, he believes that striving for intellectual perfection is the only path to achieve prophetic capability, to be preserved from harm in this life, and to obtain immortality in the next.

Gersonides believes that Job admits to being wrong in the closing chapter of the book. He sees Job as despising his previous beliefs and even regreting mourning his losses. Job purportedly comes to realize that if he perfects his intellect, then he will be able to avoid future harm.

This philosopher writes that God admonishes Job's friends because they supported a view they knew to be wrong to justify God. However, the book of Job does not support this conclusion. Job's visitors seem quite sincere in their positions. They do, however, incorrectly apply their beliefs to Job. Gersonides also concludes that Job decides there is evil and that God is ignorant of the details and cannot, therefore, deliver individual providence. Here Gersonides begins the swing back to conservative philosophers by focusing on the question of providence over an individual's well-being, as opposed to something more general over the species. Gersonides uses Elihu's voice to scold previous interpreters for stressing a position that excludes all possibility of personal providence. Such a conclusion could encourage people to be wicked and discourage people from seeking intellectual perfection.

He also seems to bend a bit to the pressure of traditionalists by favoring the reading of Scripture as plain text without the use of allegory. By mixing these two forms of scriptural interpretation, he builds a path that veers away from centuries of Aristotelian thought. Gersonides describes the contrasts between Aristotelian and traditional interpretations. He stages the controversy as a discussion of pre-Hebrew philosophy and works toward traditions established by the revelations of Moses at Mount Sinai.

Commentators and scholars have long viewed this book as a stylized debate regarding the nuances of ancient Middle Eastern religious philosophies to arrive at the foundations of the Hebraic faith. The dating of the actual writing precludes this unless an author was drawing on ancient traditions of discourse.

Gersonides presents a more sophisticated Job than some of his predecessors did. Instead of a man crying out against his fate, his champion works through specific arguments to conclude that there is no personal providence and that God cannot or will not control the evil of this world. His companions consider this resolution blasphemous. Job replies that if God were more powerful, he would have created a world without suffering. That conclusion is a debate that continues to this day.

Gersonides concludes that Elihu shows Job that his failing, his misunderstanding of personal providence, could cause potential damage to the social and theological well-being of his community. To him, Job's lack of belief in individual providence could provide others with an excuse to remain in their evil ways. For the nonbeliever, if God does not bother himself with specific behaviors or individuals, then there is no fear of reprisal, no accountability for evil. In this philosopher's mind, Job's primary defect was a lack of intellectual perfection that kept him from seeing God's providential hand, and that defect could discourage others from seeking the knowledge to gain protection from dangers in this life and to achieve immortality in the next. Gersonides believes that Job, through Elihu's message, arrives at the understanding that he deserved the suffering so that he could learn this lesson.

Gersonides then uses Job's experience as a lesson for the nation of Israel. He writes that the people of Israel experience providence when God sends a prophet, or if there is no prophet, then calamity will befall them until they are worthy of restoration. This position was a reassurance to his fellow Jews and in opposition to what the radical thinkers (beginning with Maimonides) were advocating.

He also explains that both prophecy and providential suffering can be protective and lead the individual to repentance. The end goal, in either case, is to achieve a level of faith that allows the individual to abandon attachment to material things in favor of intellectual perfection. With this opinion, Gersonides remains firmly in the Aristotelian camp.

While placing some value on the educational good of providence, in other commentaries (*Wars of the Lord*) Gersonides returns to the more direct approach that rewards only come when one achieves intellectual skill. The educational value of providence is only a desirable byproduct and not the direct cause. For this reason, he believes God rewarded Job because Job was honest in his challenge to God. Here again, Gersonides sides more closely with the Aristotelians and hints that the methods of reason are superior to the tradition of the rabbis.

In the end, Gersonides attempts to support a more traditional point of view: that individual providence does exist. However, he also believes that the operation of Providence on the individual level is relatively rare. He concludes that the best an individual can hope for is a providence that protects the species as whole, even while he feels committed to the knowledge and interpretation of prophecy to achieve personal providence.

Is it better to view Job as an allegory of our journey to reach our own highest level of virtue? Is it possible to develop our emotional and spiritual skills to the point that the cares and trials of this life do not affect us? Or would such an approach put us in danger of becoming insensitive to the trials of others? Is the book of Job written in code to reach only those that are of a mind to understand? Can it offer succor to any member of humanity suffering from the difficulties of life, be they great or small?

Suffering is a global condition that is not exclusive to Christians and Jews. Perhaps by broadening the points of reference and investigating other faiths, we can find something new that will help retell the story of Job. What lessons are available when faith teaches that the world is either arbitrary or chaotic? Or that suffering can only be mitigated when the individual finds a path that hones their spirit into greater harmony with the universe? What happens when worship does not focus on the salvation of the soul, but rather on submission or surrender to God whatever the consequences?

PART II—THEODICY AND PHILOSOPHY

Map 4

The Jewish Philosophers 882 - 1444

The Aristotelians

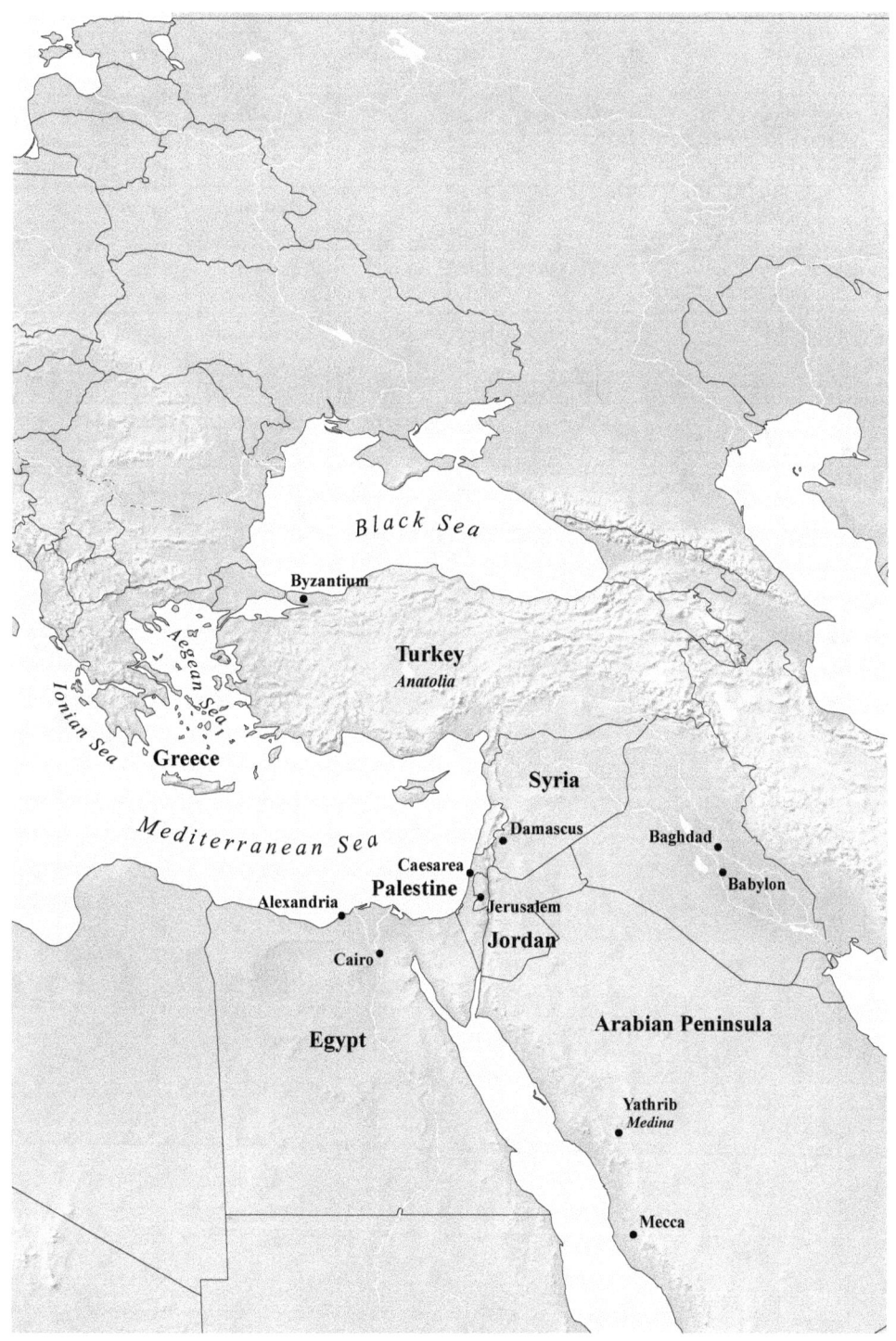

Part II—Theodicy and Philosophy

Chart 5: Key to Jewish Philosophers

Saadiah Gaon	882–942	Egypt, Syria, Palestine, Babylon	Conservative, rational	Literal, traditional
Moses Maimonides	1135–1204	Cordoba, Spain; Fez, Morocco; Cairo, Egypt	Aristotelian, rational	Allegorical
Samuel ibn Tibbon	1160–1232	Marseilles & Provence, France	Aristotelian	Allegorical
Immanuel of Rome	1261–1328	Rome, Fermo, Italy	Aristotelian	Allegorical
Zerahiah Hen	1270–1290	Barcelona, Toledo, Spain; Rome, Italy	Aristotelian	Allegorical
Levi ben Gershom (Gersonides)	1288–1344	Provence, France	Aristotelian/ Traditional	Leaning to traditional
Simon ben Zemah Duran	1361–1444	Majorca, Algiers	Conservative, rabbinical	Literal

Part III—A Different Point of View

Chapter 11

The Dawn of Religion, Preliterate, and Ancient Faiths

THIS BOOK IS ABOUT Job, a man whose story provides part of the fabric of Jewish, Christian, and Islamic teachings. Depending on the interpreter, Job's tale addresses the nature of suffering, the apparent unfairness of the world, the need to understand God, the expectation of help or hindrance from God, and a dozen other related topics. The mission of this book, however, is to retell Job's story from a human perspective, a perspective, which may have an impact on the answer Job receives. What can the beliefs of the Far East contribute? What inspiration might religious traditions with many gods, or none, contribute?

This journey began with the premise that Job is a quintessential symbol of human suffering. He and his purported patience have become part of secular as well as religious texts, ideology, and general discourse. If the story of suffering is an experience shared by all of humanity, there should be relevant material in other faiths that addresses the concept of the search for cause and effect, the burden of suffering, and the expectation of supernatural help. What non-biblical traditions say about suffering and providence might be enlightening and offer a fresh perspective for the retelling of the tale.

How a believer understands the tenets of a faith is influenced by centuries of thought molded by the theologians, philosophers, and commentators who shaped the doctrine. Even if a faith community feels the call to discard the past interpretations and seek new revelations, they are responding to the translation before them (which has its own peculiar set of interpretations) and incorporating the influence of the culture from which they come. Much of this book is devoted to investigating the development of beliefs about the subjects of suffering and providence, as well as the consequences of such beliefs. There is nothing intrinsically wrong with accepting the wisdom of forbearers in the faith or the words of modern-day pastors, priests, rabbis, or imams. However, like the optical illusion that presents one picture while another remains hidden, something of great value can be missed unless there is willingness to explore alternative views. Contrasting points of view can also serve to strengthen an existing faith or belief by clarifying core ideas and providing support for why they are so important. Therefore, understanding "a different point of view" can be invaluable in the development of thoughts and interpretations of scriptural material.

This chapter contains a wide scope of historical and religious experience. It begins with preliterate cultures where much of what is known is conjecture or derived from the study of currently existing primitive cultures (e.g., tribes of the Amazon, remote parts of Asia, the Pacific Islands, and Africa). From there, this study looks at the early history of the western hemisphere. What we know about these ancient practices is, in part, from reconstructions created through the efforts to preserve traditions with the recordings of oral histories of indigenous peoples. Some of the ancient tales are being pieced together from the monuments left throughout the world and from records which speak to the written codices long since destroyed by conquerors.

In the process of reconstructing prehistorical and early historical religious traditions, archeologists and anthropologists have learned a variety of ways employed by *Homo sapiens* to manage the realities of life. The research indicates that we have long wrestled with the travails and joys of living in this world, the purpose of suffering, and the pursuit of peace. Again, Job is representative of a fundamental human experience. What answers he receives can be rooted deep in the past as well as in the continued search for meaning and peace. Are there lessons from the distant past that will help retell the story?

Preliterate Cultures

The search for preliterate faiths for this text began with the indigenous religions of Sub-Saharan Africa. Anthropologists and archeologists believe the African continent is the root of all human existence. Researchers are discovering a contentious past and present that encompasses some of the deepest suffering known to humanity. Perhaps there is wisdom within the myriad of faiths, beliefs, and legends that were birthed and nurtured in this region.

Scholars rely heavily on research involving primitive tribes existing today to study prehistoric rituals and beliefs. There is little available in written histories, and most of our substantive knowledge comes from our attempts to interpret the artifacts found in burial sites. Although these tribes are considered primitive by our standards, their religions show sophisticated thoughts and ideas. Traditions that have been studied by anthropologists show many similarities throughout the world. Key characters may change; the geographical settings may change; however, the fundamental elements of stories regarding the creation of the world, of humanity, and of the forces that rule over that creation are replete with commonalities. Based on these commonalities, evolutionists have developed several theories about how humanity might have come to believe in the supernatural. What social and survival instincts may have made the belief in a superior being or force necessary to continued existence?[1]

Setting aside the acceptance of a purely evolutionary point of view, evolutionists have done an excellent job unpacking humanity's development of the supernatural—that is, our quest to find order in a universe that appears to have order even if on occasion it presents us with chaos. For the most part, humanity tends to seek a reason for life events. Our sciences developed through our sense of wonder, search for order, and curiosity regarding how or why something works in a specific way.

Further studies help determine if events are predictable, preventable, or useful to our own needs. If we as a species had no faith in a rational universe, we would have no basis on which to yearn for answers to questions of why or how. This argument is repeated frequently by Job himself and many of his commentators. There must be a reason, and if a person cannot comprehend what that might be, then they look to someone or something else that might know. If an event appears to be random or without explanation, then there is a need to find someone or something else able to protect and teach those affected. The question becomes, "How does one reach this entity and secure the aid required?"

In the past, there has been some disagreement among scholars regarding when monotheism developed. A substantial number of references point to the reign of Akhenaten (1353–1336 BCE). However, Akhenaten's elevation of the sun god (Aten) to a place of preeminence was more political than religious. Akhenaten was not attempting to create a monotheistic faith even though he ordered revision of any references to multiple gods on Egyptian monuments. His focus was to raise Aten above Amun in the Egyptian pantheon to reduce the power of the priesthood of Amun. The rest of Egypt's pantheon remained relatively intact.

According to the accumulating evidence from preliterate societies, Egyptian attempts at monotheism, or preeminent placement of a superior god, were not the first. A substantial majority of ancient traditions recognize a High God, a superior that is the First Cause, and that rules overall. Sometimes this personage is far removed from creation due to some infraction on the part of humanity. Sometimes the god is close to worshipers and involved in the day-to-day woes and victories of life. One of the reasons that Christianity and Islam spread so effectively is that these faiths bore many conceptual similarities with existing belief systems, especially in places such as Africa and the western hemisphere. The people did not see a great gulf between their traditions and the new beliefs. They often melded the new and the old so that the traditions remained with new interpretations.

If that is the case, then what is the source of all the gods and goddesses of this or that? At the heart of these faiths, there are lesser gods, lesser spirits, created by the

---

1. See Wade, *Before the Dawn*, for an explanation of the somewhat controversial theory of "group evolution."

Part III—A Different Point of View

High God as intermediaries between humanity and the ultimate Creator. In Christianity, one might look to angels and saints. In addition to these spirits—some good, some bad, and some rather ambiguous—ancestors come to the aid of those left behind. People created many burial rituals to ensure the assistance of or protection from those who had died.

There is a fundamental difference between the faiths of ancient Africa and the observance of modern religion. The faith, or religion, of a tribe was not something one practiced. One's faith was lived. Ninian Smart writes that modern believers think of religion or faith as a body of doctrine to which one may commit, whereas for prehistoric people, and contemporary primitive or tribal cultures, religion becomes woven into the fabric of daily existence. Faith becomes a part of life, not something a believer chooses.[2]

What a tribe believes touches every facet of day-to-day life when it comes to supernatural involvement in this world. There are consequences to this point of view. One is that conduct in this life is of little consequence upon entering the afterlife. Although not a focus of these faiths, the adherents do acknowledge an afterlife. They established many traditions and rituals to either protect from or ensure the help of deceased ancestors. The goal is not to mitigate punishment or increase reward. Life after death exists without any need for punishment or reward before or after death. Therefore, these adherents dealt with suffering and deliverance differently than individuals of Abrahamic faiths.

An example of this concept is the African religion of Yoruba. This faith traveled to the Western world during the years of active slave trade. Practitioners refashioned the faith to survive in the Caribbean and South America under the Catholic priests. According to Stephen Prothero, it is one of the largest religions in the world by number of adherents.[3] In the Americas, the faith became the basis of Santeria, Voudoun, Umbanda, and Candomblé. All four of these incorporate some aspects of the Christian faith. A movement has begun to attempt to unravel the close ties to Western faiths and to return to the ancestral practices. Prothero calls this faith the "path of connection."

Yoruba, in all its varieties, is a search for destiny, a destiny chosen before birth. There are no priests that interpret events or dreams, only diviners that give the faithful options. Diviners are often not aware of the adherent's question, only that they are facing a circumstance that requires guidance.

The problem, in the mind of the Yoruba follower (or its variants), is disconnection, and to correct that, one must reconnect with destiny, one another, and sacred power. The spirit world is a pantheon of good and evil spirits, as well as those who are neither. There is little separation between the human world and the spirit world, and spirits can and do suffer for inappropriate behavior. Natural things, rather than art, decorate the shrines. The focus is to find balance between good and evil in all things.

2. Smart, *Religious Experience of Mankind*, 27.
3. Prothero, *God Is Not One*, 203.

The Dawn of Religion, Preliterate, and Ancient Faiths

With this approach to life, the role of suffering and how to deal with the consequences are entirely different from a point of view where a God that is defined as good allows evil things to happen. Justifying the actions of spiritual powers is not a consideration. If things are going wrong, the believer must seek the path that will return them to balance with destiny.

A few excerpts from *The Good Person*, a collection of Yoruba Proverbs, may illustrate this, along with a few correlations from Job himself. For instance, Job cannot understand why the life he has lived has given him no defense against this onslaught. *The Good Person* suggests:

> If one lacks the means to reject suffering and attempts to reject it, one's suffering simply multiplies.
> (Whoever cannot defend himself or herself must learn forebearance.)[4]

In another example, Job blames no one for his suffering. Instead, he seeks answers from God. *The Good Person* suggests:

> Even if the goddess Oya sings in heaven and the god Sango sings on earth, matters cannot be so bad for the father that he will say it is all up to his dead child in heaven.
> (Even in suffering one should never disgrace oneself.)[5]

A common denominator in many preliterate cultures is that life does not end with death; it continues in some other realm. The term *numen* describes an all-pervasive spiritual power that exists in everything. Whatever change comes at death has more to do with how much numen, or spirit, resides in the person. When suffering occurs, it is due to a reduction of this power. In other words, many peoples of the African continent might say, "We are living a little." Suffering can also be due to a person, thing, or circumstance with a greater life force.

The question is if any of this information is helpful to the suffering protagonist Job. In the works of both the Christian and Jewish commentators, some scholars emphasized that the sufferings of this world should be of no account. Some composed their comments based on a firm belief in a punishment-reward system where the books become balanced at some point beyond this life. There is a large body of literature that concludes with the theory that the response Job receives is that he must wait for his answer; it will not be available on this side of the grave.

Preliterate societies did not count on benefits outside of this life. They accepted that there are good and evil influences in this current world, and they believed that it is one's duty to seek a balance. Although Job and his visitors do not come to this understanding of what balance might look like, there is a hint of the need for this approach in Job 40 and 41. In these chapters, God lays down the challenge of what

---

5. *The Good Person*, Part 1: "On humility, self-control, self-knowledge, self-respect, and self-restraint." Proverbs beginning with B.

6. *The Good Person*, Part 1: "On humility, self-control, self-knowledge, self-respect, and self-restraint." Proverbs beginning with B.

humanity is responsible for in the battle to control the evil and violence represented by Behemoth and Leviathan. Perhaps the poet of the book of Job wrote to remind his readers of a rich and long-suffering heritage while providing new insights about dealing with suffering.

Mesoamerican and South American Cultures

Anthropologists, historians, and archeologists have failed to arrive at any consensus regarding who arrived on the western hemisphere, where that landing took place, and when. Also, after years of research, there persists a belief in the primitive nature of these historical peoples even when the evidence shows advanced and creative civilizations that rival those of Egypt.

Highly developed metropolitan areas filled with pyramid-like structures span a historical period of 3000 BCE to 1532 CE. The city of Teotihuacan, northeast of Mexico City, is the home of the world's third-largest pyramid structure. Everywhere throughout Central and South America, there is evidence of sophisticated irrigation systems, terraced farming practices, transportation networks, complex social structures, and pantheons of gods and goddesses, shared and local. This heritage has something a bit different to contribute to the puzzle of human suffering, including the ability to influence it and the hoped-for aid from a supernatural source.

The peoples of Central and South America followed a belief system much like those of preliterate societies. They believed that this world and the afterworld were inextricably linked. Most of the societies maintained a vision of multiple heavens and underworlds, none of which were destinations dependent on how a person lived their life. Punishment and reward were for this life and this life alone. What did decide an individual's place in the afterworld was the position held in this life and how they died. Noblemen, warriors, suicides, and women who died in childbirth all had special places reserved in the afterworld. Some earned the honor of a second life as a hummingbird or a butterfly, both of which were sacred symbols linked with the pantheon.

If viewed from a philosophy that sins or shortcomings of any kind are all initiated and recompensed in this current life, the aspect of punishment or reward changes substantially from Judeo-Christian theology. Those differences are critical in understanding what happens when people suffer.

The geographical area encompassed by these civilizations has a violent and chaotic history. These lands are subject to earthquakes, volcanoes, hurricanes, droughts, and flash floods. Life expectancy was short, and infant mortality was high. Also, the people of these continents were subject to constant wars and conquests. Remnants of their thoughts survive the onslaught of conquerors, weather, and time. Charles S. Braden explains in his book *Scriptures of Mankind* that there is a common thread throughout human history.Individuals and cultures have recorded their feelings of weariness and disillusionment through a variety of prose, proverbs, and poetry.[6] Citizens of ancient Babylon developed a philosophy of *carpe diem* (seize the day), while other societies found little to lighten the spirit in times of great need. Large parts of Ecclesiastes would be a good example of a general malaise.

The following quotes are from *Ancient Nahuatl Poetry*:

1. Weeping, I, the singer, weave my song of flowers of sadness; I call to memory the youths, the shards, the fragments, gone to the land of the dead; once noble and powerful here on earth, the youths were dried up like feathers, were split into fragments like an emerald, before the face and in the sight of those who saw them on earth, and with the knowledge of the Cause of All.

2. Alas! alas! I sing in grief as I recall the children. Would that I could turn back again; would that I could grasp their hands once more; would that I could call them forth from the land of the dead; would that we could bring them again on earth, that they might rejoice and delight the Giver of Life; is it possible that we His servants should reject him or should be ungrateful? Thus I weep in my heart as I, the singer, review my memories, recalling things sad and grievous.

3. Would only that I knew they could hear me, there in the land of the dead, were I to sing some worthy song. Would that I could gladden them, that I could console the suffering and the torment of the children. How can it be learned? Whence can I draw the inspiration? They are not where I may follow them; neither can I reach them with my calling as one here on earth.[7]

Universal in its lament: where have the children gone? Death came in many forms, and some easier to accept than others. If there is anything that the Central and South Americans are known for, it is for human sacrifice. The Aztec gods (and priests) were insatiable in their desire for beating hearts and the blood of fellow mortals. Although records indicate there were specific occasions when the sacrifice had to come from a member of their own culture, conquest was the only way to support the mass destruction of human life. Among the reasons that the small forces of the Spaniards could defeat so many skilled warriors was this unsustainable war footing. They quickly learned how to drive a wedge between the ruling peoples and those subjugated; add a few European diseases, and conquest became unavoidable.

That said, what drove these societies to wholesale slaughter of thousands to feed their gods? Sacrifice, both human and animal, pervades most prehistoric and early historic peoples. The Old Testament remarks on the practice often. God demanded blood sacrifice of humanity to assuage whatever unpardonable sin was committed by eating of the fruit of the Tree of Knowledge. For the most part, animals filled this

---

6. Braden, *Scriptures of Mankind*, 30.

7. Brinton, *Ancient Nahuatl Poetry*, section VII, "Composed by a Certain Ruler in Memory of Former Rulers."

role. However, Scripture is also quite clear that human sacrifice, while condemned, was common.

Although God stayed his hand, there is no outcry from Abraham regarding the sacrifice of Isaac. The man who chose to bargain with the messengers of God over the salvation of Sodom and Gomorrah remains silent when God demands the blood of his son. By some accounts, it is because he neglected to give thanks to God for the boy at a celebration of his birth. Although it is easy to speculate on Abraham's thoughts and his trust in God, it is still evident that sacrifice permeated the culture.

Jephthah, a general during the time of the judges, finds himself sacrificing his only daughter due to an oath sworn before battle. Although there are alternative interpretations that indicate he sent her off to serve in the temple as a virgin for the rest of her life, the *Tanakh* is very clear that the sacrifice was a burnt offering and that the annual festivals in her name were dirges.

The prophets of many Old Testament books decry the apostasy of the inhabitants of Israel and Judah as they followed their pagan neighbors in the practice of what scholars believe to be the sacrificial offering of children.

As brutal as this history is, the Aztecs brought the practice to an entirely new level. Why?

No one knows for sure; however, it appears that the Aztecs stepped up the practice after two devastating events. In approximately 1450 CE, snow came to Mexico in such volumes that houses caved in, the lakes near and around the capital froze, and the crops failed. This catastrophe caused widespread suffering for the population for nearly four years. Just as recovery was near, another bad year struck. This time the leaders imposed martial law, and they held all the food as common regardless of the ownership of the field or source. Wild animals invaded the town, and people sold their children into slavery to eat. Repeated disasters caused suffering on a monumental scale, and the Aztecs responded monumentally.

In some perverse way, perhaps the Aztecs believed that the gods were bent on taking life, and the priests wanted to be the ones who chose which lives. Research may never explain or lead scholars to understand what created the bloodthirst of these ancestors. However, before we dismiss the practices of these priests as ancient history, perhaps we should look more closely at modern history. How many lives become a sacrifice because those who can do something choose to do nothing when the methods and the means to prevent the loss of life are available? Is humanity any less culpable in deaths due to starvation, disease, or conflict than the bloodied priests of Tenochtitlan?

Suffering, or fear of it, drove much of humanity's belief that the gods thirsted for blood. There is a pervasive sense in this theory that the gods can be bargained with to secure better times—that by practicing some form of deprivation, one can attain a better life, a more successful career, or better social position. In the case of ancient Israel, the practice of sacrifice was a lesson that failure to observe the law carried a price. Christianity teaches that Christ paid this price for all and forever.

Job's visitors do not suggest that he perform sacrifices to bargain for better times. They do make repeated statements that he will find resolution if he repents. Something went wrong, and now he must pay with his wealth, the lives of his household, and his health. As far as these men are concerned, there could be no other answer. God merely assigned Satan to extract the due sacrifice. However, in the end, God requires a sacrifice from Job's companions. Whatever their intentions may have been, they failed both Job and God.

Is this the message the book intends to deliver? In small or great ways, must there be restitution for the infractions committed in life? The Central and South American cultures believed one experienced all punishment and reward in this present life. The pain of this life was quite enough to cover the sins of the people, and they went to the grave with a new set of rules. The greater the catastrophe, the greater the repayment required. What happens to the question of suffering if bargaining for better times is not the focus? What if the goal is to take deliberate steps to mold a better life, to be a better person in the here and now?

Chapter 12

Suffering in the Far East

THE PURPOSE OF THIS chapter is not to create a treatise on comparative religions; consequently the following analysis is not exhaustive. Four systems of faith are chosen based on the level of influence each has in today's world. These are Buddhism, Confucianism, Hinduism, and Taoism.

Buddhism

According to Stephen Prothero,[1] Buddhism is a "way of awakening." The founder of the faith, Siddhartha Gautama (563–483 BCE), was a sheltered prince who lived a protected life until he reached his late twenties. His need to know more of the world caused him to embark on four journeys outside of his palace walls. During these journeys, he learned of sickness, old age, death, and the wandering holy man. Struck by the difference between his life and the experience of most of the population, he walked away from his inheritance and became a seeker of truth.

He attended every school he could find and tested his body to its human limits in near starvation. As he searched, he came to realize that the more he deprived himself, the less he could focus. So, he left the life of the ascetic and vowed to find a middle ground. Siddhartha chose to feed and nurture his body to support good health. With a stronger body, he was better prepared to seek the answer to human suffering with a clear and critical mind. After six years as a wandering holy man, he arrived in Bodhgaya, North India, and sat under a tree. He remained there for forty-nine days, determined to find an awakening, to achieve the level of Bodhisattva, or the Awakened One.

Siddhartha concludes that nothing in this life is permanent, and all is subject to change. Suffering or dissatisfaction comes from wishing things to be otherwise.

---

1. Prothero, *God Is Not One*, 169.

Suffering, then, is a result of resisting the realities of life. Everything is constantly changing and always interconnected. Buddhism focuses on the question of suffering, or the feeling that life is unsatisfactory, and the contemplation of its impact on oneself and others.[2]

One illustration used to describe what happens when the individual is out of balance with this awareness is a wheel with the hub off-center. Such a wheel cannot function as a wheel should. The key is to seek balance so that life has order. Learning to accept the changes inherent in life extends to times of success and happiness. Often, the fear of losing what is good causes dissatisfaction when it is not necessary or helpful. The Buddha listed four requisites or material possessions needful for happiness. These are food, shelter, clothing, and medicine. With these necessities, as appropriate to a person's situation in life, managing the rest of life's difficulties should be within one's grasp.

Certainly there is less suffering when an individual cultivates an attitude that subdues the passions and focuses more on moderation, compassion, and respect for other living things. As in most faiths, there are differing interpretations of Buddha's message. According to Peter Morrell, the Theravada tradition is about conducting one's life ethically, being mindful of actions and thought, and restraining excesses.[3] These practices lead to enlightenment, even if it takes several lifetimes to get it right. The Mahayana tradition focuses on attaining the stage of Bodhisattva, or of becoming the one who helps others to find enlightenment, even if it takes longer to reach personal spiritual awakening.

Dukkha is the word used in the Buddhist texts commonly translated as "suffering." However, there is no true equivalent to the English meaning. Buddhism teaches that life is unsatisfactory and that dissatisfaction has a cause. The remedy offered by Buddhism is the Four Noble Truths. These truths are not noble in themselves, rather realities that the spiritually noble come to know. They are:

1. The reality of "that which is difficult to bear."
2. The cause is grabbing or clinging.
3. Nirvana, or the point at which there is no more grasping and need for control when the mind becomes "like fire unbound."
4. The path that leads to Awakening, or the Eightfold Path, which includes:
    a. Complete or Perfect Vision.
    b. Perfected Emotion or Aspiration.
    c. Perfected or Whole Speech.
    d. Integral Action (right action).

---

2. Morrell, "Buddhist View of Suffering."
3. Morrell, "Buddhist View of Suffering."

Part III—A Different Point of View

    e. Proper Livelihood.

    f. Complete or Full Effort, Energy, or Vitality.

    g. Complete or Thorough Awareness (right mindfulness).

    h. Full, Integral, or Holistic Samadhi (concentration, meditation, or singleness of mind).

Buddha wanted those who wished to be enlightened to understand that suffering comes from desiring that which one does not have, especially when there is a failure to appreciate what one does have.

There are many similarities to these conclusions in the Judeo-Christian heritage. Augustine's writings taught that the believer should not assign value to material goods.[4] In his estimation, the loss of homes, assets, or even children should not be a matter of great concern. For Augustine, even the four basic needs of happiness should be of no concern to the Christian. Maimonides wrote that we should rise above the suffering of this world to reach higher spiritual rewards. Aristotelian philosophy describes three forms of morality that support this doctrine. The highest form of morality is intellectual.[5] Some of the commentators quoted above were insistent that the believer achieve such focus on God that the cares of this world were of no account.

Although a practical perspective of material things and a balanced view of the impact of any loss is important, it seems beyond justification to abandon material possessions. Many of the advances and comforts, even needs that are available to humanity, are the product of creative and imaginative minds. These attributes of humanity are gifts to be used effectively, gifts that can mitigate suffering.

To say that all suffering is a derivative of attachment to the material is rather superficial. The Buddha would agree. His journey taught him there are basic needs that must be met for a human being to be able to contemplate the spiritual. The views of men like Augustine and Maimonides do not address the basic needs of the human body. Attempting to look on people who are suffering as persons who are too attached to material things does little more than provide an excuse to abandon those who have a valid need. As long as *we* are safe and warm, *their* problems must be due to lack of trying, some terrible sin, or an accident of birth. Siddhartha lived at the time of the Persian Empire and less than a century before the book of Job. He understood much about the cause of human suffering. However, his answers, although reflected in Christian and Jewish interpretations, are not entirely satisfactory.

---

4. Augustine, *City of God*, 22.
5. See chapter 10, "The Aristotelians."

Confucianism

Confucius was a Chinese sage whose legacy consists of a collection of philosophical thoughts and proverbs. Prothero[6] calls this enduring tradition the "way of propriety." In all things regarding the life of humanity, Confucius taught that the paramount achievement in life is to seek the proper response. He valued learning, piety, and loyalty above profit. That commitment to education has driven the red-hot economy of Asia in the past decades.

Confucianism has no temple or congregation, although there are shrines erected in Confucius's honor all over China. The story of Confucianism begins about the same time as that of Siddhartha (551–479 BCE). Confucius, however, emphasized the practice of morality in the current world. Such morality applies to governments as well as individuals. He saw great importance in the correctness of social relationships, justice, and sincerity in all dealings. As with many western teachers and philosophers, others did not compile and put his sayings into writing until years after his death.

Patheos.com describes the Confucian way of addressing suffering and evil.[7] At least some interpretations of Confucius see suffering and evil as inevitable in this life. Suffering exists so that individuals may learn the proper way of responding. Errors are merely acts (deliberate or not) that create an opportunity to learn and to grow morally. Mengzi, a follower of Confucius, points out that the devastation brought on by great disasters creates motivation to grow morally. Earthquakes, volcanoes, and other forces of nature provide the opportunity to develop empathy for the suffering of others. Concerning governments, Mengzi saw the satisfaction of the people governed as a measure of the sovereign's right to govern.

Confucius also taught that it is the responsibility of the individual to put morality into practice. The failure to attain a moral existence and the existence of great evils are evidence of how important it is for humanity to learn the way of dealing with suffering and evil. Consequently, the occurrence of earthquakes is a way to test the moral fiber of leaders. Famines are an occasion for political dissent and even removal of the leader. The point here is that the individual is responsible for their moral development. Just as one is responsible for one's actions, governments were responsible for conducting themselves morally and compassionately. Governments can be subject to upheaval and rebellion if a catastrophe occurs in such a manner that their ability to deal quickly and fairly with mounting issues is deemed inadequate.

Reflections of these thoughts appear within the book of Job and in the commentaries on the book. Job's visitors are certain that the devastation and horror he suffers is due to some infraction that Job himself committed. Something he did was not proper. Job's companions emphasize that his troubles must be his fault, while they also insist that a human cannot meet God's standards and that sometimes we cannot

---

6. Prothero, *God Is Not One*, 101.
7. See "Confucianism."

discern God's standards. Confucius shifts the responsibility away from the wrong action (whatever it might be) and focuses on the obligation to respond correctly.

An exchange in Archibald MacLeish's play *J.B.* illustrates the perils of accepting responsibility for everything that goes wrong. The play is an interpretation of the book of Job written in the 1950s. After the couple suffers the loss of everything, including their children, J.B.'s wife arrives at the only logical conclusion regarding his attempt to accept responsibility for the loss of their children.

> *She moves toward the door, stops, turns.*
>   I will not stay here if you lie—
>   Connive in your destruction, cringe to it:
>   Not if you betray my children . . .
>
> I will not stay to listen . . .
>
>   They are
> Dead and they were innocent: I will not
> Let you sacrifice their deaths
> To make injustice justice and God good!
>
> J.B.: *covering his face with his hands*
>   My heart beats. I cannot answer it.
>
> Sarah:
>   If you buy quiet with their innocence—
>   Theirs or yours . . .
>   *Softly*   I will not love you.
>
> J.B.:
>   I have no choice but to be guilty.
>
> Sarah: *her voice rising*
>   We have the choice to live or die,
>   All of us . . .
>   curse God and die . . .[8]

A unique perspective presents itself when Job's wife is the spouse that cannot accept complicity on Job's part for the death of her children. If his actions, or lack of action, contributed to the loss of her children, he might as well have murdered them with his own hands.

One of the hardest lessons learned on a journey with Job is the lesson that not every sparrow that falls is a direct result of one's action or inaction. Yes, there are consequences for the things we do. Yes, our actions do cause heartache, pain, and suffering that we cannot heal. However, to believe that the whole question of evil and suffering rests on our shoulders is truly a misguided application of responsibility. Confucius

---

8. MacLeish, *J.B.*, 110.

taught that one must strive for balance. At times one must accept responsibility for not doing the right and just things. Otherwise, the real point is how one responds to events that occur in life.

Confucius was sagacious. He provided a structure of moral behavior that would put responsibility of an individual's actions on the individual—not inexplicable or unknowable events, rather actions, which were the cause of pain. His follower Mengzi saw the relationship between the governed and the governors to include a responsibility on the part of the governors. A government's response to natural disasters (or any large-scale disaster) is indicative of its ability, its right, to govern.

Hinduism

The ancient precursor to a formalized Hinduism was the body of literature known as the *Vedas*. In current-day practice, orthodox Hindus adhere to the *Sanskrit Vedas*. The Vedic interpretation of human suffering is important in its outlook because it does not view suffering as a problem. It is merely a state of living in a world composed of matter. The way to avoid suffering is to purify the soul and return to the gods. Why should a condition that is a natural state of affairs surprise or upset someone? Although there does not appear to be a call to ease the suffering of others, this vision of suffering may again offer a practical course of action. Natural disasters are neither acts of divine vengeance nor reward, but rather the workings of the universe.

Unlike many major religious or devotional philosophies, Hinduism does not lay claim to a single founder. It is a collection of intellectual and philosophical ideas. Some scholars believe that it is the oldest religion in the world. Western readers would associate the faith with the *Sanskrit Vedas*, the *Upanishads*, and *Bhagavad Gita*. The name *Hindu* began as a geographical term used by the Persians to indicate the peoples of the Indus River Valley.

To adherents of Hinduism, it is a traditional way of life, the keeping of a law or eternal way. According to Prothero, the faith is the "way of devotion."[9] Hinduism, according to its followers, is not a faith. They see it as the union of reason and intuition. Perhaps, like the ancient tribes of Africa, it is less a faith and more a way of life.

Essential to understanding the Hindu vision of suffering and evil is an understanding of the term *karma*. Originally, the term meant "action" and later grew to include the effect of actions. Karma is not exclusive to Hindu belief. It is also part of Buddhism and Jainism. It is a description of the fundamental law of cause and effect. In the Hindu tradition, how a person leads their life becomes the metric which informs what kind of life the person will experience in the next cycle.

In this case, an individual's suffering is a direct result of the good or bad deeds or thoughts they accumulated in a past lifetime. Those who refuse to mold their lives in

---

9. Prothero, *God Is Not One*, 131.

a devotional and moral manner will suffer rebirth as a lower life form or suffer great pain in the next life. For the Hindu, as long as the cycle continues, there is no escape from suffering.

Hindus, as do Buddhists, see desire as the root of suffering. The senses lead a person astray and cause inappropriate desire. The end of suffering is learning the discipline to control the senses and desires and avoid the effects of surrounding events. A Hindu acknowledges that one reaps suffering in accordance with previous actions. The attitude is not one of fatalism or resignation, but of acceptance that, if one strives to do good, performs selfless acts, and devotes oneself to the gods, there is a chance to improve one's circumstances in the next life.

Christian and Jewish commentators reflected on a similar philosophy. Duran, writing in the twelfth to thirteenth century, alluded to the idea of karma and referenced the Jewish philosopher Nahmanides (1194–1270) as his source.[10] He considers the idea that since Job was innocent, the only reason he could be suffering is in restitution for sins committed in a past life. Origen and his followers, Didymus the Blind among them, believed in the preexistence of the soul and that the soul only resided in a physical body as a punishment for some wrongdoing.[11]

The doctrines of the oldest and most established religions sought answers for many of the questions Job asks, even if the conclusions contained nuances that the Jewish and Christian faiths do not see. Some did not see sin as the all-pervasive problem. They saw the suffering of the world and the individual as an issue that needed to be thought through and resolved in some way that gave hope: be it in a future world, a future life, or the simple cessation of pain and woe in this current life. Hinduism presents a thought-provoking test of morality. Can a life be lived as if each thought, each action, will indeed result in payback?

Taoism

Scholars are not entirely certain that Laozi, the attributed founder of Tao, is a historical figure. Traditionally, he is said to have authored the *Tao Te Ching*, a work compiled sometime in the late fourth century BCE. Taoism is rooted in some of the folk religions of China. The faith teaches that there is a struggle between two kinds of spirits: those that wish to rise to the heavens and those that wish to be rooted in the earth. Throughout Chinese history, Taoism was popular only when the emperor was supportive.

To Taoists, wandering the earth and becoming one with nature is the highest form of achievement. Taoists do not believe in a hereafter of any kind, on this earth or any other. Therefore, one must do the best one can with what this life offers. That

---

10. See chapter 9.
11. See chapter 8.

means, in part, separating oneself from desires and seeking simplicity and peace. It means accepting things as they are and living within that reality.

Since Taoism is a tapestry of ancient and more recent religious traditions, beliefs of individuals or sects can be contradictory. Taoists in general, however, see nature itself as amoral and unconcerned about people. Sickness, aging, and death are all part of a natural cycle, and each occurs in all of nature. Such events do not portend punishment for any sins or moral error, and they are not manifestations of evil. On Patheos.com, nature is viewed as not sentimental, nor does it treat people as a sacrifice.[12] The best way to avoid suffering is to find the best way to live in harmony with nature. Taoism is what Prothero calls the "way of flourishing."[13]

There are four primary forms of Tao, and the faith has influenced both Buddhism and Confucianism. All Taoists see Tao as the accord of the universe and ever-present if one is prepared to seek it. Some Taoists see Tao as something to be revered and worshiped. For others, it is a philosophical concept, not a deity or mystical form. In all cases, if there is a deviation from the natural order, people and societies become disordered and harmful to a peaceful existence. When people and rulers live in harmony with nature, they find peace and prosperity. Suffering, then, is caused when a person does not live in harmony with the world.

Tao also teaches that not all suffering is avoidable. Sickness, aging, and death are part of the cycle of life which harmony does not resolve; in fact, such things are part of a harmonious nature. The choice then becomes to accept one's fate or suffer. Suffering is also that which occurs because of a person's actions. In this case, one must acknowledge and accept the situation and resign oneself to the consequences. For a Taoist, the best one can do is not focus on the suffering. One strives to bring life into harmony with nature and nourish the mind, body, and soul with its natural balance.

The parable of the Chinese farmer and his son illustrates the concept of the Tao. There are many versions;[14] however, they all follow a similar pattern.

> Once there was a Chinese farmer who farmed with his young son. One day their plow horse died. All the neighbors came and said to the farmer, "Oh, that is so bad, how unlucky you are."
>
> The farmer replied, "Maybe."
>
> The farmer gave his life savings to the son, who went to town to buy a new plow horse. He came back with the world's most beautiful plow horse. All the neighbors came and said, "Oh, what a beautiful horse, that was a real steal. You are so lucky."
>
> "Maybe," the farmer replied.
>
> A few days later, the son left the gate open by accident, and the beautiful plow horse ran off. The neighbors came again. "Oh, how horrible, your entire

---

12. See "Taoism."
13. Prothero, *God is Not One*, 279.
14. See, for instance, Archer, "Maybe so, Maybe not."

Part III—A Different Point of View

life savings are gone and now your horse. How will you even farm? That is so unlucky."

"Maybe," replied the farmer.

The next day the son went out to look for the horse, but instead came across a herd of six wild horses, caught them, and brought them back. The neighbors came again. "Oh, how wonderful! These are such beautiful horses! You can train one to be a plow horse, the rest you can sell. You are so lucky."

"Maybe," replied the farmer.

A few days later, the son was trying to break one of the wild horses, and the horse threw him, breaking both his legs. The neighbors came again, "Oh, how horrible! Your son has broken both his legs; how will you even farm your crops? You are so unlucky."

The farmer replied, "Maybe."

The next day the Mongolian Hordes invaded China. The Chinese army came to the small village and conscripted all the young men, to take them away for battle and probable death. Except for the Chinese farmer's son because he had two broken legs. Again, all the neighbors came to the farmer and told him how lucky he was to have his son. And the farmer thought about it for a moment, because this did seem pretty lucky.

But in the end, what he said was, "Maybe."

Tao is probably the furthest from Job's teachings. Job talks about life ending the same way for the wicked and the just, both in the grave and turning into ashes and dust. He also expects a final day of judgment, a day when his Redeemer will stand upon the earth. Neither the Christian nor the Jewish commentators suggested that seeking harmony with nature would mitigate suffering. There are several that emphasized moderation in all things. Some of the commentators presented in this book were quite adamant about the evil intrinsic in material things and in matter itself.

However, whether this world is the sole and only concern of humanity or, if there is some reward, here or in a future life or world, there is no wisdom in adding to the burden of this life with avoidable suffering. Nor is it worthwhile to dwell without ceasing on that which one cannot avoid. Taoism recognizes two kinds of suffering. There is that, which happens due to the nature of the world, and that which happens because of the actions taken by its inhabitants. Job addresses this difference in the speeches attributed to God. There, Job learns about the nature of the universe, the nature of evil, and perhaps something about balance.

The well-being of humanity depends on the ability to seek a balance with the natural world. For instance, there would be less suffering if people had access to reasonable and healthy diets. Dietary needs are so important to the Jews that large portions of Levitical law address what one should eat and how to prepare it. Christians tend to believe that the dietary restrictions given to the Hebrew nation no longer apply. However, although our lifestyles and environment have changed, the nature of the human body has not changed all that much since the nation of Israel received the law. Paul writes to the Corinthians (chapters 6 and 7) and admonishes them to purge their bodies of unclean things because they are temples of a living God. If one makes no effort to maintain physical health, what room is there to complain about the consequences?

Job's suffering included that of disease and the pain of a grieving spirit. There is nothing in the book of Job that indicates that the banquets of his children were somehow inappropriate or damaging to the soul or the body. However, survival is better assured if the individual and the culture have made the effort to seek harmony with the natural world through good health and sensible habits. Finding a sense of harmony with the universe, or with a sovereign creator, rests on the need to seek wisdom in caring for the individual and the world that nurtures the life that sustains one.

Defining the Eastern Perspective

With this brief introduction to the world of Far Eastern religions, it becomes clear that the questions of suffering and evil are universal in many ways. How these faiths chose to deal with the issues vary, and yet there is a common theme. Part of that theme is that suffering is a part of the cycle of life. It is an intrinsic part of how the world and the universe operate. Creatures get sick (or weak), creatures age, and creatures die. To resist this course is to cause pain when it is unnecessary and futile.

These faiths and philosophies also teach their followers to seek honestly those events that are a direct result of personal actions and to accept the suffering incurred as a direct result of those choices. Something can still be learned even in the case of suffering due to the actions of others. Again, it is futile to wallow in pain and suffering that is caused by actions. The best course is to find a way through the difficulty and to try to improve choices in the future. Finally, nature in all its fury causes devastation and agony. These events can test the right of rulers to rule and test the individual's ability to respond morally and helpfully.

Many ancient faith traditions have common threads, even if the conclusions may be different. Before the time of Abraham, Moses, Job, and the founders of Far Eastern faiths, the civilizations of Mesopotamia and Egypt were developing the seeds of Judeo-Christian and Islamic thought. Through trade routes and battles for supremacy, the culture of the ancient Near East laid the groundwork for the monotheistic faiths which began to reach fruition in the faith of Abraham.

Chapter 13

Suffering in the Ancient Near East

SCRIPTURE WAS NOT WRITTEN in a vacuum. Imagery used in Scripture was formed based on the times and events experienced by the authors or on traditions and legends from oral and written records. A reference such as the "ships of Tarsus" creates an image of a maritime empire, the type of merchandise traded, and some mental image of the places visited. There are similar metaphors in modern usage. German engineering should be precise, and French cuisine sumptuous. Mariachi bands bring visions of Mexico, and bullfights images of Spain. There is an unspoken lexicon of symbols, and cultural arrays, that are a part of an individual's experience. Where we live, the language we speak, the culture in which we are nurtured all contribute to our interpretation of the world.

For this reason, exploring the cultural context of the peoples of the Levant becomes crucial. Cultures described in Scripture arise from the influence and fluctuations of religious and political powers from the Indus River to the eastern Mediterranean. This region spans from the northern expanses of Central Asia to the southern parts of Arabia and on into Egypt. Israel and Judah formed, grew, and fell in the context of real history. The leaders, prophets, and historians were in communication with peoples of other nations. During their exile in Babylon, the culture, language, and rituals influenced the people of Judea and their shared heritage. Each experience added to a rich fabric of lore and imagery. Here are some of the factors contributing to that tapestry.

Mesopotamia

Babylon, Akkad, Ur, Chaldea, and Assyria were ancient kingdoms that rose and fell in the mists of time. These city-states of the Mesopotamian valley became empires that contributed much to human knowledge. Early forms of medicine, mathematics, economics, literature, and law are rooted in this valley. The Mesopotamian valley is claimed as the birthplace of Abraham, and its culture is seen as an influence for many Hebrew legends and literature.

Scripture is born from a rich heritage of human experience in the quest to find and define God. Inspired? Most certainly. However, if a body of literature, or a sacred text, is to have a lasting impact, it must resonate with generations far into the future. Finding the same themes in other literature, legend, and poetry can show something of the author's intent by seeing what the author preserved and what was left unsaid. A mere similarity between two texts does not imply that one drew from the other, especially if the themes are universal in their appeal or need for understanding. However, by contrasting texts with shared themes, it is possible to understand a bit more of what each author saw as an answer—or a lack of one.

The Babylonian version of a narrative about undeserved suffering is entitled *A Poem of the Righteous Sufferer* (*Ludlul Bel Nemeqi*).[1] The Ancient History Encyclopedia site provides a brief history of the work and its translation.[2] The poem begins with several lines describing the unfathomable power and boundless compassion of Marduk. It extols his great wisdom and relates that even the other gods cannot comprehend his purpose. This god, above all gods, throws his servant out in the street and leaves him to wander. He becomes the laughingstock of the country and subject to the taunts of his former slaves.

His agony persists for more than a year. Those that are against him prosper; those that wish to protect him suffer. The confused and battered servant enumerates all the ways he has served the gods, and yet he suffers greatly. He falls ill and lingers near death. The illness brings on a tremendous headache; he cannot speak, eat, or drink. Neither the diviner nor the exorcist can help him or determine how long he must suffer. Near death, he begins to dream.

In his first dream, a handsome young man dressed in a splendid robe appears and announces that the Lady has sent him. The sufferer tries to tell those hear him about the vision but cannot speak.

Again he dreams and sees a person who would have been a sage, a resident of Nippur. The sage pours water over the victim and massages his body, reciting an incantation.

A third dream comes to him in which he sees a remarkable young woman with the appearance of a goddess. She sits down beside him and comforts him, telling him not to be afraid, then she orders his deliverance.

One last dream comes to him of Ur-Nintinugga, a Babylonian. He is an exorcist, a young man with a beard and wearing a crown. He proclaims that Marduk has sent him. Shubshi-meshre-Shakkan sees a healing serpent slither by and feels the chains of his suffering fall away.

1. See "Poem of the Righteous Sufferer," http://www.gatewaystobabylon.com/myths/texts/life/righteousufferer.htm.
2. See Mark, "Ludlul bel Nemeqi."

Part III—A Different Point of View

The rest of the poem (and fragments) speak to the wonders of Marduk and his deliverance. The Sufferer offers thanks to Marduk for his restoration. The poem closes by acknowledging that the Sufferer never loses faith.

There is some academic literature that discounts the influence of the piece on the author of Job. Some of the differences cited to support this view are superficial such as differences in style. One piece is a poem while one a drama. The style does not preclude influence from either direction and to be precise, the biblical book is poetic drama.

Another difference is that, in the Babylonian narrative, the diviner and the exorcist deliver the sufferer, while in Job, it is God. However, both Job and Shubshi look to their deity as the source of their suffering and the source of their deliverance, whatever instrument is used to effect deliverance. There is also an interesting correlation between Elihu's angels sent to warn and help and those sent to help Shubshi back to health.

Both men suffer the loss of wealth and health, albeit in a different order. Both become social outcasts, and both reach the limit of their endurance. The Babylonian appears to have suffered for over a year. The book of Job is not precise on how long Job's suffering lasted, although Islamic sources mention seven years. Scripture notes that Job's visitors were at his side for at least seven days.

There is a difference in the way the two men view their deities. One sees his god as a leader among gods, the other as the only God. However, they both view these deities as the sources of that which is good and that which is evil. *A Poem of the Righteous Sufferer* indicates that until it was time for the Sufferer to be relieved, the diviner and the exorcist were powerless. Such was also the case with Satan and his ability to deliver the assault on Job. One crucial difference here is that Job demands justice, while the Babylonian sufferer merely submits while seeking understanding.

A Poem of the Righteous Sufferer was composed around 1700 BCE. Its preservation and presence in ancient literature is an example of the ubiquity of the need to understand underserved suffering. Examples of grief and loss abound in every age—and in every age, humanity seeks answers. In some cultures, the answer is to surrender to the powers that rule the earth. In others, seeking the mysteries of the universe to solve the problem of suffering was taboo, except among the priesthood. There is a pervasive belief that knowing God is beyond the capacity of humanity, even though we have devoted oceans of ink to do precisely that.

The author of Job is one of those who persists in the quest to understand God and his creation. In his book, God does more than deliver his suffering servant—he responds. In Job, the author of the text begins to shed light on the question of humanity's place in the universe. That is, of course, the point of this current book. What does Job teach? While philosophers and theologians searched for answers to the eternal questions of suffering, humanity was hard at work seeking answers to other universal mysteries. For thousands of years, scholars sought answers with rudimentary knowledge. Perhaps now the tools are becoming available that will help unlock the riddle of a man from Uz.

Egyptians and the Absence of Suffering

Egypt is an ever-present cultural giant in the history of the Near East with a stable and well-advanced civilization. The nation's influence is clear in the records of the Mesopotamian Valley and Canaan, as well as the empires that rise and fall throughout history.

The Egyptians did not focus on undeserved suffering. Even with the cultural, economic, and military interaction of the peoples living in the ancient Near East, Egypt seems to stand alone in ignoring this question beyond a practical focus on human behavior. Much of the information shared here is from a paper written by Daniel P. Bricker.[3] He begins by providing the basic requirements needed for a culture or a faith to develop a theodicy: a question of suffering and if it is underserved.

1. A clear standard of right and wrong.
2. Sufficient self-worth, a feeling of value.
3. If there are multiple gods, there must be a hierarchy of some sort, some order that prevents competition and jealousy.
4. Some concept of judgment in an afterlife based on actions taken while alive.[4]

These conditions should be self-evident. If there is no standard of right and wrong, then there is nothing against which to judge. There also must be a measure of what suffering is and what judgment is. If a sole deity is not responsible, there is no injustice or justice to prove.

The Egyptians did not codify their beliefs into a doctrine. There is no cultural heritage embodying what the people believed. For the most part, the aristocracy followed the rituals required by the courts of the gods. The Egyptians worshiped the pharaoh as a descendant of deity, and his word was undisputed. The pharaoh also held the office of high priest. There were many votive chapels frequented by the general population, and the common folk attended the state festivals. However, the gods and their duties or the lack thereof were not a daily concern for the Egyptian on the street.

The Egyptian concept of right or righteousness is called *ma'at*. Given the context within the writings, the word means something like truth, harmony, and justice. It is the right way to conduct oneself, and such deeds survive this current life. The goddess Ma'at represented the core idea of integrity.

The gods of Egypt lived, died, and were reborn regularly. Because the gods were so involved in life and death, the Egyptians saw this cycle as part of mortal life as well.

3. Bricker, "Innocent Suffering in Mesopotamia."
3. Bricker, "Innocent Suffering in Mesopotamia," 212–13.

Part III—A Different Point of View

The aristocracy paid dearly for the tombs and processes that would ease their entry into the afterlife. Not until after the Old Kingdom did the privilege of mummification extend beyond the elite. At that point, those with less prestigious families began to seek the promise of eternal life.

Egyptian medicine was, in many ways, more practical and less rooted in magic and superstition than that of other cultures of the time. Ancient texts show a level of understanding regarding the human anatomy that was rare. Their philosophy of being responsible for the fate that befell them may have led them to investigate the causes of disease and injury with a more practical eye. The focus on the meticulous preservation of various body parts provided a wealth of information on which to base medical research.

Egyptians rarely blamed their gods for suffering, whether deserved or not. Evil, to them, was disorder. If the gods were all about creating order, how could they be responsible for suffering? From a Middle Kingdom text attributed to a creator god:

> I made every man like his fellow.
> I did not ordain that they do wrong.
> It was their desires that damaged what I had said.[5]

Egyptian gods are created beings, not immortal, and certainly not omnipotent. Evil resides in the human heart, and there the blame must rest. Some texts attribute the creation of man to the tears of the creator god, making humanity a race destined to suffer from the start. For the Egyptian, it was unthinkable to blame the gods for the difficulties experienced in life.

In extant Egyptian texts, suffering is a direct result of violating *ma'at*. An interesting piece entitled *Dispute of a Man with His Ba* reveals something of the thinking.

The tale is about a man who is so miserable he wishes for death. His *ba* (an Egyptian representation of the life force of an individual, something more than a soul) tells him that it will abandon him if he persists in these thoughts, and he will have no peace in the afterlife. He will remain in the misery and evil of the present world. To avoid this, he takes steps to preserve his chances for peace in the future world with his *ba* intact. Making the choice to do so and taking the necessary corrective action is his decision. If unresolved injustices remain after death, then one seeks resolution in the afterlife.

The Egyptians had a firm code of right and wrong which was deeply rooted in the concept of order. Since society and cultures could not adhere to all the requirements of *ma'at* all the time, some disorder in life would occur. One does need to make sure that in the process of passing to the afterlife, all the right-doing is recorded and acknowledged. The Egyptians meet the first criteria, which is a clear standard of right and wrong.

---

5. Shafer, *Religion in Ancient Egypt*, 163.

They also had a strong perception of self-worth. Egyptians believed the gods created them and that their ruler was a divine being. They envisioned their kingdom as the center of the universe. Egyptian monuments and inscriptions indicate a sense of superiority. Consequently, self-worth is evident in their national and personal pride.

For all the multitude of gods and goddesses, these beings are rarely in dispute, and if there are disputes among them, they do not involve humanity. There are no divine wars or attacks on humanity for honoring the wrong god. Egyptians did jealously guard their right to worship the deity of their choice, and the allegiances of the royal house had a direct impact on the wealth of the priesthood attached to each of the many gods. Part of the reason for the political upheaval at the time of Akhenaten was that the favor he granted to Aten removed much of the support which had been received by the priests of Amun. To be clear, Akhenaten did not worship a god, such as that of Israel. He elevated the sun god Ra, or Aten, to a status above any other part of creation and attempted to eliminate or greatly reduce the worship of other gods in the Egyptian pantheon. His sovereign was the sun disk of Aten.

Death, however, held its power, and Egyptians invested much to ensure a peaceful afterlife with an opportunity to settle all accounts. Since all things that caused suffering were due to some form of disorder, one was responsible for setting things in order. If not accomplished in life, there was always the time of judgment in the afterlife. This final judgment of an Egyptian's life was the weighing of one's heart against the feather of the goddess Ma'at. Her symbolic feather was the scale of the final test that revealed the truth of the petitioner's life.

The Egyptian approach provides an interesting perspective from a people whose empire survived millennia. Their lives were fully dependent on the rising and falling of the Nile and the provisions of the desert oases. In their view, the gods never brought chaos or suffering into the lives of the people, and it was the individual's duty to avoid it. Suffering was not undeserved: it was a part of life and evidence of the individual's struggle to seek order. The Egyptian of the ancient Middle East would have been befuddled with the concept of theodicy and its implications.

From the heritage of the Mesopotamian valley, and the trade centers crisscrossing the ancient world to and from Egypt, a civilization arose based on trade, agriculture, and the service of a plethora of gods and goddesses. Out of this milieu, a man arose who, based on the vision revealed to him, changed the world. Abram chose to worship a God with no image, a God who had no equal. A good portion of this book analyzes the writings of the Jewish and Christian heirs to Abram's revelation. Sometime in the sixth century CE, the Arabian Peninsula saw the rise of a uniquely Arabic form of monotheism—one based on the call to return to the heart of Abram's faith.

Chapter 14

Ayyub—The Prophet of Patience

Religion, it must be understood, is not faith. Religion is the story of faith. It is an institutionalized system of symbols and metaphors (read rituals and myths) that provides a common language with which a community of faith can share their numinous encounter with the Divine Presence. Religion is concerned not with genuine history, but with sacred history, which does not course through time like a river. Rather, sacred history is like a hallowed tree whose roots dig deep into primordial time and whose branches weave in and out of genuine history with little concern for the boundaries of space and time. Indeed, it is precisely at those moments when sacred and genuine history collide that religions are born.[1]

Knowing one's history with any level of accuracy and honesty is a problematic task at best. That task can become herculean when it is necessary to understand something of the historical background of a group that is perceived with derision or fear by populations in the West. Nevertheless, as with other faiths introduced in this book, the foundation and development of the faith requires examination to understand how the followers of Islam view the story of Job. We gain wisdom from their view of a shared Abrahamic heritage. The quest to find a reliable source for information on the founding and growth of the Islamic faith led to a work entitled *No god but God* by Reza Aslan. Aslan is a controversial, bestselling author. This book does not reveal unknown or newly discovered information regarding the history and socioreligious structure of Islam. However, the work is a coherent and cohesive study of Islam that brings light to the thoughts and spiritual perceptions of the Muslim faith that will lead to some understanding of how that faith views suffering.

---

1. Aslan, *No god but God*, xxiii.

Ayyub—The Prophet of Patience

Pre-Islamic Arabia was a culmination of Mesopotamian history that included Jewish, Christian, and Zoroastrian[2] influences. Bedouins, with their caravans, built and maintained the social structure. The merchant centers that faired the best were those that grew based on the availability of water. Also, successful market centers capitalized on a socioreligious culture where the business of trade inextricably combined with religious festivals and holy sites. Although there is evidence that pre-Islamic Arabic society included the worship of a High God known as Allah, this was not necessarily a faith that excluded the existence of other gods. Max Müller[3] called this belief "henotheism."[4] The earliest evidence of henotheism on the Arabian peninsula occurs in the second century BCE in the area now known as Yemen. By the sixth century CE, a preponderance of Arabs observed some form of henotheism. They believed that Allah was the same God as Yahweh, and for many, the worship of Allah was a return to the faith of Abraham, a revered ancestor and prophet. For a sense of the geographical elements of the Arab world, see the maps found in chapters 1, 8, and 10.

Mecca profited the most from this combination of trade and festival. The success of the town was due in part to the existence of the *Ka'ba*. History does not record the origin of the initial shrine. However, by the middle of the sixth century, it was a focal point of pilgrimage and worship. The building contained representations of every god known to the people of the peninsula and included idols representing Abraham, Jesus, and Hubal (a primary Arabic deity). Christianity was not unknown to the Arabs. Whole tribal families converted through missionary efforts of both the Western Orthodox and Byzantine churches. In part due to this influence, a form of monotheism known as *Hanifism* arose, which included aspects of both Judaism and Christianity. The break from orthodox Christianity came when the Western church convened at the Council of Nicaea in 325 CE. At a conference called by Constantine to bring consistency and consensus to the faith, 318 bishops (among other doctrinal tenets) declared Jesus divine. The question of what that means is still widely debated. However, the elevation of Jesus from prophet to "very God" was cause for the Arabic believers to break away from the Western church. The Arabic understanding of God prohibited a concept of Trinity, and they could not accept a being as somehow birthed or created as divine. As Christianity became the religion of Empire, Christian communities drove the dissenting voices against this doctrine underground or silenced them. In Arabia, this fueled a nascent movement to return to the faith of Abraham and the belief in a sovereign creator with no equals.

Understanding the heart of the Muslim faith requires some knowledge of how tribal law functions. There was no codified body of law. Tribes maintained order by

---

2. See chapter 21.

3. Max Müller (1823–1900) was a Sanskrit scholar and philologist. He was a pioneer in comparative philosophy, comparative mythology, and comparative religion.

4. The worship of one god out of several, especially when the observance occurs throughout a family, tribe, or other group.

Part III—A Different Point of View

following the "Law of Retribution." Jesus refers to this ancient law in Matthew 5:38–42 when he speaks to the code of "an eye for an eye." Hammurabi's Code is the first known occurrence of the mandate.[5] Rather than a call to violence, this was a limit on the power to extract retribution. The concept of just and equal reward or retribution was the basis of a tribal ethic: an ethic that saw all members of a tribe as contributing something that granted each a just share of the tribal success. The leaders were "first among equals," who were responsible in part for resolving most issues within the tribe. The tribe with the most power resolved those issues which involved more than one tribe. By the middle to late sixth century, the power of the Quraysh family of Mecca grew to the point that the egalitarian ethic of tribal culture was nearly destroyed. As "keepers of the keys" of the *Ka'ba*, they ruled the city of Mecca, and only those loyal to them could succeed. Muhammad was born into this era of increasing inequalities.

Orphaned at an early age, Muhammed was raised by an uncle. This uncle owned a caravan and trained him as a merchant. From his travels, he became well-versed in Zoroastrianism, Judaism, Christianity, and Hanifism. Even though he served his uncle well, he could not rise in status enough to win the hand of his uncle's daughter. As a member of a branch more closely related to the ruling family, she was above his station.

He eventually attracted the attention of a rich widow named Khadija. Somewhat of an anomaly in a society that saw women as chattel, Khadija managed her wealth and hired whom she pleased. She employed the services of Muhammad to help her with the management of her holdings and to guide her caravans. She eventually married him and became his closest confidant and supporter during the early years of his prophetic career. His marriage raised him in social status in Mecca, yet he found his success troubling when he compared himself to those less fortunate. He was faithful to the support of the poor and afflicted and performed the rituals of the *Ka'ba*, yet he remained deeply troubled by the inequities that he observed. During the first fifteen years of his marriage, he often retreated to Mt. Hira for meditation. During a retreat to the mount in 610 CE, he has a vision that causes him great physical stress. Instructed from the divine to recite a message, he says:

> Recite in the name of your Lord who created,
> Created humanity from a clot of blood.
> Recite, for your Lord is the Most Generous One
> Who has taught by the pen;
> Taught humanity that which it did not know (Surah Al-Alaq 96:1–5)[6]

The vision did little to assuage his troubled mind, and it was some time before he received his second recitation.

---

5. A Babylonian code of law dated to approximately 1754 BCE.
6. Aslan, *No god but God*, 34.

Ayyub—The Prophet of Patience

To begin to understand the Qur'an in any meaningful way requires an understanding of how Muhammad viewed his mission. He did not believe he was starting a new religion. He believed that the prophets revealed God from the beginning with Adam and continued with all of those that followed him. The prophets are called *nabis* in Arabic. God commissions some *nabis* to hand down sacred texts in the way that he commissioned Moses to write the Torah and David the Psalms; Jesus is considered a *nabi* who inspired the Gospels. These individuals are more than prophets; they are messengers, or *rasul* in Arabic. Muhammad is to become one of these messengers as he continues to receive messages instructing him to recite the Qur'an[7] over the next twenty-three years. He eventually became known as *Rasul Allah*, "the Messenger of God." More precisely, he was to recite what he was given as a message for the Arabs to give a revelation to a people without a scripture. Muhammad was as reluctant as many of God's messengers; he wished to be unknown to the Meccans as a *Kahin*, or a priest of the *Ka'ba*. Muhammad's wife supported him as he struggled with his burden to deliver a message and address the inequities he saw. Without her he might have failed before he had a message with clarity and purpose.

As with the prophets of old, Muhammad's message began with the inequities of the society in which he lived. The message—the second theme informing the bulk of Muhammad's earliest recitations—dealt with the demise of the tribal ethic in Mecca. Muhammad denounces the mistreatment and exploitation of the weak and unprotected. He calls for an end to the usurious practices that enslave the poor. He addresses the rights of the underprivileged and the oppressed and declares it is the duty of the rich and powerful to take care of those less advantaged. "Do not oppress the orphan," the Qur'an commands, "and do not drive away the beggar" (Surah Ad-Duhaa 93:9–10)[8]. Allah delivered this command, not as friendly advice, rather as a warning. To Muhammad, those who were derelict in their duty to the poor, the hungry, and the oppressed would surely suffer the consequences.

By 613, Muhammad was focusing his message into a twofold profession of faith: "There is no god but God, and Muhammad is God's Messenger." The Quraysh, leaders of Meccan society and trade, are not overly bothered with the pronouncement of a monotheistic faith. However, they are not interested in monotheism at the exclusion of all else. Muhammad's message would not only destroy the fiscal strength of Mecca by striking at the root of the *Ka'ba*; he dared to speak based on his authority and not in concert with the *Jinn*[9] or *Kahin*.[10] He identified himself with the prophets that had gone before, the prophets of the Christian and Jewish faiths. He saw himself as returning to the faith of Abraham, and the bulk of Meccans revered Abraham, whatever

---

7. Qur'an translates as "the Recitation."
8. Aslan, *No god but God*, 40.
9. A genie or spirit.
10. An Arabic priest.

their religious affiliation. The Quraysh punished Muhammad and his clan for this outrage with a boycott. Relief only came when related clans defended him.

Just as he was returning to financial health, Muhammad lost both his uncle and his beloved wife, Khadija. Now he was exposed politically, and the Quraysh felt free to order Muhammad's assassination. Muhammad and his followers sought refuge, finally securing safety in Yathrib. The devout quietly slipped out of the city over several months, making the risky journey through the desert to the new community nearly three hundred miles away. By the time the Quraysh sent the assassins against him, only Muhammad and two close followers remained. They barely escaped, leaving the Quraysh so furious they posted a bounty of one hundred she-camels for his capture.

Muhammad arrived in Yathrib in 622. He cleared the ground granted by the community for use by himself and his followers and built the house that would become his home and the first mosque. On the Islamic calendar, this is year one. Yathrib becomes "the City of the Prophet," or Medina. In 630, after many bloody battles with the Meccans and intrigue within the Yathrib community, Muhammad triumphed and returned to Mecca to receive the keys to the *Ka'ba*. He immediately freed the entire population from the imposed trials of the Quraysh and released the slaves. After Muhammad cleansed the shrine of all idols, the building was re-sanctified and became the center of Muslim pilgrimage.

While in Yathrib, Muhammad built a tribal community that was inclusive of anyone who chose to join. Known in Arabic history as the Ummah, it was an ideal society structured on the tribal ethic with a few modifications required by the message revealed to Muhammad. Men and women met side-by-side in the mosque that was his home. Women could inherit and shared other freedoms not available elsewhere in Arabia. The Christians and the Jews were declared "People of the Book" and enjoyed a protected status, although nonbelievers paid a tax.

Women were not required to wear veils until approximately 627 when Muhammad felt it wise to protect his wives from prying eyes. Remember, his home was the mosque and the community center. In general, the growing faith community fiercely defended the rights and safety of all members, ensuring those less fortunate had access to their needs. Even as the faith fractured into Sunni (orthodox), Shiite (Party of Ali, or those who felt Muhammad's family should lead the faith), and Sufi (the mystic side of Islam), the ideal was a culture defined by the Ummah first established by Muhammad. Today, there is contention among the factions within Islam about what the Ummah was and how to return to the purest form possible. Believers often seek the roots of their faith and the circumstances that prevailed at the time, even when such a dream may no longer be possible.

As to the Qur'an itself, Islam believes that it is the very word of God, recited by Muhammad at God's command, and not written in the normal sense of the word. Uthman, one of the earliest Caliphs of the Muslim Ummah, collected the recitations into book form. The word, as given to Muhammad, reveals itself in poetry, which

Arabs view as the highest form of literary communication. The only decorations permitted in mosques are verses from the Qur'an displayed in calligraphy, developed as an independent art form, or geometric shapes. For the devout, the words of the Qur'an hold the same power as the day Muhammad recited them.

Also critical to the current discussion is the Muslim concept of God. For Islam, God IS. *Allahu Akbar* translates as "God is greater"—just greater, not greater than something or someone else. He is neither Thomas Aquinas's "First Cause" nor Aristotle's "Prime Mover." He is the only cause; he is movement itself. For Muslims, the act of equating anything with a sovereign God is an unforgivable sin. One God, one creation. Theodicy is a foreign concept within this view of God. There cannot be a discussion of why there is suffering in a world created by a loving God because all things are one in him. Although Islamic scholars debate the various facets of their faith as much as Jews and Christians, these core beliefs are the foundation of their faith. Muslims refer to God as merciful, and one should not question his justice.

In the Qur'an, Job is a prophet as well as a man of wisdom and great patience. Because Islam does not share in the concept of original sin, the focus of the faith is not salvation or redemption. Rather, the goal is surrender or submission to the will of God. With this perspective, how one views suffering changes.

Prothero[11] quotes the Sufi mystic Rumi as teaching that the idol of one's self is the mother of all of our idols. The Qur'an admonishes the faithful that the path to Paradise requires both faith and works. It says, "Say not, 'You have believed,' but rather say, 'We have submitted'" (Surah Al-Hujurat 49:14).[12]

The Five Pillars, usually visualized as four corner posts encircling a central support, provide more insight into Islam. The central support is the one most nonbelievers are familiar with: "I testify that there is no god but God, and Muhammad is the Messenger of God," to which Shi'a Muslims would add, "And Ali is the Master of the Believers." The four corner posts are prayer, charity, fasting, and a pilgrimage to Mecca. Muslims do not tithe as a Christian would understand tithing. They must give 2 ½ percent of their assets (excluding personal belongings such as home, clothes, and such) to the poor. Additional gifts are required to support the mosque, special interests, and the community in general. There are exemptions for subsistence levels; however, each believer must give to the needy as part of their surrender to the will of God.

In his book *Deconstructing Theodicy*, David B. Burrell explores the work of Anthony H. Johns.[13] Johns has written several papers comparing the treatment of known

---

11. Prothero, *God Is Not One*, 10.
12. Prothero, *God Is Not One*, 12.
13. A. H. Johns, PhD, is the author of papers comparing Jewish, Christian, and Muslim literature. He held the chair for Asian Studies at Australian National University from 1963–1993 and taught Islamic History and Institutions.

Part III—A Different Point of View

figures in the literature of Judaism, Christianity, and Islam. The Qur'an only briefly mentions the story of Job (Ayyub) through vignettes.

Abrahamic faiths often use symbolism and parables to illustrate core ideas. Interpreters use allegory to explain what they see as the critical idea within a passage by comparing experience known to the student with the concept not yet known. Imagery is also a way to reach an individual who is illiterate or does not have access to the source material. Islam avoids artistic representations of scriptures. For this reason, the Qur'an relies on the imagery created by the poetry of the text. As noted above, to the Arabian, poetry is the highest form of communication. Many ancient cultures revered poetry in part because of the discipline required to convey meaningful concepts within the strict control of structured poetic expression. For the Arab, the words recited by Muhammad were not only the very word of God; the nature of their form gave them power.

Two pericopes[14] mention Job, and he is included twice within lists of acknowledged prophets. The Qur'an does not replace existing scripture,[15] rather, it delivers a new revelation meant for the Arabic peoples. Consequently, there was no need to retell the history of those known from Jewish or Christian Scriptures. Allah instructed Muhammad to recite only that which was critical to a Muslim faith, while the faith of Abraham remained as the foundation. The Qur'an cites many shared traditions, which may have been preserved in a slightly different flavor as passed down through the heritage of the children of Ishmael and Esau. The story of Job imparts the lesson that God cares for his creatures and that he provides prophets to warn and instruct.

The first mention found in Surah Sad 38:41–44 records the cry of Job that Satan has touched him with hardship and pain. God tells him to scuff the earth, and a spring will come forth to grant him a cool bath and something to drink. God restores Job and tells him to take a sprig with leaves to strike in order not to break an oath. The passage ends with the pronouncement that Job is a patient and an excellent servant and one who repeatedly turns to God.[16]

This brief account poses questions that do not have immediately apparent answers. What can be determined in that Job is not a prophet that brings a message, rather his life becomes the message. He asks for help, which he receives. God tells him to consummate a yet-to-be-revealed oath, and Job receives praise for his compliance. There is no challenge to the heavens and no antagonistic visitors. The message is not clear about what Job's trials were nor why they occurred.

Muslims believe that the Qur'an is the very word of God, who commanded Muhammad to recite it as given. Finding the backstory to the Arabic version of Job's trials

---

14. An extract from a work, more commonly used in scriptural references.

15. Muhammad believed that there was an all-encompassing holy book that was only partially revealed through Jewish and Christian Scripture. The Qur'an was the message to be revealed to the Arabians.

16. Burrell, *Deconstructing Theodicy*, 55.

requires a search through commentary and compilations from later years. Al-Imam ibn Kathir provides some interesting details.[17] The version, as told by Imam Imaduddin Abul-Fida Ismail ibn Kathir, is very similar to the tale familiar to Judeo-Christian heritage with a few exceptions. One is the encounter between Job and his wife. He has suffered for seven years before his wife comes to him (after Iblis [Satan] whispered in her ear) and begs him to ask for mercy. For what he perceives as lack of faith, Job tells her that if he is restored, he will punish her with one hundred strokes. He refuses to eat or drink anything from her hand.

Now, the brief mentions of Job found in the Qur'an come together. The sprig of leaves provided by God is a way for Job to strike lightly against his deceived wife while still fulfilling his oath. Two balanced exchanges complete the elements essential for a Muslim. First, Job is destressed; God tells him to scuff his foot to bring forth water so he might be restored. Second, there is the unstated presence of an oath given; God tells Job to fulfill with oath with kindness.

In addition to brief notes about the lessons of Job, two separate rosters describing the prophets include his name. The prophets are grouped according to the type of message delivered. His name is among the *nabi* as opposed to the message-bearing prophets (*rasul*). Job is the message. His message is about patience and the belief that God is merciful even when circumstances appear otherwise. In the Islamic tradition, Job makes no demands of God and is guilty of nothing. There is no basis for an argument about theodicy, providence, or how or why suffering occurs.

Islamic Theologians and Philosophers

In Arabic, the word *Islam* means something akin to surrender or submission. However, the root, *salam*, also gives it a meaning of peace and safety. The deeper sense of seeking this peace is the act of surrender to God's will. Surah al-Hujurat 49:14 translates roughly as "It was far better to be able to declare you have surrendered than that you believed."[18] In the act of surrendering to God's will, there is little room to doubt the mercy of God. As in other faiths, this passage has not precluded centuries of vigorous debate on the nature of God and his creation.

In chapters 9 and 10 of this book, there are brief descriptions of two Islamic schools of theology, both of which influenced the Jewish philosophers of medieval times. The effects of Islam during the culturally advanced and politically stable periods of European history run deep. Muhammad taught that Christians and Jews were "People of the Book," *dhimmi* (protected persons). Within the Muslim Empire, followers of these faiths paid a tax and were free to pursue their faith—*if* they did not proselytize. For Muslims, an infidel (*kafir*, the ungrateful ones) was a person who denied the existence of God. Jews and Christians, of course, did not. As the empire

17. See ibn Kathir, *Stories of the Prophets*.
18. For an English translation of the Qur'an and some annotation see quran.com.

Part III—A Different Point of View

spread into Europe, Arabs took control of the centers of learning. They supported education, literacy, and the translation of ancient texts.[19]

Because of this great thirst for knowledge, such places as the courts of the Khazars in Turkey and the Caliphate of Córdoba in Spain provided the intellectual freedom and the resources to explore philosophy, theology, and the sciences in earnest. The Caliphate of Córdoba reached its peak during the last years of the tenth century and early eleventh century, and it was foremost in providing asylum to Jews and Christians considered heretical by the papacy. With a population that had better access to education, learning, and religious freedom, the hold of the Catholic Church weakened. Living within the Caliphate provided some protection from the growing trend to enforce orthodoxy. Understanding how Islam developed throughout this period provides the background to the philosophy and theology of the Christian and Jewish thinkers of the time.

The Mu'tazilah school of theology believes that it is possible to determine all matters of faith by reason.[20] In some ways, this approach resembles the Aristotelian viewpoint. The adherents to this philosophy lived mostly in the cities of Basra and Baghdad, both in modern Iraq. Their most influential era was during the eighth to the tenth centuries. A fundamental tenet of their position was that because God (Allah) was of a perfect and eternal nature, the Qur'an must have been created and not have been coeternal with God. If the Qur'an were eternal, it would contravene the idea of God as singular. As noted earlier, the Qur'an was not initially a written revelation: it is a compilation of the recitations of Muhammad as given to him by God. The Qur'an was the speech of God, but it was not God. The Mu'tazili determined that since the Qur'an was not coeternal with God, the purposes and demands of God were attainable through rational thought. Knowledge, then, comes from reason, and reason helps distinguish right from wrong.

For this Islamic group of thinkers, the problem of evil in the world was due to the free will of individuals to act. God was not ultimately evil. He could not and does not demand evil of any individual, or the whole concept of punishment is rendered nonsensical. They did not deny that suffering goes beyond the simple cause-and-effect relationship of doing the wrong thing. In such cases, they looked to a Christian teaching which states that God does not test his people beyond their capacity to handle temptations or trials.[21] There may be acts which God permits that serve a greater good or prevent a greater evil. Whatever the outcome, these Muslims believe that, ultimately, a coherent and rational choice will lead to accountability in the present life and beyond.

The Jewish philosophers saw this interpretation in the words of Bildad. Although Bildad may begin with the position that the pure and upright can plead with the

---

19. See Bendiner, *Rise and Fall of Paradise*.
20. Valiuddin, "Mu'tazalism."
21. 1 Cor 10:13.

Almighty for relief, he shortly moves on to a position that Job must have committed some infraction, or he would not be suffering as he is (Job 18). In Job 25, Bildad declares that no one can be righteous before God. Consequently, it is Job who is a far better example of one who believes that if a person looks upon the world with some rational sense of making the best choices possible and follows those choices faithfully, such a person should be able to stand in the face of universal justice and declare innocence with integrity.

As with the Christian and Jewish philosophers, some Arabic philosophers see reason as a tool of humanity and not of God. The Ash'arites[22] held that reason must be subordinate to revelation. To them, the content of the Qur'an was coeternal with God. Similar to the Christian fathers, the Ash'arites saw the nature and attributes of God as simply beyond what any individual could reason or understand. They believed that humanity possesses free will or freedom of intention while lacking the ability to create. Creation is the province of God and only God. The Ash'arites taught that moral truths, interpretation of scripture, and the correct application of values derive from revelation and were only available through the authority of religious scholars, hopefully through some form of consensus.

As with many divisions of who believed what, both doctrinal camps borrowed and followed some tenets of their opposition. Neither was or is completely rational or traditional. Maimonides looked to Job's friend Zophar as a representative of the Ash'arite philosophy since he was the champion of the unknown and unknowable God of the universe. Zophar, as were his compatriots, was shocked and incensed that Job should dare to question his Creator or the fate that he suffered. Within the confines of a theology which teaches that above all the believer must surrender to the will of God, there is little room for questions or challenges when it comes to what befalls the believer. Such a believer must trust those with an insight to the divine and who, through revelation, can guide the faithful to answers.

Islam, the Way of Surrender

Interpretations of the life of Job within Islamic schools of thought agree with some of the ideas put forth by Jewish and Christian philosophers and theologians. The church fathers believed the material goods of this world were of no account and, therefore, were not a real loss. Some of the Jewish philosophers agreed.

In Islam, the creed of surrender arrives at a similar conclusion. Several of the commentators discussed in Part II also looked at God as beyond human comprehension and held that his power was beyond our knowledge. They felt that the effort to understand him was beyond our reason. Some of the Islamic thinkers would agree, others most decidedly not.

---

22. Hye, "Ash'arism."

Part III—A Different Point of View

The main tenet of Islam makes the entire question of human suffering a vehicle of spiritual awareness and growth. The justice of God is assumed. Therefore, if there is suffering, there is cause, whether one understands that cause or not. If the focus of faith is to submit or surrender to whatever life brings, there is no why.

Although total surrender to a sovereign creator can grant peace in times of need or suffering, it seems difficult to believe this would entirely quell the need to *know*. Humanity has the undeniable gift of reason. The most incredible and far-reaching discoveries of science and mathematics throughout recorded history have been made by men and women in search of the face of God. There must a better answer than quiescence, something more than the quiet resignation of a soul crushed by the weight of a universe. God applauds those who turn to him. In Hebrew Scripture, he commanded Job to gird himself and answer—as a man (human).

There is a way in which scripture (from many faiths) leads us to focus on the full implications of deeds and thoughts. The accumulated wisdom of the ages works to show the logical outcome of these deeds and thoughts, both the good and the evil. However foreign it might seem in a study of Scripture, it is important to look at how believers of other faiths respond to adversity. If Job is to fill a universal role, then we must use a universal light to discover the root of his message. A scholar, using the Hebrew language of his time, and the legend of a man who was not an Israelite, wished to deliver a message, perhaps even to challenge us to think. With this accumulated information, it is now time to look at what modern commentators can contribute to the meaning of the book. What new, or old, ideas do they present from a modern perspective in explanation of the riddle of Job? Have recent insights found a way to retell the story effectively and with a message useful to the modern individual?

Part IV—Recasting Job

Chapter 15

Is Job Really about Theodicy?

THIS BOOK BEGAN WITH simple building blocks used in the interpretation of Scripture and in the study of who may have written the book, when, and perhaps where. In previous chapters, an analysis presented the works of representative commentators of the Christian and Jewish faiths within the context of the times in which they lived and taught.

Additionally, the previous section introduced some of the disparate approaches that humanity has developed to address the impact of undeserved suffering. That section closed with the viewpoint of Islam. For the most part, the Muslim faith sees no reason or purpose in challenging God or his ways regarding the suffering of humanity, although Islamic scholars debate such issues as vigorously as any philosopher or theologian. However, modern experience and a more widely informed public has demanded more from the book of Job than the answers of the past. Remember, theodicy is the vindication of divine goodness and providence in the face of apparent evil. Is the book of Job about theodicy or something else entirely different?

In the modern world, suffering, in all its varied forms of distress and agony, is far more palpable. The modernization of communications has brought the starving, war-torn, battered, and disease-ridden world into the front rooms of anyone with access. The plights of rape victims, cancer patients, dementia patients, wounded war veterans, and peoples of developing countries across the globe are now very much within our shared experience. Add to this a better understanding of losses to sickness, accident, deliberate violence, and natural catastrophe, and the rational person begins to wonder, "Why me, why them?" Does Job still have the power to give comfort?

What if Job is not about suffering, good and evil, and what humanity's and God's part in the struggle might be? Is there an answer to the undeserved suffering of the starved child, the battered wife, the raped man, woman, or child, or the wounded veteran?

Part IV—Recasting Job

Deconstructing Theodicy—
Is Job Really about Suffering and Providence?

One source that looks at this question from a philosophical point of view is a work entitled *Deconstructing Theodicy: Why Job Has Nothing to Say to the Puzzle of Suffering*. Some of the literature within this book is challenging in both terminology and thought. However, it does provide a solid introduction to modern philosophical approaches to undeserved suffering.

David Burrell is a professor emeritus at Notre Dame University. His academic background and focus are in philosophy and theology, and he has an impressive publications list. His writings address the academic audience and the serious layperson willing to become familiar with the nomenclature and terminology of the field. In addition to his thoughts, he analyzes the works of Terrence Tilley[1] and Marilyn McCord Adams.[2]

Burrell postulates that the classic theological and philosophical interpretation of Job as a book about testing, or reward and punishment, is unfounded. He points out that Job's visitors push him into an unsolvable conundrum by demanding that he confess to some erroneous deed or thought. However, if Job confesses knowing there is nothing to confess, the commission of a *prima facie* lie damns him. Job cannot admit to doing wrong, or he loses his case. Some of the commentaries reviewed above acknowledged a similar idea. The supposition is that God's displeasure with the arguments put forward by Job's visitors is because they fabricated reasons for Job's suffering to defend God. Job's companions pursue an argument that will force Job to lie. They persist in their belief that Job is refusing to address the wrong he has committed and pressure him to create a lie (even if they do so unknowingly) with a groundless confession.

Job listens to his visitors and then tells them he never asked for their help. Yes, what they say is true. Nevertheless, their explanations do not match his circumstances. He turns his back on them and addresses God. That is whom he wishes to speak with, and no one else will do.

Burrell builds his thesis by pointing out that Job correctly identifies the One who has given the gift of the covenant as the only One who can answer regarding its precepts. He does not consider the thoughts of his fellows as a suitable answer for him in his current situation. Job never denies that what his visitors say has merit. However, he strenuously denies that punishment, reward, and testing have anything to do with his current circumstances.

---

1. Terrence Tilley is the Avery Cardinal Dulles, SJ Professor of Catholic Theology at Fordham University, Rose Hill Campus, New York.

2. Marilyn McCord Adams was the Recurring Visiting Professor at Rutgers School of Arts and Sciences, Department of Philosophy, New Brunswick, New Jersey, and an Episcopal priest.

Is Job Really about Theodicy?

Job declares his companions a hindrance to his cause and tells them that they offer no succor. In his opinion, the only entity in the universe that can answer truthfully regarding his suffering is the One who permitted it to happen. So, if the poem does not address suffering and providence, then what does it teach?

One alternate explanation is that it is about communication between the Creator and the created. In support of this position, Burrell and others rely on Job's constant plea to be heard. Job is heard; and God does respond. In this interpretation, the only meaning that God's response has is to bridge the gulf between Creator and created while honoring the call to "Hear me, Oh Lord." Job receives an answer, and by that answer, we can know that God hears. The poem is not meant to resolve, or even address, the mystery of calamities and sin. To Burrell, it is a plea that God does hear, and he can answer. Burrell determines that the point of the discourse is that within the relationship between the Creator and the created, there is an implication that communication should exist. Either side should have the facility to ask a question and receive a response even if the only response is "I hear."[3]

This argument stems from the presumption that the question of suffering, and avoiding or mitigating it, depends on the Creator's foreknowledge of all events. There are some reasons to assume that a sovereign Creator must be omniscient. For one, it is difficult to believe that anyone can have control over a situation unless one is fully informed. At least that is what a person might perceive. Scripture tends to support this thought with several passages, including, "Indeed, the very hairs of your head are all numbered" (Luke 12:7), or, "Are not two sparrows sold for a penny? Yet not one of them will fall to the ground apart from the will of your Father" (Matt 10:29).

There is a vast body of literature which attempts to reconcile this position with a firm belief in free will. How else can an individual be held accountable unless there is a choice? The Calvinists suggest the answer lies in predestination, which resonates with preliterate societies. To resolve the issue of choice, Calvinists say that the individual cannot know the future. Therefore, an individual remains accountable for the thoughts and deeds of his or her life. Whatever byway or thoroughfare we journey, we are placed in a position of justifying God's actions in the court of humanity. For many new schools of thought, this is absurd on its face.

Burrell and those in his ideological corner define a polar shift in thinking about the book of Job. Instead of a treatise on suffering, they see the book as a discourse on the right of the created to address the Creator—and get a response. That communication is fundamental to these philosophers, whether they believe it has merit in and of itself (God does hear and does answer) or that it leads to an ability to deal realistically with the evil found in the world.

Burrell introduces Terrence Tilley, author of *The Evils of Theodicy*. The basis of the following analysis of Tilley's text derives from Burrell's comments, review material in the *Journal of the American Academy of Religion*, and excerpts from the Burrell's book.

3. Burrell, *Deconstructing Theodicy*, 105.

Part IV—Recasting Job

Tilley defines theodicy as a product of the Enlightenment. He declares it is a failure in resolving the problem of evil. If anything, this philosophy has created the need to justify God. Tilley challenges academia to undermine the whole effort to explain evil in a world created by a benevolent God and questions whether God is even involved in the process. His premise is that the question never was about how a good and loving God could permit evil in his creation. However, once academia became engaged in the question, there appeared a need to seek and prove a reason for the hypothesis.

In part due to this focus by academics, authors of material related to the question of suffering co-opted a wide range of literature to support the theodicy point of view. For Tilley, this was the philosophical equivalent of the adage, "If one has a hammer, everything looks like a nail." Tilley refutes these positions by analyzing several classical and theological works used in support of theodicy. Among them, *Enchiridion* (Augustine, 420 CE), *The Consolation of Philosophy* (Boethius, 523 CE), *Dialogues Concerning Natural Religion* (David Hume, 1776), and *Adam Bede* (George Eliot, 1859). Tilley believes that these works of literature were hijacked and put to a purpose that the clear text of the books and dissertations did not support.

Tilley's book begins with several chapters using *Speech Act Theory* to analyze the book of Job. Speech Act Theory is a way to explain how language accomplishes intended actions and how the person spoken to understands what is said. For instance, think about the number of popular books written to explain the different communication methods and interpretations between men and women. People speak with intent. That is, they understand what they want others to understand. However, once heard, the other person may not come away with the understanding that a speaker intended. One path to certain miscommunication is the "victory for the point of view" problem. Instead of debating an issue to learn, people will debate with the sole goal of claiming victory over the other person's point of view. Neither party learns much, and communication, as defined, does not occur.

The terms used in communication theory are specific to each part of the act of communication. Scholars who view the book of Job using the processes of communication see the book as dealing more with what the author expected the reader to understand and do, not the philosophical discussion of various theological doctrines. Tilley suggests that speech, in this context, may be viewed in part as prayer, preaching, pledging, swearing, or confession. Each style has a different end goal and a different personal investment. When looking at Job, Tilley cautions that the reader should look to Job's focus to determine something of what he hopes to accomplish.

In the second portion of his book, "Remembering Disremembered Texts," Tilley explains how selected texts became misappropriated to the cause of theodicy. What he describes is a method of analysis which uses inductive rather than deductive reasoning. In other words, inductive reasoning starts with an overall premise and goes in search of support. Deductive reasoning looks at the elements and allows the conclusion to develop from the information provided. More simply, "If all you have is a hammer . . ."[4]

Tilley believes that at best, Job is a warning to the reader *not* to seek ultimate answers. Knowing that there is communication between the Creator and the created does not carry a presumption that the created will receive the answer that is sought. Tilley argues that the book of Job is a stumbling block for theodicy and offers no consolation for its readers. In his opinion, if the book supports any doctrine, the voice of Job must be silenced by the reader or God himself. There must be no more seeking of eternal truths, only the assurance that there is someone who knows and is willing to support us in our need.

In addition to Job, Tilley analyzes *Enchiridion* (Augustine, 420 CE), *The Consolation of Philosophy* (Boethius, 523 CE), *Dialogues Concerning Natural Religion* (David Hume, 1776), and *Adam Bede* (George Eliot, 1859). He concludes that if the reader gets lost in a maze of reconciling the presence of evil in a world created by a presumed all-loving God, the reader will lose the original message the author wished to convey. For instance, in George Eliot's novel, the author uses the character of Hetty Sorrel to direct the reader's attention to the power of confession. She focuses on the dialogue that permits the condemned to lose the fear of death without denying death's power, and on how confession and forgiveness incite others to overcome evil. Hetty does not yearn to figure out why there is evil; she concentrates on the actions required to deal with evil.

For Tilley, the point is that Job chose to speak *to* his Creator, not *about* him. Consequently, Job's message rests in the act of seeking answers from the source, as indicated by God's approval of him, not in the blathering of persons purported to justify the actions of the Almighty. (Although that does appear to be a consuming pursuit of various members of humanity). By analyzing the speech patterns of Job, Tilley illustrates that Job begins with laments and curses then moves to a much more assertive position of challenge. Unlike the timid approaches of earlier scholars, Tilley sees Job state a demand for justice and declare a right to speak directly to his Judge and Jury. For Tilley and his colleagues, there are two primary points:

1. There is an intrinsic relationship between Creator and the created.
2. Accordingly, that very relationship demands the ability to communicate.

Whether answers are forthcoming or considered helpful is a different issue. Tilley would silence the questioner and respond that perhaps the answer is available, just not now. If there is an answer, the knowledge of being heard should be enough. However, it seems odd that we should consider communication effective if it does not convey useful information. Without meaning-making, and, importantly, acknowledgment of meaning-making, there is an absence of utility.

4. Tilley, *Evils of Theodicy*, 86.

Part IV—Recasting Job

Tilley concludes that the focus to justify evil in creation is not the point at all. What we should learn is the real benefits of communication in the religious context: prayer, confession, preaching, and the act of communicating with each other and the Creator so that we might find a way to deal with the world as it is.

Burrell then moves to the work of Marilyn McCord Adams, *Horrendous Evils and the Goodness of God*. According to Burrell, she takes the same point of view regarding the right of communication yet uses that process for an entirely different goal. She does not completely throw out theodicy; she works to redefine it.

McCord Adams, who was a priest in the Episcopal Church, focused on philosophy of religion, philosophical theology, and medieval philosophy. Although some of her work is directed primarily to academia, she also addresses the same subjects within the pastoral realm. She makes a genuine effort to apply academic knowledge to the reality of people's lives. Climbing down from the ivory tower is useful for seeing if academic thoughts have verity in the day-to-day struggles of *Homo sapiens*.

In the referenced work, she develops the notion that attempts to justify the coexistence of both evil and a beneficent God are futile. Instead, she feels the focus should be on what good God can make of evil. To her, the function of determining the relationship between God and evil is intrinsic in the experience of the victim. It is the victim's viewpoint that is critical, and all other discussion occurs in a vacuum. How does that translate in the pastoral context?

As a pastor as well as a philosopher, McCord Adams realized that the most common strategies for solving or mitigating truly horrific evils in this world fall far short of success. Given rape, disfigurement, abuse, starvation, murder, and a host of other crimes humanity perpetrates on fellow beings, how can platitudes and homilies reach the heart of an injured individual and give meaning to a now traumatized life? What strategies can one employ to provide solace to those who suffer?

She defines these strategies as such (this author's interpretation follows in italics):

1. One approach is to acknowledge that the coexistence of God (at least one that is all-knowing and all-loving) with the evident evil in a world he purportedly created and watches over is logically impossible. *This issue is discussed in far more detail later. However, defining God and then being concerned that he doesn't fit well within that definition is counter-productive at best.*

2. Another view is to redefine the parameters of the discussion by saying that God is not all-powerful (e.g., limited through the exercise of free will or some other factor). *Some of the earliest writings on Job introduce this argument. However ancient, it does little to assuage suffering experienced on a personal level. The issue is that more often than not, we tend to define God to meet our own end goals and become surprised or feel let down when the expected outcome does not occur.*

3. The third strategy is to search for a reason or reasons why God might permit evil. *My book is full of possible answers that fit this category. These might include*

such thoughts as "This is the best possible world, and evil is somehow necessary to an overall pattern of good." Or, "Allowing free will demands that God allow some actions to reach fruition regardless of the impact on other lives."

To McCord Adams, the process of explaining to a bereaved parent that the loss of their child somehow contributes to the overall freedom of humanity to choose does little more than turn God into a monster. The same result occurs if one tries to explain that a catastrophic flood or a volcano is somehow supposed to help the victims grow in character and understanding. Many agnostics and atheists would agree with her. Her goal is to find a way to show a person suffering from trauma how to integrate their experience of evil into their relationship with God in a manner that makes sense and that allows God to make good out of the evil.

William C. Placher clarifies these ideas in his review of *Horrendous Evils*.[5] In his words:

> She rightly, I think, rejects Kenneth Greenberg's often quoted line that in such matters we should say nothing that it would be inappropriate to say in the presence of the burning children of Auschwitz. Is there anything you can say in the presence of burning children? But after the burning has ended, she notes, survivors have to deal with their experiences, and they may have questions to which a philosopher can say something helpful.[6]

Placher summarizes the strategies listed above by using the arguments of philosophers J. L. Mackie, Nelson Pike, and Alvin Plantinga, who, respectively, have dealt at length with each of the three viewpoints noted. McCord Adams states that arguments framed in moral terms are problematic. Moral terms describe the goodness of God. From a philosophical viewpoint, the evils used in the explanations provided by these philosophers are morally evil acts perpetrated by humans. She believes the purely philosophical interpretation fails the victim. In her words, when horrors occur that wound deeply, the individual may have a reason to doubt whether life can be worth living. She cites such events as rape, dismemberment, child abuse, child pornography, incest, starvation, war, and torture of any nature. These are events that betray trust or loyalty and that crush the individual and strip them of whatever makes them who they are. McCord Adams urges that horrendous evils such as these are "so pernicious" because of their "life-ruining potential, their power *prima facie* to degrade the individual by devouring the possibility of positive personal meaning in one swift gulp."[7] The lesson, then, lies in the impact on a human life and whether that impact is so severe that no good can come of it—for that individual. What does the event mean to the victim, rather than within the scope of society in general or end-time resolutions?

---

5. Placher, "McCord Adams's *Horrendous Evils*," 461.
6. McCord Adams, *Horrendous Evils*, 185, 188.
7. McCord Adams, "God-Who-Does-Nothing," 107–31, 112.

Part IV—Recasting Job

One of the ways that McCord Adams redirects this pain is to use it as a personal identification with the suffering of Christ. If, as a Christian believer, a victim accepts that Jesus did indeed take to himself the suffering of the world on the cross, then the pain suffered right now, at this moment, is part of that pain. Personal suffering, then, is a real and intimate connection with God and his Son. Ignatius of Antioch, as well as many historical martyrs, saw their persecution as an opportunity to suffer with Jesus and to draw closer to him. By adding this nearness to God to a firm belief in a balancing of the books in the afterlife, a Christian finds a far deeper meaning in personal heartache and calamity. McCord Adams also proposes that the perpetrators of horrors will find succor and personal forgiveness in learning that Christ identified and recompensed their acts on the cross. They find redemption in the knowledge that God can and will find a way to convert the horror into a contribution to the redemptive plan.

This approach is problematic in that it distorts the message at the heart of the Christian faith. Christians believe that, at one point in history, God offered the only perfect sacrifice to atone for the many failings of his creation: the life of his perfect Son. According to Christian theology, this was the consummation of the blood sacrifice established in the garden of Eden. Therefore, substitution was no longer required. By accepting the true and only perfect sacrifice, the believer is set free from the obligation of payment for the failings of this life; this is the definition of divine grace.

Primarily due to the teachings of Paul, the nature of suffering took on a new meaning for Christians. Now a believer did not suffer because of sin; rather, a believer suffered to draw nearer to Christ. Any reading of the stories of the martyrs of the first centuries, or *Fox's Martyrs*, shows that those who suffered did not go to their deaths unwillingly. Many went believing they were experiencing only some small part of what their Savior had and considered it an honor. Deep in the throes of a belief that they were unworthy, suffering was to be accepted, even sought out.

This vision has driven many to seek solitude, such as membership in cloisters. The need to pay, in some small way, inspires some to fast or to seek deprivation of some human comfort. In such cases, some seek self-inflicted discomfort or outright suffering to draw nearer to God. There was, and remains, a need to seek some way to pay for a presumed sinful nature, whether any actual sin is committed or not. Job's companions would have been quite pleased.

However, attempts to define God have created a paradox. If Christ paid the price, then why must others? Does suffering in vicarious communion with the ultimate act somehow defile the pure sacrifice? What sort of presumption is it to attempt to identify with a sacrifice said to stir nature itself, through our willing or unwilling suffering?

The problem with McCord Adams's approach is that it reverses the intent of shared suffering. In many hard-won victories for freedom and human rights, the organizers suffered. Anti-slavery, women's rights, civil rights, and labor rights all had leaders who suffered, even died. The energy of the movement that carried it through to fruition was the *shared* suffering of the proponents. The sacrifice of the few encouraged others to press forward to ensure that the sacrifice was not in vain. Deep in the heart of the battle cry "This is a good day to die!" is the implication that the soldiers will do everything in their power not to die, yet go into battle with the knowledge that what they are doing is right and good and worthy of the risk.

For a Christian, the power of the cross set humanity free. The focal point of the sacrifice on the cross is that the most important thing in the world is to love enough to risk loss and to sacrifice safety. However, the goal of that risk is to become all we were created to be: reasoning, compassionate beings who seek solutions to suffering. At the very least, believing that we can make ourselves part of the ultimate sacrifice is presumptive, especially since Christ's sacrifice was perfect and complete in and of itself. If the penalty is paid in full, then what should be shared is a life of service to the people Christ loved.

Placher finds merit in McCord Adams's work; however, he does have some reservations, one being her position regarding the intrinsic evil of humanity. Humans are created finite, and scripturally, this was declared good by God. Being human does not make us evil. Whether we use our finitude to create good or evil is an entirely separate matter. Evil, or sin, changes our natures. If creation acts within its nature, there is no evil. A lion is not evil when it pulls down its prey—this action is within its nature.

Another issue Placher has with McCord Adams's presentation is that she tends to see both the victim and the perpetrator as needing the same mercy. Placher differs. He agrees that when we look on the horrors of the world as Christians, we should pray that God has mercy on them all. However, he still feels there are differences in meeting the needs of those injured versus those who cause those injuries. Placher, like many troubled Christians, views himself as an abuser because he lives in privilege while so many children in the world go hungry. He feels that he is contributing in some way to suffering simply by not being in the place and time where others suffer. Therefore, there must be some difference between the mercy afforded the victim and that afforded the perpetrator. Placher writes that the intent of those who contribute to the suffering guides any such mercy.

These are intriguing thoughts. If we follow this rationale, there is no need to wrestle with who or what each of Job's visitors represents. They are all merely background noise setting the stage for the real point. What, precisely, God says is no longer of great import because the point is that God spoke, and he identified with his creation. There is no conundrum about what God does or does not know about individual lives because that knowledge is less important than the support offered in an hour of need. From a philosophical point of view, this may represent a tidy answer. However, it dismisses vast portions of Job. Focusing on the aspect of communication with the Creator is important, yet we lose something fundamental to the message if we ignore the content of that communication.

Chapter 16

God on Trial

ANOTHER WAY TO APPROACH the story of Job is from the viewpoint of a court challenge. Is the book of Job a court case in which Job, and by extension, humanity, puts God on trial for creating a world where there is unearned, unrelenting suffering? Does Job deserve an answer in the courts of heaven, and does Satan have a valid case in challenging God's judgment for creating a world that permits misery?

Putting God on Trial by Robert Sutherland is the source for the material in this chapter. He holds a Bachelor of Arts in history from the University of Toronto and a Bachelor of Laws degree from Osgoode Hall Law School. He is a practicing attorney in Canada with many successes before the bar. As a jurist, he views the book as the description of a suit against God brought by Job. Sutherland concludes that Job's trial is a test of selfless love. Job, however, must wait until the end of time to receive his answer; otherwise, the test has no validity.

Sutherland sees Job as blameless, and everything that follows must rest on that fact. To ignore this key point is to muddle the entire book. Understanding this connection is one of the reasons that there are still scholars that view the book as one work, not two patched-together writings. Given this premise, Sutherland points out that any interpretation that calls Job's integrity into question is a nonstarter. The same is true of any interpretation that attempts to create a need for Job to grow in character. Job himself agrees with his visitors on all their points except when it comes to his current experience. He does not argue with the belief that sin requires punishment. He also acknowledges that God might test those who love him. However, if God is omniscient, would he not know the heart of the believer without testing?

If Job has committed no infraction of the moral code, then even his challenge is not in error. Nothing in the closing statements from God indicates that Job was wrong to ask, even demand, an answer to his query. Scripture declares that he spoke rightly (42:7).

Based on these parameters, Sutherland sees four items essential in examination of the text: a) Satan's challenge, b) Job's oath of blamelessness, c) God's response, and d) Job's response to God. Sutherland sees the book of Job as representative of Nietzsche's conclusion that if you stare into an abyss long enough, it will stare back at you.[1] Nietzsche's point is that we must be careful when fighting monsters to avoid becoming one. Sutherland feels that more than any other book in the Bible, the story of Job will tell you what kind of person you are by the choices you feel forced to make.[2]

Sutherland bases his analysis of Job on the ancient right of an oath of innocence. In this case, Job swears the oath against God. In the traditions of the ancient Near East, this lawsuit required no formal court. The oath of innocence was sworn to God (or gods) as the sole judge. There was no need to find the defendant or seek a statement, nor were witnesses required. The swearing of the oath provided all the details needed. Job was within his legal and traditional rights to swear out an oath of innocence, even against God, and expect a response. Scripture defines the rights deriving from the oath in 1 Kings (8:31–32), 2 Chronicles (6:22–23), and Deuteronomy (1:17).

The legal codes of Babylonian, Hittite, and Jewish traditions codified this principle. Egyptian mythology uses it in the final judgment as described in the *Book of the Dead*. An oath of innocence establishes a lawsuit in cases where the defendant is not available or, if found, cannot be forced to appear in court to answer charges.

To set the stage, Sutherland casts Job as the new Adam, and Uz as a new Eden. The most important difference between this Adam and the one of Genesis is that Job is a mature human being, fully developed and aware of the moral obligations he has toward his compatriots and God. He is the best *Homo sapiens* has to offer, utterly righteous and blameless.

To continue his commentary, Sutherland introduces the Jewish festival of *Rosh Hashanah*, or Head of the Year. It is the first day of the Ten Days of Awe during which God reviews the actions of each man and woman. Each person then has ten days to repent and receive absolution from God. The tenth day is the Day of Atonement, or *Yom Kippur*.

Sutherland uses this fall festival cycle as the backdrop against which he interprets the book. There are two plaintiffs in this court: Satan and Job. Sutherland supports his analysis by framing the commentary within a ten-day chronology (Days of Awe). He starts with counting three separate days on which Job receives news of his losses (Job 1:13; 2:1; and 2:13), then he adds the seven days and nights during which Job and his visitors are in silent mourning. Satan lays his case at the beginning of the passage, challenging the very existence of creation and God's plan for it. After Job's test, Job lays his case before the court, and he makes his stand. Job is unaware that there is another plaintiff off-stage: the one who has delivered such misery into his life.

---

1. Nietzsche, *Beyond Good and Evil*, 69, aphorism 146.
2. Sutherland, *Putting God on Trial*, 19.

Part IV—Recasting Job

Job's speeches describe his search for three representatives who might help him in his plight. These are a mediator, a witness, and a redeemer, all of whom have a unique place in scriptural definitions of an oath of innocence. During the first round of dialogue with his visitors, he looks for a suitable mediator (9:33). A mediator, or arbitrator, is a person who brings the parties in a suit together to attempt to resolve the issues at hand. Such a process usually is legally binding by consent of the parties. Job investigates and dismisses his hope for an individual who can stand between himself and God and press his case for undeserved suffering. He concludes that the only mediator who meets his requirements is God.

Job moves into the second round of exchanges with his visitors. Attempting to ignore them and speak directly to God, he begins to build his case, knowing that he risks a sin of presumption. He still declares his right to know why he suffers so. In Job 13:15, he pleads, "Though he slay me, yet will I trust Him."[3] Some translations of this passage result in an ambiguous or contradictory message. Context dictates that Job is willing to risk it all to get his answer. In a manner that had many Christian commentators looking for allegory, Job is defiantly pressing his case. Whatever the cost, he wants an answer from God: why does he permit suffering, most especially for those who serve Him?

Old Testament Scripture supports such a challenge. Abraham bargains with the messengers sent to destroy Sodom and Gomorrah. He argues that it is not just to destroy the righteous with the wicked. Through his challenge, he gains a commitment to preserve the lives of the righteous. This bargain is in contrast to much of Scripture which emphasizes that catastrophe falls on the wicked and righteous alike.

Another example is that God prepared to destroy the whole tribe of Israel before they traveled far from Egyptian borders. Moses challenged God with a logical conundrum. How can he show his power to the Egyptians if he rescues his people only to destroy them? Interpreting this passage as an argument for the benefit of God or Moses is difficult. Was God teaching Moses, or was Moses begging for the lives of the Israelites? Scripture records that Moses wins his point, and the nascent Israelite nation survives.

Much of Hebraic theology was structured around communication, even debate, with God. These debates are based on the human need to know as much as possible about why the world operates as it does. Hebrew theology carries the act of debating with it as a deep-seated tradition that survives in Jewish studies to this day. Although not all scholars support debate, for the most part the Jewish philosopher defends the right to question and the right to speak truth, even to God.

During his second speech in the second cycle of dialog, Job explores the possibility that a witness might intercede on his behalf (16:18–22). The option of a witness appeals to Job because God sees everything, even the heart. God knows Job is blameless and can testify to that. Because a witness would know Job's life, his heart, and his

3. Alternate translation, *Tanakh*.

mind, he would also know that Job has a moral right to understand why he is suffering and why there is evil in the world that afflicts even the righteous. Certainly, a witness would support his case.

As Job reaches the end of the second round of dialogue, he abandons the search for a witness as insufficient and looks for a redeemer (19:25) who can act as a prosecuting attorney, pressing Job's case against heaven in his stead. Such a person in Hebrew law was morally and legally obligated to protect the rights of a defendant and to restore the person suffering loss to their original status. A kinsman-redeemer might settle debts, purchase the individual out of slavery, or avenge a wrongful death. Unlike a mediator or even a witness, a redeemer was under obligation to see justice done. (Note: as the book of Job reports, Job was indeed restored to his original status. Under this interpretation, was he vindicated in the end?)

According to Sutherland's analysis, Job concludes that he will only see justice on the Day of Judgment when his Redeemer stands to defend him. At that time, God must provide a vindication for allowing a creation that contains evil. If the reason is not sufficient, then Job is within his rights to condemn God for the treatment he has received (and Satan wins his case as well).

Job is not willing to accept that he must wait until all human history plays out to receive his answer, yet he sees no other way to press his case. God is his Mediator, Witness, and Redeemer, and he sees no other solution than to wait until the Day of Judgment to get the answer he seeks. He still presses his case. Whether the answer comes now or later, he knows that his integrity demands it. He cannot preserve that integrity by falsely accepting that he has done wrong. In Sutherland's words, this is Job's sworn oath of innocence.

Job's claim is this: God was the author of undeserved evil in the world. Job has a right to know why that evil exists, yet God has not provided an answer. That oath expressed in Job 27:2–4 is "By God who has deprived me of justice! / By Shaddai, who has embittered my life! / As long as there is life in me, / And God's breath is in my nostrils, / My lips will speak no wrong, nor my tongue utter deceit."

Throughout chapter 31, Job makes his evidentiary statement by listing all the things he has done rightly. His words echo the Egyptian oath of evidence presented to Osiris at the weighing of the soul after death. He also denies concealing sin, unlike his predecessor Adam. Sutherland suggests this provides scriptural ambiguity for the concept of original sin. Here, a human being does have the capacity to lead an upright life and to stand on that integrity in the courts of heaven.

As per the passage, Sutherland agrees that Satan claims that Job is only faithful because he is blessed. If he is afflicted, he will curse God to his face. Part of the resolution of the oath is that a curse will be brought down on the defendant should the case be settled in favor of the plaintiff. Satan would then get his wish: Job would curse God. If God cannot defend the purpose for unearned suffering in his world, he loses everything.

Part IV—Recasting Job

Unlike the Jewish commentators investigated earlier, Sutherland completely discounts the speech delivered by Elihu. Placed in the context of the passage, he is abrupt, unruly, angry, young, and anything other than someone prepared to deliver wisdom in any situation. He blurts out that the Almighty will not answer, and then proceeds to answer for him.

Elihu presents the same case that Satan did in the prologue. No love for God is entirely free of selfishness. Also, God would be wicked and unjust if he did not reward the righteous. In Elihu's opinion, Job has committed the worst sin of all, rebellion.

Then God speaks. Commentaries about Job throughout history do not represent the voice of God with depth. Sutherland's work is intriguing, at least in part, due to his focus on these chapters. His education in the history of ideas brings a unique perspective.

Sutherland writes that God's response, in each facet of his sovereignty, delivers points seven at a time. First, God lists cosmic creations: the wonders of the sea, Sheol, snow and sleet, rain, the heavens, and lightning.

Next, God lists seven examples from the animal world: lions, goats, asses, oxen, ostriches, the warhorse, and birds of prey. Sutherland explains that these animals manage on their own, sometimes their lives involve violence, and that violence helps sustain other creatures. The process does not require input from humanity.

Absent from these verses is any mention of the human world, of civilization, or anything that might be managed by the might and ingenuity of a rational mind. Sutherland believes this litany is a deliberate move to put Job in his place, to include him with the *merely* created. Of course, Job has never claimed omniscience, and much of his dialogue focuses on acknowledging God's power, as evidenced in the wonders of creation. In the terms of a court case, this is no more than an opening statement, a speech to establish the facts and to remind the court who is speaking.

Since Sutherland's premise is that this is a trial of selfless love, he cannot allow God the room to be loving. He points out that the Creator is battering the witness. Even if bound by a challenge from God to avoid being direct with Job, the lawyer in Sutherland feels it is overkill to repeat an answer to every statement Job has already conceded.

In the creation myths of the ancient Near East, creation is not something that comes from nothing. It is the imposition of order on chaos, and the imagery used is that of great battles. Sutherland points out the correlation of the terms and images used in Job with Psalms 89 and 104. He draws out the story of creation from the Psalms and uses those images to set the stage for the second speech and the introduction of Leviathan.

Sutherland draws two conclusions: God's language in describing the physical world defines purposes; and God measures, commands, controls, separates, and designs things. God also alludes to providence as he provides for the animal kingdom—ensuring his creatures have food, freedom to pursue their needs, and protection for the young. The implication is that God's concern has a purpose and that it is ongoing. The illustrations used to describe this care seem to deliberately ignore the needs of humanity and, in fact, confound them. God points to the rain that falls where no one lives; riders can barely control the war stallions prepared to do battle, and predators destroy life to assuage their appetite.

Job? He responds that he was already aware of these things and had said as much in very clear language. There was nothing more to be said on these issues. However, Job still has not received an answer to his question. If God cannot provide one, then he must concede the suit.

Sutherland begins his analysis of the second speech from God with the background of the Leviathan legend. Leviathan is a myth with roots deep in Near Eastern mythology. As previously noted, the creature is the embodiment of evil. The creation myths of Babylon and Canaan involved similar creatures. The defeat of Leviathan is part of the Jewish apocalyptic vision of the restoration of Israel. The name means "twisting one," such as a serpent. Occasionally, Leviathan represents Satan himself, and it is another name for the Jewish chaos monster, Rahab.

Leviathan (according to Sutherland) is a proper name, and behemoth is a common name. Behemoth means "great beast." Behemoth is also plural in usage, although combined with singular verbs. The intent is to include all of evil within one embodiment, a being in direct contrast with the fullness of God. That is, Leviathan is the name of the beast described as behemoth. Some interpretations use behemoth as a separate beast representing the Canaanite beast of the recreation. Sutherland points out that within the Canaanite mythology, Satan, Leviathan, and behemoth represent an echo of the unholy trinity of Revelation.

And here is the confession. Job 40:19 clearly states that behemoth or evil "ranks first among the works of God, the One who made it" (NET).[4] Leviathan, then, is a created being just like Job. Sutherland draws an interesting picture of Leviathan as representative of the ugly parts of evolutionary history, the function of life feeding on life, and the necessity of death for the world to function. These translations show that from the Hebrew perspective, Adam (or Eve) did not bring evil (death) into the world. It existed as the first act of creation.

From the Babylonian point of view, this beast represents chaos, and chaos is evil, part of the very fabric of creation and part of a plan for the world. The difference brought to the picture by the Hebrews was linear eschatology (the study of a final destiny), rather than the cyclic versions of many Near Eastern legends. For the inhabitants of the Near East, the gods could control chaos, not defeat it. In Hebrew legend, God could and would finally banish chaos.

The Hebrew apocalypse works well into Sutherland's interpretation of Job as it represents the final judgment. Per the legend recounted in Isaiah (chapter 27), God

---

4. Or, from the *Tanakh*, "He is the first of God's works; Only his Maker can draw the sword against him."

will draw the chaos dragon out of the water and capture it. He will slay it, and it will become the messianic banquet feast at the final judgment. At the court following the meal where all people, of all time, appear for judgment, God will answer all questions.

Sutherland sees God's second speech as a direct reference to the ancient tales of the full resolution of the question of evil. It is also an indirect answer to Job. "Not now. Not at this moment. But, one day, you will know, and on that day you can judge."

God on Trial presents detailed arguments with supporting material to arrive at these conclusions. Sutherland builds a strong case that if the book as it stands is not able to provide comfort, then perhaps it can provide some peace. Based on his analogy, as well as the Hebrew, God is the author of evil, and there is undeserved suffering in the world that has nothing to do with the righteousness of the sufferer. Sutherland supports his conclusion by referencing the prologue where Satan must ask permission to unleash evil on Job's life. Also, Job is clear that God is the only source and arbiter of his circumstances. Sutherland concludes that evil had to exist to develop the selfless love of God.

Sutherland brings out in detail what others allude to as an interpretation—that Job is putting God on trial through the legal mechanisms of his time. The source is rich in historical support for the imagery of the passage, yet it falls short of providing an answer. In the end, Sutherland concludes that no answer is available in this lifetime. Some scholars would agree that Job never receives an answer. There are others that go a step further and posit that Job, or even the Bible as a whole, fails to answer the question "Why do we suffer?"

Chapter 17

When It Gets Real

THIS BOOK BEGAN WITH a question: when caught in the crush of suffering, when faced with unexplained evil, do platitudes, clichés, and prayers offer any real comfort? Or do they deepen the pain? If this book accomplishes anything, it cannot be a simple compilation of accumulated academic, philosophical, and theological musings from across the world. There needs to be something tangible to hold on to while dealing with the real pain experienced in life or as seen in major disasters around the world. If the goal is to find a functional answer to suffering, one must be prepared to step out of the ivory tower and stare deeply into the eyes of a battered woman, a rape victim, or a man who has lost his job and doesn't know how to feed his family. Whatever the solution, it must survive contact with reality.

Bart Ehrman is the James A. Gray Distinguished Professor at the University of North Carolina at Chapel Hill. He grew up a devout Evangelical, attending both Moody Bible Institute and Wheaton College. He obtained his masters and his PhD at Princeton Theological Seminary and spent years studying Greek, New Testament exegesis, and the history of the early church. He has written several popular books on these subjects. At least in his earlier efforts, he wrote with clarity, honesty, and a fervent respect for his material. Somewhere along the line, he developed a crisis of faith. Not willing to disavow the existence of divinity of any kind, he remains an agnostic. However, one question alone drove him away from the God of his youth—the question of evil in the world. His book *God's Problem: How the Bible Fails to Answer Our Most Important Question—Why We Suffer* is the primary resource for the issues presented in this chapter.

Many have written volumes on what Job's sin might have been or what character flaw he might have suffered, even in the face of clear assertions within the book that his suffering was undeserved. Why is there this deep-seated need to blame him in some small or great way for his suffering? Is the assumption that suffering is punishment for sin so ingrained in our cultural and religious DNA that we have no room

Part IV—Recasting Job

for other possibilities? Has the reward and punishment paradigm been driven into our hearts and minds by Scripture, commentaries, pastors, rabbis, and millennia of Judeo-Christian heritage to the exclusion of all alternative answers? Or is it possible that if blame must assigned, and we can accept we are not to blame, then we are faced with the frightening idea that God is the only possible source of the suffering we see and feel?

Ehrman explains that throughout the Old Testament, students find the consequences of disobeying God. The theme of the Pentateuch, the historical books, the prophets, and much of the wisdom material is the penalty required when God's precepts are ignored or broken. Take careful note of *how* a person can disappoint God. According to Scripture, God punishes his people primarily when one of two things happens: there is some misstep in the manner of worshiping God; or his people ignore those in need of help, such as widows, orphans, and the indigent.

According to Scripture, any believers who broke the rules of worship or mistreated a fellow being who needed help were worthy of the wrath of God. Considering the very strict rules of tithing established by the Islamic faith, the same is true for Muslims. According to a long tradition of scriptural interpretation, the people of Israel suffered because they forsook God and failed to care for those who needed help. Above all else, it was the neglect of those with a solvable need that was worthy of punishment, not a breach of the hundreds of detailed instructions regarding sexual behavior, misbehaving children, proper clothing, or dietary requirements.

The belief that God delivered suffering to punish his people for breaking his code was so ingrained in the Hebrew psyche that even the vagaries of history and the course of natural disasters were placed firmly at the feet of God. Bad things happened when God became angry, and sinners must pay the price.

Ehrman turns to the present day and asks: why should a man, woman, or child living anywhere on this globe suffer starvation, disease, war, and abject poverty? What evil thing have these individuals done to deserve their fate? Was the starving child born in the wrong place at the wrong time? When fate is the cause, is the assumption sin? A sin punishable by death? Taught to him from an early age, the depiction of an avenging God began to bother Ehrman as he learned and experienced more of suffering. He provides the illustration of a personal moment to reveal when this seeming injustice became clear to him.

During a thanksgiving prayer for the food laid before him, he realized his life was rather worry-free with enough food, clothing, and shelter to meet his needs. However, how could he thank God for giving *him* these things when so many millions of others were not so lucky? What special thing did *he* do to deserve the shining face of God, while God withheld his sustaining grace from others, and for no apparent reason?

Another illustration he uses to draw out the inequities of claiming the special favor of God relates to a survivor of a disaster. For Ehrman, the event that drove home this fallacy was a plane crash. One of the survivors was thanking God for his deliverance, yet so many others had died horrible deaths. Ehrman (as well as the author of this book) shuddered at the presumption of such a statement. Why you? What could these others have done that deserved this horrible death? Why should their loved ones need to suffer so? Why does God spare one child in a school shooting while others are left bleeding and dying on their classroom floor?

Any acceptable answer to the existence of evil must deal with this paradox. Why do people who really don't deserve to suffer, suffer so greatly? If God can answer prayers to alleviate suffering, then why not answer all supplications for relief? Where is he when an infant dies at his mother's breast because she has run dry from her starvation? Ehrman doesn't deny the possibility that divinity exists, but he has concluded that a just and loving God cannot defend the existence of undeserved evil. A Greek philosopher named Epicurus (341–270 BCE) was one of the earliest to consider the trilemma formula in response to suffering. The logic-statement rejects the idea of an omnipotent and omnibenevolent god. Paraphrasing multiple sources, the premise goes like this:

> Is god willing to prevent evil but not able? Then he is impotent.
> Is he able but not willing? Then he is malevolent.
> Is he both able and willing? Whence, then, evil?

Such doubts are not limited to the individual. The culture which developed from the Western European Renaissance also suffered a crisis in faith. For the reasoning mind, believing in an omniscient, omnipotent, benevolent Creator requires answers. Over the centuries, philosophers and theologians developed the free-will defense, which is the basis of Leibniz's work on theodicy.[1] For him, it was the core reason for suffering and the subsequent action of Providence.

From the late 1400s to the early 1700s, Europe became a breeding ground for new thinkers, philosophers, and theologians who focused on the human ability to reason. Religion and science went under the microscope of human reason. Men such as Francis Bacon (1561–1626), Galileo Galilei (1564–1642), Rene Descartes (1596–1650), Isaac Newton (1642–1727), and Martin Luther (1483–1546) contributed to the classical works of our growing knowledge. The combined works of these men helped create a form of monotheistic faith called Deism. The movement, which began in the first half of the seventeenth century, was developed further by philosophers such as Edward Herbert (1582–1648). There were only two central beliefs to this view.

1. The existence of one God who designed the world and established some system of rewards and punishments; and

2. The obligation of humans to virtue and piety.

---

1. See Leibniz, *Theodicy*.

Part IV—Recasting Job

Leibniz (1646–1716) used this parameter to look for an explanation of undeserved suffering and the presence of evil in the world. He, as well as deists in general, did not believe that God was directly involved in the day-to-day lives of humanity.

Leibniz's solution rested on the existence of free will. God could have created any world he cared to. However, the very best of all worlds required that humans have free will. Humanity needed to be free to choose between God and mammon. Modern philosophers also rely on this answer, often wrapping it in the terminology of the profession. The results can be difficult to follow through the sometimes obtuse and circular reasoning. Also, the arguments fail when they hit the streets in any poor side of town, in a developing country, or the middle of a heartbreaking accident with the resultant death and injury.

The free-will defense does seem rational, at least on the surface. The argument goes like this: There is undeserved suffering because people have the free will to choose how they will act. Some choose to act badly to their fellow beings. For instance, a person might decide to drive while intoxicated and cause a traffic accident resulting in death and injury. However, why should one person's choice trump another's right to life and health? The argument is that this would be a less than perfect world if humanity did not have the option of free will. In other words, if a commitment to God has meaning, the choice to follow God must be a choice.

This defense, as offered by Leibniz and his followers, is woefully incomplete. To the best of our ability, thinking within the confines of the finite mind, free will does exist. However, it is not simply a tool to provide a choice between good and evil. Free will is the engine that drives imagination and produces creative solutions. Reason, the ability to choose and grow in knowledge, is the only path to fully understanding the universe so we can then use the knowledge to fix problems and reduce suffering.

Human beings do horrible things to each other and cause untold suffering. However, free will also allows others to exercise their choice to intervene and offer solace, restitution, or restoration. In fact, within Scripture, God commands people of faith to step in and alleviate the suffering around them. According to the Old Testament prophets, resisting the call to do so is subject to punishment by God.

Ehrman introduces another scriptural response to the purpose of suffering: the elusive greater good.[2] The hope of a greater good is the belief that even though suffering may be terrible, God can create some good from it. The option to seek the greater good was an answer supported by Marilyn McCord Adams as well as many of her colleagues. The reasoning is that no matter how bad things get, there is assurance that God will create some greater good out of the situation. Scripturally, Ehrman gives the examples of the early Christian believers. According to the Gospels, they were to scatter and spread the word throughout the world. Instead, they hunkered down in Jerusalem. When the persecution began, they left the city to preserve their lives. The greater good was the spread of the gospel.

2. See Rom 8:28.

Scholars call this line of thought redemptive suffering, meaning that even tragedy can be used by God to achieve his divine plan. Ehrman provides additional examples from Scripture. For instance, how can it possibly be right or good that Joseph's brothers beat him and sold him into slavery? According to Genesis, this allowed Joseph to provide for the family of Jacob and those living in Canaan and Egypt during a great famine. Of course, even in this interpretation, people did indeed suffer as crops and herds failed for seven years.

Another scriptural explanation of suffering is that some suffer so that the solution will glorify God. According to the story of the exodus, sometimes Pharaoh hardened his heart against the Israelites, and sometimes God hardened his heart. Even after Pharaoh released the Israelites, he pursued them. God declared that this happened so that he could destroy the Egyptian armies, and all the world would know that by his sovereign power he delivered the Israelites.

A similar scenario occurs in the New Testament with the death of Lazarus. Jesus is informed well in advance that his friend is very ill and near death, yet he waits until his friend's body is rotting in the grave. When he arrives to console the grieving family, he raises Lazarus from the dead—so that greater glory might accrue to God.

Scripture also teaches that suffering is a path to salvation. By the law of Moses, animals for sacrifice and consumption are slain in a manner not to cause fear. Predators or scavengers were not acceptable at all. Modern science can show that these stipulations avoid the consumption of large amounts of adrenalin. The crucifixion of Jesus was not what a Hebrew would call kosher. Beaten, bloodied, hung on a tree, and suffering in the extreme, he was the perfect sacrifice. Christians have long viewed Isaiah 53 as a foreshadowing of the crucifixion because the passage resonates timelessly: "Yet it was our sickness that he was bearing, / Our suffering that he endured" (v. 4). Suffering, from this interpretation, is a requirement for redemption.

These are all versions of something good coming from something bad. There are times when a setback beneficially changes our course. Such as an unexpected sickness which bars us from pursuing our normal activities. When prevented from doing what we want to do, we might find time to rethink our goals and, perhaps, choose a different path. Or, getting scared because we wake up from too much partying and realize we have a drinking problem. If we choose to do something about the problem, or despite it, the suffering has a positive effect.

Ehrman draws the line when asked to look at the suffering of others as having a good impact on someone other than the one suffering. To say that suffering exists in the world to test our willingness to give is egocentric, arrogant, and probably a sin. Ehrman (and this author) views this interpretation as repugnant. Must others starve so that someone else can enjoy the occasional cheesecake? Must others grow sick and die so that others have the advantages of a vaccine? This viewpoint is not an acceptable answer if, indeed, the *primary* cause of suffering is to invoke action on the part of an observer. However, the reaction to assuage that condition may still be part of the ultimate answer.

One of the many issues that influence Ehrman's interpretation of the book is the premise that the beginning and ending prose of the book came from the remnants of a folk tale and that the poetic discourse in the middle came from a different author. In this rendering of the passage, the two are disjointed and have different messages to deliver. This view also sees a disconnect with the third round of discourse. Bildad's response seems too short, Zophar is completely missing, and Elihu pounces into the middle of the scene. These scholars believe that something was muddled up in the transmission to modern texts.

The folktale portion of the text, then, explains that the suffering of Job is a test of faith. To Ehrman, God, in the closing verses, is affirming what Job has said and condemning what the friends have said. He feels that God's response cannot refer to the dialogues as preserved. In them, the friends defend God, and Job challenges him. This view fundamentally changes the interpretation of the book. In the commentaries explored earlier, God condemned Job's visitors precisely *because* they defended God—by assuming guilt where none existed.

Ehrman agrees that God is the admitted source of the suffering. At no point in the book of Job is the responsibility for Job's troubles assigned to any other than God. Job, of course, knows this, and that is the basis of his challenge. Due to this acknowledgment, God caused the loss, the pain, and the agony.[3] Ehrman then wonders what sort of God this serves. What sort of God would maim people, destroy property, and even slaughter innocent children and servants to prove a point? Is a new batch of offspring any consolation for those who were lost?

With the advent of Christianity, the concept of testing a believer's faith becomes more intense. Christians actively pursued occasions to suffer for their faith, even when it was not necessary. There are historical accounts from the time of the Caliphate of Córdoba (929–1031 CE) that even under the most tolerant of rulers, some Christians sought to provoke the Caliph and his advisors for the sole purpose of being persecuted. Such events occurred even when political, economic, and religious freedom allowed Christians, Jews, and Muslims to enjoy a thriving and peaceful kingdom. There is this drive to suffer as Christ suffered—even though he was supposed to take on all the suffering of the world.

Turning to the poetic dialogues of Job, Ehrman determines that the answer to suffering is that there is no answer. Whatever the discussion throughout the book may hold, the answer is there is no answer as to why Job might suffer if he has done no wrong. Part of the response within the book is that God is so great and mysterious that humans cannot understand the "why," and they have no business asking. In Ehrman's view, God does nothing to answer Job and, instead, grinds him to dust. The reader

---

3. See Isa 45:7.

When It Gets Real

is left to ask, "If God is so far above his creation that his creatures have no chance of understanding him, then why are they so plagued?"

This line of thought leads Ehrman to the book of Ecclesiastes, generally but not exclusively credited to Solomon. The book is a collection of thoughts describing life as it appears from the view of a man observing day-to-day events, with the conclusion (per Ehrman) that all is vanity. Nothing survives, and what we choose to enjoy or suffer in this life is all that there is. Nothing is remembered; nothing can be preserved. For the teacher of Ecclesiastes, one must enjoy what blessings are received and deal with sorrows as best as life affords. The Teacher of Ecclesiastes would have us do more than avoid suffering; he suggests that we seek to revel in what we find in life without expectation of reward or punishment at life's end.

Ehrman takes on one more scriptural interpretation of why there is suffering: a school of thought called "apocalypticism." This term is familiar to many Christians who have studied Daniel and Revelation. These are books that tell us that evil rules the current age—specifically Satan and his minions—though one day, God will send his own messiah to destroy the forces of evil and reign supreme over the righteous. Apocalypticism, however, has its roots in ancient history. Ehrman places its beginning around the time of the Maccabees, who won independence from Antiochus Epiphanes ca. 150–175 BCE.

There was a reason for the growing focus on apocalyptic thinking during the time of the Maccabees. Throughout the history of Israel and Judah, the prophets taught that if God's people would return to him, worship in the manner set out by Moses, and care for those who needed help as dictated in the Law, God would return to his people, and they would, again, be prosperous. History shows this did not happen. No matter how hard they tried or how much they repented, they remained subjected to foreign rule and oppression.

Antiochus sparked a long-smoldering fire when he entered the temple in Jerusalem and defiled it with a pig (ca. 168 BCE). He then instituted laws that prevented the observance of any of the Jewish rituals and demanded that they worship the gods of the realm. This absolute intolerance was too much for the priesthood to bear, and they felt the only recourse was rebellion. The Maccabees led that revolt. In time, they won independence and re-sanctified the temple. When the Maccabees were successful in recapturing the temple, they needed to relight the menorah. A search of the temple only produced enough purified oil for one day, yet the lamp burned for the full eight days required to consecrate more. The Jewish holiday of Hanukkah celebrates this event. However, even after this great effort to return to God, the people suffered.

Ehrman sees this historical point as the beginning of apocalyptic thought. Those who believed in God had to come up with a reason they were still suffering when they were doing everything possible to act rightly and according to God's law. Previous commentators and the description of the legends of Leviathan given in chapter 24 indicate otherwise. The eschatology of apocalyptic thought may have gained a wider following as the remnant dealt with a world of suffering and oppression. However, the seeds of a reconciliation of some sort at the end of times was already well planted in Hebrew thought.

The tendency to look to the future for a solution is also evident in the Apocrypha and New Testament passages attributed to the sayings of Jesus and in the writings of Paul. Ephesians 6:12 says, "For our struggle is not against enemies of blood and flesh, but against the rulers, against the authorities, against the cosmic powers of this present darkness, against the spiritual forces of evil in the heavenly places." Paul's teaching to the gentiles was that God had stepped out of the equation and that humanity was dealing with a different source of trial and tribulation. For many New Testament writers, it was only at the end of time, when the messiah returned in glory and destroyed evil, that the world would be at peace. Then there would be no more suffering, disease, or oppression.

Redefining Job is not about eschatology. However, addressing this aspect is an important part of an explanation for undeserved suffering in our current world. First, *apocalyptic*[4] theology assumes that somehow God has temporarily relinquished authority over this world. He only intervenes occasionally, and the purposes and timing of that intervention (providence) are a mystery. *Eschatology* is a term that encapsulates all studies relevant to an end-time philosophy or theology. The term *apocalypticism* is a specific type of eschatology that involves the presence of evil in the world and the final removal of that evil in some end-time scenario.

Some form of a final apocalypse runs deep in religious and spiritual history. The word means "revelation" and only took on the sense of widespread destruction during the development of Christian theology. The Greeks, the Coptics, other early Christians, and some of the medieval philosophers believed that deterioration is the destiny of this world of matter. The early church fathers and Jewish philosophers used the term *privation*, which meant that matter, which has a finite lifespan, was inherently defective. In some cases, they thought of matter as evil. This world of matter is doomed and, therefore, finite. Only in spirit, only beyond the grave, can the soul reach its potential and know God.

In this view, there is nothing that can eliminate or help us understand evil and suffering. The best that we can accomplish is to survive until death and then hope for a reward in heaven or at the end of time. However, this cannot be the answer if the very thought of *not* being an active part in the mitigation of suffering and evil is anathema to everything stressed from Genesis to Revelation. Even if the apocalyptic view of the end of history is some part of the total mystery, it is certainly not the answer. Not even those who preached the imminent arrival of the Christ throughout the New Testament allowed their followers to step away from the obligations of caring for those who

---

4. "Apocalyptic" derives from the Greek "apocalypse," which means "to uncover" or "an uncovering."

needed some form of help. How a person treated others was a clear demarcation for those accepted or rejected by the Son of Man.[5]

Ehrman addresses these questions in the effort to find a satisfactory solution for undeserved suffering. He also believes that seeking direct aid from God may not be helpful, if even possible. To Ehrman, whether as a poignant plea or an angry demand, all our philosophy and theology are nothing if we cannot look in the eyes of a sufferer and offer relief, or if we cannot take the hand of a suffering individual and provide real comfort. However, what if the ancient Hebrew author had no intention of discussing the deep subjects of suffering and God's part in the cause or relief of pain? What if the author of Job was writing a work of uniquely Hebrew comedy? Keeping in mind this is a Hebrew Scripture, what are the possible interpretations of Job's story if the distinctly Jewish perspective of using a comic vision to mitigate the horrors of life is the focus of a least some of the prophets of old? What is comic vision as it pertains to Scripture?

---

5. See Matt 25:35–40.

Chapter 18

Can Job Be Understood through Comic Vision?

THIS BOOK IS ABOUT retelling the story of Job and how that might help decipher a new message from the poem. Storytelling is part of what makes us human and an art form we have developed since the first recorded cave paintings. Each culture develops unique approaches to the art, even as a shared thread of themes, characters, and styles remains. The Greeks began to record and produce plays around 770–750 BCE (a few centuries before the book of Job). Their contribution to the dramatic arts included the characterization of plays through the muses Thalia (Comedy and Idyllic Poetry) and Melpomene (Tragedy). As dramatic arts matured, the classification of works of theater and written tales fell into three categories: tragedy, comedy, and satire.

Satire is the easiest of the three to define. Comedic satire is a type of story that uses the tools of comedy, such as irony, exaggeration, or ridicule, to criticize. Such stories rarely offer solutions since the intention is to use wit to draw attention to a problem and to disparage a situation, person, or group. Satire often stings by wrapping truth in ridicule. Many classical writers used barbed humor to point out the inequities and failures of an idea or practice. Some authors of note are Voltaire (*Candide*,[1] 1664), Jonathon Swift ("A Modest Proposal," 1729), Molière (*Tartuffe*, 1758), C. S. Lewis (*Screwtape Letters*, 1942), and Shirley Jackson ("The Lottery," 1948). For centuries, men and women with a critical eye toward the issues of their time chose humor, sometimes lighthearted, sometimes dark or satirical, to deliver a message that their audience may not have received otherwise. However, although the story of Job does include aspects of the absurd, there is also a clear attempt to resolve Job's questions. Satire, then, fails as a model for Job's story.

Arriving at a clear distinction between tragedy and comedy is a challenging task, especially when it becomes important to include the Hebrew sense of humor, carnival,

---

1. See chapter 19.

and satire. John Morreall[2] devoted much of his career to evaluating the fundamental principles that constitute comedy versus tragedy. He loosely defines the idea of "comic vision" as a counterpoint to tragedy rather than with a set of specific rules. Morreall teaches that humor is a crucial piece of humanity's coping mechanism and that it provides identifiable physical and mental benefits, including the relief of stress. Humor provides relief from negative emotions and can allow a person to think through solutions to a problem rather than to dwell exclusively on the problem. Humor is a social lubricant, making many interactions less confrontational and more open to cooperative solutions. Humor can also short-circuit conflict and make dealing with difficult people an easier task.

Based on his work, Morreall developed what he calls "the cognitive psychology of the tragic and comic visions." Not all aspects of the list are universal, although some concepts relate to Job's story. In contrast to tragedy, comic heroes tend to be malleable and dynamic, not binary and static. Comic plots permit a higher level of disorder or a randomness in which simple solutions do not wrap things up neatly. Morreall writes that humor is possible only when there is ambiguity.[3] Comedy does not have to make sense even as it often calls attention to incongruities. Comedy makes room for a better grasp of realities in the world by avoiding clear-cut principles, ethical abstractions, and moral goals. Comedy sees the gray areas, the less than perfect. In the tragedy, the protagonist is restricted by predetermined rules and goals which prevent the hero from fulfilling a standard that is intrinsically out of reach. Comic heroes tend to make up the rules as they go along, or at least become wary of generalization. Humor is a survival technique. By seeing the absurdity of a situation, an individual can reduce the pressure and suppress their instincts long enough to determine if those instincts are the best response. The question becomes whether the Hebrews availed themselves of humor to deal with the vagaries of life within Scripture.

J. William Whedbee was the Nancy J. Lyon Professor of Biblical History and Literature and professor of religious studies at Pomona College, Claremont, California. His work in literary criticism brings a sensitive eye to the literature as well as the theology of biblical texts. His work *The Bible and the Comic Vision* is a compilation of his studies and is the source material for much of this chapter. Whedbee references the work of scholars that have contributed to the limited literature about comic vision and Scripture. These commentaries approach passages such as Balaam's talking mule, Abraham's and Moses' bargaining with God on various subjects, and the books of Jonah and Esther. Whedbee understands the reluctance to view comedy within Scripture; however, he asks his reader to view Scripture in the light of the culture within which it took shape in hopes of finding a new understanding of the message.

---

2. Doctor of philosophy and emeritus professor of religious studies at the College of William and Mary in Williamsburg, Virginia. He operates a website, www.humorworks.com.
3. Morreal, *Comedy, Tragedy, and Religion*, 54.

Part IV—Recasting Job

Whedbee believes Job is a tragic tale and that the comic vision embraces the tragic dimension without rendering the calamity impotent.

Whedbee describes four elements that are necessary to a comic vision. The plot of a comedy usually begins with everything in harmony, then a test comes, which challenges the status quo, and, finally, the story ends with the protagonist returned to a society or situation made whole. These story elements create a U-shaped plot that contrasts with a tragedy, which ends in irretrievable loss. Comedy ends in carnival and the happily-ever-after. For instance, the origin of the Jewish festival of Purim is a celebration of the victory of Esther (and her uncle) over Haman, the king's royal vizier. Purim is a celebration with costumes, masks, and merrymaking and is observed as a carnival of joy and restoration.

Second, there are usually one or more characters that fill the roles of a simpleton and a trickster. These personages abound within the pages of Scripture in the roles of Jacob, Rachel, Balaam, King Ahasuerus, Nebuchadnezzar, and many others great and small who learned lessons through the action of ineptitude or highly developed skills of manipulation. The image of the trickster is at the heart of comedic ambiguity—sometimes mischievous, sometimes manipulative, always in possession of secret knowledge which can help (or hinder) the protagonist. For instance, Jacob acted the trickster when he manipulated his uncle into surrendering a substantial share of his flocks. Simpletons carry the plot forward by consistently missing the point, which causes them to end up in situations with no understanding of what happened or why, at least not until the plot is revealed. Esther and her uncle manipulated King Ahasuerus to save their people.

Third, the language of comedy uses puns, plays on words, parody, hyperbole, and repetition. Sometimes the tale incites joyous laughter while others are sardonic or dark. In the latter case, the observer is laughing *at*, rather than *with*, the protagonist. When comedy is a parody or satire, the humor uses ridicule to bring down the arrogant who threaten the free pursuit of life in all its joyous flair. Satire sits apart from comedy since there is no effort to resolve the problem the protagonist faces, and there is no restoration.

Fourth, comedy is a chameleon, finding a unique place in each circumstance and presentation. Comedy can support the status quo or to tear down and subvert the established norm. Voltaire, Swift, Molière, Lewis, and Jackson were artisans who used satire and parody to draw attention to practices and ideologies they found unsupportable or even abhorrent. In the case of C. S. Lewis, he used parody to illustrate how evil might celebrate the calamities of life and rejoice in the misguided soul.

Whedbee develops a criterion by which to analyze the story of Job and to seek a message behind the tragedy and pain that may provide a useful view of how to deal with suffering. He understands that his reader may be uncomfortable with the suggestion that Job, of all the stories in Scripture, is comedy. However, he asks that we not confuse laughter with comedy; comedy can be serious and is often the consummate tool for dealing with chaos and suffering. For him, dark comedy is a clear example of this variety.[4]

Whedbee begins to build his case by using the prose narratives from the beginning and ending of the book. Job's tale begins as a fairy tale, a once upon a time story about a man in a mythical land whose possessions are perfect in number and kind. Even the delivery of the discussion between Satan and God and the catastrophes that follow encompasses a rhythm of twos and fours. To bring out the U-shaped plot, Whedbee emphasizes that in the end Job is restored with his wealth doubled, a new set of children, and a long and healthy life.

To flush out the comic vision, Whedbee spends some time analyzing the characters. Satan presents as the trickster, both in Hebrew legend and in much of Scripture. However, for comic vision, buffoons, or simpletons, are also required. For this part, Whedbee chooses Job's rather useless friends. MacLeish also cast J.B.'s visitors in this role.[5] They are antagonists who keep pressing points of view that have no relevance to Job's situation. They insist on speaking at cross-purposes, nearly babbling in the background while Job tries to sort things out.

The next element in this vision is ambiguity, which is richly represented by God. Throughout the discourse of the poem, God is a disciplinarian, one who should care for those who love him yet seems dispassionate about the loss of life and property caused by his authority. Job laments in 9:22 that God destroys the guiltless and the wicked without predilection. For some readers, the lack of a definitive answer from the Almighty adds to the ambiguity and is less satisfying than no answer at all.

This interpretation also sheds a far different light on the part played by Job's wife. For Whedbee, her contention that Job should curse God and die is the pivot in the plot. Before this exchange, Job is depressed, in mourning, and resigned to whatever his fate may be. Once his wife issues her challenge (and immediately disappears), Job's tone changes. Even as he curses the day of his birth, he begins to seek, even to demand, answers. Whedbee references the work of Ilana Pardes, who sees Job's wife as the fulcrum that moves the narrative from the lament to the driving urgency of the dialogues.[6] She compares Job's wife to Eve, who challenged her husband to think beyond the black and white dos and don'ts and to seek a path to knowledge. Even if this interpretation is debatable, the point is that when Job's wife intervenes, the story changes dramatically. At that point, the dialogues begin with Job no longer resigned to his fate; instead, he develops a growing conviction that he is due an answer.

Job begins the quest for answers by cursing the day of his birth. By invoking the legends of Leviathan and Yam, he may be declaring that all of creation should return to chaos, perhaps because order seems to be an illusion he can no longer afford. Job, crushed by the weight of his loss, is plagued with the "comfort" of his companions.

---

4. Whedbee, *Bible and the Comic Vision*, 224.
5. MacLeish, *J.B.*, 114–32. See also chapter 19 of the present volume.
6. Pardes, *Countertraditions in the Bible*, 151.

Part IV—Recasting Job

Job's companions repeat their choruses of penalty and discipline with increasing intensity. Although they have slightly different visions of the nature of their Sovereign, each concludes that Job has committed some terrible sin of omission or commission and needs to repent. Each of them becomes so enamored of their argument that they wax eloquent on the sad state of the wicked and the need for God to punish, correct, and guide his beloved. They become cruel caricatures of harpies, speaking to hear themselves speak and to press their point of view as true, even if there is no evidence to support their claims.

The more they insist they are right, the more sardonic Job becomes. The text is, indeed, clear as he mocks their supposed wisdom.

> Indeed, you are the [voice of] the people,
> And Wisdom will die with you.
> But I, like you, have a mind,
> And am not less than you.
> Who does not know such things? (Job 12:2–3)

Or:

> But ask the beasts, and they will teach you,
> The birds of the sky, they will tell you . . . (Job 12:7)

And:

> You would help without having the strength;
> You would deliver with arms that have no power.
> Without having the wisdom, you offer advice
> And freely give your counsel.
> To whom have you addressed words?
> Whose breath issued from you? (Job 26:2–4)[7]

Within the comic vision, the dogmatist offers general maxims that nearly always miss the mark, and in the process, shows himself to be a fool. Commentators that see Job within a comic vision believe the poet created a brilliant, cutting satire of Job's comforters. In their perceived role as wise men, they become ridiculous parodies as they insist on repetition of profound statements which have no relevance to Job and his situation.

Elihu reinforces this mood as he bursts on the scene with accusations against the presupposed wisdom of the graybeards—then proceeds to repeat much of what they have said. "Here I have waited out your speeches, I have given ear to your insights, while you probed the issues; But as I attended to you, I saw that none of you could argue with Job, or offer replies to his statements" (32:11–12).

---

7. Although Whedbee associates this passage with Job, the Hebrew is singular, leading scholars to believe it is a misplaced portion of Bildad's responses directed at Job

The poet deepens the atmosphere of crosstalk by having Job respond incongruously to his tormentors. Job delays his answers to his companions by ignoring what they just said and arguing a point presented much earlier. Whedbee provides the example of 9:2: "Indeed I know that is so, / Man cannot win a suit against God," which Whedbee sees as an answer to 4:17, "Can mortals be acquitted by God? / Can man be cleared by his Maker?"

Job also shifts the target of his conversation in mid-speech. The transition at 13:19–20 brings this sudden shift into focus. "For who is it that would challenge me? / I should then keep silent and expire, / But two things do not do to me, / So that I need not hide from You . . ." Job goes from asking a question of his companions to beseeching God. Job is juggling his defense against his companions with his pleas to God for an answer. Whedbee knows that Job is convinced his suffering is not due to sin. He sees the issue as something far deeper, something related to the workings of the universe. He assails God and holds nothing back. Within his plea for answers, he draws the picture of an uncaring tyrant who may have no answers.[8]

Whedbee believes Job is most eloquent in his parody when he uses the hymn of praise to point out the pervasive chaos and disorder in the universe (9:2–10). Throughout the passage found at 12:17–25, Job delivers contrasts between the good and wise attributes of God and the counterintuitive evidence in nature and life as humanity finds it.

For Job, if there is no justice to be found, then he must be vindicated and declared innocent of any cause that would warrant the death and destruction leveled against himself and his family. Then comes another twist in the comic plot. At the end of chapter 31, Job has finished his speech. He has drained his soul and his mind, and the expectation is that, from this place of defeat, God will step in with an answer. Instead, Elihu pops in, declaring none can speak with or for God—but he, of course, can.

Although Elihu repeats much of what the previous antagonists have argued ad nauseam, he brings in the additional hint of avenues of providence. He speaks of mediators and signs that God sends to warn against impending disaster. Although he ultimately misses the mark by repeating the error of Job's friends, he may provide a window into the ultimate answer, a window which points to awareness of the world as a tool to prevent or mitigate suffering.

Finally, God enters the picture. Even within the community of those who see the comic vision in Job, the interpretations vary. For scholars such as Gerhard von Rad,[9] Job's answer is the overwhelming grandeur of the universe and his inability to understand all its workings. Although this interpretation is typical, some academics believe this answer is too tidy and does not do justice to the irony laced throughout the book.

---

8. Whedbee, *Bible and the Comic Vision*, 237.
9. von Rad, *Wisdom in Israel*.

David Robertson[10] presents the Yahweh passages within the larger context of the book. Job has already proclaimed that if he did speak with God, God would only overwhelm him with questions he could not answer. Job goes to great lengths in Job 9 to describe how God would respond, and in the main, this is what happens. God's opening statement is a demand to answer questions Job cannot. Robertson also argues that Job's repentance is tongue in cheek. He has already stated that, if God should appear, he would declare himself guilty when, in fact, he is not. The meaning of the book, per Robertson, is found in the poet's attempt to develop a strategy for coping with "man's fear of fate, his destiny, the unknown." That coping mechanism is to ridicule the object feared, a way of telling the universe that, though crushed, one's integrity remains inviolate whatever the cost.

Whedbee does not entirely agree with Robertson's caustic interpretation. Job may predict a Creator who is overpowering, who brings chaos where there is order, but God's response is one that shows order even if it is not immediately evident to Job. He also sees joy and festivity in the portrayals selected. The stars sing together. The ostrich may be laughable, but she laughs at horse and rider (39:18). Whedbee points out that even the description of Leviathan uses sporting terms. In Psalms 104:26, the poet says that God formed Leviathan for sport. God can speak to the joyful, sometimes chaotic order of the universe with humor because he is in control. Within that control, the Creator has built in the capacity to laugh. Throughout the discourse, creatures laugh at the cities of men (39:7), other creatures (39:18), fear itself (39:22), and at the javelins thrown to bring them down (41:29). Read from this perspective, the universe is alive with the joy, and the carnival of life is lived in ordered chaos.

Within the commentary on the Yahweh discourses, Whedbee does not believe that Job receives an unambiguous answer. To him, God sidesteps the legal vindication of Job and offers one of order. From a Hebrew perspective, order involves justice. This justice transcends humanity and encompasses the entire creation. Edwin Good translates God's speech as "Would you even annul my order, treat me as wicked so you can be innocent?" (40:8).[11] Whedbee asks if we must condemn either Job or God so that the other can remain innocent. Good resoundingly answers, "No." He explains that the question of moral presumption is not the way the world works; it is not the question Job should be asking.[12] Within this context, the exegetes determine that although the poem follows the trial motif, with the author occasionally representing the defendant as Job and occasionally as God, the tone changes. The Yahweh speeches broaden the scope and propel the discussion out of the courtroom and into the theater of creation.

In Whedbee's words:

---

10. Robertson, "Book of Job."
11. Good, "Job and the Literary Task," 471–75.
12. Good, "Job and the Literary Task," 471–75.

> Job's new perception, I would argue, is rooted in a comic perspective, which comes only when Job has a double view—i.e., a divine and human view—of himself and the world. . . . He sees God and through God's eyes he now sees the world; he sees the mysterious and marvelous interworkings of the universe; he sees the seeming superfluity which is nevertheless required for the larger needs of life in the cosmos; and he sees that humanity only constitutes a small part of the cosmos.[13]

Of all the insights offered by the comic vision into the book of Job, Whedbee is at his best when he writes that Job now sees the great expanse of creation in all its wonderous exuberance and joyous laughter. Creation is full of life, and the actions within that universe are not wholly dependent on the creatures known as *Homo sapiens*.[14] I would add that Job begins to see that creation and destruction intertwine within an ever-creating universe. At the end of his tale, Job no longer sees from an egocentric point of view. He now has the keys to a universe in constant motion and can rest in the freedom that he is not the focal point. He is not the cause of all evil, nor is he always responsible for the evil that befalls others. He is a contributing partner to an ever-changing, ever-creating order.

Although looking at Scripture through the lens of comic vision may be challenging, the exercise allows the reader to see a different perspective of both the question of suffering and the context of Hebrew literature. Stepping back from a situation and letting humor shine a light on the questions can provide powerful coping tools when life's events are trying or traumatic. Graveyard humor is a trademark of people in dire situations. The ability to see the carnival can help responders and those involved in calamity to deal with great catastrophes or provide the needed push to survive a great loss.

From 1972–1983, the American television series *M*A*S*H* became one of the top ten programs and stayed in the top twenty for its full run. One of the hallmarks of the show was the ability to find humor in a world gone mad with death and destruction, suspicion, distrust, and the uncertainties of serving a cause that was not well defined. There were many serious episodes in which the characters made it clear that the humor did not disparage or minimize the true suffering inherent to military action, but it also reveled in the human ability to rise above loss and find joy, if only to cope and survive to fight another day.

Whether in tragedy or comedy, humanity continues to seek a cause for suffering and to find ways to respond effectively. Moving from the scholar to the authors of classic literature, what lessons exist in the fictional world that provide support and guidance in a world of suffering?

---

13. Whedbee, *Bible and the Comic Vision*, 251.
14. Whedbee, *Bible and the Comic Vision*, 251.

Chapter 19

Suffering in Literature

ONE OF THE THINGS that makes literature enduring is that it allows a reader to experience hopes, dreams, worries, and fears in a safe place. The best authors, the ones whose work survives for many generations, create that safe place and build pathways to solutions in a fictional world. The storyteller can place the reader in a situation that tests an idea or preconception against real-life outcomes. What better way to explore feelings about suffering than to watch a character deal with familiar situations? What better way to test multiple theories of scholars and thinkers within the workings of the world than through the test tube of literature?

Many classical works explore suffering. Some works ask specific questions to challenge a long-held orthodoxy, and some use satire to bring out the impracticality of one theory or another. Some stories spark a conversation and unsettle the complacency of the cultural expectations of the author's contemporaries. If a story achieves the longevity of a classic, then many generations benefit from the musings of the author. In each case presented here, the author chose to challenge what he believed to be grievous errors in the common beliefs of his time.

Candide, Francois-Marie Arouet (Voltaire, 1694–1778), 1759

Voltaire was a French satirist, a risky profession in the years leading up to the French Revolution. He used his writings to shine light on the dogma of his day and the overpowering influence of the Roman Catholic Church. He was a firm advocate of the freedom of religion and expression, and he supported separation of church and state. He also poked his satirical pen at the philosophers of his day. One such target was Gottfried Wilhelm Leibniz.

Voltaire wrote the story of *Candide* as a direct response to the philosophy of the time in general and that of Leibniz in particular. Leibniz took the hints and thoughts expressed by philosophical predecessors and arrived at a codification of something he called theodicy. According to Leibniz's opinion, the only explanation for suffering in the world was that God saw it necessary to grant humanity free will. Leibniz further believed that free will is prerequisite to a creation model for the *best* possible world. During the age of the Enlightenment, the thinkers of Europe were certain that humanity held fast to the reigns of its destiny.

Then catastrophe struck, not in some far off, heathen place, rather at the heart of Lisbon. In 1755, Lisbon suffered an earthquake, a tsunami, and the fires of All Saints' Day. These events shook the very foundations of the philosophies and theologies of the day. The theological and philosophical positions of the time supported a benevolent God, certainly one that protected his own. Such things should not happen to a Christian nation. These events caused misery on a massive scale, and there was no apparent evidence that free will had any part in the destruction.

In answer to the devastation, Voltaire wrote *Candide*. He opens his tale with a description of the perfect life, in the perfect castle, with all things ordered most perfectly. Voltaire writes that Pangloss, the teacher, "proved admirably that there is no effect without a cause, and that, in this best of all possible worlds, the Baron's castle was the most magnificent of castles."[1]

In the best of all worlds, Candide falls victim to the wiles of a young woman and is expelled from the castle. Exiled from home, Candide begins to wander the world in search of life's answers. What he finds is one misadventure after another as his firm belief in the "best of all worlds" leads him into trouble at every turn.

Candide and his companions finally arrive home, and once they are safe and secure, they find life empty because there are no more challenges. After a discussion with a successful Turkish farmer, who owns no more than twenty acres and has no interest in the politics of the city, Candide arrives at his conclusion. The piece closes with this:

> [Pangloss] "There is a concatenation of events in this best of all possible worlds: for if you had not been kicked out of a magnificent castle for love of Miss Cunegonde: if you had not been put into the Inquisition: if you had not walked over America: if you had not stabbed the Baron: if you had not lost all your sheep from the fine country of El Dorado: you would not be here eating preserved citrons and pistachio-nuts."
>
> "All that is very well," answered Candide, "but let us cultivate our garden."[2]

In the eyes of Voltaire, blindly following the tenets of optimism and believing that "all things work to the good in this most perfect of all worlds" is a travesty. To him, it was impossible to ignore the real suffering in the world and senseless to belittle the cost with the prattle of philosophers and theologians. He does not know the answer; he does know that whatever this life holds, one does best to cultivate

---

1. Voltaire, *Candide*, 2.
2. Voltaire, *Candide*, 168.

one's garden. *Candide* suggests that one should avoid the presumption of a kind and benevolent Protector and yet remain vigilant in the search for the best possible world. The remaining hope is that the search will benefit others.

The Brothers Karamazov, Fyodor Dostoyevsky (1821–1881), 1880

Dostoyevsky, born of aristocracy, was educated in many of the best Russian institutions of the time and became a member of the elite of Russian literary societies. His membership in these associations got him into trouble with the tsar's political police. Barely escaping a death sentence, they shipped him off to Siberia, where hard labor increased the severity and frequency of the seizures he had suffered for years. On release, Dostoyevsky served a mandatory military tour where, eventually, his health and the diagnosis of epilepsy made it impossible for him to serve any longer. Freed from prison and military service, he traveled and wrote. He was not always in the best of circumstances, and that contributed to his views on life, philosophy, and psychology. His insights have earned his works the status of literary classics.

In the tale of *The Brothers Karamazov*, Dostoyevsky uses the interactions of four brothers to work out his thoughts on suffering and the philosophies prevalent in his time. The brothers are Dmitri (a hedonist who takes after his father), Ivan (the agnostic who demands answers for the cruelty in the world), and Alexei or Alyosha (the devout Russian Orthodox monk). Last is Pavel, believed to be the bastard son of their father, Fyodor Pavlovich Karamazov.

The plot involves several twists and turns, including love triangles and the murder of Fyodor. The eldest son, Dmitri, is arrested, tried, and convicted of the crime. As the story develops, the reader learns that Pavel is the murderer. In a confession to Ivan, Pavel justifies the murder based on Ivan's insistence that everything is permitted in a world without God.

The author does more than challenge the current status quo; he subjects his characters to circumstances that are in direct contrast to their beliefs. When the senior member of the monastery where Alyosha serves dies, his body decays even though the devout monks believe him to be righteous enough to prevent decay from happening. The monks are reluctant to relinquish the legend that the truly righteous do not decay; consequently, they choose to discard the teachings of the departed abbot. Among these is the belief that no sin occurs in isolation and that we are all responsible for the suffering that we cause, however far removed we may be from the effect.

Ivan, in the chapter entitled "Rebellion," expounds on his thoughts of suffering and brotherly love. He believes true brotherly love is impossible once one sees the face of the sufferer. In other words, we can love one another in the abstract but not as individuals. He determines that perhaps Jesus could—but he is God and we are not.

Ivan focuses on the suffering of children because "in the first place, children can be loved even at close quarters, even when they are dirty, even when they are ugly."[3]

Ivan goes on to describe the cruelty of the Bulgarian war, calling it an injustice to the beasts to call it bestial. He details the reports he has heard of the particular cruelty to the children, innocent of all wrongdoing, yet made sport of and murdered before their mothers' eyes. He goes on to describe a case of child abuse so severe that when the victim reaches adulthood, his crimes are worthy of death. He has collected an entire library on the travesties visited on children, even in the most affluent of homes. Of all the misery in the world, it is the cruelty visited on these most innocent that strikes him deepest.

Ivan details his struggle with the belief that, in the end, we will all know that this world was created for the ultimate glory of God, and there will finally be harmony. Ivan does not want to pay the price of even a single tear from the eyes of a child to reach that harmony; for him, even that one tear is not worth any amount of glory in this life or the next. Ivan tells his brother:

> "Is there in the whole world a being who would have the right to forgive and could forgive? I don't want harmony. From love for humanity I don't want it. I would rather be left with the unavenged suffering. I would rather remain with my unavenged suffering and unsatisfied indignation, even if I were wrong. Besides, too high a price is asked for harmony; it's beyond our means to pay so much to enter on it. And so I hasten to give back my entrance ticket, and if I am an honest man I am bound to give it back as soon as possible. And that I am doing. It's not God that I don't accept, Alyosha, only I most respectfully return him the ticket."[4]

Neither Dostoyevsky nor Ivan can countenance the suffering in the world with the vision of a benevolent God. They cannot accept that humanity must purchase eternal harmony, bliss, and salvation at such a high cost, a cost that includes the fragile, innocent lives of children. Such moments force a compassionate heart to face all the pretty theories and test them to the extreme. Job demands that we see the suffering of the world honestly without the veil of theology or philosophy. Is it any wonder he demands an answer from the only source he deems knowledgeable enough to respond?

Till We Have Faces, C. S. Lewis (1898–1963), 1956

C. S. Lewis was a prolific and beloved author of Christian apologetics and fantasy. A reluctant convert, he sought to avoid dogma and explore the wider aspects of what it meant to believe in the Christian God. Of all his writings, readers consider *Till We Have Faces* one of his best. He shared that opinion with his reading public. The book

---

3. Dostoyevsky, *Brothers Karamazov*, 180.
4. Dostoyevsky, *Brothers Karamazov*, 186.

is an interpretation of the Greek myth of Cupid (love) and Psyche (spirit or soul), a hero's tale of a woman who overcomes obstacles to reunite with her only true love. At the heart, it is a tale of undeserved suffering.

The story of Cupid and Psyche is quite old. The tale gained recognition from the Latin classic *Metamorphoses (The Golden Ass)*, written in the second century CE by Apuleius. The tale itself must be quite ancient since depictions of Cupid and Psyche appear in Greek art as early as the fourth century BCE. The story is about a king with three daughters, each quite beautiful but none as beautiful as the youngest. Although the older sisters marry, the youngest finds only worshipers, no lovers. So great is the attention she receives that she draws the ire of Venus. Venus sends her son Cupid to end the competition with the young woman's death. Cupid falls in love with her and takes her away to a hiding place. He provides her with all her needs, and his only request is that she never try to discover his identity.

Time passes, and the young bride tires of being alone all the time and begs to see her sisters. Her lover grants her wish. However, the visit is disastrous. Her sisters become quite jealous of her new lifestyle, and they coerce her into revealing the identity of her husband. By exposing him, she brings the wrath of Venus down upon herself and her husband. Venus forces Psyche into a quest designed to drive her to extinction, but she prevails against the jealous goddess and eventually returns to her beloved Cupid.

A life-changing event can trigger personal suffering. These kinds of events cause us to build public faces to protect us from scrutiny. Often these changes build a wall between the sufferer and those whom they know and love. Those who suffer see this wall as protection from further pain, a protection against vulnerability. There are several reasons a survivor might not share their inner turmoil. Depending on the events creating the trauma, the survivor's life experiences, and previous reactions, sharing may be viewed as either a burden on the listener or an exposure of some weakness or failing.

Individuals also build walls to push away those who are suffering. For instance, like Job's companions, those who observe suffering seek to understand a reason, if only to avoid the situation for themselves. Humanity tends to seek order and is often uncomfortable when events appear arbitrary. For some individuals, the need for order is a search for God (or gods). In others, the search for order is an explicit effort to eradicate even a hint of the divine.

C. S. Lewis uses the plotline of Psyche and Cupid and retells the story. In his version, the tale becomes the story of an over-protective half-sister who fails to trust her sibling when it counts most. Her story is the search for justice. In Lewis's tale, the town sacrifices Psyche (Istra) in a high mountain meadow to assuage the troubles that have come upon them. She is tied to a tree and left to die. Her true love finds her and spirits her away. Her older half-sister, Orual, is unwilling to accept that Istra may have died, and she returns to the mountain to find her.

Suffering in Literature

Orual finds her sister not far from the site of the ritual in a mountain valley. She is happy and quite healthy. However, to Orual, she appears to be suffering from a delusion about a beautiful palace appointed for her comfort and care. In Lewis's interpretation, Orual does not see the palace. She believes that Istra is quite mad. To find evidence to support her sister's claim, Orual searches her memory of lessons on the goddess and in Greek philosophy. In the end, Orual cannot reconcile her knowledge with what she can see with her own eyes. Although Orual can tell Istra is quite happy, for Orual there is only contradiction and doubt. Orual finally decides to coerce Istra into revealing the identity of her newfound husband, someone sure to be a tramp or a highwayman. As the betrayal becomes a reality, Orual glimpses a palatial home through the mists of the valley and comes to realize the damage she has caused with her persistence to know what is real.

The results are disastrous. Orual now knows that her sister was quite sane and that she is responsible for sending Istra into the wilderness to be tested by a jealous Venus. Stunned and grieving, Princess Orual returns home. A few days later, at the death of her father, she becomes Queen Orual. Shaken to the core, Orual vows always to wear a veil so that none can see how homely she is. Slowly, Orual extinguishes that part of her that was the caring and loving protector of her beloved little sister. She lives in constant fear that the gods will strike her down for the heartache she has caused. Orual never allows herself to love again.

Queen Orual is a wise ruler. She reverses the policies of her father and finds ways to protect the country from the vagaries of nature, to build their treasury, and to protect their borders. An excellent fighter, she rides with her armies when required. The kingdom finds peace, yet she suffers. By chance, during a casual trip taken for pleasure, she happens upon a temple built in honor of her little sister, Istra. The local priest tells her the story of the wandering lover. She recognizes the tale in part, but she is stunned that the legend is missing crucial information about the part she played. The priest blames Istra's nameless sister for all the tragedy faced by the young woman. Orual vows to write her own story—the full truth—and to seek justice from the gods.

The tale is compelling because it is a search for an elusive answer to the question "Why are there trials, suffering, and retribution?" Like Job, we tend to believe we are doing our best, that we make appropriate decisions based on the knowledge we have. Then we discover we did not have all the relevant facts. No matter how hard we seek answers, we only see the things in this world darkly. Then, like Job, we reach a point at which we begin to demand answers. We want answers not because we do not believe, rather because we do.

In Lewis's tale, the queen muses as she writes, "There must, whether the gods see it or not, be something great in the mortal soul. For suffering, it seems, is infinite and our capacity without limit."[5]

---

5. Lewis, *Till We Have Faces*, 277.

Part IV—Recasting Job

No, not so different from the real world where we often seek guidance, follow the precepts we have learned, and yet we suffer. Looking beyond ourselves, we see a world in pain and note that much of what happens is an accident of birth or tragedy based on lack of knowledge. Is there any wonder that our highly developed, rational minds seek answers? Is it not inevitable that we reach a point when we stop and demand of the universe, of God, "Why?"

The queen chronicles her tale to challenge the gods, to ask them to tell her what more she could have done with the information she had. In the end, she learns that her love for her sister and her own experience of suffering throughout her life brought solace during Istra's years of wandering. Through her suffering, Orual provides support during times of Istra's trials. When the final test comes, Istra has grown in spirit, and even Cupid cannot sway her from the task at hand. Istra does, in the end, earn the approval of the gods and wins back her place at Cupid's side. Orual learns she no longer needs the veil that she has worn most of her life. Her life of service and sacrifice has only enhanced the beauty she has never known nor believed she possessed.

For Lewis, although we often suffer the consequences of ill-informed decisions, we still have a chance to build on our failures and turn them into something productive. We gain *face* by what we do about suffering and how we treat those in pain. Something is redeeming in how we use the tools at hand to make the world a better place, however small that improvement may be. When we strive in this way, we earn the right, the obligation, to stand and "gird our loins like a [rational being]" so that when asked, we can inform. That search for understanding can never end. Else, why did God give the gifts of a reasoning mind, a spirit of wonder, and a will to seek truth? Perhaps there is redeeming value in suffering that grants us the absolute right to demand an answer. Orual concludes, "I saw well why the gods do not speak to us openly, nor let us answer. Till that word can be dug out of us, why should they hear the babble that we think we mean? How can they meet us face to face *till we have faces*?"[6]

Does the book of Job provide an answer? Is there a moment when humanity earns the right to stand in the courts of heaven and require an answer for unrelenting and undeserved suffering? Is there a time when suffering, which may occur because we did not have all the information necessary, becomes resolved—and to our satisfaction?

J.B.: A Play in Verse, Archibald MacLeish (1892–1982), 1958

Archibald MacLeish was an American poet, playwright, and writer. He was a librarian of Congress and received three Pulitzer Prizes. He was devoted to literature and the development and sharing of the arts. *J.B.* is the story of Job cast in the America of the

---

6. Lewis, *Till We Have Faces*, 294.

Suffering in Literature

1950s. There are a few plot twists, but MacLeish stays with the primary elements of the storyline as presented in the biblical book.

Two old carnies narrate the play: one represents Satan and one God. Throughout the play, they attempt to remain behind their masks when in character, though there are times when they seem to be in deep conflict regarding their parts.[7] Even with foreknowledge, they find it difficult to watch the devastation of J.B. and his family. The format of the verse leads the reader to see a slowly unfolding accident which they are powerless to stop.

The play begins with J.B. and his family sitting down to a Thanksgiving dinner. Each family member is offering thanks for the good things they have. J.B. emphasizes that his success is not due to luck. He is successful because he has always been a worshiper of God. His wife expresses concern that the children may not understand as well as she would like and feels that their thanks are superficial and merely a concession to get on with the meal.

In due time, multiple disasters strike the family. A son, who is deployed in a war which just ended, dies before he can return home. Two children die in an accident caused by a drunk driver, and the youngest is raped and beaten by an addict. Bricks falling from a building due to an unknown catastrophe crush the remaining offspring. The catastrophe has also destroyed J.B.'s bank and the entire block where it once stood. Devasted by his losses, J.B. grows ill.

As the broken man begins to lament this turn of events, he seeks a reason for the rapid-fire tragedies visited on himself and his family. He seems unable to find anyone or anything to blame but himself. J.B.'s wife refuses to allow him to take the blame for the loss of their children. In her eyes, if he insists on blaming their calamities on himself, that all this misery is due to something that he did or did not do, he might as well have been the murderer. She cannot accept this thought and consequently leaves him.[8]

MacLeish's comforters are anything but, and they represent individuals from the clergy, medicine, and a kind of everyman. They are all worn, broken, and ready to torment J.B. even further. They push hard to get him to doubt and capitulate to reason—certainly there can be no faith in God worth having in the face of the consequences.

The conversations between the carnies can be very challenging from a scriptural and spiritual point of view. Mr. Zuss (God) declares that nothing will make J.B. turn from God. Nickles (Satan) whispers, "Why must he suffer then?"[9] Mr. Zuss replies, "So that J.B. might praise God." To which Nickles replies that he already does, "like a canary." Nickles becomes forceful in his speech, noting that we are born into bright delusion, believing God loves and cares for us, but suffering teaches us the truth. As the conversation intensifies, Mr. Zuss admits that God would not permit the test unless he knew the outcome. Nickles again presses, "Then why the test?" Mr. Zuss replies,

---

7. Macleish, *J.B.*, 97.
8. See chapter 14.
9. MacLeish, *J.B.*, 48–50.

Part IV—Recasting Job

"So that J.B. will know." The carnies put on their masks, perhaps because they cannot bear to see human faces say the words of Satan's challenge to God to test J.B.'s loyalty.[10]

In the end, Sarah, J.B.'s wife, returns. She has been wandering about the desolation of what was once their prosperous town. J.B. is not immediately happy to see her, asking her why she left him. Her response, "I loved you. I couldn't help you anymore. You wanted justice, and there was none—only love."[11] She left him to preserve that love because she could accept no other answer. In the end, the only response MacLeish has for the suffering we endure is that we endure. We pick it all up from the ashes and rebuild, not because we understand but because we love. In the end, it is all we have left if we choose to preserve it.

Commentary, as expressed by scholars, theologians, and philosophers, is not the only valid source for understanding Scripture. Literature created to place the questions humanity faces into a contemporary framework or to work out the consequences of a specific belief or theory also helps to provide understanding. If Scripture is to have meaning for every person in every age, then it must have meaning wherever we encounter life in all its glory and degradation. How can it be of comfort if it does not reach deep within us and touch our souls in the face of reality? With all the references and tools explored in this text, can the puzzle of Job be solved? Or must we wait for an answer that, even at the end of time, might not satisfy our need to understand?

---

10. MacLeish, *J.B.*, 50.
11. MacLeish, *J.B.*, 151.

Part V—Redefining the Conversation

Chapter 20

The Gordian Knot

THE LEGEND OF THE Gordian knot originates from Alexander the Great's march to take Asia. On his march through Anatolia (modern-day Turkey), he arrives in Gordium, the capital city of Phrygia. There he finds a monument to the founder of the city. The statue is a chariot tied to a pole using an intricate knot. Legend has it that the person who unties the knot will go on to conquer Asia. Various recorded solutions include Alexander slicing through the knot with his sword, finding a way to extract the pole, or—per the instructions left behind—finding the hidden ends that untie the whole mess. Whether the incident is historical or not, the term "Gordian knot" has come to represent a complex problem that usually contains a paradox of some kind, and that requires a solution which acknowledges that contradiction. Properly retelling the story of Job then requires a solution which addresses the "loose ends." Any solution which does not address the loose ends of the argument or use them to resolve the puzzle will not suffice. Resolving theodicy, undeserved suffering, and the role of Providence requires more than brute force destruction of the knot. All the connecting points need to be found and put in the proper place, thus loosening the knot and allowing us to retell the story with new meaning.

From a Judeo-Christian point of view, and the perspective of some other faiths, certain attributes define God (or the supreme god). The sacred works of all faiths try to characterize a sovereign deity in such a way that supports developed tenets. Following is a list of generally accepted attributes, as presented in Christian literature. A summary analysis of how these aspects fit within the various interpretations of Job's search for answers follows.

PART V—REDEFINING THE CONVERSATION

A supreme Creator must be omniscient, or all-knowing.

For the Abrahamic religions, God is all-knowing in part because he is either outside of time or is somehow part of the very fabric of time. Since a finite existence does not constrain God, he can *know* all that was, is, or will be.

One way to think of this concept is to think of time as eternally now. There is no tense in eternity, so all is knowable in the same moment. We can get a taste of this experience by using discoveries from physics and astrophysics. When astronomers look deep into the night sky, they are looking at light that has traveled light-years to reach the lens of the telescope. Light consists of photons moving through space at a measurable rate of speed. We measure astronomical distances in light-years, that is, the distance a photon travels in one year. Since light travels at 299,792 kilometers per second (186,000 miles per second), in a single year it travels 9,460,730,472,580.8 kilometers. It takes a full eight minutes for light to travel from the sun to earth, and 4.37 years for light to reach earth from Alpha Centauri, earth's nearest interstellar neighbor. Light recorded by earth or near-earth instruments sees Alpha Centauri as it was 4.37 years ago, not as it is in earth's *now*.

The farther away astronomers explore the further back in time they see.[1] Looking forward into the future requires predictions using, among other things, what we know about physics and mathematics. Julian Barbour, a theoretical physicist, proposes that there is no real time at all.[2] That is, everything occurs in an *eternal now*. Each now is complete and whole. Even with Newton, Einstein, and hundreds of highly qualified physicists working on a theory of time, defining time still eludes us. With our growing knowledge about time, we have a better grasp of what is meant by the word "omniscient." All things are known in the now—whatever now is currently existing.

Job 37:16 says, "Do you know the marvels worked upon the expanse of clouds, / by Him whose understanding is perfect?" Scripture teaches that he counts the hairs on our heads (Luke 12:7) and that no sparrow falls without his knowledge (Matt 10:29). Passages such as these support the notion of God's perfect knowledge. Nevertheless, what does perfect knowledge mean in an individual's life? Physicists and mathematicians have calculated that to comprehend all the information in the universe, we would need a computer as big as, well, the universe. If we need a computer as big as the universe to comprehend the universe fully, then how can we limit God to some defined space? Have we lost something critical in attempting to define God's omniscience in terms of our understanding?

Further, does knowledge of the future demand action to alter the outcome? Certainly, as mortals, we do not always allow an assured outcome to deter us from a chosen course. Humanity is notorious for not acting in the face of suffering, real or

---

1. Recent research has indicated that the speed of light may not be constant; see Grant, "Speed of light not so constant after all."
2. See, Barbour, *End of Time*.

predicted, and individuals and cultures sometimes actively resist action. The question is, if the mitigation or cessation of suffering is well within the purview of humanity, why, then, demand that God fix the problem? Even if he is all-knowing and foresees all the difficulties, why must he be held accountable for not doing what we are fully capable of doing ourselves?

A supreme Creator must be omnipotent, or all-powerful.

This attribute is only partly dependent on a belief in miracles. A miracle is an occurrence that defies logic or current practical understanding. Conventional wisdom holds that water does not become wine unless the laws of chemistry are changed or suspended. Suns do not delay their course across the sky unless the laws of physics are changed or suspended. People do not rise from the dead or receive immediate healing unless the laws of biology and microbiology are changed or suspended. Using this logic, one cannot have miracles unless someone breaks the rules.

First, set aside the trivial arguments that ask such things as whether God can, for instance, make a rock so big he cannot lift it. C. S. Lewis addresses this issue succinctly in *The Problem of Pain*:

> His Omnipotence means power to do all that is intrinsically possible, not to do the intrinsically impossible. You may attribute miracles to Him, but not nonsense. This is no limit to His power. If you choose to say, 'God can give a creature free will and at the same time withhold free will from it,' you have not succeeded in saying anything about God: meaningless combinations of words do not suddenly acquire meaning simply because we prefix to them the two other words, 'God can.' It remains true that all things are possible with God: the intrinsic impossibility are not things but nonentities. It is no more possible for God than for the weakest of His creatures to carry out both of two mutually exclusive alternatives; not because His power meets an obstacle, but because nonsense remains nonsense even when we talk it about God.[3]

The issue is that we create a quagmire once we attempt to set boundaries on something not fully understood. Learning does not occur when we set boundaries based on our current understanding; learning occurs when we discover our boundaries and move past them.

Are there miracles? Quite possibly there are. Do they require that the laws of this universe be broken, changed, or suspended? Not necessarily. What scientists have discovered in physics and quantum physics is that what is possible may not be easily determined based on current knowledge. Research indicates that things do not become reality until observed or measured. Recent observations indicate that the particles that

---

3. Lewis, *Problem of Pain*, 18.

make up the universe may have a will.[4] These are the questions that drive scientists and mathematicians to devote lifetimes to discovering what makes the universe tick.

We attempt, from our finite point of view, to define something infinite. There is nothing particularly wrong with that if we do not assume that the infinite must fit within the resulting definition. Viewing the universe from outside of a finite, egocentric lens is extremely difficult, not impossible. Each year we learn more about the universe, how it came to be, and how it functions now. What can be determined is that God's power, in whatever way evidenced, is not a universal fix-it. God's power is an intelligent, creative force that continues to operate in the now.

The author of Job (42:2) tells God, "I know that You can do everything, / That nothing you propose is impossible for You." The list of passages that assure the believer that God is in control is quite long. Jeremiah 32:7 asks if anything is too hard for him. In Mark 10:27, Jesus says that all things are possible with God. We need to ask, however, "Just because something is possible, is it the *fitting* thing to do?" As individuals, our point of view is limited, often necessarily so. What we cannot do is presume we know how God will choose or why. Tevye, the milkman in the Broadway production and the movie *Fiddler on the Roof*, sings a query to God. He reflects on what life would be like "If I Were a Rich Man."[5] The question is whether it would disrupt some great cosmic plan if he, a poor Russian Jew, were a wealthy man. With our present knowledge, we really cannot know, can we?

A supreme Creator must be omnibenevolent, or all-loving.

Jews, Christians, and Muslims all believe that God loves them and, within differing doctrines, all he has created. Exactly what this means is entirely dependent on the interpreter's background, religious faith—or lack thereof—and their philosophical and theological perspectives of the world.

The idea of omnibenevolence stems from the concept that God is both perfect and morally good. Not all faiths believe that their deity (or deities) exists in perfection. The definition of *morally good* varies from culture to culture as well. Defining morals in this context can be complex and an exercise in futility. Consider how we define a moral individual, and then see if any of those attributes apply to a sovereign creator.

Morally good can mean just. One could presume that an eternal judge who knows all the relevant facts is in a special position to judge rightly. For this reason, those things that befall a believer must be justified in some way, even if the "why" is not understood. In other words, even if justice is deserved, mercy can still prevail. Sometimes the actions taken have created more suffering than the perpetrator can

---

4. Bloom, *The God Problem*, 427.

5. *Fiddler on the Roof* is a 1964 Broadway musical, also adapted to film in 1971 (directed by Norman Jewison), based on "Tevye and His Daughters" (or "Tevye the Dairyman") and other tales by Sholem Aleichem. The song referenced occurs in the first act of the musical.

resolve. How does one "fix it" if, through a deliberate or negligent act, a wildfire destroys property in the billions and takes the lives of dozens? Then sometimes, as in the case of Job, the penitent arrives at court with clean hands and a burning desire to know why a life of righteousness is not enough to protect one from the vagaries of the world.

There is also a school of thought that renders the term as meaning that God is perfect and desires goodness. If that is the case, then why would God not pursue every means to make *it* (however that may be defined) happen? If God loves his creatures, then why not fix whatever the problem is?

The book of Job approaches the love of God from the view of justice by asking, "Is God just?" Other passages within Scripture address love from a caring and nurturing or protective view. These passages teach that humanity is loved by the Creator even as a parent loves a child. The question is, do we understand love, however it is defined, even when experienced among ourselves? Given the uncertainty faced in day-to-day relationships, how can we define, with certainty, how a universal love might look?

A vast amount of literature uses these three attributes (all-knowing, all-powerful, and all-loving) as crucial to sorting out the causes of undeserved suffering. The question remains whether, in the quest to define God, we lost him. To answer that question, we can compare the answers explored in this book with the criteria established by the defined aspects of a creator. As this book has shown, we have expended centuries of commentary and philosophical thought to offer solutions to the question of Job's suffering and what that answer might mean to individuals. Following is a summary of those proposals and how closely they fit within our notions of a sovereign deity.

The Crime and Punishment, or Penalty and Reward Theory

One of the most often quoted reasons for suffering is that someone somewhere did something wrong, and now the penalty must be paid. This argument is the primary argument of Job's visitors. Whether Job knows it or not, there is some blemish in his life that requires his avowal. If he would repent of this unknown crime, things would be set right.

There is no doubt that there is a price to pay for breaking a code, be it moral, cultural, or personal. All cultures, to some extent, enforce this tenet. We do so to the best of our ability, even though that ability often falls short of the mark. Is theft of bread or milk to feed a starving child the same offense as stealing money from a house-bound senior? Is the act of securing a shoreline to protect a home during floods the same offense as corporate destruction of resources for economic gain? What if deterioration of that shoreline is not due to natural causes? Are we godlike in knowing, always, precisely who did what and why? Should we have the power to end a life because of a crime committed, even if we do know beyond all doubt that we have the right person? These are the reasons we have courts, lawyers, judges, and juries whom we entrust with the duty to work in concert and arrive at a fair decision. The problem is that the justice served often seems unsatisfactory. Public opinion often weighs in on the fairness of a sentence or a pardon, an opinion which is subjective depending on the circumstances and emotional investment in a case. For instance, a rape victim may serve time for assaulting or murdering her assailant, while a rapist gets off with a few months in jail and community service. A corporate executive or political figure may get a few months in a minimum-security facility for financial crimes while a person of color selling cigarettes on a corner gets beaten to death.

Things get even stickier when we try to interpret divine justice. Job's visitors press this case diligently, and so does Job. They contend that God, the omniscient creator of the universe, knows all and is the ultimate judge regarding punishment. We do not suffer unless he has deemed it appropriate. Job agrees. However, his position is that God *knows* that he is innocent. He declares emphatically that he has committed no sin of commission or omission and that he stands before the bar with clean hands, yet his Lord permits, even directly inflicts, suffering.

Given a sovereign whom we believe to be omniscient, omnipotent, and omnibenevolent, it is not a stretch to believe that he would discipline those he loves so that they might become better people. For instance, as parents and caregivers, we attempt to discipline our children. Although we tend to fail miserably, we also struggle with ways to rehabilitate society's criminals. These are concepts more easily understood than implemented.

The problem arises when the punishment appears to be arbitrary and without explanation. What lesson can we learn from inexplicable discipline? How can God hold us accountable for a code we cannot know? According to Job's tormentors, there could be precepts established by the creator which we cannot comprehend (Job 11). How, then, can a just God condemn us should we trespass a hidden code?

Punishment and reward, then, can only be a partial answer to the suffering in the world. Job's visitors failed in their analysis primarily because they could not see beyond the dogma of the past. In their attempt to justify God, they created a theory that blamed the blameless. Consequently, they offered no succor—only more suffering.

The Free Will Theory

The concept of free will is at the root of theodicy as developed by the Enlightenment philosopher Leibniz.[6] Free will is a natural development of thought from the punishment and reward philosophy presented by the prophets of the Old Testament. How can one be punished for something if there is no choice involved? We saw this argument in the commentaries written by some of the church fathers as they debated the implications of Augustine's doctrine of original sin. Many could not countenance the

---

6. See chapter 5.

thought that the action of one man condemned all of humanity. In their view, each holds the choice of right or wrong firmly in his or her grasp and is, therefore, responsible and accountable.

Leibniz goes further. He hypothesizes that God permitted free will because it was an integral part of a perfect creation and the only path to the best of all worlds. A substantial percentage of humanity would beg to differ.

Free will is a concept that is far more complex than it might appear. Does free will limit the power of God? If he can and would interfere with the consequences of a free will choice, does that limit free will? If there is divine interference, is there any way to understand why God might interfere in one case and not another? Even though collective choices may create disasters, not all disasters are known to occur due to specific choices. For instance, generations of destruction of the wetlands in the Mississippi River Delta have left the coast more susceptible to destruction by hurricanes. There are many clues that some of humanity's practices add to the instability of our geophysical world; there is less certainty regarding what types of actions can directly cause catastrophes such as a volcano, at least as of now.

The choices of one generation, or a definable segment of society, can severely limit the choices of the next generation, or of people or persons in some other location or circumstance. The destruction of the forests in Indonesia for palm oil farms causes a severe environmental crisis as far away as Singapore. Whose free will should take priority—those who feel there is no other way out of poverty or those who would like to be able to breathe on the way to work without a mask? What about the natural habitat that supports the environmental balance of the earth as a whole? Should there be a collective effort to protect these shrinking resources, to assuage the impact of humanity on the ecosphere?

What about the sins of our ancestors? If an individual has the free will to abuse and batter a child, the chances are statistically consequential that child will carry the legacy into later life. Recent research has found statistically diverse results for children suffering from mental, physical, or socioeconomic challenges. There always remains the possibility that the survivor overcomes his or her past. Again, whose free will should take priority? And if one generation chooses to squander the wealth of resources and commerce available to them, what limitations does that create for the following generations?

Philosophically and scientifically, we are beginning to understand free will and what it implies. Chapter 24 provides some detail regarding current research into how our brains operate and what influences our behavior. Brain chemistry does play a part in how we respond to our individual life experiences. However, the same research indicates that we can consciously change our responses and interpretations if we choose to do so. Any answer that we derive concerning the existence of suffering in the world must consider the impact of an individual's choices on themselves, other individuals, and the world. It may even be possible to glimpse something of the role a creator might play in balancing the contradictory impacts of all those independent choices. Consequently, the agency of free will could well be a piece of our answer.

The Redemptive Suffering Theory

Redemptive suffering centers on the thought that when bad things happen, the circumstances provide an opportunity for better things to occur in the future. This point of view looks for the greater good or sees that pain and suffering can be the cause rather than the effect. It is a realignment of perspective where suffering is the beginning rather than the ending.

This theory is another way of saying all things work together for the greater good. It brings out the omnibenevolence definition that sees God's perfection and desire for goodness. He acts, at least in part, to create greater good out of the suffering inherent in the world.

From a practical perspective, this aspect can be an viable outcome. There are times when something happens that keeps us from our first desire yet opens doors to other opportunities. In his book *God's Problem*, Ehrman shares the story of a summer when hepatitis kept him at home. Instead of spending the summer deep in his first love of athletics, he read. He chose to research the subjects posted for the upcoming year's debate team. It changed the course of his life and did so in a manner that pleased him.[7] Sometimes the setbacks and heartaches in life foster a greater good. Individuals are wise to learn from mistakes or create a better path using the circumstances in which they find themselves.

Can we always turn suffering into some greater good? Who decides where the balance lies between the suffering of one individual and deliverance of another? Even if the death of a child encourages changes to laws or practices that protect others, is the suffering of that child or the loss to those parents recompensed? We should always seek ways to convert the agony we find around us into something positive. However, does that outcome justify the pain of the afflicted? Is it possible to derive something good from the suffering of one starving child, let alone millions? Why must they starve?

The Sufferings of Love Theory; Testing Loyalty and Love

There are two aspects to this theory: testing loyalty and testing character. They overlap somewhat, yet the core ideas are different. In the prologue to Job, Satan believes Job is only loyal to God because he is the recipient of God's bounty. Take away his wealth, his family, and his health, and all that loyalty would go up in smoke. Job, of course, could not know this is a test, or it would be no test.

---

7. Ehrman, *God's Problem*, 154.

Job's response is resounding. Job 1:21, "Naked came I out of my mother's womb, and naked shall I return there; the Lord has given, and the Lord has taken away; blessed be the name of the Lord." Again, in Job 2:10, "Should we accept only good from God and not accept evil?" And from 13:15, "Though He slay me, yet will I trust in Him." How many times is Job required to declare his loyalty to have it accepted?

How do we fit the omniscience of God into this scenario? If God knows everything, certainly he knows whether we are loyal. Are we tested to prove to others that we are loyal? Must we somehow prove to Satan and the rest of the world that our private loyalty is sufficient to carry us through trials which seem to target us specifically? Is the current agony only a test to know ourselves with a deeper understanding, to know what we are capable of and more of what frightens or weakens us?

The book of Job is not clear on what inference Satan may draw from such a test. That leaves the record of history as a testimony for the effectiveness of this approach. No overwhelming evidence indicates anyone has a positive interpretation of the suffering of Jews, Christians, or Muslims. On the contrary, history indicates that the general belief is that individuals or groups of individual Jews, Christians, or Muslims did something wrong (as Job's visitors assumed), or they are delusional.

Research indicates that throughout history, those religious or cultural communities with laborious initiations were the communities that inspired the maximum loyalty. Theoretically, that which does not cost a great deal has little value.[8] Historically, initiations tended to strengthen loyalty to one group as opposed to another. So, perhaps, such trials are a test to intensify existing loyalty to a creed or faith.

We can accept that there is a certain benefit in having to prove loyalty to a cause or faith to gain acceptance as a member of that group or institution. There is some personal gain in testing the foundations of our commitments and knowing where we stand and what we are willing to give up for a belief or an idea or a way of life. Nevertheless, can we seriously believe that the sovereign Creator of the universe is going to grind us to dust to prove we are still willing to believe? Current research is giving us a better understanding of codependency and abusive relationships. We know that in some cases, the abused partner remains because they sincerely love their abuser and continue to hope for change. Sometimes they remain knowing that leaving can be the final trigger to fatal violence. In any case, these types of relationships are not healthy for either party. Subjecting oneself to abuse to preserve a relationship or attempt to seek validation is dangerous emotionally and physically. Such a relationship is not a pretty picture when one seeks a Creator to love.

In *J.B.*, MacLeish suggests that the test is not for God's benefit but our own so that we know the extent of our commitment.[9] Perhaps, but at what point does that test become counterproductive? What sort of response would we expect from our

---

8. Wade, *The Faith Instinct*, 40.
9. MacLeish, *J.B.*, 50.

children if we tested them in this manner? Can a test be valid if it is without explanation or justification, even after the test ends? How broken must we be to prove worthy?

We see some implications of these same feelings in the church's teaching of suffering in Christ. The belief that they were suffering with Christ was what sustained the martyrs of the church throughout history and what sustains many of them now. Suffering in love is the underlying belief that none of us should fare better than Christ and that whatever we suffer is merely a drop in the ocean of his suffering. We show our love for him by sharing, in some small way, in the cost of that love.

What constitutes suffering with Christ is a question that only a believer can answer. Following in the steps of Jesus does require sacrifice and suffering. In some areas of the world, that cost can be life itself. However, Scripture teaches that he paid the full price for that suffering. If we propose that human suffering is required, then are we saying that the sacrifice is insufficient to the cause? Theologians say that the price was both backward-looking and forward-looking; it was an all-inclusive moment. If that is the case, then remembering that sacrifice should produce a sense of freedom, not more suffering.

Choosing a course of faith does require sacrifice, whatever that faith may be. That sacrifice can incur suffering in some small or great way. It cannot, however, adhere to an interpretation that the creator of this universe would take the notice and the time to grind the believer to ash to prove their loyalty. There may be elements we can take from this interpretation. However, as an answer to undeserved suffering, it fails horribly. Perhaps Satan's part in the story is to set up the foil, to introduce the commonly held belief so that the author can explore alternatives.

The Test of Character Theory, or Growing through the Pain

Nietzsche, in his *Twilight of the Idols*,[10] states, "From life's school of war: what does not kill me makes me stronger." Even if the sufferer is a member of Nietzsche's defined elite, such a sentiment does little to assuage suffering and may make it worse. It is true that, as we go through life, whatever events we experience shape us into something that is uniquely us. Whether we choose to allow life's tribulations to build our character or crush us is, to some degree, our own choice. However, tribulation, as a builder of character, works far better if there is a discernible cause and effect. At some point, we must get the message that, due to this choice, these things happen, whether the choice is ours, or someone else's.

Maimonides believed that suffering was required for the individual to attain intellectual virtue.[11] To him, as well as some of the church fathers, suffering in this world was not real. The loss of physical things held no pain for the individual that aspired to intellectual virtue and eternal life. In his view, this was the lesson Job needed to learn.

10. Nietzsche, *Twilight of the Idols*, 3.
11. Maimonides, *Guide for the Perplexed*.

Nothing he held on this earth, including the lives of his children, was of account in the greater scheme of things.

To Maimonides, this was the source of providence. The individual must aspire to develop the ability to concentrate on God while living in the current world in such a way that suffering did not affect them. Although that sounds marvelous, most people would have great difficulty dealing with the effective application of this theory. Siddhartha realized that to become enlightened, he could not separate himself from life. Persons who choose to live a life of devotion in a monastery or convent of whatever religious bent can separate themselves from this world. However, for most of humanity, living on the cusp of that conversion experience all day, every day would be a bit like our brains on drugs.

There is also the issue of empathy. Most, if not all, religions have some maxim to love others and to care for those who face challenges in this life. One could argue that it is important to understand and accept some level of suffering to understand the pain of others better. One should also avoid becoming so overwhelmed with the pain of others that they are incapable of constructive assistance. What happens if one becomes so immune to suffering that another's suffering no longer has impact? Can a moral person, in good conscience, ignore the suffering of others with the attitude that all debts become resolved in the next world? The Old Testament prophets tell us that we do so at the risk of our eternal souls.

There is no doubt that, when subjected to the crucible, we do build character. A substantial part of humanity's heritage, both in legend and in myth, expresses precisely that. Our stories illustrate how humanity has overcome obstacles and created something newer, stronger, better than what has gone before. When a character or an individual prevails against challenges we love to tell the stories so that others might benefit from the experience. Consequently, retelling Job's story from this perspective could be some part of the answer. However, the suffering of the poverty-stricken of the world does not build character as much as it fills graveyards.

The "Suffering for a Better Heaven" Theory

Suffering for a better afterlife is slightly different from the apocalyptic view described below. It is a theory drawn out in Job only obliquely. The Old Testament does not evidence a highly developed concept of life after death. What it does describe is a vision of Sheol, where all things are equal, and there are no high or lowborn. Sheol is a place of rest and freedom from tyranny and oppression; however, this place of freedom was not a goal to seek except for peace and cessation of constant woe.

The church fathers of the early centuries often wrote of the need to suffer a little in this life to increase our rewards in the afterlife. Somehow, God is showing his love by allowing his creatures to build up credit for better rewards in the hereafter.

This interpretation is disturbing. Now, instead of worshiping God for the good things he brings in this life, we are worshiping him to store up treasures in the next life. Again, the notion of being so "heavenly minded you are of no earthly good"[12] is problematic. Many faiths share the belief that there is some direct relationship between our journey here and what happens once we lose our grip on this life. However, a better afterlife should not be the sole goal of our conduct during this life, nor the cause for suffering. If an atheist can live a life of moral integrity for the rewards or accomplishments of this life alone, can a person of faith do any less? Job is not in search of a better afterlife; he is in search of an explanation for the trials of this one.

There Is No Reason; Life Is Vanity

Epicurus, a Greek philosopher who lived from 341–270 BCE, believed that the purpose of philosophy was to achieve a tranquil life free from fear. He also believed that death brought the end of the soul and the body, which we should not fear. The gods did not reward or punish human beings, and the universe was infinite and eternal. In his view, all things occur through the motions and interactions of atoms moving in space. Epicurus would have been quite at home in many scientific academies of today. Maimonides would have rejected this perspective. He believed that we must strive to learn to be worthy of eternal life and not abandon a hope for providence.

According to Ehrman,[13] the Teacher, the author of Ecclesiastes, also sees all life as vanity. Since good and bad have no preference, we suffer only by chance. All life is vanity, and the best we can do is live well, do what we can for our fellow beings, and die.[14]

As unsatisfying as this answer may seem, it does demonstrate a fundamental truth. There are some things we cannot control. We see in the world that those who are wicked do prosper, and those who are ethical do suffer. We know that we cannot rely on the gentlemen's rules of dueling in the middle of a street fight. Sometimes the best we can do is live well with what we acquire and use our wealth and influence in the most ethical way possible. Scripture alludes to this philosophy by teaching us that sometimes we overthink situations and end up losing what influence we might have to make life a bit better for those around us. The final words in Ecclesiastes are, "The sum of the matter, when all is said and done: / Revere God and observe His commandments! / For this applies to all mankind."[15]

Although this may be sound advice, it is not a satisfactory answer to the undeserved suffering of the world. When we dine and enjoy each other's company, servants

---

12. Attributed to Oliver Wendell Holmes, Sr.

13. Ehrman, *God's Problem*, 189.

14. Interpretations of Ecclesiastes vary; however, the book begins with a lament that all is vanity and ends with the admonishment to live well, care for those who need it, and leave the rest to God.

15. Eccl 12:13.

and workers are laboring to make our lifestyle possible. In other words, someone worked to produce the clothing we wear and the food on our table. This response to a presumed arbitrary and unknowing universe is not an ultimate answer; it is a response that Candide would understand. Voltaire admonished us to tend to our garden, and from our success, we may be able to tend to others and assuage some of the pain in this world.

The "Not of This World" Theory

Apocalyptic interpretations posit that God has allowed the forces of evil to rule this current world for some yet-to-be-disclosed reason. In this case, we are placing all our bets on some answer at the end of time. The theory rests on the hope that, at the end of history, God will provide an answer that will sufficiently explain why he has permitted this to be and why all the millennia of suffering experienced by humanity was required.

The theology of the afterlife is a view whispered in the Old Testament and buried in the imagery of Leviathan. It comes to full fruition for Jewish believers during the time of the Maccabees and Christian believers in the New Testament. The New Testament tells us that we deal with principalities[16] and that someday Christ will return to reclaim the earth. This theological interpretation also carries the seeds of gnostic and Aristotelian thought. Matter is inherently finite, it represents deprivation, and we will not be whole until we leave this world of matter and privation behind. As previously noted, to some philosophers there is no real loss in this world unless one loses one's soul.

In Job, we see this answer in his cry: "I know that my Vindicator lives; / In the end, / He will testify on earth" (Job 19:25). An end-time resolution of all questions is also the theory presented in *Putting God on Trial*.[17] In the end, Job and the rest of humanity will get a satisfactory answer to the question of suffering.

Perhaps we will see all things more clearly in the future, and perhaps our explorations into the universe and the science of how things work will provide some answers. The question remains: will it be enough? How do we tell the broken, raped woman that her terrifying experience was all part of a greater end-plan, and God promises he'll make it all up to her? According to some versions of the Christian faith, if she has never heard of Christ, then this is only the beginning of her suffering. There is much more to come.

When we were younger as a race, when humanity had yet to reach the beginnings of understanding of the universe and our place in it, this answer may have been enough. The author of Job wanted more. And so should we.

---

16. Eph 6:12.
17. Sutherland, *Putting God on Trial*, ch. 16.

Part V—Redefining the Conversation
The "God Is Too Great a Mystery" Theory

The central point of this theory is the view that we will never figure out the mind of God, that we should accept the arbitrary behavior of the universe and hope for the best. I need to get more personal here and state that I utterly reject this interpretation, in part because I cannot see how we can be held accountable to answer to something we cannot comprehend. This view proposes that we can never have a full understanding of the law and may not even have the capacity to understand that parts of it even exist.

It is also anathema to my thought process to believe that humanity has developed a rational mind and remains barred, somehow, from knowing the universe in which that mind matured. Yes, we are finite, and yes, the very idea of understanding all there is to know about the universe is beyond our comprehension. However, the discoveries of science over recent centuries indicate that the universe is *not* arbitrary. The cosmos is *not* a mindless, uncaring, frothing cauldron of chaos. The universe that we inhabit has order, creative force, and basic rules under which it operates. Of all the arguments that peppered my youth, it was the proposal that there was no way to truly understand God or why there was suffering in this world that drove me to the journey that resulted in this book.

This chapter presented the primary attributes of God and summarized current interpretations of theodicy and views on the causes of suffering. As evident in my response to this last theory, what follows is a shift from the more general conversation between writer and reader to something more personal. Most of this book dissects the literature that relates to suffering, theodicy, and providence. I have mentioned frequently how the theories presented were not entirely satisfactory to me. I also do not expect them to satisfy any other serious observer. We started this book with the exercise of taking apart the story of Job and rebuilding it from the ground up. Now, to solve the riddle of what the author may have had in mind as these words formed on the page, we need to see what information may have been available. What might they have known intellectually, philosophically, and theologically as they mused about the trials and tribulations of our weary soul, Job? To finish the task of retelling the story, we must revisit the author at their desk. What was it that drove the Persian-period philosopher on a journey to explore Job and his travails?

Chapter 21

The View from the Author's Window

REITERATING A COMMON THEME in this book, the authors of Scripture did not compose their works in a vacuum. Although some of the authors focused on local geography, culture, and politics, not all of them did. Authors, ancient and modern, use imagery familiar to their target audience. For the authors of Scripture, the imagery would have provided meaning for any reasonably informed person of the era and the location. Each author who contributed to the body of Scripture had a unique background, perspective, and mission. Chapter 3 described the author of Job as a well-educated person living somewhere around 400 BCE. They knew Hebrew intimately, although it is not their first language. The author's execution of the poetic drama is exquisite. We have before us a scholar.

Poetry is the style used for much of the philosophy of the ancient world. The sacred writings of many religious traditions use poetry, and the Greeks favored it for studies in multiple disciplines. What would a scholar, most likely living in the Levant around 400 BCE, know about the world, the cosmos, and how things work? What follows is a brief look at the cultural and political background of the period, as well as the scientific and philosophical thought, which developed a century or so before the author of the book of Job lived.

The Achaemenid Persian Empire (550–330 BCE)

As established in previous chapters, scholars date the composition of the book of Job to ca. 400 BCE. Their conclusion takes into consideration internal evidence of the language and structure of the book. However, there is more evidence within the book itself to support this conclusion. The historian in me wishes to place the author in the world in which they wrote. Where and when this individual lived would have influenced the interpretation of the discourse within the book and might shed light on the poet's intent.

Part V—Redefining the Conversation

The Achaemenid Empire spanned the Asian, African, and European continents.[1] It encompassed Egypt and its neighbors, parts of Eastern Europe, Lydia (Turkey), the eastern Mediterranean, Central Asia, Mesopotamia, and as far east as India. It was a cohesive and well-maintained realm with periodic royal review of assigned governors (satraps).

The Persian king Cyrus the Great founded the empire. When he secured his throne in Babylon, he set the political prisoners free and restored the local temples. The edicts of Cyrus were the historical event behind the scriptural migration of the remnant of Israelite peoples back to Judea in the Levant ca. 539 BCE. As with all large empires, there were revolts to put down and peoples to subdue. For the Persians, the hottest trouble spots were Egypt and the Greek city-states. The Greeks, much like the Hebrews, were fiercely independent. Although the Greeks shared a language, a religion, and an intellectual heritage, they had great difficulty committing to anything more structured than an alliance of city-states. The political volatility of the peninsula caused coalitions to form and fall apart many times, even when the Greeks were at war with outside forces.

Current day Iran and Iraq were the heart of the Persian Empire. Archaeological research has not been an easy task since the political and cultural nature of Iran and Iraq remains unpredictable. Consequently, a great deal of what we know about the Persians and their rule derives from Greek records. The Greek accounts of the Greco-Persian Wars (499–449 BCE) provide some of that history. Historians record court intrigues (regicide was a popular form of ascending the throne throughout ancient history), moral decadence, and excess within the empire. However, such events occurred in the history of many empires. Once an empire gains stability, an aristocracy with appetites soon follows.

Greek reticence to Persian rule aside, the empire was a stable political influence. Cyrus the Great, the founder, is remembered as a strong and tolerant ruler. He permitted conquered peoples to speak their language, practice religion as they saw fit, and maintain their unique culture. He also created a Charter of Human Rights that applied to all the subjects of the realm, with men and women holding equal status.[2] Cyrus wished to build an empire based on mutual respect and a stable civic authority.

An interim of unrest ensued when Darius I ascended the throne in 522 BCE. Once he had secured his position, he contributed much to the continued stability and success of the empire. During his reign (lasting to 486 BCE) Darius I undertook the construction of the Royal Road. He also enlarged the system of satraps to govern the outlying areas efficiently. The Greeks recorded that Persian building projects used paid labor rather than slaves and that women received equal pay.[3] Equality of the sexes was a fundamental tenet of Persian law as well as their faith.

1. See maps in Part II.
2. A translation of the original clay cylinder can be found at http://www.farsinet.com/cyrus/.
3. Mark, "Women in Ancient Persia."

The View from the Author's Window

As the Persian Empire grew, it contributed to the character and cultural foundations of Near Eastern and Western Civilizations and the languages of the Mesopotamian valley. While the regional languages of Egypt, the Mediterranean, and Mesopotamia became the purview of the priests and scholars, Aramaic became the official language of the realm. Aramaic is one of the languages of our scriptural heritage. It belongs to a family of Semitic languages that includes Canaanite, Hebrew, and Phoenician. Greek and Aramaic are the original languages of the New Testament.

The Persians bequeathed one other powerful influence: the gift of their primary religion, Zoroastrianism. The faith survives in small pockets of Iran, some areas of India, and scattered congregations throughout the world. Though not strictly monotheistic, it is a faith structured around one supreme creator god, and it contains many similarities to the tenets found in Jewish, Christian, and Islamic beliefs. Founded by Zoroaster in the sixth century BCE, it teaches dualism, the battle between good and evil, with the presupposition that good (represented by the creator god) will win in the end.

For Zoroaster, free choice temporarily limits God's omnipotence. Therefore, humanity becomes part of the cosmic struggle in return for that gift. To these believers, the ethical choices of humanity have both a cosmic effect in the war between good and evil and a direct effect on an individual's eternal destiny. There are familiar themes in the writings of Zoroaster, such as heaven, hell, angels, demons, resurrection of the body, and a messiah. This faith includes the tenet of a virgin birth and a divine redeemer. The word "magi" as used in the nativity recorded by Matthew derives from *magus*, which is a member of the priestly caste of ancient Persia.[4]

The seeds of the concepts of apocalypses, free will, and battles between good and evil forces within the universe run deep in our heritage. The author of the book of Job drew from this heritage as he contemplated the world, divine action within that world, and humanity's response. While Persia provided a relatively stable political and religious background, the Greeks were developing the foundations of modern science. What would the author of Job know about science?

Thales of Miletus (624–546 BCE)

Thales, sometimes referred to as the first scientist, lived in the Greek city of Miletus, located in modern Turkey. Most of what survives of his work comes through the writings of Aristotle, which means we are not entirely sure of what is pure Thales and what is an interpretation or extrapolation of Thales. What we do know indicates that he sought answers from nature regarding how things were rather than assigning

---

4. Magi is a plural form of magus, the title given to a member of the hereditary priestly class among the ancient Medes and Persians. Zoroastrianism was the state religion at the time.

supernatural causes. He was a "monist," a term that describes belief in one transcendental god who is eternal and acts through other influences rather than directly on an individual.

In search of a universal material found in all things, he settled on water, something modern scientists believe is essential to the development of life. Some of his other contributions are more difficult to discern. He devoted much of his life to the study of natural phenomena in search of non-supernatural explanations. He watched the actions of ships on the bay to determine that the earth floated on a great sea and reasoned that waves moving across this vast ocean were the force that caused earthquakes. He was one of the first to accurately predict an eclipse and to understand the cycle of the 365-day year. Neither of these concepts appear to be natural conclusions from the perspective of landmasses floating on a global sea. Understanding the astrophysics of eclipses and annual cycles requires the premise of a spherical earth. Thales writings do not specifically state a shape for the earth. However, others were working on that question from observable evidence.

Pythagoras of Samos (569–475 BCE)

The life of Pythagoras is shrouded in legend and bits of recorded history, at least in part due to the extreme secrecy practiced by the cult he organized on Samos. History places him in Egypt ca. 535 BCE, where he went to study the ancient wisdom of the country. When Persia invaded Egypt around 525 BCE, he was captured and taken to Babylon. Wasting no opportunity, he studied with the priests of Mesopotamia. When released, he returned to Samos and, sometime after 520 BCE, formed his school, calling it the Semicircle.[5] After a few years, he left Samos to avoid becoming involved in politics and moved his school to Crotona. Some of his followers were vegetarians who lived in the community with no personal possessions. Others lived outside of the community with their possessions and ate what they chose.

Finding anything else more definitive about the Pythagoreans and their leader is rather difficult. Plato and Aristotle both reference the work of the founder and his followers. Although the Greeks, in many ways, considered the pursuit of knowledge a divine vocation, the Pythagoreans viewed their practice as a mystery to be shared by only a few. One incident that led to their designation as a cult was the sacrifice of an ox in celebration of discovering the forty-seventh proposition of Euclid.[6] They enmeshed their study of mathematics and philosophy with their study of metaphysics. They believed the only way to free themselves from an endless cycle of death and reincarnation was to obtain an understanding of the universe. In pursuit of this knowledge, they came to believe that mathematics was the basis of knowledge and that geometry

---

5. See "Pythagoras."
6. In any right triangle, the sum of the squares of two sides is equal to the square of the hypotenuse (the longest leg). It is the basis of squaring the base of a monument, such as a pyramid.

was the highest form of mathematics. The Pythagorean interpretation of the world, like the Zoroastrians, was dualist. The world depended on the interaction of opposites such as male and female, light and dark, hot and cold.

Disentangling the theories of Pythagoras from those that bear his name but were developed by community members is difficult. Later generations of his followers always attributed their work to the founder and no one individual. In any event, the Pythagoreans developed the mathematical proofs of the relationships inherent in the right triangle. Although the Babylonians and Egyptians had used these concepts for centuries (as in the building of pyramids), the Pythagoreans worked out the abstract mathematical proof. Pythagoreans also defined the five regular solids: tetrahedron, cube, octahedron, icosahedron, and the dodecahedron. In their view, the sphere represented ultimate perfection.

In cosmology, Pythagoras taught that the Earth was a sphere in the center of the Kosmos. In his view, the planets, stars, and the universe must be spherical because that is the most perfect solid figure. Consequently, he determined that the paths of the planets should be circular. Pythagoreans also determined that Venus was the morning star and the evening star. The group taught that music was another path to understanding since it is so intimately related to mathematics. Pythagoras's work in harmonics revealed the symmetry of relationships between notes. The Story of Mathematics website provides some background and explanation of these concepts.[7]

In approximately 450 BCE, the Pythagoreans felt compelled to change their position on a geocentric Kosmos. Although the system they developed was rather complex, they explored and defended a heliocentric universe. Their theory stood for some time, even with the strained explanations required to predictably describe the motion of sun, moon, and planets. They had come to believe that the earth revolved around a central fire. Two thousand years later, the scientists and theologians of medieval times fought against the belief that the earth was flat and the prevalent misconceptions of which celestial body orbited which—if, indeed, the earth was round. Evidently, against all other evidence, the belief in a flat earth remains to this day.

Anaxagoras (500–428 BCE)

Anaxagoras is known for his cosmological theory of origins. He taught that the original state of the universe was a mixture of all its ingredients and that the mixture was not uniform. Everything apparent to the observer consisted of different amounts of each ingredient, and the ingredients became mixed in different ways. At some point, a "mind" initiated movement, and the ingredients separated, becoming the parts of the things we observe today. Anaxagoras did not approach this theory with a religious connotation, and he did not fully define what he perceived as mind. His writings

---

7. See "Pythagoras of Samos."

indicate that his perception of mind was something purer than all the rest of the elements making up the early universe.

Although Thales could predict an eclipse, Anaxagoras was the first to give the correct explanation of an eclipse. His work proposed that both the sun and the stars consisted of some fiery iron or other material that burns at great heat. Further, the moon consisted of the same materials as earth. These were his recorded findings two thousand years before Galileo Galilei.

Empedocles (490–430 BCE)

Empedocles defined four elements—earth, fire, air, and water—and postulated that all change was a shift of relationships between these elements. He postulated that there were two divine powers, Love and Strife, which together acted as the moving influences within the universe, causing the observed changes. Conceptually, he was far ahead of his time in the perception of scientific and mathematical principles. Empedocles determined that light traveled at a finite velocity. He also developed a form of the law of conservation of energy and devised a theory to prove constant proportions in chemical reactions. He developed these conclusions through reason and observation. His work received little attention until long after modern scientists, physicists, and mathematicians proved its validity.

Democritus (460–370 BCE)

Along with Leucippus, Democritus was the founding father of atomic theory. Much of what we know about his work comes from those who disagreed with him (such as Aristotle). From the surviving record, scholars are fairly certain he was the first to determine that very small, indivisible, and indestructible building blocks made up all matter. He called these building blocks atoms and believed they combined in different ways to make up the things we saw. He was the first to posit that the celestial body called the Milky Way was a formation consisting of distant stars. Democritus believed that, along with his many stars, there were many worlds, some of which might be inhabited.

Hippocrates (450–380 BCE)

Hippocrates is the father of modern medicine. The writings attributed to him are likely a combination of his work and the work of those who built on his theories and practices. He offered a biomedical methodology, a system of diagnosis, and a foundation of professional ethics. The oath taken in the medical field today derives from his creed and his commitment to serve the gods and goddesses with faith and integrity. The quote "First, do no harm" is not expressed explicitly.[8] His writings were a fundamental shift away from the world of magic and superstition toward the world of empirical evidence and direct experimentation.

The Greeks and the Author of the Book of Job

Why is this summary of Greek thought important to the retelling of the story of Job? The few scholars mentioned here were changing the way that humanity viewed the universe. In the rich cultural atmosphere of Persia and Greece, scholars were redefining how individuals perceived the universe and how we fit within the story. The author of Job was a scholar residing somewhere in the Levant.[9] The work of the neighboring Greeks and the philosophies of the reigning Persian Empire were part of the cultural, theological, and intellectual fabric from which the message of the book of Job emerged.

Job contains precepts drawn from ancient legends about undeserved or inexplicable suffering visited on the righteous and the innocent. The content of the debates draws from the wisdom of the prophets and lawgivers of the Israelites. However, internal evidence indicates that this book is much more than a simple retelling of an ancient legend. To understand the message of the book of Job, we need to place the author within the context of the Levant (possibly Judea or one of the coastal cities), ca. 400 BCE. From that, we can postulate something of what a scholar of that age might have known and how that might have contributed to recorded thoughts. A fundamental part of inspiration is the vessel that delivers the message. If God is the inspiration for Scripture, then the author of that work was likely chosen for their unique ability to speak to the subject.

The ideas of free will, dualism, rewards, punishment, and afterlife were already in the theological lexicon. These concepts were not a theological interpretation confined to a small enclave trying to rebuild an identity on the shores of the Mediterranean. For me, the key to understanding Job was to see the author of Job as part of a cultural background. The author chose to debate theology and philosophy by combining the established interpretations of Hebrew faith with the religious thoughts of an empire and the intellectual explorations of the Greeks and their fellow scholars. Through these staged debates, the author found something important to say about our responsibilities as we gain new knowledge and understanding. Also, the author's treatment of the natural sciences indicates a familiarity with the work of the Greeks. Men and women[10] of reason, both from the viewpoint of practical application and from philosophical thought experimentation, were stretching our knowledge of the universe and how it worked.

---

8. See "Greek Oath."
9. See chapter 3 and maps provided in Parts I and II.
10. See Wider, "Women Philosophers."

Part V—Redefining the Conversation

Why it took two thousand years for the concepts of our universe explored by these Greeks to make it into the general conversation is anyone's guess. By the time such men as Copernicus and Galileo were presenting their views to the public, the philosophies of Plato and Aristotle had become well ingrained in church interpretations of the cosmos. Perhaps the church and various other cultic practices are to blame for clinging tightly to the interpretations they found most useful. Perhaps it was a fear that humanity was an insignificant part of the big picture and not the center of all things good and evil. In the end, we do ourselves a great disservice if we apply Scripture without understanding the context that contributed to its message.

What we can deduce is that our author, a scholar, living in the crossroads of intellectual and theological thought of his time, had questions. The sage advice of the prophets and lawmakers of centuries past were no longer enough for those who sought knowledge. The author saw a need to build a bridge between the wisdom of the past and the evolving knowledge of the time. When we begin to retell Job in the context of its times, we can prepare to redefine Job for our times. To begin the retelling, a summary of the book of Job from this new perspective will help support a new interpretation.

The dissertations of Eliphaz, Bildad, and Zophar are not the pivotal arguments in this book. Even Elihu misses the point. For all their knowledge and experience, they miss the heart of the question. Even today, we deal with those who see Scripture as somehow separate from the lives and experiences of those who contributed to the content. Such a method of interpretation can be a costly error. The author of Job characterizes the protagonist as a man who acknowledges there is wisdom in the understanding of sin and punishment. Job then turns away from his visitors as it becomes clear they cannot expand their view beyond ancient dogma.

The fulcrum of Job's argument begins when, in the face of silence from the heavens, he asks, "Where can man find wisdom?" (28:12). Above all, no answers can be forthcoming until we can redefine the question, a question reconfigured for a time of emerging knowledge. Where, then, do we begin? Job's Ode to Wisdom (Job 28) provides some clues.[11]

Some key verses in the chapter derive from other passages in the Old Testament, most notably Psalms and Proverbs. Wisdom is a recurrent theme within Scripture, and it is the heart of the Talmud. There are two versions of the Talmud, one Babylonian (fifth century CE) and one earlier form known as the Jerusalem Talmud. The Talmud is a body of literature that defines Jewish civil and ceremonial law and legend. The purpose is to interpret the written law and to understand the obligations established by that law. These writings are the search for wisdom and understanding. In Job

---

11. Modern scholars of Joban literature such as David Clines of the University of Sheffield and Edward Greenstein, quoted elsewhere in this work, have reached a conclusion that Job 28 is actually Elihu's concluding argument, or it is a separate work and not an expression of Job's point of view. In either case, the questions raised and answered within Job 28 have meaning within the context of conclusions drawn within this text.

28:28, the speaker's closing statement is, "See! Fear of the Lord is wisdom; / To shun evil is understanding." Shunning evil takes understanding of the law. Still, what is "fear of the Lord"?

A word defined by the cultural context of one language can lose meaning in the cultural context of another, Hebrew being a prime example of this issue. To apply an English meaning to a generally accepted translation can lead to confusion. The Hebrew word used in the phrase "the fear of the Lord is the beginning of wisdom" is *yirah*. This word does not represent an attitude of fear and trembling. The *Jewish Encyclopedia* describes the usages of the Hebrew word translated as "fear" from a different perspective.[12] Within Jewish practice, this word is a way of drawing nearer to, not shrinking from, God. The term used implies love and service, not dread, not service in need of reward, not fright.

The Ode to Wisdom found in Job 28 describes our search for wisdom under every rock and in every crevice—created or manipulated. There is a mine for silver and a place for gold, iron, and copper. Everywhere, humanity pushes the boundaries of the known and strives to light the darkness to recreate the world to suit what the species believes it needs or wants. The beasts are confounded as we overturn the very mountains, carve through the bedrock, and seek out every precious thing—or at least those things we deem to be precious. We exercise control on all the waterways and reveal what lies below the waves.

Nevertheless, where is wisdom? Does it reside in the land of the living? Is it even possible to find wisdom as a mere mortal?

Job ponders the reality that all we have discovered and created will not buy wisdom. Even as the Greeks pursued the knowledge and wisdom that helped build Western Civilization, their city-state kingdoms waned. Wisdom, according to Job, cannot be found in the deepest sea. Even our knowledge of death, the abyss, and Abaddon[13] provides only whispers.

Job concludes that God—and only God—possesses wisdom. He has measured out the world, set the courses of nature, and formed the fabric of our universe. Therefore, God is the only source of wisdom, the only answer. To Job, God is as far above us as we are above the beasts. If humanity can work with the beasts to tame the world, is there hope that God has a plan for humanity to do the same? As Job turns away from his visitors, we begin to see the conflict the author is working to resolve. Job's compatriots see his quest for answers as blasphemy because, in their view, the wisdom of the past requires submission. Through Job, the author struggles to incorporate the advances of his age within the wisdom of God. If sin and deprivation are not the only causes of suffering, then why do they occur?

As Elihu comes to the end of his lengthy case against Job, he returns to the theme of looking to the marvels of God for answers. In 37:14, Elihu describes how the sun

12. Guttmacher, "Fear of God."
13. The Hebrew name of the angel of death.

can hide and then be revealed by the wind, the forces of nature can cause warmth or cold, and the heavens can look as "firm as a mirror of cast metal."

He closes his case with this (37:23–24):

> Shaddai—we cannot attain to Him;
> He is great in power and justice
> And abundant in righteousness; He does not torment.
> Therefore, men are in awe of Him
> Whom none of the wise can perceive.

Neither Job nor God responds to him. Of further note, Elihu's version of God's wonders is simplistic and mythical; there is no depth to his descriptions. Elihu is not interested in deeper knowledge; he prefers the mystical, unknowable God. How does one respond to someone who states that wisdom cannot be obtained, while Scripture indicates that we are to seek it? How does one respond to someone who declares they are the final authority on any subject, even if they have talked past the issue at hand? If the search for wisdom is a waste of time, why, then, do we reason? Why are we driven to begin a quest we cannot complete?

Here is where I diverge the furthest from what might be considered a consensus on the interpretation of Job. Most traditional commentary emphasizes Job's predicament. He is faced with the overwhelming power of God, and although he is not being accused of crimes of any sort, he is being crushed to dust and told he must wait. Someday, there may be an answer. But I see a different story. I hear a challenge in the question, "Have you considered?" I hear an invitation in the demand, "Come, I shall ask, and you shall answer." God's response redirects our attention; it is a tutorial on how and where to look to seek our answers. Again, although Job may be humbled, he is not humiliated. God instructs and guides Job; he does not grind him down. These are the reasons I see Job as a hero and not a penitent.

Even before I felt convinced that the author was, indeed, a scholar of the Persian period, I felt the power of that opening challenge: "Who is this who darkens counsel, / Speaking without knowledge? / Gird your loins like a man; / I will ask and you will inform Me. / Where were you when I laid the earth's foundations?" (38:1–4). My response was not to cower under the incomprehensible power of the creator of the universe—I saw an invitation, rather, a demand, to view that creation and reason out what it taught me, to learn the secrets of its workings so that I could better understand the heart of its creator.

Was this the intent of the author? I sincerely believe so. He lived in a period when the precepts of an enlightened philosophy and theology guided an empire. He lived at a time when science, as we know it today, was birthed and developed by men and women of reason. It was a time when scholars respected the wisdom of the past, even as they pursued knowledge with vigor and expectation. God, or some form of supreme intelligence, still ruled the universe. However, it was a universe that reason said had purpose with discernible patterns, a universe we could come to know. In such a universe, what was the purpose, the meaning, of suffering?

Can we use this knowledge to seek out the answer to our current quest? Why is there suffering in the world, and can we expect any help in our struggle against it? The next three chapters look at how the author perceived the nature of the world, the universe, the beasts of the field, and Leviathan with his companion Behemoth. To retell the story for the modern reader, I will build on knowledge available to the author of the book of Job and combine it with modern research and philosophy. If the meaning of Job is to teach us to grow in understanding of creation as a path to wisdom, then what does that quest teach us? Can we use the wonder and probing of an author from twenty-five hundred years ago to guide us in a search through modern science for a better understanding of how the universe works and what our part in it might be? Is there an answer in our age to the conundrum of suffering?

Chapter 22

Consider the Measure of the Earth

THE NEXT THREE CHAPTERS provide an analysis of Job 38–42 using the knowledge available to an author writing around 400 BCE. That information, as recorded here and in previous chapters,[1] is then broadened using the knowledge that modern science and medicine have contributed to how the universe functions. I believe that these chapters are crucial to the understanding of the author's goals. Job finally gets his wish to engage El Shaddai in conversation. In these chapters, the author works through the need to incorporate the growing body of humanity's knowledge with a new perception of who the Creator is and what his role might be. To retell the story of Job, we need to redefine how we look at God.

Predominantly, commentators on the book of Job do not see an answer in this exchange beyond the belief that God tells Job he cannot understand until the end of time when, perhaps, he will. I found this view unacceptable. I am not alone, since for centuries we have continued to revisit the ash heap and attempt to draw something more from Job and his experiences. Perhaps now, by turning the point of view inside out and retelling Job's story, we can find an answer. Is it possible that the book of Job is about the balance of faith and science? Was this author in search of answers that have meaning within the knowable universe while acknowledging a Sovereign Power capable of its creation? Can we learn to understand suffering within the context of a constantly creating cosmos?

I am not attempting to prove that the Bible contains science, accurate or otherwise. I do, however, believe that the authors used the world as they saw it as a tool to think about things of the spirit, even as we do today. The imagery of what we see helps us understand that which we cannot see; this is the basis of allegory, metaphor, symbolism, and logic. It is how our minds work.

There are enough hints within the poetic discourse to legitimize seeing these next chapters as an answer. Repeatedly the poet points toward the workings of nature,

1. Most specifically, chapter 21.

the relationships of its creatures, and the fundamental workings of the cosmos. God responds by pressing home some of the points that Job has already made while adding several more. The focus is to look, to learn, and to find answers. El Shaddai invites Job to open his mind and reach for comprehension as his understanding of the physical world expands. Paul writes to the Romans (1:20), "For since the creation of the world his invisible attributes—his eternal power and divine nature—have been seen, because they are understood through what has been made. So people are without excuse."[2] As noted in the previous chapter, knowledge of the world was not entirely based on mythology and legend when the author retold the legend of Job. A well-educated scholar of 400 BCE had access to the reasoning of the Greeks, the Egyptians, and the Persians. That is a large body of information, some of which forms the foundations of scientific pursuits today.

Acknowledging accuracy in the ancient sciences of any sort poses several problems. First, it was an ingrained philosophical dogma that perfection in the cosmos reflected perfection here on earth. We are not built to accept arbitrary circumstances; we are constantly in pursuit of patterns. However, to keep our patterns in line with expectations, we also like to make assumptions based on what evidence we choose.

Some of the scientists of Newton's time wanted to look more closely into the past to determine if the ancient historical records were accurate or flawed in some way. The debate at Newton's time centered on the accuracy of the records kept by Babylonians, Egyptians, and Greeks. Many scientists of the day thought that if we were to develop a reliable cosmology, it needed to account for events recorded in the past as well as what was evident through current observations.[3] Astronomical records that predated the time of the Babylonian king Nebuchadnezzar were considered suspect by Newton. They described events that were not possible in a universe believed to be steady and consistent. In the end, those who wished to test new ways of interpreting the cosmos against historical data lost to the clockwork universe of Newton.

Fear of an unstable world permeated our thought process. From the Greeks to Newton, we sought perfect elements, perfect spheres, and perfect celestial mechanics. We see evidence of this belief in scriptural commentators such as Zerahiah Hen (1200 CE), who dismissed the historicity of Job because it reported fire from the sky. Such a thing was beyond his imagination but did indeed exist.

This ideological doctrine is also evident in the search for a perfect cosmos and a perfect morality. It was a view rejected by some of the writings explored above. One case in point is Voltaire's *Candide*; we *do not* live in the most perfect of worlds, and there *is* something else going on. We have a right and an obligation to understand the

---

2. From the NET Translations. This passage is often pulled from context to condemn homosexuality when Paul is actually referring to the need for order and understanding.

3. Nicolas Freret (1688–1749), Secretary of the Academie des inscriptions, was a contributing researcher among scholars attempting to sort myth from fact in ancient writings. There is some contention regarding what writings he authored.

workings of this world and to use that knowledge to create a better world. Newton was not wrong; he was working with incomplete information.

Today, we can use Newton's physics to launch spacecraft into interstellar space while understanding that we are still exploring the field of subatomic physics where the rules get very interesting. As we learn more about the universe we live in, we know that reality does not consist of perfect geometric shapes dancing in perfect time to a metronome started before the dawn of humanity.

That fundamental need for stability was not limited to the likes of Zerahiah and Newton; it permeated the church. As the church formed and councils determined the shape of the faith for future generations, Aristotelian and Platonic philosophy contributed to the basis of that faith. In both science and philosophy, the church became a supporter of the perfect universe. In the mind of many of the church fathers, God's creation was perfect; therefore, humanity's moral life should be perfect and well-structured. The root of Galileo's battle was to incorporate what he observed with what he believed. He believed—his faith did not move—but he knew, without a doubt, that the Earth did. He knew the orbs were not perfect forms, and he knew that creation was far more interesting than the church wanted to admit.

"Where were you when I laid the earth's foundations?" (38:4)

The book of Job gives us a sweeping, poetic description of Earth. God measures the foundations and lays cornerstones. He forms the world as the morning stars sing together and all the divine beings shout for joy (38:7). Then the author of Job declares that the globe hangs on nothing (26:7). In 400 BCE, mathematicians and philosophers were developing mathematical proof that the Earth was globular and surrounded by space. Our scholar drew on that knowledge and used it to revisit our relationship to the universe and its Creator.

The intellectual drive to measure the earth began in very ancient times. By reconstructing the measuring units used, French scholars of the eighteenth and early nineteenth centuries were able to show that the circumference of the Earth had been estimated even before the Greeks. How accurate those measurements are is still up for debate. By the time of Eratosthenes (240–194 BCE), the calculated circumference of the earth was within 2 percent or less (which represents less than five hundred miles) of the modern measurement (24,901 miles).[4]

Today we know the measurement of the earth with such precision that we can use the timing between satellite signals to pinpoint our location anywhere on the globe using GPS. We know the height of every mountain and the depth of the sea. We know how far we are from the sun, how deep our atmosphere is, and how large our magnetic shield is. We know how fast we circle the sun and the path of our solar system's

---

4. See "Eratosthenes (273–195 B.C.)."

journey within our galaxy. We know something of how the earth is formed, to its very core, and what that means in the movement of landmasses and bodies of water.

We also know something of those wandering orbs detected by the Babylonians and named *planets* by the Greeks. We have also learned a great deal about how the foundations of those planets take form. We know why, to some extent, some planets are rocky, and some are gaseous. We have added many bodies to that original catalog, and we have even sent our ships and satellites out into the solar system and interstellar space to learn more. Just about fifty years ago, we landed on our closest neighbor, and our knowledge grew.

Homo sapiens was not present when the foundations of this world were laid, although we have been observers as other worlds formed.[5] The search for knowledge continues, and the more we know, the more we know how much we do not know—but that does not give us cause to be discouraged. It feeds our desire to know more, to rephrase the questions, to incorporate each fact we learn into the formulation of the next theory. God tells Job, "I will ask and you shall answer" (38:3). The search for truth continues.

"Who closed the sea behind doors?" (38:8)

When the book of Job was penned, the Greeks had several theories regarding geography and geology. Some of them were mythological, such as Thales's idea that the earth itself floated on a large ocean. He also observed that water was a primary element without which nothing could survive. The reasoning developed by the Babylonians, the Egyptians, and the Greeks is the foundation of modern sciences.

Recent experience has taught that sometimes the sea does not remain within its boundaries, and when it escapes, the earth and those who dwell on it can suffer tremendous damage. We came to know something of the "why" of those forces because we witnessed the effects in action and then learned to find the evidence of past catastrophes in the geological record. Much of our learning occurred as we plied the oceans as merchants, explorers, and conquerors. The lore of humanity's interaction with the seas and oceans of this planet comprises many volumes of human history. Here, again, we are still learning.

Even in the fields of history and archeology, we are still not certain of who arrived on what landmass when. However, through these fields we learn much about our species, the drive to discover, to seek a place to call home, and to find treasures yet unknown—or to avoid the problems we faced in that place we left behind.

We know something of oceanography and of the creatures that live in the waters of this globe, both great and small. We do not know the full path of the migrating

---

5. See "Watching How Planets Form."

whales, nor do we know how some species can survive in near-ice conditions at the poles or in the heat of a sea vent, which reaches 750° Fahrenheit (400° Celsius).

We know of the tides, the moon's effects on the heartbeat of our globe, how ocean currents contribute to our weather, and the way corals and the life of the sea protect us and feed us. We know that the gravitational forces of the sun and moon can combine to create super-tides (perigean tides),[6] which can cause anything from spring floods to terrifying waves of destruction. As with our reach into space, we build complex machines to take us to the very bottom reaches of the sea.

Though initially we saw the ocean as teeming with life, we have come to learn that we can and do change the ecology of the seas by over-fishing, destroying the reefs, and creating artificial floating islands of debris. We have learned that vast expanses of the sea are liquid deserts with little life above that of a microscopic scale. Also, that microscopic life has a variety far beyond our expectations and imagination.

We have also learned that the oceans play an important role in the origin of life, here and most likely elsewhere. Whatever the source of their insights, the ancients did see something of the truth of the matter. As far as we know, without water of some kind, life can neither begin nor prosper. We also know that the oceans contribute a crucial piece to the stability of our climate and that catastrophes can occur when the historical balance of our oceans change.

"Have you ever commanded the day to break?" (38:12)

Of all the things that drove our curiosity to *know*, the movements of those amazing bodies in the sky must have been prime irritants. From the time we first looked up and felt the warmth of the sun, knew the chill of its absence, learned the cycles of the moon, and watched the slow, majestic dance of those dots of light in the night sky above us, we sought reason, order, and understanding. No, we cannot command the sun to rise. However, we have learned a great deal about why and how it does so. And we are getting ever more efficient at harnessing its power to fuel our homes and enterprises.

With many starts and meanderings, we arrived at the mechanics of our solar system. There are Greek, and perhaps older, records which indicate that philosophers and scientists knew the cause of an eclipse and understood something of the orbits of the earth and the planets.[7] At the very least, they had discerned patterns in those movements. We also know that the struggle to understand even the basic mechanics of the solar system with provable mathematics took centuries. However, once we began to break free from the need to have a perfect, stable, and unchanging cosmos, knowledge of the universe expanded exponentially. Learning that the lack of perfection does not destroy the balance of nature itself is a lesson we can use in interpreting

---

6. See "What Is a Perigean Spring Tide?"
7. See chapter 21.

the philosophy and theology of Job—forcing the notion of a perfect model on an active and constantly creating universe leads to blind alleys.

In recent times, we have learned something of how mass and gravity affect the motions of everything from the smallest particle to the attraction of massive galaxies and black holes. The field of physics is finding questions faster than answers at this point in our history. The last century has seen major advances in our understanding of how stars, solar systems, galaxies, galaxy clusters, and even atoms form, and something of how they die. The astrophysicists of today search the skies to learn more about the earth, its neighborhood, and what we can expect for the future. No, we cannot call the sun to rise, but we do know why it does.

"Can you tie cords to Pleiades?" (38:31)

The stars and all their mysteries have begun to reveal themselves to us. Although they are still out of our reach physically, we know something of the location of stars in the night sky and why they move as they do. We understand that some of those points of light are more than another distant sun; they are vast colonies of suns. We know that our galaxy is a relatively small one with a wavy spiral shape and that there are uncountable numbers of galaxies of all sizes and a few different shapes. We know that galaxies collide and stars explode. We know that the very fabric of space consists of things we can only glimpse in our mind's eye. Curiosity drives us on to ask more questions and to seek more answers. We cannot tie a cord to the Pleiades, but we do know the path to their door.

"Which path leads to where light dwells?" (38:19)

Empedocles, a Greek philosopher, had already hypothesized that light had a measurable velocity as the author of Job penned his verse. The Greeks studied, as best they could, what made up light, how it interacted, split into colors, refracted, or became patterns. Light has probably fascinated us since the first starry night and the first warm campfire, and yet it still holds mysteries.

Now we know that light consists of photons, and we know how fast it travels, although there are recent experiments that indicate that its speed is changeable.[8] We know that refraction and gravity bend light. We are beginning to understand that light is some combination of a particle and a wave and that it has unusual properties when measured or observed. We know that it can teach us about the universe, including how big it is, what the chemical composition is, and perhaps how old it is.[9] Internet

---

8. Grant, "Speed of Light Not So Constant."

9. This author recognizes that there are open scientific debates regarding how we estimate the life of the universe. Even acknowledging that there are unresolved issues in details about big bangs, or big bumps, or details in how physics changed in the first few moments of the universe to allow the

sites and libraries devoted to Hubble, space exploration, astronomy, and physics are all excellent resources to further research what light spectra teach us about our universe.

We also know that light provides energy. As the light of the sun reaches us, it interacts with plant life through photosynthesis. Sunlight brings life-giving energy to the biological creatures of this globe. It helps drive the process of evaporation and condensation that waters the far reaches of the ecosystem, and it gives us warmth. Light is so mysterious and pervasive that, early in our history as a species, we looked to the sources of light as deities responsible for our existence and survival.

No, we were not born when the cycles of light and darkness were established. Nor did we exist when the stars and planets were first revealed to the surface of our world. Nevertheless, we have learned where the light dwells, what it is, and how it travels, and we know something of the darkness that surrounds it.

"Have you penetrated the vaults of snow?" (38:22)

Climate—how it operates, where it drives the forces of weather, how it changes—is crucial to a healthy ecosystem. Then, as now, knowing when to plant, what to plant, and when to harvest is a matter of survival. Does one set sail today or next week? Will the wells be productive during the coming summer? How do I feed my household in drought, during floods, or after devastating storms?

The need to know the coming of the rain and snow or warmth and cold was a contributing factor in the development of astronomy. On every inhabited continent, our first historical records contain some account of the search for order in the coming and going of the sun and moon. The need to know and understand these cycles is one of the reasons the winter solstice was of such great importance. It signified a time when the sun was indeed climbing back into the sky and the promise of summer was certain. The seasons for Egypt were more dependent on the rise and fall of the Nile, yet weather still attracted concentrated study.

Some populations today no longer fear a freezing night or a burning sun. At least one can expect reasonable comfort given sufficient economic status to allow for adequate shelter and a means to control the climate in that shelter. However, the workings of weather have a direct effect on our lives. Meteorology, as a science, has suffered derision as the predictions of a sunny day can dissolve into a downpour. Climatology, though, is getting far more precise. We can easily take for granted an increase in accuracy, but predictability of the weather can now drive major economies. It can offer great surpluses or predict shortages which put basic food needs beyond the reach of marginal populations.

---

combinations of particles, or details in how matter survived antimatter, there is still a preponderance of science that indicates we are on the right path. Perhaps, in the end, none of our current theories will survive in their current state. I do firmly believe that the answers are buried in the cosmos around us.

Consider the Measure of the Earth

We know that solar cycles, the Earth's orbit, and the tilt of its axis influence how much of the sun's radiation reaches the earth and, consequently, affects our climate. We know how volcanoes, ocean temperatures, glaciers, and currents in the air and water can cause the general climate of a region to change with varying levels of permanency. For some time now, we have understood that the earth is an integrated system that operates based on the balanced laws of nature and that when a change in that system occurs, it affects the entire system. We are also learning more of how our actions can impact the balance which has supported and nourished us for many centuries.

We can seed the clouds, and we have learned to harness some small part of the sun's energy, the wind, and the rain for our purposes. However, we have yet to conquer these forces of nature or learn how to protect ourselves from their destructive power. Yes, we have learned where the vaults of snow reside, but we have yet to force them to do our will. Considering our tendency to be quite shortsighted when it comes to our comfort, this is probably a good thing for now.

We will not hear from Job quite yet. However, this is a good place to see if we can understand something of what the author is saying. Was part of his message hidden within these broad strokes describing forces and heavenly bodies we barely understand, let alone control? Is this passage meant to crush us with the grandeur of it all? Or is it a challenge to learn, discover, create, and perhaps begin to understand the forces that rule this cosmos? I intend to show that it is a challenge. Recall the moment in C. S. Lewis's myth when we stop babbling about what we think we know and we go about the business of learning. The time has come to find our faces.

These forces, these celestial objects that occupy our universe, all have benevolent, life-giving attributes. For centuries, we sought their perfection. Even in the past century, some scientists wished to prove a steady-state universe where all things remained in balance and would do so for eternity.[10] However, the consensus of physicists today tells us that we do not live in a balanced, stable universe. The author of Job would have had access to scholars that saw perfection and stability in the workings of the universe, and used that knowledge to draw our attention to God's creation. If we truly want to know the nature of God, then we need to look closely at his works. Both through ancient and modern science, we have learned that this universe is a well-functioning creation machine. Sometimes in the process of creating, what already exists is destroyed or changed. That change can be slow and methodical or sudden and cataclysmic.

We have learned Earth is not a safe, perfect sphere. There is a body of literature that argues this planet is created specifically for our benefit and development. Academic literature refers to this theory as the "anthropic principle," a philosophical argument which states that the observations of the universe must be compatible with the conscious and sapient life that observes it. Although an interesting concept, I view this theory as circular reasoning, a "chicken or egg" type of question. If the earth did not exist as it does now, we would not be here to know how perfect, or near perfect, it

---

10. See Hoyle et al., *Different Approach to Cosmology*.

Part V—Redefining the Conversation

is. Intellectual integrity, then, demands that we look at how this globe, this universe, operates and then see what that can teach us about our trials and tribulations.

Our tiny globe is close enough to our sun to nourish us while simultaneously protecting us from the destructive cosmic forces of the sun by a magnetic field generated by our iron core. Without that protection, we would radioactively fry in nanoseconds. We know this because we have ventured beyond our atmosphere and we have some idea of what awaits us there.

Science has shown us that, for all the destructive power of a volcano, the molten rock that spews from the earth is high in mineral content, and once the landscape cools, it can be far more fertile than it was before—the gift of life from a force that can change the global climate for a decade. The seismic activity of our earth can bury civilizations and spark tsunamis that travel for thousands of miles, wiping out hundreds of thousands of people. However, the geologic movements of our crust are part of what keeps this earth a fertile environment both on land and in the sea.

We also now know something of the instability of our solar neighborhood, of how comets swing in huge orbits around the solar system, and how the orbits of asteroids and meteors can deteriorate and threaten our very existence. Rocks falling from the sky was not a generally accepted concept until recent times. Fire did not come from the sky; at least we hoped not. In 1994 we witnessed the breakup and collision of Shoemaker-Levy 9 as it impacted the surface of Jupiter.[11] Studies of this event gave us a better understanding of how gravity influences comets and other objects in the solar system, including the impact on the planets in their courses. Still an open field, there is controversy regarding the role the gas giants play in this dance. Although scientists originally thought that their magnetic fields protected Earth from incoming missiles with their magnetic fields, new research indicates that the opposite may be true.[12]

In 1908, a meteor exploded over the Tunguska River in Russia. The force from the explosion flattened some seven hundred and seventy square miles of forest. All this from an explosion that occurred perhaps three to six miles above the forest floor.[13] The Meteor Crater in Arizona is nearly one mile across.[14] The impact of this meteor occurred around fifty thousand years ago.[15] As we have improved our aerial surveillance, we have improved our ability to find even more evidence that the earth has had encounters with unwelcome guests with varied results. Scientists are now sure that the dinosaurs and much of the life on Earth at the time became extinct during the impact

---

11. See "Comet Shoemaker Levy."
12. Byrd, "Jupiter Protects Earth?"
13. Phillips, "The Tunguska Impact."
14. For more information, visit https://meteorcrater.com/.
15. See Turney, *Bones, Rocks and Stars*, for a discussion on the various methods available to scientists for dating and which methods are best applied where.

and aftermath of a meteor or meteors. The impact site most likely for this event is near present-day Mexico.[16]

Beyond our local neighborhood, we study the stars and look for other planets where we might yet find life. Although the practice of astrology seems to persist long after we have discovered that the constellations are our constructs based on our point of view from the outer rim of our galaxy, there are those among us who cannot shake the belief that the stars somehow control our destiny. The stars do contribute to our destiny in a fundamental way.

Stars are born when the force of gravity reaches a point at which it can crush the hydrogen within an interstellar cloud into a compressed ball, and a nuclear fusion plant ignites.[17] The death of a star depends on its internal mass. As the core heats up and it runs out of hydrogen fuel, it begins to fuse heavier elements. One of these elements is carbon, the basis of life on earth. If the star's mass is comparable to our sun, then it will become a red giant. Its outer shell expanding well into planetary orbits and consuming the planets that once depended on it for life. All the while, it creates some of the elements that made those planets possible.

Some stars are so massive that, when their cores heat up, they form heavier elements. Once the element iron begins to fuse, the star will die a violent death. With no fuel to hold the outer shell steady, gravity takes over by collapsing the star's mass in a cosmic explosion. The size of these explosions is massive and beyond what we can comprehend. With ever more sophisticated computer modeling, we are learning about the complex physics and fluid dynamics of how a star explodes and what determines the outcome.

Stars burn with the heat of nuclear fusion and explode in the process of creating the building blocks of matter itself. Some collapse into black holes that devour everything that wanders within range of their event horizons, including light. We know now that black holes reside in the center of galaxies, contributing to the gravitational force that holds them together. In the center of some galaxies, the action of the black hole is so violent that it spews gamma rays in amounts so large we can view the plume from earth.

This brief trip through astrophysics and planetary science illustrates that these forces are both immensely destructive and immensely creative. As our knowledge grows, we formulate and solve the math and program computers to model results, which we can confirm by observation. However, it is difficult for our minds to grasp, for instance, the force of an exploding supernova. A supernova is an explosion so great that it may rip a hole in the fabric of space-time. The forces that attend the explosion of a star can drive the elements forged deep in the heart of the star far out into space. These elements form everything we know of in the universe. Without this cosmic forge, this violence of creation, Earth and all that depends on it could not exist.

16. Hand, "Scientist Gear Up."
17. See Lang, *Life and Death of Stars.*

Part V—Redefining the Conversation

Can we believe that the author of Job was trying to direct us to the study of astronomy and planetary science? Certainly they could not conceive of where science has taken us today. However, there must be a reason that they drew our attention to the nascent sciences of Earth and cosmos.

By describing the vast known and unknowable, the author appears to be suggesting that we cannot build a world or a cosmos with a fairy-tale-perfect plotline—at least not from our egocentric point of view. The forces that create our universe are violent, even while they may create something beautiful in the agony of destruction. Without those forces, creation does not occur. The interactive ecology of earth would not function without its climate, its geology, or its interaction with its solar neighbors. There would be no way to replenish the minerals in our soil or the oxygen and nitrogen in our air. When we look for places in the universe that might have life, we look for worlds like our own, worlds that have geologic activity, water, and the forces that make that mix a home for the spark of life.

Knowing that catastrophes are part of living on this planet does not mean, in any way, that responsible people can ignore human suffering that is caused by the impact of nature. Whenever a volcano, a hurricane, a tsunami, or a drought occurs, Scripture demands of us whatever actions alleviate that suffering. The moral obligation of the believer is to bring comfort to those who suffer and to help rebuild.

Also, we can no longer ignore the impact we have on this earth. Whether heaven is knocking on the door or not, we are called to nurture, to maintain, and to care for the creation with which we are entrusted. We have a responsibility to find ways to preserve the forests that give us air to breathe, to maintain the waterways in a manner that nourishes ourselves and our planet, and to find those means that *are* within our ability which might protect and preserve our home.

The author of Job penned a wisdom poem to place us within the context of an active, vibrant, and sometimes violent universe so that we can better understand the source of some of our suffering. Sometimes we must step back and realize that the situation is not egocentric, that the problem is not all our fault, and that, this time, we are not in control. Sometimes we are part of the story, not the focus.

Perhaps the forces in this universe are perfect for the creation and survival of life. However, without them, no life would exist to ponder the question. New physics and astrophysics indicate that the odds of our current universe coming into being may be astronomical or even nonsensical if there was only one chance to create this cosmos. However, if multiple opportunities are possible, then the creation of this one combination of physics was inevitable. One thing is certain; any definition of God that does not include a vision of the vast possibilities within a knowable universe fails as an apt definition of its Creator. We might as well worship the wooden or golden idols of the ancient Middle East. Knowing this, we can begin to understand the "why" of suffering and what actions might alleviate the impact.

There are other ways that the author challenges us to rethink the "why" of suffering and what our response might be. The next portion of the book provides examples from nature and the lives of the creatures that share this planet with us.

Chapter 23

Consider Nature

NOT ALL THAT LONG ago, those who wrote, spoke, and protested about preserving the balance of nature and the ecosystem were considered little more than Chicken Littles: prophets of doom with questionable lifestyles and spirituality. Even in today's political climate, the premise that the earth is at our mercy and that, although there are other contributing factors, our actions directly affect the health of our ecosystem, does not find universal agreement. Science, however, has been accumulating mounting evidence that humanity has a role in global climate change.[1] To retell the story of Job, we must redefine our place in the universe.

In the past several decades, scientists who focus on the environment and the biodiversity of the planet have accumulated data which indicates that we do, indeed, impact the earth. We are destroying the balance established to protect and nurture our home, and we are doing it with amazing rapidity. Sorting out how much of an effect humanity has on the ecology is not a simple problem. Changing our ways without forethought would destroy whole economies and place an even heavier burden on those who suffer in poverty with all its attendant miseries.

Changing our habits is only one piece of the puzzle. There are external factors that contribute to changes in our ecosystems. As our planet travels around the sun, the poles shift, causing changes in climate that affect agriculture and lifestyles. Acknowledging these changes allows us to plan how to approach the management of agricultural resources, water supplies, and shelter. Science is also uncovering a feedback loop among the elements that cause climate change.[2] We know that volcanoes influence

---

1. For resources regarding the science behind the growing consensus regarding climate change, see "Scientific Consensus." Note that some references can change based on U.S. government mandates.

2. Climate change is a more accurate description than global warming since it accounts for the change in weather throughout the globe. For instance, winters are far worse in some places because the Arctic is warming and pushing the polar streams southward. The same action creates the drought conditions in the South Central portion of the United States. See Pierre-Louis, "As the Arctic Gets Warmer."

climate, and increased volcanic activity in our oceans wreaks havoc with our global temperatures. Recently, however, scientists have found evidence in the geological record that rising ocean levels can contribute to increased volcanic activity, creating a feedback loop which speeds up the effects.[3]

We are learning that the balance of nature is not a counter-culture obsession; it is a vital part of our survival. We also know that there are components of the issue that we control and some that we do not. We may not be able to influence the frequency or intensity of under-sea volcanoes; we can control how much we impact the air and water on which we depend to survive. Whatever path we choose to alleviate the consequences, there is a price to pay. That is what the next few chapters in Job are about: the price of balance and how that affects our lives.

Job responds to Zophar (12:7–8), tongue-in-cheek, that Zophar must be "the voice of the people," and wisdom will surely die with him. He then calls on all of nature as witness to his innocence. He demands of Zophar, "Who among all these [creatures] does not know, / that the hand of the Lord has done this?" (12:9) In these next few chapters of Job, God cross-examines the witnesses. Predator and prey domesticated and wild, each has a part, and sometimes that part appears cruel and unforgiving.

From 38:39 through chapter 39 of Job, the focus shifts from the broad strokes of the cosmos and Earth itself to the animal kingdom. A cursory reading may leave the impression that the birds and animals selected are random choices. However, to believe so would not do justice to the author. These choices have symmetry and a nuance that bears a message intrinsic to the selection.

The Birds

The author begins his nature lesson with a raven (38:41), a hawk, an eagle (39:26), an ostrich, and a stork (39:13). Although scientific research into the intelligence factors of the members of the animal kingdom has only been a serious pursuit in the last few decades, science is confirming what animal lovers and owners have known for centuries: animals are not dumb. Some are smarter than others, and each species has a unique personality that is evidenced by how its members respond to the world around them. What was known by observation, legend, and anecdote rooted in prehistory is now beginning to find support in the lab. The knowledge of the current age may shed light on the choices the author made for this portion of the text.

The raven, a member of the genus *Corvus*, is a very intelligent bird. Given tasks that require logical problem-solving skills, these birds will manage to find the solution with few, if any, errors. They adapt to any environment. They are scavengers as much as foragers and will eat whatever seems appropriate to the ecology where they settle. Scripture asks, "Who provides food . . . / when his young cry out to God?" (38:41).

---

3. See "When the Ice Melts."

With its well-developed avian brain, this bird has learned to forage and scour the earth for foodstuffs that do not endanger her health or that of her family. Science has shown that this species has learned to use tools to acquire food and to play. The raven also studies risk. Ravens have funerals, of a sort, and scientists postulate that the purpose is to study the demise of their compatriots to avoid such an end for themselves. Through the creative forces of nature, the raven has found a niche that it alone can fill.

The hawk and the eagle are both predatory birds that set their homes high in the cliffs where few predators can cause trouble. Birds of this type can see fish in moving water from several hundred feet above the surface. When they dive to collect that prey, they can reach 125 and 100 miles per hour, respectively.[4] Trained since ancient times to hunt for their handlers, they are carnivores that depend on meat wherever they can find it. Scripture describes these predatory birds with the succinct statement, "His young gulp blood" (39:30). They survive based on their skill and the strength of their wings and eyes. People of many cultures may have learned to partner with predatory birds, yet they do not control them. When these birds hunt for their masters, a carefully managed bond develops so that the handler can expect both obedience and respect when the avian is set free to seek its prey. Again, nature has seen to it that a creature fills a specific place in the cycle of life by allowing this aerial hunter to develop the skills and attributes required to survive.

In contrast, the author presents the ostrich. A native to Sub-Saharan Africa and Asia Minor, this bird shows no singular intelligence. Scripture states that she beats her wings "joyously" (39:13) even though her plumage is worthless for airlift. The adult ostrich can reach speeds of up to forty-seven miles per hour. The ostrich is not known as a nurturing parent. The hen drops the eggs on the warm sand, she may cover them up, and then she leaves them to live or die. The author of Job tells us that "God deprived her of wisdom" (39:17), and yet she and her species survive.

In this cross section from the avian world, we see representatives of the smart, the skillful, and the inept, each with a specific niche to fill, a skill set uniquely developed for survival. Although there are natural catastrophes that disrupt the balance of nature within a localized ecosystem, humanity can also have a direct effect on the efficiency of the course of nature when the carefully orchestrated pieces no longer fit and the ecosystem begins to break down.

The Beasts

The author then turns to the mammalian kingdom. He selects representations of the predator and the prey, the domesticated and the wild, and a few that, like the hawk, require a relationship between the beasts that serve and the master that uses them.

---

4. A Peregrine falcon can reach two hundred mph, a Golden Eagle around one hundred and fifty.

Lions (38:39) hold a place in lore as monarchs of savanna and forest. Within the pride, some of the females care for the young and some hunt. Male lions rigidly control the line of succession. Those that are not born within a natural order of succession must either become solitary wanderers or seek a pride which they can win through strength and cunning. Should a lone male win the leadership of a pride, he will destroy all the existing cubs. The destruction of existing cubs serves three purposes. First, this reduces the possibility of challenge. Second, it secures his place by eliminating genetic descendants from the defeated leader. Third, lionesses are more willing to mate if they are not nursing. This behavior is a cruel path, yet if the male does not follow his instincts, he will not survive long as a leader, and his chances of survival on his own are substantially less.

As noted, the females are primarily responsible for hunting. The process is violent and bloody. Many a nature film shows the chase as predator pursues herd animals and attacks without mercy. Even with the easy availability of nature films that portray the struggles that occur daily in the wild, most of us find it hard to internalize the destruction of an animal, whether it be an elk, a snowshoe rabbit, or a field mouse. Watching the last unsuccessful attempts of a starving lynx cub or a mother Arctic fox is just as difficult.

The author changes the point of view from predator to prey by asking Job if he knows the season when the mountain goats give birth or the hinds calve. The ibex of the Levant is a wild mountain goat that lives in the nearly vertical desert-mountain cliffs. The gestation period is five to six months, and a newborn is already strong enough to jump about on the rocky slopes. After four weeks, it can join other kids while being trained to navigate the slopes. The kids wean at four to six months and remain dependent on their mother for at least a year. Even an unweaned kid can avoid a predator with amazing agility. However, some are captured and become the needed nourishment of a carnivore, whether four-footed or winged.

Hinds (39:1), or the red deer, travel in herds. When they give birth, they leave the herd and stay sequestered until the young hind is ready to run with the group. Usually weaned at four months, they might still suckle for a time even when they are no longer dependent on their mother's milk. Many deer species hide their young while they are foraging, which works well since the fawns have no smell and cannot be easily detected, at least not until they move. Hidden in plain sight, they have a different kind of survival technique.

This tension between predator and prey creates a balance between the species within each ecosystem. When prey is bountiful, the predators also flourish. During years when the prey population drops, the predators die off. Conversely, if the predator population dwindles, due to disease or over-hunting, the prey population explodes and destroys the environment through overuse of the resources. Many specialized ecosystems form the global biosphere. The interaction of these ecosystems provides a home we can thrive in, even if the mechanics of the process are repellent or heartbreaking.

The author then turns his attention to those animals that might serve humanity. In this case, the illustrations are quite personal. While God describes the difficulties of domesticating ass and ox, he might be reminding Job of the investment in time and effort lost when the raiders took his herds.

God begins with the wild ass (onager). We cannot easily tame the ass. He forages for food in the wilderness and avoids domestication (39:5). The stubborn wild ass (donkey) is a legendary archetype. The prophet Balaam had issues with a donkey that would not follow orders, even though it was presumably domesticated.[5] Donkeys are a good choice as a burden-bearing beast since they are sturdy and able to navigate mountain passes. They are not always open to guidance.

Recent scientific research has discovered something quite interesting about the animal, an explanation for a personality trait that resonates well with the story of Balaam. Donkeys are not stubborn, at least, not without cause. If they do not follow directions, it is often due to something suspicious which is causing them fear or distrust.[6] That is, when a donkey refuses to submit to the lead, there may be some danger the driver needs to assess. As part of their survival toolkit, these animals have a heightened sense of danger, a wariness that serves the beast attempting to avoid being a meal for a prowling predator or taking a misstep that may cause injury.

The wild ass is not the only reluctant servant of humanity. The wild ox, in its natural state, cannot be domesticated (39:9). Generations of targeted breeding and training are needed to use the animal in tasks best suited to its strength. Wild oxen are hard to capture, capable of defending themselves and their herd, and are well equipped to find their food. The sick, the weak, and those who wander off unprotected are subject to attack. The ox is powerful enough to resist domestication yet lives under the same rule that nature applies to all its creatures: eat or be eaten.

God asks, "Do you give the horse his strength?" (39:19). The horse is uniquely suited to domestication, and thousands of years of breeding have developed a wide variety of horses suited to innumerable tasks. Some are good riding horses, some have the strength of an ox and can haul great weights, some work in ranching or entertainment. Some breeds are racers or suited for endurance in desert or mountainous terrain. Among all of the types of horses bred and trained by humanity, none compare to the warhorse.

The warhorse is no longer as crucial in the conduct of war, although many events, such as jousting tournaments, mimic their past. For centuries they were fierce and fearless participants in the conflicts of humanity. Charging into battle against an enemy bent on creating mayhem requires a unique set of skills and a different

---

5. Num 22:21–39.
6. Hart, "Understanding Donkey Characteristics."

temperament than any other animal which has submitted to domestication.[7] *Breaking a horse* is the process of training a wild horse to the harness. Breaking a horse without breaking its spirit is a talent and a hard-learned trade. Once trained, they are loyal, hardworking, and dependable. God asks, "Do you make him quiver like locusts, his majestic snorting [spreading] terror?" (39:20). No, we can only harness the power that nature has created.

By considering the predator and the prey, we have an opportunity to understand something of the balance of nature and the price paid for that balance by both sides of the equation. By considering the variety of beasts that can serve humanity versus those that seem better suited as partners than servants, we learn something of what we can control. Perhaps the lesson here is that we are not the masters of the universe, even though we can productively manage some parts of nature's bounty and power.

Remembering Nature

The chapters describing nature and its inhabitants deliver a compelling message about the world we live in, a world that is sometimes beautiful and sometimes cruel. In this section, the author describes a world where more variety, more diversity, exists than we know—even now—after centuries of digging into every corner we can reach.

The author illustrates some basic things about how nature functions. There are very real concerns when we choose to upset the balance maintained in the ecosystem. We may see nature as sometimes cruel or unfair, yet the balance remains within margins when the cycle of life is operating correctly. An excellent example of this point is the reintroduction of wolves into Yellowstone National Park in the Western United States.

Ranchers in the area were justifiably angry about the possibility of wolves killing their livestock—wolves they could not kill to protect that stock because it was against the law. The management of the interface with nature had to meet the needs of neighboring families so they could protect their livelihood. Similar situations are occurring all over the world, and sometimes, with creative thinking, we find effective ways to build that interface with nature. In the case of Yellowstone, once the conflict between interests resolved, the scientists watched as the reintroduction of wolf packs changed the ecology and geography of the park.[8]

When the program began in 1995, the wolves had been absent for seventy years. There were, of course, expected shifts in the ecology. However, the observed changes were broader and more intrinsic than anticipated. The deer herds that had over-grazed the grasslands changed their habits. The wolves did kill some deer, which altered the feeding habits of the surviving deer and strengthened the herds in the process. The deer returned to higher slopes, allowing the grasslands to grow thick and to squeeze

7. Other than dogs.
8. Farquhar, "Wolf Reintroduction."

out the non-native grasses. The change in grazing range allowed more trees to grow and forests to regenerate.

Reforestation brought back a variety of birds. With increased timber growth, the beavers returned, which, in turn, developed an ecosystem for otters, badgers, fish, ducks, and other wildlife. Wolves also reduced the coyote population, which allowed the small rodent population to return to previous levels. Small rodent populations drew back the eagles and the hawks. Bears returned to the valley because the revitalized grasslands and forests produced more berries and greater dietary variety.

Along with the changes in the ecosystem, the geography began to shift. With more vegetation and more mature forests, the soil stabilized, the riverbanks became firmer, and the rivers, rather than meandering all over the landscape, formed narrower channels with fresher water. Cleaner water supported a diverse and stable aquatic ecosystem. All these changes took place over time due to the reintroduction of a few wolves. They were a piece in a larger puzzle, one we are only beginning to understand.

Is it realistic to believe that the author was contemplating these ideas while writing the script for God's speech? In 400 BCE, wise people were looking at the world around them and determining through reason how the world worked and what possible causes would result in the observed effects. Nothing was exempt from the probing mind and the inquiring spirit. The style and content of the writing of Job indicates that the author was well-educated and knew the thoughts of some of the best minds of the time. We should look at the imagery used to convey the author's thoughts. What was this individual trying to say by evoking the savagery of the lion, the precision of the hawk, the grace of the hind, the plodding, reluctant service of the ass and ox, and the passionate and fierce skill of the warhorse?

In response to Job's quest to find an answer to suffering, the author asks Job to consider the suffering required to maintain a flourishing ecosystem and reminds him that some things are controllable, and some things are not. Nonetheless, each thing, each piece of nature's puzzle has a part in a greater scheme. Perhaps, our author suggests, we must look at our suffering with a broader perspective. This approach may remind us of the explanation that all things work together for the greater good, but it is far more than that. It is the development of a more mature attitude that sees a universe integrated at an essential level. Perhaps even organized as a living thing. We are only a part of this system, and sometimes we suffer and become subject to privation. At other times, it is our part to create, support, and build.

God gave humanity dominion over the earth in Genesis. The interpretations of that command are almost as complex and diverse as interpretations of the book of Job. However, in most cases, dominion is a form of power that requires stewardship and responsible interaction, even as it demands a realistic view of appropriate control. We can mutilate the forces of nature to the point of our destruction—or we can become a contributing partner in the cycle of creation.

Consider Nature
What Does Job Say?

Job responds to these lessons in the expanse of the universe and broad sweeps of nature with only a brief statement recorded in 40:4–5, "See, I am of small worth; what can I answer You? / I clap my hand to my mouth. / I have spoken once and will not reply. / Twice and will do so no more." Is Job admitting that he is completely insignificant in the overall scheme of things and is in no position to answer God when questioned? Or is he pointing out the obvious to his Maker and calling on him to answer? If Job is so insignificant, then why does he suffer so?

MacLeish would suggest that Job covers his mouth to hide a laugh, a response that Whedbee would appreciate. In *J.B.*, Macleish's carnies discuss the incongruity of Job's response. In a scene where the character says that God never laughs (which may be debatable), there is a hint in this scene that Job does. He may *say* he is abashed, but by putting his hand to his face, he may also be covering an impulse to laugh.[9] Does he think the answers simplistic, a mere echo of points he has already made? Or, is he now catching a glimpse of the beauty of a simple answer? Perhaps relief that the whole weight of the world is not on his shoulders and that there are things, ordered things, over which he has no control?

God's response changes the tone of the conversation. God brushes aside Job's dissembling and claims of insignificance and demands he respond to the core question:

> Gird your loins like a man;
> I will ask, and you will inform Me.
> Would you impugn My justice?
> Would you condemn Me that you may be right? (Job 40:7–8)

Understanding our place in the universe helps us gain perspective on suffering. Once we view ourselves as part of a bigger picture, we become equipped to discern the cause of suffering and our part in alleviating its impact.

El Shaddai does not allow Job to throw up his hands in defeat and walk away without complete understanding, nor does he permit Job to walk away with a misplaced conviction that he is insignificant and unworthy of his quest. Even if Job is starting to understand, there is more to know. Job must stay and continue to learn, for there is one more piece to the puzzle.

Now that God has instructed Job in the physical aspects of the world in which he lives, the author pushes the conversation forward to explore the spiritual aspects of that world. There are forces within us that we can control, even if we cannot conquer them. We, unlike Job's tormentors, must acknowledge that evildoers prosper and the righteous do suffer. What, then, is the nature of evil?

---

9. MacLeish, *J.B.*, 8–9.

Chapter 24

Consider Leviathan and Behemoth

JOB HAS ONE MORE testimony to hear before we can reach a conclusion about suffering, why it happens, and what we are supposed to do about it. Leviathan and Behemoth are creatures of myth and legend and the ultimate allegory for evil and chaos. Understanding the mythos of these beasts as portrayed in the ancient Middle East and Scripture is essential to the imagery of these chapters. The author is using this symbology to ask questions and express ideas that were being changed by the discoveries of nascent science. Here, too, we can learn a great deal from exploring what modern research has discovered about the mind and how it makes decisions. To retell the story of Job, we must redefine evil and understand our part in reducing its impact.

Are human beings accountable for their actions, or are they subject to the consequences of some ancient sin, or are they slaves to a biological makeup determined before birth? By investigating both the origins of the Leviathan and Behemoth legends and by looking at scientific breakthroughs of recent decades, we can begin to understand something about this thing called evil. Understanding how the mind works adds to the knowledge of what causes suffering. As we learn more, the act of agency, of making a choice, becomes clearer. The degree of accountability for any action taken by an individual is a daily battle in medicine and law. Logically, without accountability a person cannot be punished for failing, whether by society or by God. The need to determine accountability is at least one of the core issues in the battle waged over interpretations of Job.

From Scripture and the Talmud

This portion of the book of Job addresses the characteristics of two legendary monsters, first, Behemoth, "whom I made as I did you" (40:15) and who is called the first of God's works (40:19). Second, Leviathan, who is so fierce he is untouchable. Even an attempt to assault him is asking for certain death. His skin is made of armor with scales so tightly laid that not a breath can enter. He breathes fire and causes the ocean to boil. He is so fierce that he even frightens divine beings (40:15—41:26). No one can stand against this great sea serpent.

Throughout Scripture, Leviathan is used as a metaphor for evil and chaos, even as it is made clear that the beast and its land-dwelling counterpart, Behemoth, are essential parts of creation. In Genesis 1:21, sea monsters are among the life created to fill the seas. Psalms 104:26 says God created Leviathan to "sport with."

The act of defeating Leviathan becomes a metaphor in Scripture which represents the conquest of evil and the eventual rise of Israel. In Isaiah 27:1, the prophet draws a picture of an apocalyptic restoration of Israel on the day the Lord will punish Leviathan, defeat him, and purge the sin of Jacob. In Psalms 74:14, the poet cries out to God to deliver Israel from her enemies before she becomes a laughingstock. Only God can deliver Israel because only God can crush the head of Leviathan (evil). In Revelation (13:1 and 20:2), the beast reappears as the ancient serpent of the sea and, once Christendom assimilated the legend, this beast became associated with Satan.[1]

Scripture, then, describes a beast of destructive and chaotic power that only God can eliminate, a beast that represents Satan incarnate (for Christians) and all the evil associated with that image. Throughout the Old and New Testaments, this beast is the ultimate feast of a restored Israel, a main course in a banquet to celebrate the ultimate victory of the righteous. The author of Revelation uses the imagery of the "beast out of the sea" and the "beast out of the earth" to convey both the depth of evil the world can attain and the power of ultimate victory over that evil.[2]

The Babylonian Talmud also describes Leviathan. As the Rabbis taught, "his eyes are like the eyelids of the morning."[3] The Talmud goes on to explain that, as in all the rest of creation, the Lord created male and female. He knew, however, that if these beasts mated, they and their offspring would destroy the whole world. To avoid this outcome, God castrated the male and killed the female, preserving her flesh in salt for the righteous in the world to come. At that future time, the Lord would slay both Leviathan and Behemoth. According to legend, Behemoth and his mate suffered the same fate as their ocean-dwelling counterparts. The important points here are that these creatures represent all that is evil on the land and in the sea and that the Lord created them. In Hebrew tradition, before all else, the Lord created chaos and evil. He then controlled and limited the power of these creatures.

These creatures were not the invention of the Hebrew tribes. They are rooted deep in the mythological tradition of the ancient Levant and Mesopotamia. To understand the images drawn in Job, and what the author's intent might be, it is important to understand the source and history of those symbols.

---

1. It should be reiterated that Jewish theology sees Satan as a trickster, not evil incarnate, whereas Leviathan is chaos and evil. The two are not interchangeable.

2. Rev 13, 17.

3. b.B.Bat. 74a, http://www.come-and-hear.com/bababathra/bababathra_74.html.

As Job begins his journey through suffering, he curses the day he was born. His lament invokes several images which have caused consternation to many commentators. In a lament that expresses his desire to remove that day from the course of history, he calls on several powers, including "those who cast spells upon the day damn it, / those prepared to disable Leviathan" (3:8). In chapter 3 of this book, there was a translation of this passage given by Greenstein,[4] which he uses to show the poetic strength of the Hebrew use of thought rhyme.[5] In this case, Greenstein understands Yamm and Leviathan to be virtually synonymous, two names of the mythological Canaanite sea monster. Such a direct reference by the author indicates that the symbolism is important, and the history of that symbolism could contribute to understanding the story of Job.

From Middle Eastern Mythology

Yamm derives from an ancient Semitic word meaning "sea." It is an Ugarit word used by the Canaanites to describe their god of rivers and seas. Yamm represented the chaos of the sea and its power. In Canaanite mythology, Yamm is the king of all gods until he becomes tyrannical and takes the wife of another god. The god Ba'al defeats Yamm and sends him into exile. Ba'al also defeats Lotan, another sea monster so closely associated with Yamm that he may be just another aspect of the serpent.[6] Lotan is a seven-headed sea serpent: a familiar image from Scripture.

Babylonian mythology records a similar tale of disputes among the gods. In this case, Marduk, a late-arriving deity, ascends to primary importance by slaying the more ancient goddess of chaos, Tiamat, a sea monster.[7] After defeating the serpent in a battle using a combination of his powers and those of other gods, Marduk breaks Tiamat's body in pieces to form the earth and its inhabitants. In the context of the Babylonian creation myth, *Enuma Elish*, Marduk earns the right to be the god of creation by defeating chaos.

The shared theme among these myths is that the sea and its notorious serpent represent chaos, unquenchable hunger, and evil. In each of these creation tales, overcoming chaos permitted the Earth and its inhabitants to take form. In each of these legends, the monster is preserved, subdued, resurrected, or somehow made a part of a victory banquet later in history. This theme is key to understanding the third speech from God: evil was, is, and shall remain a part of creation. It is not, however, a free

---

4. Greenstein, "Language of Job," 651–66.

5. As noted, this is a poetic device where Hebrew authors match different words (sometimes from other languages) with the same underlying meaning to rhyme the "thought" rather than the sound of the word.

6. See "The Baal Cycle," an ancient Semitic legend, translated from clay tablets found at Ras Shamra (Ugarit) and dated to 1400–1200 BCE.

7. There are many differing depictions of Tiamat depending on the location and culture of the worshipers.

agent. The Lord of Israel is powerful enough to sport with it, and Scripture is clear that he alone can overcome the beast and free the world of its nature. The question remains, whether chaos and evil are required elements of a successful universe, or if these aspects are merely plagues on the existence of humanity, with no meaning or resolution satisfactory to the soul.

From Recent Research

In the ancient Middle East, evil and chaos were the purview of the gods. Only a deity could control the power of evil, and only a deity could destroy it. On the surface, the chapters devoted to Leviathan and Behemoth describe forces beyond the control of humanity. However, as the book develops, the author utilizes words and images that direct the reader to look and think beyond the old traditions. There is no reason to believe the author has given up the search for wisdom at this point simply because the knowledge of his day could take him no further. If humanity was already expanding the boundaries of knowledge in 400 BCE, is there any reason to believe that the author assumed Leviathan and Behemoth would keep their power untested forever?

The author of Job, as did many of the commentators presented in this book, puzzled over the question of how a creature with the power of reason should respond to the existence of evil. Research into the biological and psychological workings of the mind is finally beginning to answer that question. Understanding the tension between biological predisposition and conscious choice will aid in clarifying when an individual is fully accountable and when valid mitigating circumstances are contributing to their actions. Agency and accountability come into play once that individual understands that they are responsible for the changes necessary to make better choices.

A case in point might be the treatment of people with schizophrenia. First, the individual must accept that there is an issue, something inherently difficult with this condition. Second, finding the correct cocktail of medications is time consuming and can result in terrible side effects. Third, once they reach a stable place and the symptoms are more manageable, the individual tends to think the medications are no longer necessary or are too much of a burden given side effects. People with schizophrenia can have trouble holding down a job, maintaining a relationship, or even avoiding crime. Agency comes in when the person must decide if they will continue a maintenance program to avoid actions they may not remember or cannot control. Whatever the biological predisposition may be, there is still usually a point when a person understands the choices. If it becomes apparent that, for whatever reason, there never was a path to understanding, a moment to decide, then society, to protect itself, must step in and make that choice.

Part V—Redefining the Conversation

Some of the source material used here comes from an episode of the TV series *Through the Wormhole*, entitled "Can We Eliminate Evil?"[8] The segment presents several scientists in the fields of neuroscience and psychology. Researchers in these fields are probing the interaction between stimulus and response within the brain.

In Amsterdam, at the Center for Building a Culture of Empathy, Christian Keysers and his team study empathy and its impact on our choices.[9] Through a series of tests, using fMRI[10] scans, Keysers has identified the parts of the brain that activate when we are in pain. These same parts are activated when we see that someone else is in pain. In other words, pain is a shared experience at a level far deeper than expected. Where our brains are concerned, the pain of others is our pain. Keysers contends that this is the basis of empathy, that sharing the burden of others is hardwired into our brain structure.

Not all people feel the same amount of empathy. As in all measurements regarding the nature of an individual and how they think, there is a spectrum which is dependent on experience, culture, expectations, age, and a host of other elements. Some people feel empathetic pain more acutely than others. A surprising discovery made by Keysers's team is that sociopaths do feel empathy; the difference between them and the general population is how they channel that empathy. They tend to use their skill to read their mark and to create the situation they need to harm someone in order to fulfill their own needs.

People can control their baser emotions, whatever their level of empathy. The question becomes whether there is some regulator in our make-up to guide our decisions. Does this code come from a religious conviction, a societal contract, or some other standard? At what point do we learn an ethical code? What influences our ability to control the emotions (or lack of) that cause a person to commit theft, or even murder?

Karen Wynn of the Yale Department of Psychology seeks to answer that question by studying babies a year old or younger.[11] She wants to discover how early in a child's life the influence of language, society, parental control, or any other contributing factor changes the response to stimuli. Wynn is seeking the answer to when an infant develops a moral compass and when the pressures of society begin to have greater impact.

To extract answers to abstract questions from those who have yet to develop a language, let alone much of an abstract thought process, she structures experiments

---

8. Sayenga, "Can We Eliminate Evil?"

9. See Keysers, *Empathic Brain*.

10. fMRI stands for "functional magnetic resonance imaging." MRIs scan for structure by imaging the water molecules' hydrogen nuclei and providing a look at tissue types, whereas fMRIs calculate the levels of oxygen in each area of the brain, which provides a researcher with a map of what parts activate under what circumstances.

11. The Infant Cognition Center, http://campuspress.yale.edu/infantlab/.

using different colored puppets. One color of puppet helps another puppet as it tries to get into a box. A different colored puppet interferes with the action and slams the box lid down. Then the baby is presented puppets of the same colors to choose. Eighty to ninety-five percent of babies five to six months of age will choose the helpful puppet. For Wynn, this means that there is an inherent moral compass that guides even the undeveloped mind in the general direction of ethical behavior. An alternate conclusion may be that even at this young age, the mind understands that those not helpful to others are unlikely to be helpful at all. As we grow older, the questions become more complex.

David Eagleman[12] is a neurologist at the Baylor College of Medicine. He studies the brain, how it responds to external stimulus, and how it makes decisions. He points out that the loss of a thumb, though inconvenient, is not life-changing. However, the loss or damage of a thumb-sized piece of the brain can be very devastating. Depending on what part of the brain is affected, damage can (but not necessarily) forever change such attributes as risk-taking, empathy, and executive control of an individual's actions.

As an illustration, he provides the history of Charles Joseph Whitman, an engineering and architectural student at the University of Texas in 1966. Whitman murdered his mother, wife, and fourteen random victims on the university campus before police stopped him. In his suicide note, he requested an autopsy. The autopsy revealed a brain tumor located in an area of the brain that affects self-control.

Whitman's story reveals several contributing factors that may have led him to make the choices that led to his death and that of others. He had a demanding and perfectionist father that abused his mother. Admitting any weakness would have been difficult. He left home for the military as soon as he could enlist. He started his college career in mechanical engineering and was called back to active duty due to poor grades. Returning to the university in 1965, he switched to architecture. In 1966 he was suffering from severe headaches and consulted a university therapist over concerns for his mental health. Records show that he scheduled a follow-up appointment; it was an appointment he did not keep. The notes he left behind indicate a man in turmoil, a man who thought he was protecting his family from the horror of what he was about to do. All of which indicates he knew what he was doing yet felt helpless in the process. Proclivity and agency, a subtle battle fought each day by every individual in great and small ways.

Eagleman's team does not stop at finding some of the reasons behind aberrant behavior. Their goal is to understand how to teach individuals to use their experience, both the bad and the good, to make choices based on an appropriate use of short-term and long-term thinking. Using something they have developed called the *prefrontal gym*, Eagleman and his students can help train people to avoid actions that create problems in their lives and the lives of those around them. With the use of an fMRI,

12. See Eagleman, *The Brain with David Eagleman.*

a subject can see a feedback loop from a baseline response to stimulus. For instance, when the subject sees pictures of drug use, a feedback monitor shows the level of desire based on brain activity. As the subject resists the unwanted impulses, the feedback monitor indicates a reduction in desire. In this way, a patient can learn to control the impulse and to reprogram the brain. A similar process occurs in mental health sessions where a counselor works with a patient to develop stronger life skills and to work out problems with the past. However, Eagleman's process is far more targeted and provides visible results. Such a procedure could open a door to rehabilitation of persons caught in situations where they have difficulty controlling themselves. The process is a viable tool when an individual is willing to work hard to change. Anyone that has worked in a field that requires reaching out to persons with neurological issues, including a mental health diagnosis or addictions, knows that nothing can help the person who does not desire that help. However, the arsenal available to help those who choose to seek help is growing exponentially.

Defining the balance between agency and predisposition is a developing field in neuroscience research. As technology develops imaging tools of greater accuracy, it becomes possible to determine who might be at risk for developing a propensity to harm themselves or others. James H. Fallon is a neuroscientist, a professor of psychiatry and human behavior, and the emeritus professor of anatomy and neurobiology at the University of California, Irvine School of Medicine. His journey to the root of evil became personal. During a series of studies conducted on the PET scans of sociopathic killers in 2006, he thought he had accidentally mixed some of the scans in with research he was conducting on his own family. He was using PET scans to search for markers of Alzheimer's disease in his family tree. The scan that drew his attention turned out to be his own. His PET scan indicated the same brain-imaging pattern as the sociopathic test subjects.

Fallon did not take the information too seriously until he attended a public talk at the University of Oslo on bipolar disorder. When he returned home to Southern California, he subjected himself to both genetic and psychological testing. The results were that his profile indicated a predisposition towards sociopathic tendencies. He determined that, among other influences, it was his formative years within a family that supported him in developing the tools required to make pro-social choices. Fallon, then, evidences agency by choosing alternatives to what could have been a tendency toward sociopathic behavior. Among his personality traits are the tendency to maintain control over situations and the choice to manipulate others if he believes it will help him succeed.

Some 3 percent of the population is subject to sociopathic traits. Those traits can be traceable to the structure of the brain and the genetic makeup of the individual. This knowledge does not free the individual from choice. Medicine has long understood that brain chemistry can and does influence our actions. Our ability to alleviate those symptoms and restore a higher level of agency in the individual is part of what can mitigate suffering, both that which is experienced by the individual and any harm that might occur to others. Perhaps you can think of it in this manner. A quadriplegic or amputee cannot get behind the wheel of just any commercially produced vehicle and drive safely. However, if the appropriate training and equipment is in place, persons facing this type of challenge can become successfully mobile.

Fallon illustrates what he perceives as the differences between the sociopath and the ideologically normal brain with the picture of a casual drive down any city street. During the day, everyone can see everyone else. People are recognizable and, perhaps, may exchange greetings with the driver. During the same drive at night, the people on the streets are shadows in the darkness. People become mere moving objects, which can be either obstructions or useful implements toward some end goal. The driver also hides in the shadows, and their intentions cannot be seen or understood until it is too late. As imperfect as the example might be, Fallon is using a common experience to convey a sense of the "disconnectedness" a sociopath may feel toward fellow beings.

Fallon reports that he realized he was not the person he thought he was. He found that buried deep in his genetic makeup was a person who could be evil. From his experience and education, he believes that nurture outweighed nature in the end, and he was able to make the choices that led him to become a productive member of society with sometimes annoying, usually funny, personality traits.

Instead of being a stabilizing influence, the atmosphere in which we are reared can have the opposite effect. There are times when society changes the fabric of what we see as moral. Karen Wynn discovered that the influence of others can begin to affect our choices before we reach the age of one. She was saddened by her results, feeling that we were born with a tendency to look out for each other, yet we quickly found the need to be accepted overruling our empathy for others. Perhaps, though, her results are a demonstration that we see the actions of others as a forewarning of whom we should avoid.

Again, staging her morality plays with different colored puppets, Wynn offers babies a choice of graham crackers or beans. Once she knows which is preferred, her puppets take the stage. The puppeteer makes it clear that one colored puppet agrees with the baby's preference, and the other does not. Almost without fail, the baby chooses the puppet that agrees with her choice. This result is not surprising since, even as adults, we tend to associate with people that have similar likes and dislikes. Social media is a prime example of this tendency. Wynn expresses surprise when she tests the strength of that preference. Once a favored side is selected, the baby will often support punishment for the puppet that does not agree with her choice.

Our need to belong, to be part of some group, can and often does override our inner sense of morals or ethics. When we allow the need to belong to overrule our inner moral compass, we lose our individuality and control. Such a frame of mind can create a mob, a group of people drawn up in the activity that is not defined by them individually and in which (on any other day) they would not choose to participate.

Part V—Redefining the Conversation

We are a social species and we long to belong, sometimes to the point that we find the need to separate those who are "with us" from those who are not. Sometimes those divisions are arbitrary, but they are no less powerful. The power of the group, the "belonging," can lead us to actions we would not ordinarily take.

One author that wrote about the need to belong and the formation of movements was Eric Hoffer. The best known of his works, *The True Believer*, was published in 1951.[13] Hoffer claims no formal education. He lost both parents by the time he reached the age of eighteen. In 1920, he moved to California and found work as a migrant farmworker and manual laborer. He joined the longshoreman's union in 1943 so that he could work a few days a week and read and write the rest of the time. His philosophy comes from his experiences and direct observation of people, movements, and social change. With the publication of his first book, he found celebrity. His writings explore the tendency to be accepted, to be part of something, and to take on the dogma of the group as one's motivation.

Our membership in a group is only part of the equation of how we view evil. Owen D. Jones, a professor of biological sciences and an attorney at Vanderbilt Law School, has been studying how we determine punishment for people who break society's codes. In Jones's experience, jurors and judges tend to look to the outcome, not the intent.[14]

One research study conducted by Jones used a scenario with two drunk drivers, both of whom were in an accident, both of whom had the same alcohol level. However, the sentence imposed on each driver was vastly different. One driver hit a child before he hit the tree. If all other factors appear to be equal, such as the age, socioeconomic background, or education of the drivers, the emotional impact of an injured child, rather than the intent of the drivers, influences the level of punishment delivered. Both defendants chose to drive intoxicated; both caused damage which they could have avoided. The jury becomes influenced by the outcome of the choice rather than the choice itself. Perhaps this is fair; the penalty should be greater for personal injury than for property damage. The issue is both drivers need to make different choices. Their histories (if this not the first time) and their willingness to accept responsibility should carry weight in the final decision regarding punishment. This, Jones proposes, is where judges and juries need to reassess how they decide punishment and any expected results from punishment or rehabilitation.

In another study, Jones introduces a scenario where he attempts to murder his friend by ordering a salad for her covered in poppy seeds. He believes she is allergic to poppy seeds and will die of anaphylactic shock. She is allergic to peanuts, not poppy seeds. When the chef prepares her salad, he includes peanuts, and she dies from her reaction. Jones found by presenting this case to student courtroom scenarios that a jury is far less likely to convict him of murder because she did not die through his

13. Hoffer, *True Believer*.
14. The following information is from Sayenga, "Can We Eliminate Evil?"

specific effort, even though he intended to harm. Decisions made on whether to convict an individual occur in an analytical and cognitive part of the brain. However, when individuals assess the type of punishment due, it is the emotional part of the brain that decides the severity.

Jones believes that with training juries and judges can better align consequences with crimes. He contends that training individuals to understand intent as well as outcome can facilitate the process of seeking justice. In this way, jurors and judges can better decide between punishment and rehabilitation. An individual who steals bread to feed their family and an individual who steals for personal gain would receive a just decision. By learning to detect the nuances of intent and motive, we better equip ourselves to lock away the true criminal while finding ways to support or rehabilitate those who wish to choose differently.

Another experiment in the dynamics of the human mind and what influences motivate us occurred in 1961. Stanley Milgram of Yale University conducted a study to determine if the Nazi defense of "just following orders" completely negated agency.[15] Please note that there are many factors which contribute to how an individual responds in any specific situation. The following results and conclusions are given based on the source material noted in the footnotes.

The experiment itself was simple. One person sat in a booth connected to electrical leads. Another person sat outside of the booth and controlled the amount of shock delivered to the individual in the booth. The study participant was to initiate a shock at any time the subject answered a question incorrectly. Each wrong answer demanded an increased shock level. The person operating the controls did not know that the victim did not receive the intended shock. The moderator dressed to look like a doctor, or lab technician, to establish an authority figure. If the participant became uncomfortable, researchers instructed the moderator, even against written contracts and releases the participant had signed, to inform the participant they were obligated to complete the experiment.

Milgram then polled his colleagues and graduate students at the university and elsewhere. He questioned how many subjects would fully punish the victim to the extent the authority figure demanded. Overwhelmingly, poll respondents believed that only a small fraction of the subjects would choose to inflict pain on someone at the command of the moderator. They were wrong, horribly wrong. Despite witnessing victims who demonstrated signs of distress, including cardiac arrest, 65 percent of the participants administered what they believed to be a 450-volt shock for the crime of answering a question incorrectly. Although no one was physically harmed, there was substantial outrage over Milgram's methods and a general outcry regarding his professional ethics.

---

15. See Philip Zimbardo, "Foreword," in Milgram, *Obedience to Authority*, para. 6.

Nearly fifty years later, psychologist Jerry M. Burger performed the same study and found the results to be similar.[16] However, in a modified experiment, Burger discovered that it did not take a great deal of encouragement to convince some of the subjects to avoid inflicting the ultimate punishment on the victim. If another person in the room with the subject spoke out against the authority figure in the room, some participants were more willing to back away. A few just got up and left, no matter what the moderator said about the contract. Burger discovered that if there is the least bit of support to make the moral or ethical choice, we will stand up to an authority who is asking us to harm others. Even one dissenting voice matters. At crucial junctures, the support of someone else who shares our moral and ethical standards helps us to make the better choice, to hold to our standards whatever the circumstances or consequences. For those who wish to reduce the suffering in this world, becoming that voice is not an option.

I feel it is imperative that we strive to understand the difference between a predisposition to cause harm to ourselves or others and the choices we make which are products of biology, neurology, and chemistry. Sexual behavior, desires, identity, and tendencies, or anything on the spectrum of human sexuality and identity, is no more a choice than the color of our skin, eyes, or hair (at least at the roots). However, a difference of opinion on lifestyles, regardless of the source of that choice, is not a valid basis to cause harm and suffering to another. The pedophile is still a criminal, as is the person who uses their sexual status to harm anyone based on that status.

The Beasts That Dwell with and within Us

The author of Job used established imagery to define the shape of evil. At that time in history, Hippocrates had only just begun to explore medicine as a science. In his writings, we see indications that he believed the lifestyle of the patient contributed to their attitude and appetites (in physical health as well as mental). He also felt that some diseases affected the actions of some of his patients and caused them to lose the ability to make responsible decisions.

As we learn more about how our minds work, we understand more about the roots of evil in the human spirit. Sometimes we are the vehicles of suffering, as we knowingly or unknowingly inflict on others what we so desperately wish to avoid ourselves. Sometimes we are the victim. Learning more about how the inner universe of the mind functions and how it reacts to the world around us could give us tools to help fight the beasts.

We also endlessly debate what level of responsibility humanity has. If we are not able to defeat Leviathan, how can we protect ourselves against evil? What amount of responsibility can a person have for the choices made?

16. See Burger, "Replicating Milgram."

Note that the author of Job raises this question: how much evil is due to choices made, and how much is intrinsic to creation, a force over which humanity has no control? If the individual has no control, how can they be held accountable? The author of Job prods us with the question even if knowledge available at the time was insufficient for an answer. How do we balance agency against predisposition, and whom do we hold accountable when an individual will not make the right choices themselves? What we can or cannot do to control evil is a work in progress. Even now, we are learning how to harness Leviathan if we have the will to do so.

We are about to hear Job's final speech, his acceptance of the challenge to consider the creation laid out before him, and his confirmation of an inalienable right to ask questions and receive answers.

Chapter 25

Before I Heard, But Now I See

AT THE END OF his battle of wits with God and his visitors, Job proclaims:

> Who is this who obscures counsel without knowledge?
> Indeed, I spoke without understanding
> of things beyond me,
> which I did not know.
> Hear now, and I will speak;
> I will ask, and You will inform me.
> I had heard You with my ears,
> But now I see You with my eyes;
> Therefore, I recant and relent,
> Being but dust and ashes. (42:3–6)

In direct contrast to Job's speech after the testimonies of Earth's attributes and nature, Job declares that now he sees. Before, he admits, he could say no more. Now he states he will continue to ask questions and expect answers. He will do so with a better understanding of his finitude, of his place in the cosmos.

Historically, interpretations left Job with a Gordian knot. Many of the conclusions provided came with a set of mutually exclusive conditions. The issues related to arriving at this conundrum derive from falling into the trap of logical fallacies. Two such examples are the "joint effect fallacy" and the "insignificant fallacy."

These are errors made in the process of developing a logical argument. The "joint effect fallacy" occurs when one thing is held to cause another, when in fact, both the cause and the presumed effect are the result of an underlying cause. The error occurs when we assume that because X happens after Y, then X must be a result of Y. For instance: A doctor tells a parent that a child's fever is causing a breakout of spots when both symptoms could be caused by the measles, a far more critical issue. To be effective in the quest to reduce suffering, or to understand the source of undeserved suffering, it behooves us to be brutally honest about the underlying contributing factors. Otherwise, we will exacerbate rather than mitigate suffering.

The "insignificant fallacy" occurs when one thing is held to cause another, and while it may well contribute to the outcome, it may be insignificant compared to other contributing factors of the effect. For example, we realize that our choices may indeed cause suffering. However, those choices may be insignificant when compared to the creative and destructive forces of nature. When we choose to vacation in Florida during hurricane season, we may experience a hurricane. However, the choice to take the vacation in that location does not create the storm. In other words, the belief that it is our actions that are the sole cause of the effect before us may be an honest assessment of the situation, or it may be the result of an egocentric point of view that does little to solve the problem. Assuming we are the sole cause prevents us from seeing opportunities to become a part of something greater. Removing ourselves from the center allows us to help others and ourselves without focusing on blame.

Job's search for answers only results in revealing the effects of some underlying cause. His petition to God was to find that root cause. Job's final speech indicates that he has found the answer or, at the minimum, a way to actively pursue it.

The literature interpreting Job 42:3–6, quoted at the beginning of this chapter, includes a wide spectrum of ideology. Throughout history, commentaries have seen Job's declaration in these verses primarily as his surrender to his innate inadequacies. Some commentators see this speech as a *mea culpa* that the whole affair was a misguided attempt on Job's part to understand the world and its Creator, an undertaking beyond a lowly speck of dust. Interpreting these verses as Job's surrender to a life without answers bends the passage into a preconceived notion of God and his creation. Job rises from the ashes knowing that he *is* getting answers and with the assurance that he *is* beginning to understand. He reiterates that he will continue to ask those questions *and expect answers*. The New Testament tells us: "But if anyone is deficient in wisdom, he should ask God, who gives to all generously and without reprimand, and it will be given to him."[1] His acknowledgment of his mortality and his finitude does not prevent him from speaking truthfully or from seeking truth and wisdom.

In Greenstein's paper "Truth or Theodicy?" he explains his growing conviction that the book of Job is about more than suffering.[2] It is also about *how* we speak to God. Although he points out that the language used throughout the dramatic discourse is the language of communication, he disagrees with the views of Tilley and McCord.[3] Structurally, as the debate escalates, Job becomes aware that his companions are not only missing the point, they are also fundamentally incapable of seeing his point. Despite this, they grow more aggressive in their approach, doing their best to keep him from outright blaspheming God. They are not pleased with his tone (a quality of

---

1. Jas 1:5, NET.
2. Greenstein, "Truth or Theodicy?" 238–58.
3. See chapter 15.

speech). Neither were many rabbis who, through the ages, contributed to Talmudic wisdom. In their opinion, Job stepped over the line and did so repeatedly. The church fathers tried to put a gentler face on Job's demands to avoid the same conflict. Both camps gave him leeway for being under extreme duress. Many believers still interpret Job's crises as teaching him that God owes explanations to no one.

What Greenstein determines is that Job did not affront his Creator. The book teaches us *how* to speak about the issues, as well as what those issues are. Greenstein concludes that Job invoked divine pleasure because he spoke truthfully, and he did so regardless of the consequences. His paper also points out the difference between truth, which is empirical, and truthfulness, which is ethical. Job may not have had complete command of the truth, but, throughout his ordeal, he did remain truthful. For Greenstein, as well as for many others, God accepts Job's (and our) need to know.

Communication theory states that effective communication has several key elements. It must be clear, concise, easily understood by the receiver, honest, and complete. Job's frustration with his companions was due to the inability to communicate. They had something to contribute; nevertheless, they were not addressing his core question—they were talking past him. God, however, did understand Job's need to know. When God provided his answer, God did so in such a way that Job could draw conclusions based on what Job knew and could learn. Job's question, his challenge, is "Why does suffering manifest in the world, and why is it so out of proportion to what one might expect?"

To answer that question, we have retold the story of Job. We have placed the author in a time and place so that we could better understand the knowledge available to him. We have redefined how we look at God by working through the chapters describing creation and how it reveals the creator. We have redefined our place in the universe, learning to be neither the pinnacle nor the smallest worm. Finally, we redefined evil and what capabilities we have developed to control it. Now we can redefine the conversation and see how the book of Job teaches us to seek the answers we need each day of our lives.

The Appropriate Place for Tradition and Dogma

There is nothing intrinsically wrong with the responses of Job's companions. Their views were accurate within a narrow perspective. There are consequences when individuals do the wrong thing. That is why we are wise to look closely at our actions, our attitudes, and our thoughts to determine if we are responsible for the suffering we see. If there is a knowable reason for the predicament we find ourselves in, then we should find a way to change or mitigate the situation and to try to repair the damage.

Through adversity, whatever the source, we can strengthen our character. Whether evidenced in compassion, a better sense of our capabilities, or a deeper understanding of the grief of others, we should use suffering to become a better person or to find a greater good. Suffering, then, can provide a path to deeper understanding.

However, the problem with the answers of Job's companions is not confined to their need to find some way to justify God. They also err by not responding to Job's direct question. Everything they offer is an *effect* of some cause when it is the cause that Job sought. They also show a lack of compassion for Job and his situation. The lessons of Scripture show more interest in how we respond to those who need us than it does in a developed ability to correctly ascertain blame.

The Testimony of the Earth, and the Universe Beyond

For many centuries, humanity, in its effort to define the role we play in the universe, has created a dichotomy. Even with the variety of cultural and religious convictions throughout history, we tend to gravitate to one extreme or the other. In one case, we believe that the earth is the center of creation (physically and morally) and the focus of all the gods or God. As part of this view, the idea developed that a predefined perfection exists in the heavens, and humanity must strive to replicate that state on earth. The planets move in perfect circles, any disease or disability was and is a direct result of the individual's actions, and the inability to succeed in life is due entirely to the individual's actions in opposition to God's will as defined by the prevailing orthodoxy. Clinging to that pinnacle of existence cost us dearly in ethical development and scientific discovery. At least in part, wanting the universe to be perfect in every way led us to wrong conclusions about how the solar system works, what our place in the cosmos might be, and how and when to take care of our sick and injured.

Each step of discovery from an earth-centric paradigm to one of an expanding universe was hard-won. Scientists and the general population alike did not easily accept the change from being the most important thing in God's creation to becoming merely another life-form on a small planet on the outskirts of a rather small galaxy. Science also led us to relinquish our death-grip on the perfection of the heavens. The better our instruments became, the more precise our information became regarding the universe we could observe.

When unable to cling to the vision of an egocentric universe, the human spirit tends to swing in the opposite direction. When no longer certain that humanity is under the special protection of the gods, we reduce our importance to that of the lowliest bit of life imaginable. The psalmist considers himself no more than a worm (22:6), and Job wishes he had never even been born. People haven't changed much. There is still a strong tendency to think of ourselves either as rulers of the universe or insignificant bits of floss floating in a sea of random circumstance. God's speeches to Job make it clear that neither is the case.

Certainly at least part of God's speech regarding the power and expanse of the earth and its place in the immediate heavens provides Job with an illustration of how finite Job is. However, God tempered that speech with the command to gird up, listen, and respond. The book of Job is a challenge to discover our true place in creation, which is neither in the ultimate center of that creation nor in a place of insignificance.

Physicists are professional dreamers. It is their job to look at the universe and seek answers, only to find themselves redefining the questions. Through theoretical physics, we have discovered the four forces that maintain our universe. These are the strong interaction, the electromagnetic force, the weak force, and the gravitational force. Without the relationship each of these has with the other forces, our universe would not exist.[4] Theoretical physicists, when exploring the possibility of multiverses, work through the mathematical probabilities of a viable universe that does not have the same forces interacting in the same way. Some of these models work on a mathematical level even though they would not support life. We must conclude, from what we know at this point, that all the working parts of the cosmos must function as we see them, or life itself would not exist.

Within an isolated system (our entire universe), there are laws of conservation. One of those laws is that energy cannot be destroyed; it only changes form. Locked inside every atom is the energy required to hold it together. When matter converts to energy, it does so violently. What we view as the death of a star is the conversion of its mass to energy, and in the process, it releases elements that allow other things to form, including life.

God's lesson on the forces and physical aspects of the Earth is a window into how creation works. The principles of that creation are vibrant and ever-changing within knowable rules which a creature with the gift of reason can discern. The responses attributed to God step back from the focus of a single person in pain and examine the interactions necessary to make that life possible.

We can frame and resolve questions about our existence and the world. There are things we can change once we understand them. We are learning how to predict when a major catastrophe is on the way. Now we must learn to protect or move those who are subject to those catastrophes. As our knowledge grows, we can plan for volcanoes, earthquakes, tsunamis, and life-threatening weather. Even now, we have some of the answers necessary to slow down the changing climate and to protect our resources. There are times when we do not have to suffer; we can solve, prevent, or mitigate the problems. This view of the cosmos also gives us a broader sense of what God is—a creator who has set in motion a constantly creating changing universe controlled by simple, repeatable rules. Seeing God in this role changes how we see him as a protector and a judge.

---

4. See "Possible Discovery of Fifth Force."

Before I Heard, But Now I See

The Testimony of Nature

God's second lesson focuses on something more immediate: the balance of nature. Humanity's search for how nature developed so many different species, each so uniquely fitting a niche within an ecosystem, has gone on nearly as long as our search for meaning in the skies. The struggle between creation science and evolution did not begin with Charles Darwin. Recorded thought on the process starts in approximately 520 BCE with Anaximander. There were many centuries when God's creative power was not challenged, whatever vehicle he chose to use to accomplish that creation. Many Christian biologists hold the belief that God is the author, whatever method chosen. We call their view theistic evolution.

Sorting through conflicting information can be difficult. All the more so if one has a sincere desire to know how the world of science interacts with the world of faith. Science and faith are not mutually exclusive. Faith can give light to knowledge, while science seeks proof of knowledge. In that search, scientific research aims for a self-correcting method of study. In the end, new paradigms find their way into the literature because scientists in different places can test the findings published by others. However long it takes, and however rooted a reputation may be in any theory, science, through observation and replication, clarifies the issues and asks new questions. What this process has taught us is that nature is an integrated whole. A species does not survive unless it can find shelter, food, and a mate, manage disease, and control predators. That process can appear to the human eye as cruel and unforgiving.

Job's lesson about nature graphically illustrates the balance between one life and another. It also describes humanity's interaction with nature: what can be controlled, what cannot, and what types of partnerships achieve a better existence for all inhabitants of this globe. The key is to learn the way nature operates and use that knowledge responsibly and effectively. When it comes to the question of suffering, nature can be brutal in the process of obtaining balance. Sometimes humanity needs to step back from the result to understand the cause. In no other way can we determine if there is a way to mitigate or avoid the suffering.

Blessed with reason, we can seek solutions that protect the balance of nature and alleviate human suffering. Even though a child on the African savanna may be at risk of a lion attack, we can still seek ways and means to coexist with the lion. With effort and a genuine concern for the nature around us, we are learning how to let the lion live and still preserve the lives within its reach.

Understanding nature should not result in allowing hundreds of thousands of human beings to starve. Nor should they die due to curable or preventable disease or lack of clean water. As we learn how the earth's biosphere works and what is required to maintain the balance, we become more responsible for solving the issues that cause suffering. Developing sources of clean water, delivering reliable medical aid, and discovering new and more productive ways for agriculture and husbandry to assuage the suffering of the world are ethical and moral obligations.

The Existence of Evil

Scripture describes Leviathan as a creature with which God "sports." In Hebrew tradition, Satan is not evil incarnate, nor is he a fallen angel. He is a tester, the one who challenges us to temper the strength of character and conviction. The "tester" is the part he plays in the garden of Eden and the part he plays in Job. The images of Behemoth and Leviathan are representative of true evil—images of chaos barely controlled.

God wants Job to see that he did create the best of all universes, one in which life was possible. There is, however, a price to pay. Within the natural and physical laws required to provide for life, there are processes which, at least to humanity, appear to destroy or cause harm and suffering. The ancients believed that matter was finite. According to the laws of physics, it isn't; it is a different form of energy. The interaction between matter and energy are often violent and destructive—even as the process creates. The first cause of suffering is rooted in the creative requirements of producing the very fabric of this universe. What, then, can be done to counterbalance the destructive effects of creation?

The desire for a perfect world has clouded our perception of God specifically, and reality in general. We have difficulty seeing beyond the grandfatherly figure that protects us from all the monsters in the world, and we conclude that if he doesn't, we did something wrong, or maybe he doesn't care. When we are saved from devastation, it is because we are special. Even though some of our neighbors are not. We are blessed because we pray right, give to the right charities, and abhor the sins of others. We live or believe we wish to live in a religionist's version of *Pleasantville*.

Pleasantville is a classic film from 1998 that is considered the definition of the changing social mores between the 1950s and the 1960s.[5] Scripted as a grayscale 1950s sitcom, the inhabitants of Pleasantville exist in a perfect world where nothing ever goes wrong. By an accident of obsession with the TV world, two modern teenagers end up trapped in that perfect 1950s town.

The influence of these teenagers changes the world of Pleasantville in many ways. One by one, the inhabitants of the perfect little town change from black and white caricatures to Technicolor beings. They each find a way to realize that there is a world beyond Main Street and that sometimes the player misses the perfect shot. Beyond the message of the emerging social revolution of the time, the movie uncovers inherent traits that make us unique: passion, wonder, and the power of agency.

Pleasantville is a tale about finding that thing which fills the individual with enough passion to become the deliberate vehicle of change, to become a part of the

---

5. *Pleasantville* is a 1998 film written, produced, and directed by Gary Ross, most frequently described as a metaphor for the 1960s.

Technicolor world. For the population of Pleasantville, becoming Technicolor was their version of "gaining faces," as C. S. Lewis describes in his book.

In pursuit of that change, we will put ourselves at risk and will, occasionally, even die for our convictions. Humanity does not fear suffering, in and of itself, but rather the great mystery of why we suffer.[6] Sometimes when threatened with a choice between the expectation of pain and the action required to change, we do nothing because we have difficulty determining the relevant value of personal integrity or conviction versus the pain. Is suffering the crucible what makes us greater, that drives us to do heroic and compassionate deeds? Or is it the anvil that crushes us and makes us demons, the carriers of evil passed on through communities and generations in the effort to cleanse ourselves of pain by inflicting it on others?

In the end, it is neither and both. According to Job, creation took a specific path, one supported by science, as we know it. A physical universe became and developed through the operation of simple physical laws based on a specific balance of four fundamental forces. That process can cause devastation as energy and matter interact. As creation grew and life became a factor, the balance of nature was required to ensure each species operated within a niche that provided food, shelter, offspring, relative safety from predators, and a way to adjust to or modify the climate.

This creative process is certain to cause loss, death, and suffering. There must be a reasoning mind that can understand the process and respond in a manner that reduces suffering. The residents of Pleasantville could not imagine an event when a firefighter might have to put out a fire. They could not see beyond the predetermined walls of their existence. God saw that to understand the universe, humanity needed the ability to see evil and destruction and to know that these terms were not always interchangeable. To reach an understanding of when and if evil is the root of destruction and suffering, humanity must have the ability to choose.

Redefining God

To understand suffering, we needed to understand something more of the Creator. Through dogma and doctrine, we have developed a definition of a sovereign ruler of the universe that is not big enough to be its creator. Far too often, we build a box, hang a sign on it, and expect God to live there. We fail in understanding when we insist on creating anthropomorphisms and decide that God is or must be this way, or he isn't God. How can we discover answers, or know the power of wonder, if we begin by setting boundaries?

Perhaps Maimonides was correct. There are parts within the story of Job which can provide the reader with some comfort. Or, if there is no comfort, those that suffer can retreat to a position that the mind of God is beyond our understanding. However,

---

6. See Lewis, *Till We Have Faces*.

for those who choose to accept the challenge, there is a definable reason for suffering. Not only is there a prime cause, there is a solution. However, it requires action on our part, and Scripture tells us what that action should be.

Judeo-Christian Scripture is insistent that we offer aid to those who need us. Caring for those who face challenges of whatever nature is a teaching that is not limited to the New Testament. Proverbs 21:13, "Who stops his ears at the cry of the wretched, / he too will call and not be answered." Ezekiel 16:49, "Only this was the sin of your sister Sodom; arrogance! She and her daughters had plenty of bread and untroubled tranquility; yet she did not support the poor and the needy." Zechariah 7:9–11, "Thus said the Lord of Hosts: Execute true justice; deal loyally and compassionately with one another. Do not defraud the widow, the orphan, the stranger, and the poor; and do not plot evil against one another—but they refused to pay heed. They presented a balky back and turned a deaf ear."

From Babylon and Ur to the Large Hadron Collider, our perception of the cosmos in which we find ourselves has undergone many changes. That knowledge should inform us to accomplish more than to engineer better tools of exploration and destruction; it should teach us how to better combat suffering.

The voice from the whirlwind is a call to look at the cosmos and get a better grip on cause and effect. The scriptural warning that the sins of the fathers visit later generations is not a prophecy—it is a statement of fact. Although studies show that the socioeconomic and cultural background of a child does not always determine their future, we do know that the odds can be against a child raised in poverty, violence, and discrimination. We know that dumping chemicals into the ecosystem causes sickness. Now we need to find ways to prevent more occurrences or to avoid pending outcomes.

When we choose a course of action that is sure to end in catastrophe, we are disingenuous at best to blame God for not protecting us from the consequences. What the voice in the whirlwind is trying to teach us is that with our drive to name cause and effect, we often get the two confused. If we continue to fight against nature, it will fight back. No supreme being of the universe should be held responsible for rearranging the laws of physics so that when you get behind the wheel of a vehicle drunk, your life and the lives of those who share the road will be spared. How arrogant can we possibly be?

Yes, sometimes, "miracles" occur. Perhaps this time, the driver of the other car is alert to danger and understands that the world can be a cruel and unforgiving place and sees a way to avoid or moderate disaster. For these times, when a split second can change our lives, all the teachings and experiences of our lives make the difference.

That moment of understanding, skill, and knowledge is that moment when Providence steps in, when God does hear the cry of our hearts. First, we learn. We learn about the laws that make the world function and that are required to create a viable ecosystem for us to live and for us to reason. Once we learn, we must actively pursue ways to change the things within our power to change. For life in this universe to flourish, there was an absolute necessity for a creative mind that could assess situations, find solutions, imagine alternatives, and *choose* between the outcomes. Free will may be a participatory cause of suffering; however, it is also the answer. We are not fruit flies in a jar of honey, eating and reproducing our way to destruction; we are sapient beings with choices.

I believe that God has responded in the past and continues to respond to suffering in our time. However, his response requires an active partnership between the Creator and the created. That means that humanity must take an active role in learning how suffering occurs and how to respond. Intellectually we know there might be things beyond our comprehension; that is no excuse to stop looking. Emotionally we know that suffering impacts us and those around us. God gave us the choice to be a part of the solution to suffering rather than a vehicle of suffering. Job's visitors made the wrong choice.

We are offered the opportunity to become a creative force that finds a path through the violence and cruelty of nature to compassion and restoration, to reduce the suffering inherent in the processes that drive our universe. Will we choose to become part of the creation story, or will we die off as an ignoble, failed experiment in consciousness and its ability to build a better world?

Scripture teaches us that this choice is an obligation, the price we pay for our reasoning minds. It is an obligation for the here and now, not some future world. From Genesis to Revelation, we are commanded to love one another, to have compassion, to reduce suffering. It is a personal commitment. Medical practitioners have used "First, do no harm" for centuries.[7] Mahatma Gandhi said, "If we could change ourselves, the tendencies in the world would also change. As a man changes his own nature, so does the attitude of the world change towards him. . . . We need not wait to see what others do."[8]

What I hope to have accomplished with this book is to show that the universe is not an arbitrary, unknowable chaos. Because we can come to know, God directs us to understand, to use our reason to see the path to mitigation, restitution, and compassion. The foundation of free will is to choose a path more right, more in keeping with a universe that celebrates life even as the very existence of life is threatened. In *The Hobbit: An Unexpected Journey*, Gandalf explains that it is not great power that defeats evil; it is the everyday acts of ordinary people.[9]

I wrote this book to explore the conundrum of suffering and possibilities of providence. Also, the intent was to discover if a knowable balance existed between God's

---

7. This is not an actual quote from the Hippocratic oath. The original reads (per one translation), "I will follow that system of regimen which, according to my ability and judgment, I consider for the benefit of my patients, and abstain from whatever is deleterious and mischievous." Shmerling, "Myth of the Hypocratic Oath."

8. The quote "Be the change you wish to see in the world" has not been verified as coming from the writings of Ghandi. The quotation noted above is the closest to the sentiment conveyed. It is found in Gandhi, *Collected Works*, 13:241.

9. Jackson, *The Hobbit*, movie version, 2012.

Part V—Redefining the Conversation

participation in the process of suffering and the individual's response to suffering. Throughout these pages, I examined the writings of ancient and modern interpreters. Some ideas were considered part of the solution, although not the penultimate solution; some were dismissed completely. In this last chapter, I have summarized the interpretations and conclusions I have learned within the context of a modern world. These conclusions arrive at two fundamental obligations: to learn, and to use the learning to care for ourselves and others, whoever they may be. In October of 2017, David Gerrold posted a statement on Facebook which was a succinct definition of the core values presented in this book:

> It's in our behavior that we demonstrate who we are, who we really are. And if I had to pick the single most important aspect of consciousness, I'd focus on empathy. When we recognize the self-ness of others, their ability to feel, that changes the way we treat them. It changes us. Everywhere we go. It changes how we treat animals and children and the disabled and elderly and people who look different or dress different. It changes how we behave in the world. It changes us. The more we practice that change, the more it becomes a part of us, the defining part. Because—it's so obvious. Practice makes permanent.
>
> And this is my point. Sentience—true sentience—by its nature, cannot be malevolent. It cannot be evil. Because in the recognition that others can hurt, it takes on the responsibility of not being the cause of that hurt.[10]

The difficulty is in the definition of "sentience." Sentience is the capacity to feel, perceive, or experience subjectivity. Philosophers have used the term to distinguish the ability to think or reason from the ability to feel (sentience). Gerrold believes that if we truly understand the pain of another, we cannot neglect our obligation to help resolve that suffering.

God answered that both reason and sentience are critical to how we live our lives. Humanity is neither the central point of the universe nor an insignificant bit of stardust. There are times when we must face the consequences of our failures or misguided steps. There are times when the forces of humanity and nature conspire to create undeserved suffering. However, by receiving the gifts of reason and sentience, it becomes incumbent on the us to look outward, to learn, and to find solutions.

---

10. Quoted by permission from David Gerrold, a prolific author of fiction and winner of both the Hugo and Nebula Awards for SF/F work. He was also awarded the lifetime achievement awards Forry Award (2007) and Sylark Award (1979). Facebook post, Oct., 2017. Reprinted with permission.

Bibliography

Aquinas, Thomas. *Expositio super Iob ad Litteram* [Commentary on the Book of Job]. Translated by Brian Mulladay, edited by Joseph Kenny. Rochester: Aquinas Institute, n.d.

Archer, Marlo. "Maybe So, Maybe Not. We'll See." http://www.drmarlo.com/?page_id=181.

Aristotle. *On Soul.* Translated by J. A. Smith. Overland Park, KS: Digireads, 2009.

Aslan, Reza. *No god but God: The Origins, Evolution, and Future of Islam.* Updated ed. New York: Random House, 2011.

Augustine. *The City of God.* Edited by Marcus Dods. Urbana, IL: Project Gutenberg, 2014. http://www.gutenberg.org/ebooks/45304.

"The Baal Cycle." https://emp.byui.edu/satterfieldb/ugarit/The%20Epic%20of%20Baal.html.

Barbour, Julian. *The End of Time.* London: Weidenfeld & Nicolson, 1999.

Barnes, Albert. *Barnes' Notes on the Bible.* 14 vols. 1834. https://www.sacred-texts.com/bib/cmt/barnes/job000.htm.

Barrick, William D. "The Authorship of Deuteronomy 34: Moses or a Redactor?" Paper presented to ETS Annual Meeting, Nov. 14–16, 2001.

Bendiner, Elmer. *The Rise and Fall of Paradise: When Arabs and Jews Built a Kingdom in Spain.* New York: Dorset, 1990.

Bloom, Howard K. *The God Problem: How a Godless Cosmos Creates.* Amherst, NY: Prometheus, 2012.

Braden, Charles S. *The Scriptures of Mankind: An Introduction.* New York: Macmillan, 1952.

Bricker, Daniel P. "Innocent Suffering in Mesopotamia." *Tyndale Bulletin* 51.2 (2000) 193–214.

Brinton, Daniel G. *Ancient Nahuatl Poetry, Containing the Nahuatl Text of XXVII Ancient Mexican Poems.* Urbana, IL: Project Gutenberg, 2004. http://www.gutenberg.org/ebooks/12219.

Burger, Jerry M. "Replicating Milgram: Would People Still Obey Today?" *American Psychologist* 64.1 (2009) 1–11. https://doi.org/10.1037/a0010932.

Burrell, David B. *Deconstructing Theodicy: Why Job Has Nothing to Say to the Puzzle of Suffering.* Grand Rapids: Brazos, 2008.

Byrd, Deborah. "Is It True That Jupiter Protects Earth?" Nov. 25, 2015. http://earthsky.org/space/is-it-true-that-jupiter-protects-earth.

"Comet Shoemaker-Levy Collision with Jupiter." http://www2.jpl.nasa.gov/sl9.

"Confucianism." https://www.patheos.com/library/confucianism.

Copleston, Frederick. *A History of Philosophy.* Vol. 1, "Greece and Rome." Garden City, NY: Image, 1962.

Dembitz, Lewis N. "Widow." http://jewishencyclopedia.com/articles/14892-widow.

Bibliography

Dostoyevsky, Fyodor. *The Brothers Karamazov*. Urbana, IL: Project Gutenberg, 2016. http://www.gutenberg.org/ebooks/28054.

Eagleman, David. *The Brain with David Eagleman*. Six-part PBS documentary. Aired Oct. 14–Nov. 18, 2015.

Ehrman, Bart D. *God's Problem: How the Bible Fails to Answer Our Most Important Question—Why We Suffer*. New York: HarperOne, 2008.

Eichhorn, Johann Gottfried. *Introduction to the Study of the Old Testament*. Mishawaka, IN: Palala Press, 2016.

Eisen, Robert. *The Book of Job in Medieval Jewish Philosophy*. Oxford: Oxford University Press, 2004.

"Eratosthenes (276–195 B.C.)." http://hosting.astro.cornell.edu/academics/courses/astro201/eratosthenes.htm.

Farquhar, Brodie, "Wolf Reintroduction Changes Ecosystem in Yellowstone." https://www.yellowstonepark.com/things-to-do/wolf-reintroduction-changes-ecosystem.

"Fight, Flight, Freeze Responses." http://trauma-recovery.ca/impact-effects-of-trauma/fight-flight-freeze-responses/.

Fischer, John Martin. "Nelson Pike, 'Divine Omniscience and Voluntary Action' (1965)." *Philosophical Papers* 38.2 (2009) 27–46.

Foster, Benjamin R. *Before the Muses: Myths, Tales and Poetry of Ancient Mesopotamia*. Bethesda, MD: CDL Press, 1995.

Foxe, John. *Fox's Book of Martyrs*. Urbana, IL: Project Gutenberg, 2007. http://www.gutenberg.org/ebooks/22400.

Gandhi, Mahatma. *The Collected Works of Mahatma Gandhi*. 98 volumes. New Delhi: Publications Division, Government of India, 1999. https://www.gandhiashramsevagram.org/gandhi-literature/collected-works-of-mahatma-gandhi-volume-1-to-98.php.

Good, Edwin M. "Job and the Literary Task: A Response." *Soundings* 56 (1973) 471–84.

The Good Person: Excerpts from the Yoruba Proverb Treasury. University of Nebraska. http://yoruba.unl.edu.

Gottheil, Richard, et al. "Captivity, or Exile, Babylonian." http://www.jewishencyclopedia.com/articles/4012-captivity.

Grant, Andrew. "Speed of Light Not So Constant After All." *Science News*, Jan. 17, 2015.

"Greek Medicine." https://www.nlm.nih.gov/hmd/greek/greek_oath.html.

Greenstein, Edward L. "The Language of Job and Its Poetic Function." *Journal of Biblical Literature* 122.4 (2003) 651–66.

———. "Truth or Theodicy? Speaking Truth to Power in the Book of Job." *Princeton Seminary Bulletin* 27.3 (2006) 238–58.

Guttmacher, Adolf. "Fear of God." http://jewishencyclopedia.com/articles/6045-fear-of-god.

Halley, Henry H. *Halley's Bible Handbook: An Abbreviated Bible Commentary*. 24th ed. Regency Reference Library. Grand Rapids: Zondervan, 1965.

Hand, Eric. "Scientists Gear Up to Drill into 'Ground Zero' of the Impact That Killed the Dinosaurs." *Science*, March 3, 2016.

Hargus, Coyt David. "Theories of the Israelite Occupation of the Land of Canaan." Masters diss., University of Texas at Austin, 2000.

Hart, Ben. "Understanding Donkey Characteristics." https://www.thedonkeysanctuary.org.uk/.

Hastings, James. *Hastings' Dictionary of the Bible*. Ada, MI: Baker, 1994.

Hirsch, Emil G. "God." http://www.jewishencyclopedia.com/articles/6725-god.

Bibliography

Hirsch, Emil G., et al. "Chaldea." http://www.jewishencyclopedia.com/articles/4213-chaldea.

Hoffer, Eric. *The True Believer: Thoughts on the Nature of Mass Movements.* New York: Harper Perennial Modern Classics, 2010.

Hoyle, Fred, et al. *A Different Approach to Cosmology: From a Static Universe through the Big Bang towards Reality.* Cambridge: Cambridge University Press, 2005.

Humphreys, Justin. "Aristotle." http:/www.iep.utm.edu/aristotl.

Hungerford, Lynda. "Dialect Representation in *Native Son.*" *Language and Style* 20 (1987) 3–15.

Hye, M. Abdul. "Ash'arism." In *A History of Muslim Philosophy*, vol. 1, book 3, ch. 11. E-book. New York: Columbia University Press, 2004. https://www.al-islam.org/history-muslim-philosophy-volume-1-book-3.

ibn Kathir, Imaduddin Abul-Fida Ismail. *Stories of the Prophets: Peace Be Upon Them.* Translated by Rashad Ahmad Azami. Houston: Dar-us-Salam, 2003.

Irenaeus. *Against Heresies, or On the Detection and Overthrow of the So-Called Gnosis.* In Ante-Nicene Fathers 1, edited by Alexander Roberts. www.ccel.org/ccel/schaff/anf01.html.

Jackson, Peter, dir. *The Hobbit: An Unexpected Journey.* 2 hours 49 minutes. New Line Cinema, 2012.

Jacobs, Joseph, et al. "Ezra, Book of." http://www.jewishencyclopedia.com/articles/5968-ezra-book-of/.

Jastrow, Morris, Jr., and Wilhelm Nowack. "Bildad." http://www.jewishencyclopedia.com/articles/3296-bildad.

Jastrow, Morris, Jr., et al. "Deuteronomy." http://www.jewishencyclopedia.com/articles/5132-deuteronomy.

"JEDP Theory." www.theopedia.com/jedp-theory.

Kahneman, Daniel. *Thinking Fast and Slow.* New York: Farrar, Straus and Giroux, 2011.

Kaufman, Stephen A. "Aramaic." In *The Semitic Languages*, edited by Robert Hetzron, 114–30. New York: Routledge, 1997.

Keysers, Christian. *The Empathic Brain: How the Discovery of Mirror Neurons Changes Our Understanding of Human Nature.* Kindle edition, n.p., 2011.

Kiernan, Thomas P., ed. *Aristotle Dictionary.* New York: Philosophical Library, 1962.

König, Eduard, and Emil G. Hirsch. "Eliphaz." http://www.jewishencyclopedia.com/articles/5679-eliphaz.

Kutscher, Eduard Yechezkel, and Raphael Kutscher, eds. *A History of the Hebrew Language.* Jerusalem: Magnes Press, The Hebrew University, 1982.

Lang, Kenneth R. *The Life and Death of Stars.* Cambridge: Cambridge University Press, 2013.

Leibniz, Gottfried Wilhelm. *Theodicy: Essays on the Goodness of God, the Freedom of Man and the Origin of Evil.* Translated by E. M. Huggard. Urbana, IL: Project Gutenberg, 2005. http://www.gutenberg.org/ebooks/17147.

Lewis, C. S. *The Problem of Pain.* New York: HarperOne, 1996.

———. *Till We Have Faces: A Myth Retold.* New York: Mariner, 2012.

Loyola Productions Munich. "Marilyn McCord Adams - What can Christian Theology say to the problem of evil?" *YouTube*, July 25, 2016. https://youtu.be/iwMdWx5yysY.

MacLeish, Archibald. *J.B.: A Play in Verse.* Boston: Houghton Mifflin. 1989.

Maimonides, Moses. *The Guide for the Perplexed.* Translated by M. Friedländer. Overland Park, KS: Digireads, 2010.

Bibliography

Mark, Joshua J. "The Ludlul-Bel-Nimeqi—Not Merely a Babylonian Job." https://www.ancient.eu/article/226/the-ludlul-bel-nimeqi--not-merely-a-babylonian-jo/.

———. "Women in Ancient Persia." https://www.ancient.eu/article/1492/women-in-ancient-persia/.

McCord Adams, Marilyn. "Evil and the God-Who-Does-Nothing-in-Particular." In *Religion and Morality*, 107–31. Ithaca, NY: Cornell University Press, 2020.

———. *Horrendous Evils and the Goodness of God*. Cornell Studies in the Philosophy of Religion. Ithaca, NY: Cornell University Press, 2000.

Milgram, Stanley. *Obedience to Authority: An Experimental View*. Kindle edition. New York: Harper Perennial Modern Classics, 2009.

Morreall, John. *Comedy, Tragedy, and Religion*. Albany, NY: State University of New York Press, 1999.

Morrell, Peter. "A Buddhist View of Suffering." http://www.homeoint.org/morrell/buddhism/suffering.htm.

Nietzsche, Friedrich. *Beyond Good and Evil*. Translated by Helen Zimmern. Urbana, IL: Project Gutenberg, 2009. http://www.gutenberg.org/ebooks/4363.

———. *The Twilight of the Idols and the Anti-Christ: Or, How to Philosophize with a Hammer*. Translated by Anthony M. Ludovici. Urbana, IL: Project Gutenberg, 2016. http://www.gutenberg.org/ebooks/52263.

"Origin of Dromedary Camel Domestication Discovered." *ScienceDaily*, May 9, 2016. www.sciencedaily.com/releases/2016/05/160509191839.htm.

Pagels, Elaine H. *The Gnostic Gospels*. New York: Vintage, 1979.

Pardes, Ilana. *Countertraditions in the Bible: A Feminist Approach*. Cambridge, MA: Harvard University Press, 1993.

Parkinson, R. B. *Voices from Ancient Egypt*. Norman, OK: University of Oklahoma, 1991.

Pfeiffer, Robert Henry. *Introduction to the Old Testament*. New York: Harper, 1948.

Phillips, Tony, ed. "The Tunguska Impact—100 Years Later." http://science.nasa.gov/science-news/science-at-nasa/2008/30jun_tunguska/.

"Physicists Confirm Possible Discovery of Fifth Force of Nature." https://phys.org/news/2016-08-physicists-discovery-nature.html.

Pierre-Louis, Kendra. "As the Arctic Gets Warmer, Our Winters Get Colder." *Popular Science*, July 10, 2017.

Placher, William C. "An Engagement with Marilyn McCord Adams's *Horrendous Evils and the Goodness of God*." *Scottish Journal of Theology* 55.4 (2002) 461–67.

Plantinga, Alvin. *Where the Conflict Really Lies: Science, Religion & Naturalism*. Oxford: Oxford University Press, 2011.

Prothero, Stephen. *God Is Not One: The Eight Rival Religions That Run the World*. New York: HarperOne, 2010.

"Pythagoras." https://www.mathopenref.com/pythagoras.html.

"Pythagoras of Samos." www.storyofmathematics.com/greek_pythagoras.html.

Ratner, Robert J. "Morphological Variation in Biblical Hebrew Rhetoric." *Maarav* 8 (1992) 143–59.

Rendsburg, Gary A. "Linguistic Variation and the 'Foreign' Factor in the Hebrew Bible." In *Language and Culture in the Near East*, edited by Shlomo Izre'el and Rina Drory, 177–90. Leiden: Brill, 1995.

Robertson, David. "The Book of Job: A literary Study." *Soundings* 56 (1973) 446–69.

Ross, Gary, dir. *Pleasantville*. 2 hours 4 minutes. New Line Cinema, 1998.

Rubenstein, Richard E. *When Jesus Became God: The Epic Fight over Christ's Divinity in the Last Days of Rome*. New York: Harcourt Brace & Company, 1999.

Sayenga, Kurt, dir. "Can We Eliminate Evil?" Narrated by Morgan Freeman. *Through the Wormhole*. Season 3, episode 7. Aired July 18, 2012.

"Scientific Consensus: Earth's Climate is Warming." https://climate.nasa.gov/scientific-consensus/.

Shafer, Byron E., ed. *Religion in Ancient Egypt: Gods, Myths, and Personal Practice*. Ithaca, NY: Cornell University Press, 1991.

Shmerling, Robert H. "The Myth of the Hippocratic Oath." https://www.health.harvard.edu/blog/the-myth-of-the-hippocratic-oath-201511258447.

Silberman, Neil Asher, and Israel Finkelstein. *The Bible Unearthed: Archaeology's New Vision of Ancient Israel and the Origin of Its Sacred Texts*. New York: Touchstone, 2002.

Simonetti, Manlio, and Marco Conti, eds. *Job*. Ancient Christian Commentary on Scripture, Old Testament 6. Downers Grove: InterVarsity, 2006.

Singer, Isadore, and Jacob Zallel Lauterbach. "Josiah." http://www.jewishencyclopedia.com/articles/8927-josiah.

Slocum, Robert Boak. *The Anglican Imagination: Portraits and Sketches of Modern Anglican Theologians*. Surrey, UK: Ashgate, 2015.

Smart, Ninian. *The Religious Experience of Mankind*. New York: Charles Scribner's Sons, 1969.

Jewison, Norman, dir. *Fiddler on the Roof*. 3 hours 1 minute. United Artists, 1971.

Stewart, Rhea Talley. "A Dam at Marib." *Aramco World*, 29.2 (1978) 24–29. http://archive.aramcoworld.com/issue/197802/a.dam.at.marib.htm.

Sutherland, Robert. *Putting God on Trial: The Biblical Book of Job*. Victoria, B.C.: Trafford, 2004.

Tanakh—The Holy Scriptures. Philadelphia: Jewish Publication Society, 1988.

"Taoism." https://www.patheos.com/library/taoism.

Tilley, Terrance W. *The Evils of Theodicy*. Eugene, OR: Wipf & Stock, 2000.

Toy, Crawford Howell, and Casper Levias. "Hebrew Language." http://www.jewishencyclopedia.com/articles/7453-hebrew-language.

Turney, Chris. *Bones, Rocks and Stars: The Science of When Things Happened*. New York: Macmillan, 2006.

Valiuddin, Mir. "Mu'tazalism." In *A History of Muslim Philosophy*, vol. 1, book 3, ch. 10. E-book. New York: Columbia University Press, 2004. https://www.al-islam.org/history-muslim-philosophy-volume-1-book-3.

Voltaire. *Candide*. Urbana, IL: Project Gutenberg. http://www.gutenberg.org/ebooks/19942.

von Rad, Gerhard. *Wisdom in Israel*. New York: Bloomsbury, 1993.

Wade, Nicholas. *Before the Dawn: Recovering the Lost History of Our Ancestors*. New York: Penguin, 2007.

———. *The Faith Instinct: How Religion Evolved and Why It Endures*. New York: Penguin, 2009.

"Watching How Planets Form: Anatomy of a Planet-Forming Disc around a Star More Massive Than the Sun." https://www.eso.org/public/usa/news/eso0636/.

Waters, Larry J. "The Authenticity of the Elihu Speeches in Job 32–37." *Bibliotheca Sacra* 156. (1999) 28–41.

Wedgwood, C. V. *The Thirty Years War*. New York: New York Review, 2005.

"What Is a Perigean Spring Tide?" http://oceanservice.noaa.gov/facts/perigean-spring-tide.html.

Whedbee, J. William. *The Bible and the Comic Vision.* Cambridge: Cambridge University Press, 1998.

"When the Ice Melts, the Earth Spews Fire: Researchers Discover a Link between Climate and Volcanic Eruptions." https://phys.org/news/2012-12-ice-earth-spews-link-climate.html.

Wider, Kathleen. "Women Philosophers in the Ancient Greek World: Donning the Mantle." *Hypatia* 1.1 (1986) 21–62.

Yahalom-Mack, Naama, and Adi Eliyahu-Behar. "The Transition from Bronze to Iron in Canaan: Chronology, Technology, and Context." *Radiocarbon* 57.2 (2015) 285–305.

www.ingramcontent.com/pod-product-compliance
Lightning Source LLC
Chambersburg PA
CBHW081417230426
43668CB00016B/2262